HISTORIC PHOTOS OF
SAN FRANCISCO

TEXT AND CAPTIONS BY REBECCA SCHALL

TURNER
PUBLISHING COMPANY

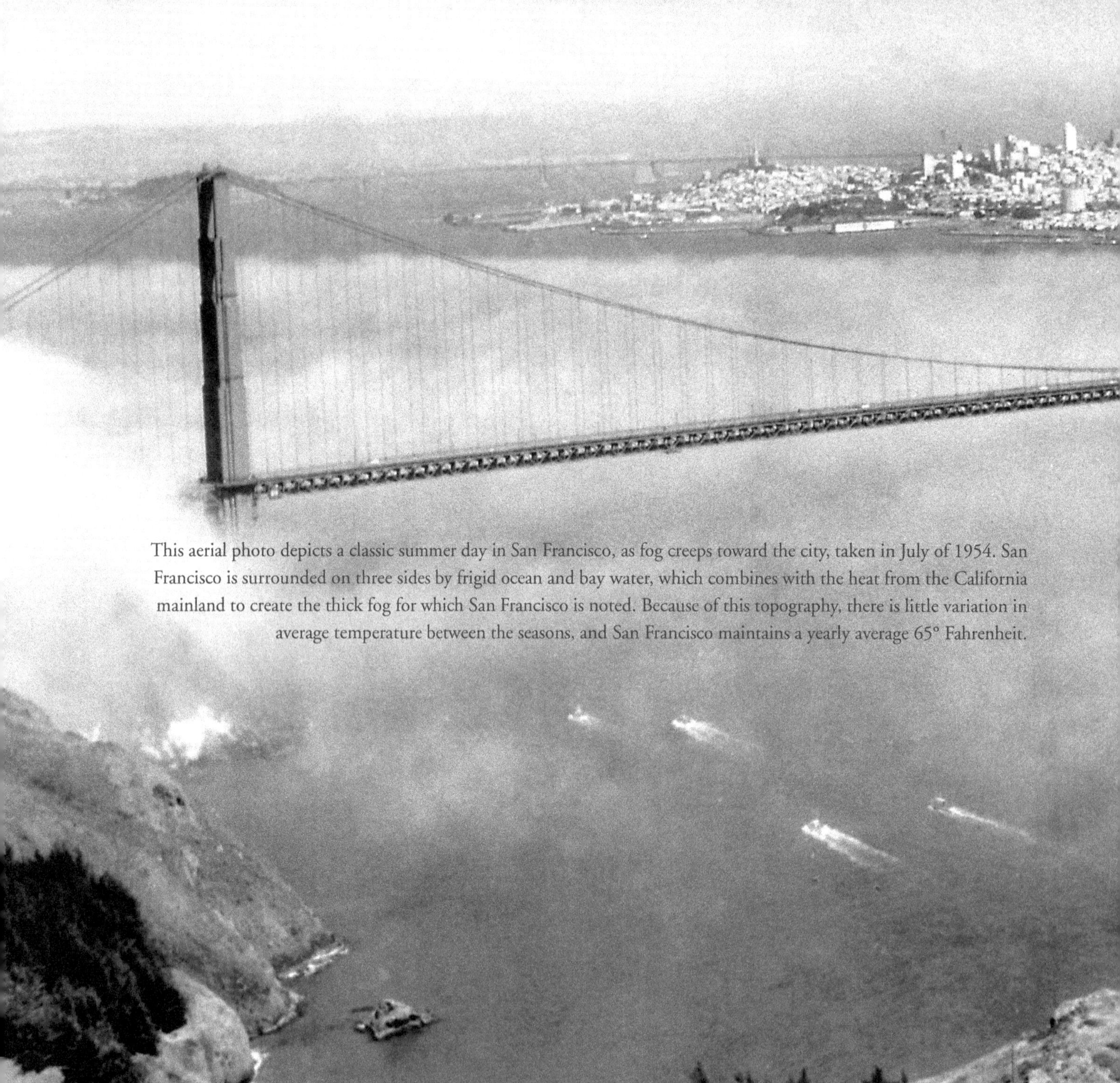

This aerial photo depicts a classic summer day in San Francisco, as fog creeps toward the city, taken in July of 1954. San Francisco is surrounded on three sides by frigid ocean and bay water, which combines with the heat from the California mainland to create the thick fog for which San Francisco is noted. Because of this topography, there is little variation in average temperature between the seasons, and San Francisco maintains a yearly average 65° Fahrenheit.

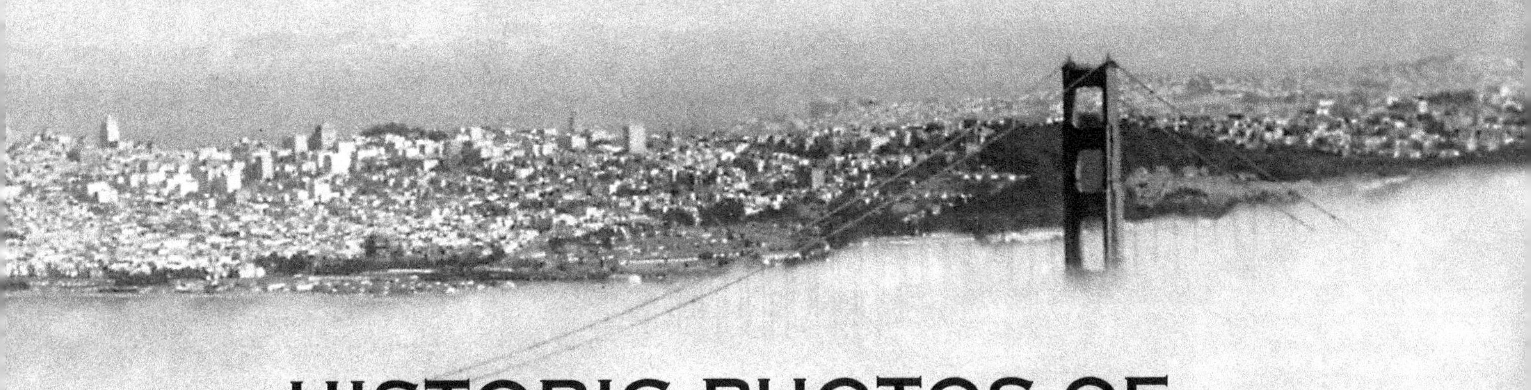

HISTORIC PHOTOS OF SAN FRANCISCO

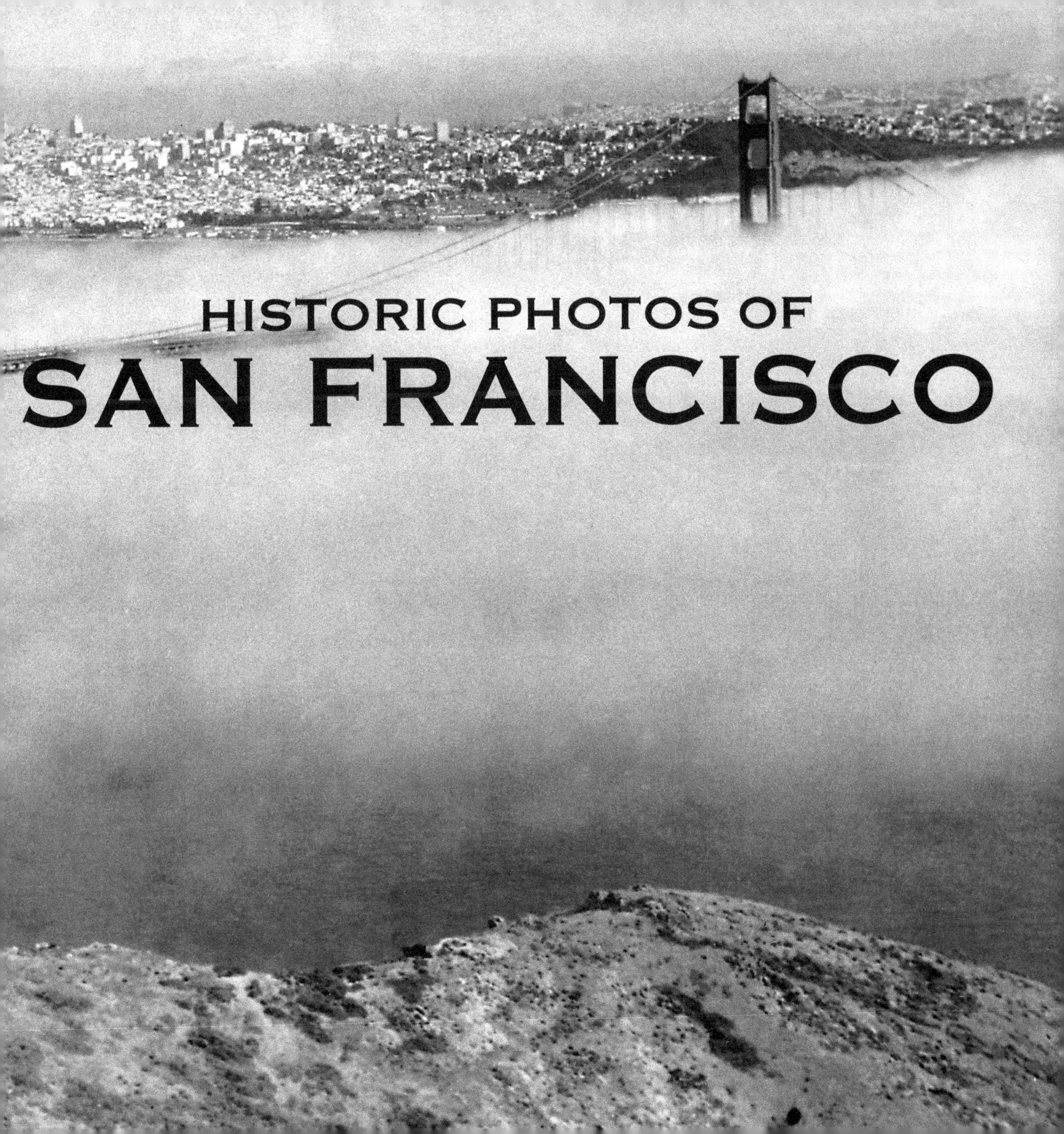

Turner Publishing Company
www.turnerpublishing.com

Historic Photos of San Francisco

Library of Congress Control Number: 2006934479

ISBN-10: 1-59652-307-7
ISBN-13: 978-1-59652-307-4

ISBN 978-1-68336-938-7 (hc)

Contents

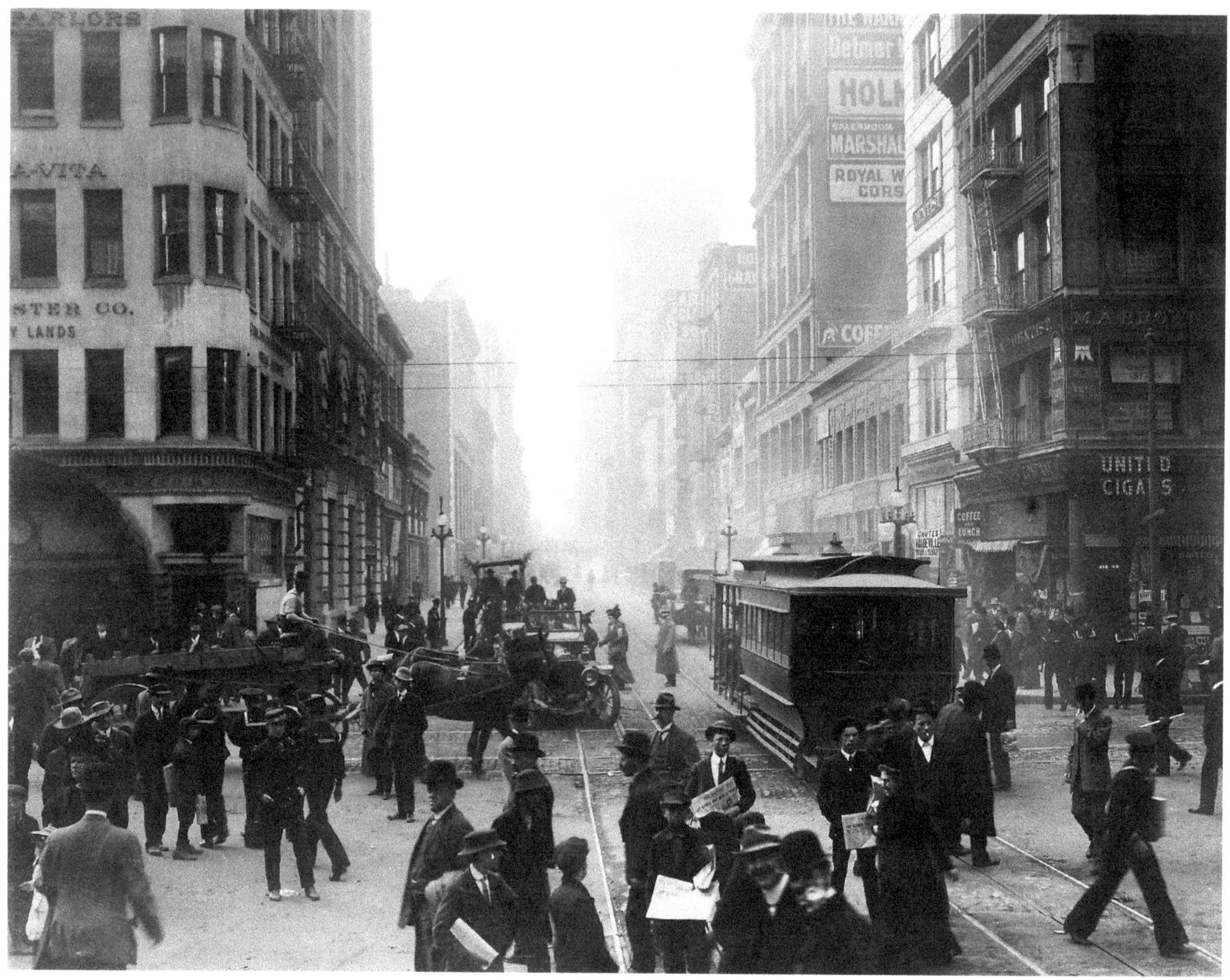

Well-dressed people are coming to work along Kearny Street, in this 1909 picture. Many of the businesses nearby that were destroyed by the earthquake and fire of 1906 stand rebuilt, including the nearby Palace Hotel, which reopened in 1909.

Acknowledgments

This volume, *Historic Photos of San Francisco,* is the result of the cooperation and efforts of many individuals and organizations. It is with great thanks that we acknowledge the valuable contribution of the following for their generous support.

San Francisco Public Library

Robert Chandler

Teddy Schall

Fran Schall

Gerry Schall

Janice Pivnick

Andrew Lack

This book is a tribute to my family, and a celebration of San Francisco.

Mom, for your dedication and generosity; Dad, for your kindness and patience; and Teddy, for your intellect and wit—thank you. I love you. *Rebecca*

Preface

San Francisco, California, has thousands of historic photographs that reside in archives, both locally and nationally. This book began with the observation that, while those photographs are of great interest to many, they are not easily accessible. During a time when San Francisco is looking ahead and evaluating its future course, many people are asking, How do we treat the past? These decisions affect every aspect of the city—architecture, public spaces, commerce, and infrastructure—and these, in turn, affect the way that people live their lives. This book seeks to provide easy access to a valuable, objective look into San Francisco's history.

The power of photographs is that they are less subjective than text in their treatment of history. Although the photographer can make decisions regarding subject matter and how to capture and present it, photographs do not provide the breadth of interpretation that text does. For this reason, they offer an original, untainted perspective that allows the viewer to interpret and observe.

This project represents countless hours of review and research. The researchers and author have reviewed thousands of photographs in numerous archives. We greatly appreciate the generous assistance of the archivists listed in the acknowledgments of this work, without whom this project could not have been completed.

The goal in publishing this work is to provide broader access to sets of extraordinary photographs that seek to inspire, provide perspective, and evoke insight that might assist people who are responsible for determining San Francisco's future. In addition, the book seeks to preserve the past with adequate respect and reverence.

The photographs selected have been reproduced in black and white to provide depth to the images. With the exception of touching up imperfections that have accrued with the passage of time and cropping where necessary, no other changes have been made. The focus and clarity of many images is limited to the technology and the ability of the photographer at the time they were taken.

The work is divided into eras. Beginning with some of the earliest known photographs of San Francisco, the first section records photographs from before the Civil War through the end of the nineteenth century. The second section spans the beginning and earlier part of the twentieth century. Each section to follow spans a decade of life in San Francisco, with the last chapter covering the 1960s.

In each of these sections we have made an effort to capture various aspects of life through our selection of photographs. People, commerce, transportation, infrastructure, religious institutions, and educational institutions have been included to provide a broad perspective.

We encourage readers to reflect as they walk in front of Lotta's Fountain at the Palace Hotel, along San Francisco Bay, the Golden Gate Bridge, through the bustle of the Ferry Building lots, or along California Street. It is the publisher's hope that in utilizing this work, longtime residents will learn something new and that new residents will gain a perspective on where San Francisco has been, so that each can contribute to its future.

—Todd Bottorff, Publisher

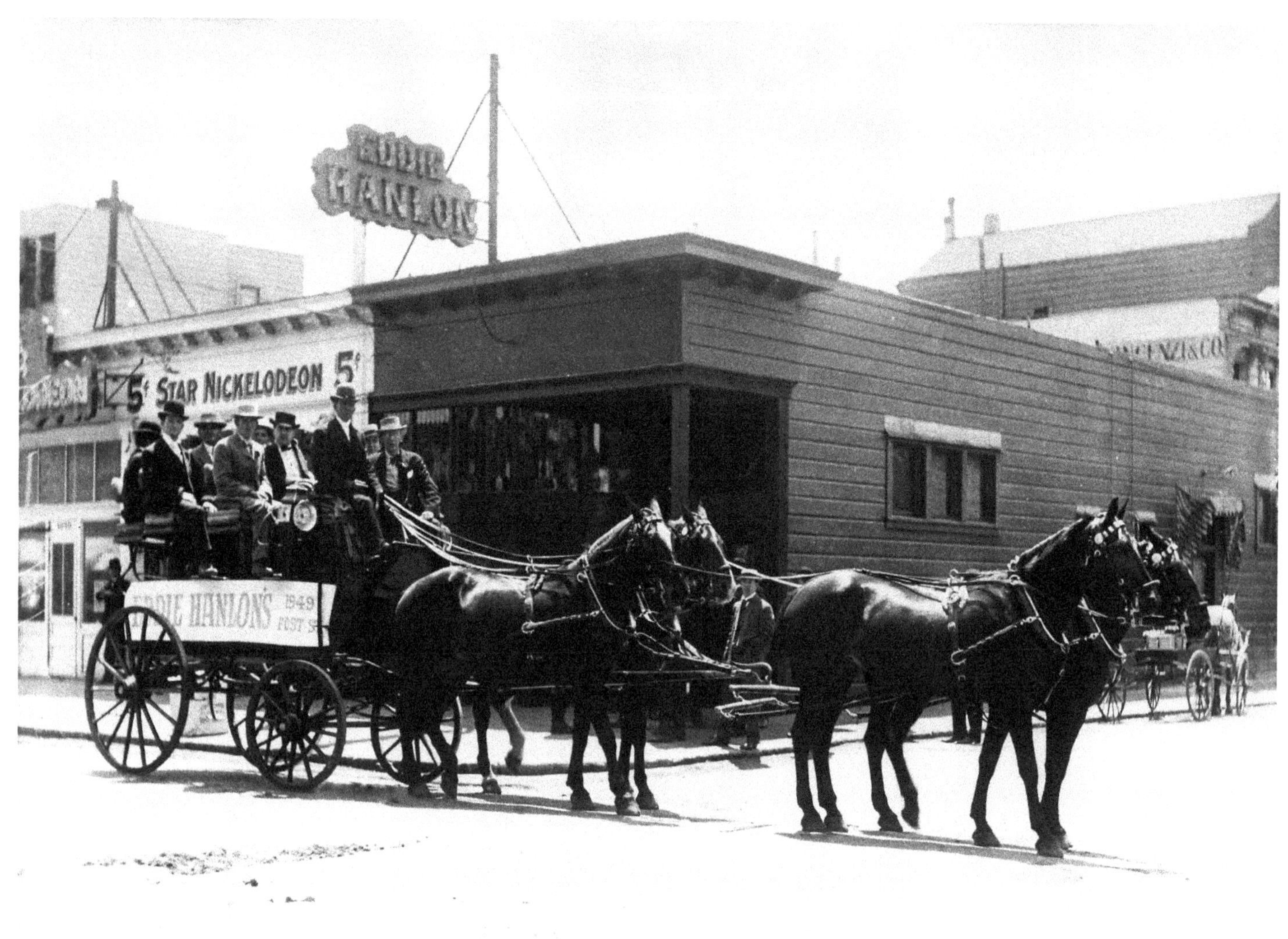

Eddie Hanlon's bar was located at 1949 Post Street between Fillmore and Steiner, here seen in 1908. Jones Memorial United Methodist Church now rests on this site.

The Paris of the West (1860–1899)

The San Francisco area had been inhabited for thousands of years by Native Americans before the first European, Don Gaspar de Portola, discovered San Francisco Bay in 1769. In the 1770s, Spanish missionaries settled in what would become San Francisco, and the city remained a detached outpost of the Spanish Empire for the next half century. After gaining independence from Spain, San Francisco—then known as Yerba Buena, after the fragrant herb abundant in the area—became part of Mexico's quiet Alta California province in 1821. In 1847, during the Mexican-American war, American settlers occupying the city renamed it San Francisco.

After the discovery of gold at Sutter's Mill in the Sierra foothills of California in 1848, fortune hunters and adventurers the world over rushed to California in one of the greatest human migrations in history. In 1850, as California joined the Union as the 31st state, San Francisco, its population exploding, was becoming a melting pot in which people from distant lands, distinct traditions, different political views, and varied ways of life lived and worked together. Due to its territorial isolation, an atypically complex and dynamic society evolved. Although the gold supply in the Sierra Nevada foothills was depleted by the mid 1850s, silver discoveries over the next several decades in Nevada created even greater fortunes, which poured into San Francisco and accelerated its development. Residents grew passionately attached to life in California, and the future of the state rested not on gold, but on agriculture, commerce, and industry.

Although not the state's capital during the Gold Rush, San Francisco emerged as the mining capital of the West and the state's center for commerce and the press. California's factories, banks, and other businesses prospered in San Francisco in the early years of its statehood. A spirit of entrepreneurialism and capitalism emerged that has survived in California for the past 150 years. Mass migrations brought entrepreneurs to San Francisco who created companies that still exist today, such as Levi Strauss and Company, Boudin Bakery, Shreve and Company, Wells Fargo Bank, and the Ghiradelli Chocolate Company. As a result of its sundry population, San Francisco acquired an international flavor, and the attitudes of its citizens were often as varied as the cities from which they came.

San Francisco's strategic position on the West Coast helped it to protect the entire nation and provided a gateway for trade with Asia and other parts of the world. Throughout the second half of the nineteenth century, a city of sand dunes and shanties would be transformed into what is now among the nation's most desirable real estate. The city progressed with the introduction of the cable car in the 1870s and erection of monuments like the Palace Hotel and City Hall. With the outbreak of the Spanish American War in 1898, San Francisco became the most important military base in the West. As the twentieth century drew near, San Francisco emerged as the West's first metropolis, becoming financial competitor to New York and cultural rival to Boston.

A group of people stands in front of the first office of Wells, Fargo, & Co. at 424 Montgomery Street, between California and Sacramento, in the 1850s. Founded in 1852 by Henry Wells and William Fargo, the bank earned a reputation for its dependable service and security. It was also the company of the famous Pony Express. The Wells Fargo building burned in the fires after the earthquake, but the bank's vault and credit remained unscathed. After the quake, the bank committed to help rebuild the city. Today its headquarters remains on this block, at 420 Montgomery.

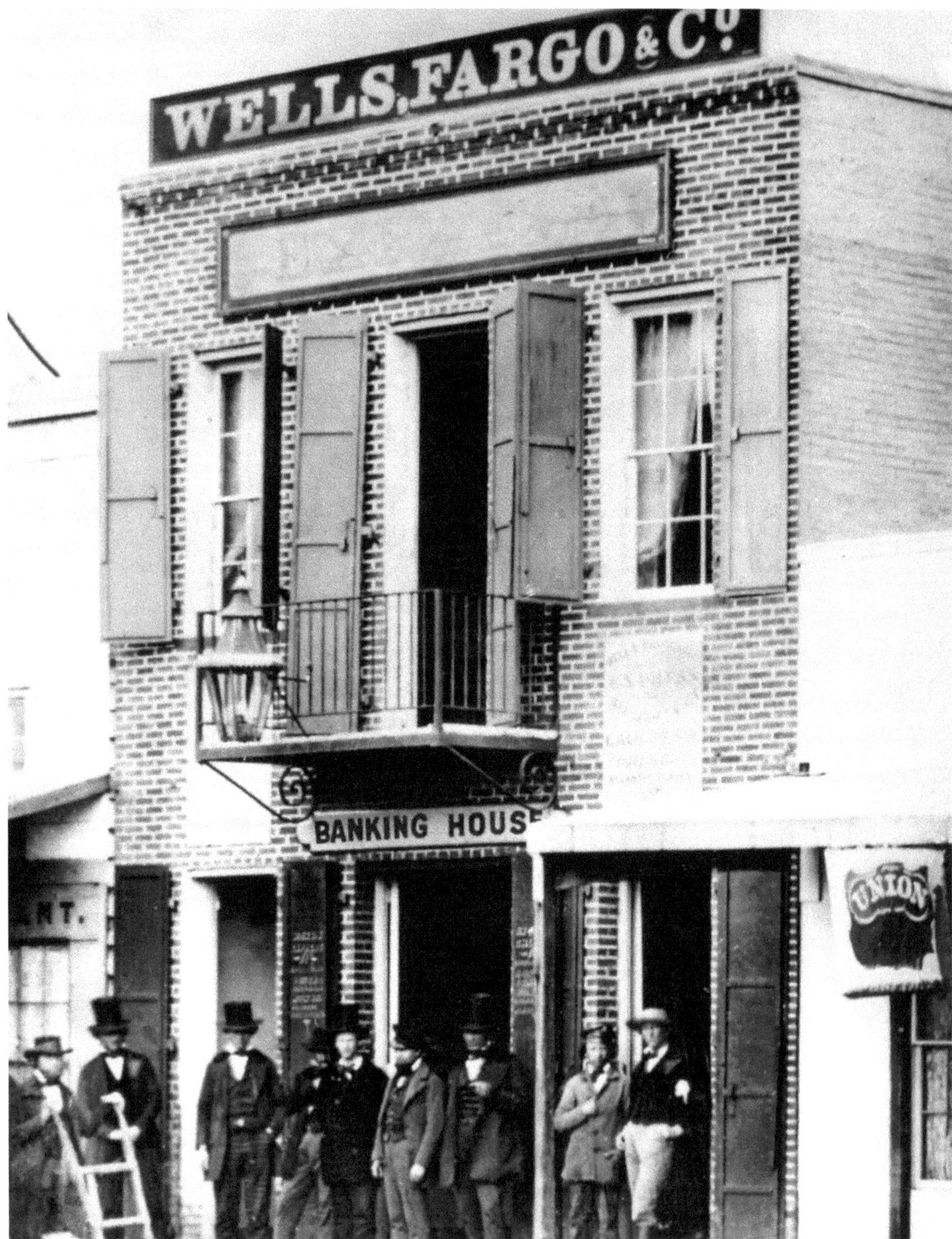

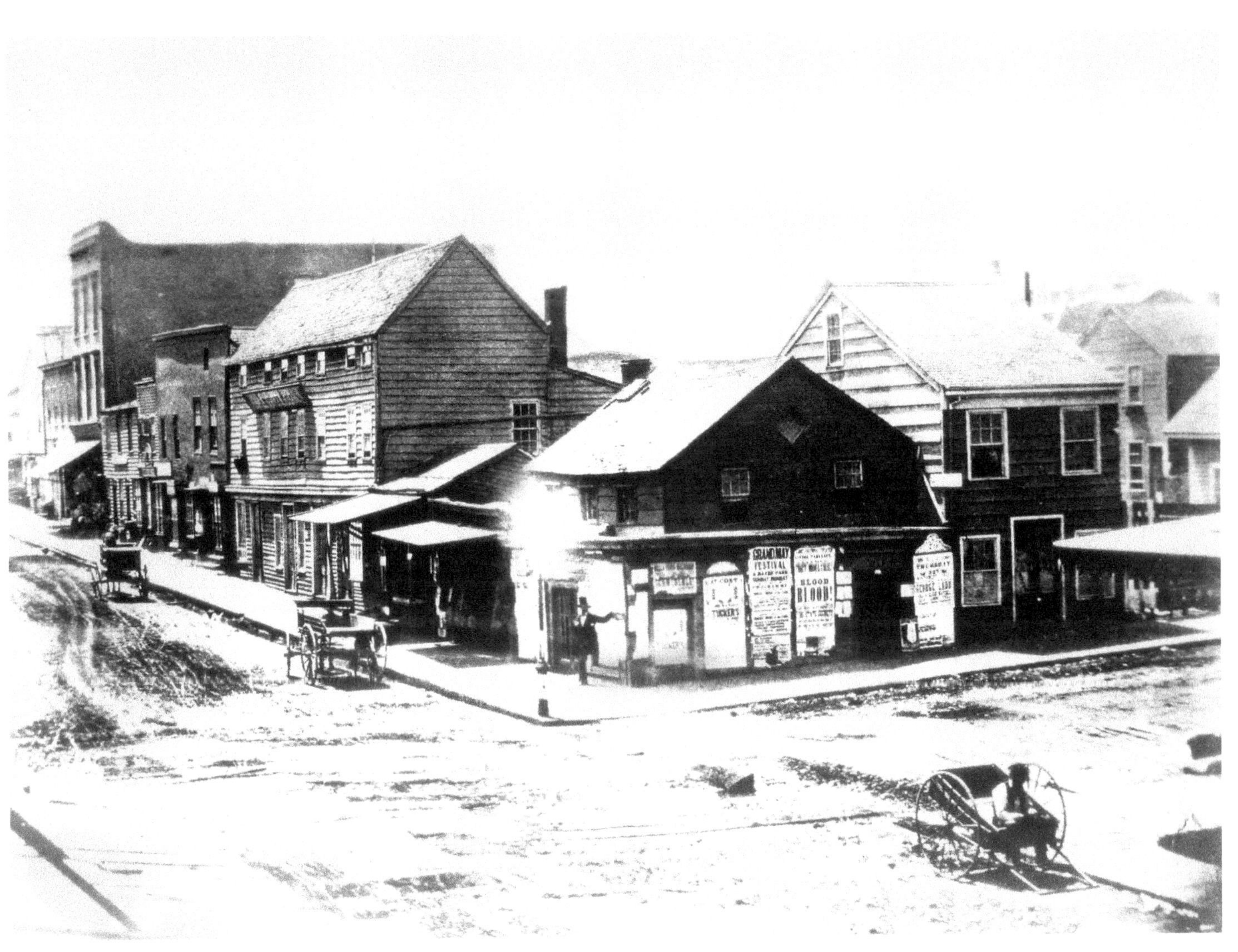

In the early 1850s, local jeweler Christian Russ built the Russ House, a hotel on Montgomery between Bush and Pine streets in the Financial District, shown here in 1860. In 1927 at this location, the 31-story Russ Building was built. Modeled after Chicago's Tribune Tower, the Russ Building was the largest building west of Chicago for 30 years.

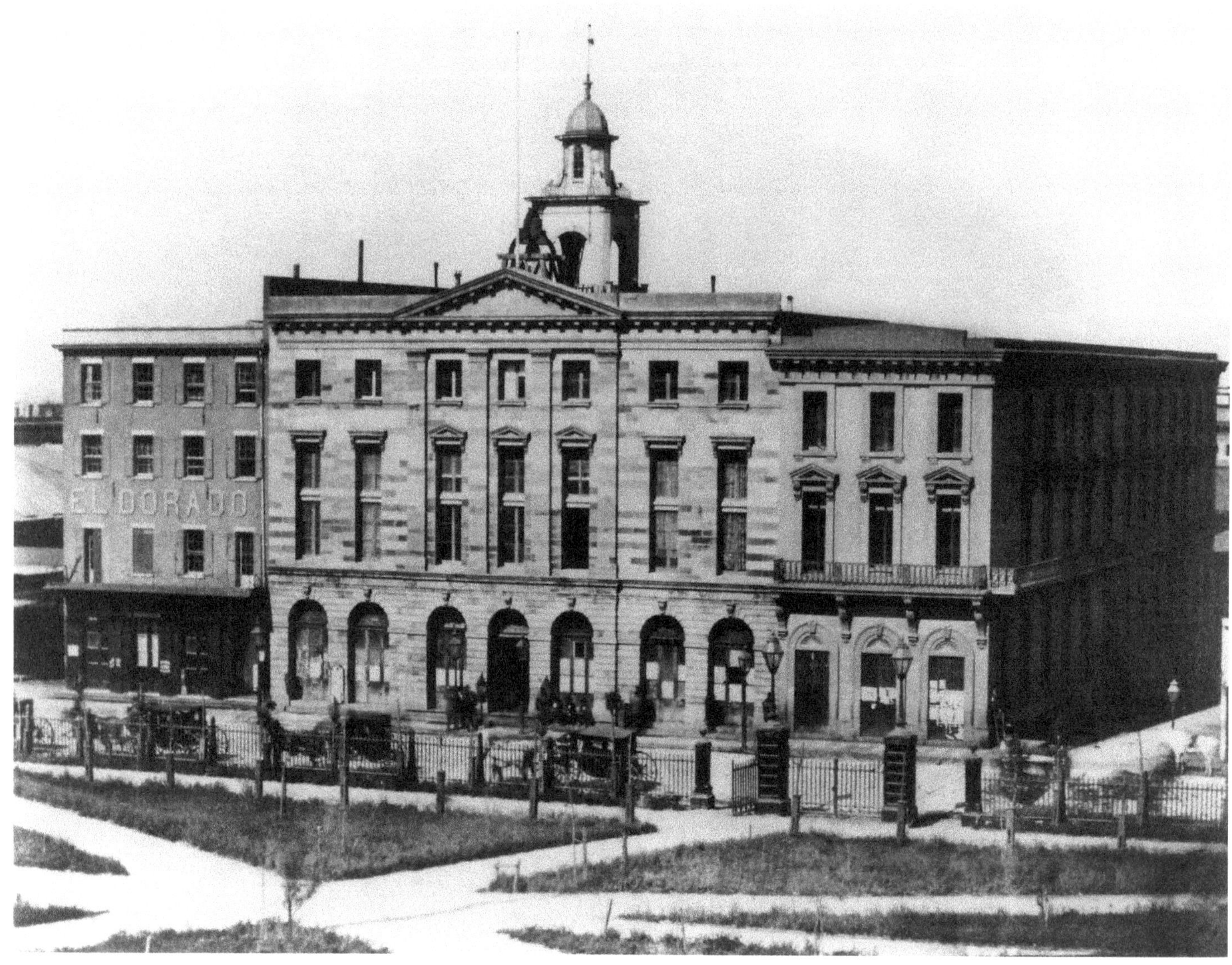

Portsmouth Square was the town center of the Mexican pueblo of Yerba Buena, and is the site where Captain John B. Montgomery planted the American flag on July 9, 1846, and claimed the port for the United States. Also here in 1848, Samuel Brannan ran through the streets yelling "Gold, Gold, Gold from the American River!" marking the start of the Gold Rush. During the Gold Rush, Portsmouth Square brimmed with gambling halls, theaters, and saloons. Shown here in May 1855 are McGuire's Opera House, the Union Hotel, and the Eldorado, one of the more famous of these establishments. The Parker House nextdoor served as San Francisco's city hall, and the Eldorado became the city's Hall of Records and then the Hall of Justice. On this site now stands a tourist hotel, regarded by many as a lackluster successor. Portsmouth Square, now a hub of Chinatown and one of the area's only wide-open spaces, is always crowded with tourists and Chinatown residents doing tai chi or playing chinese chess.

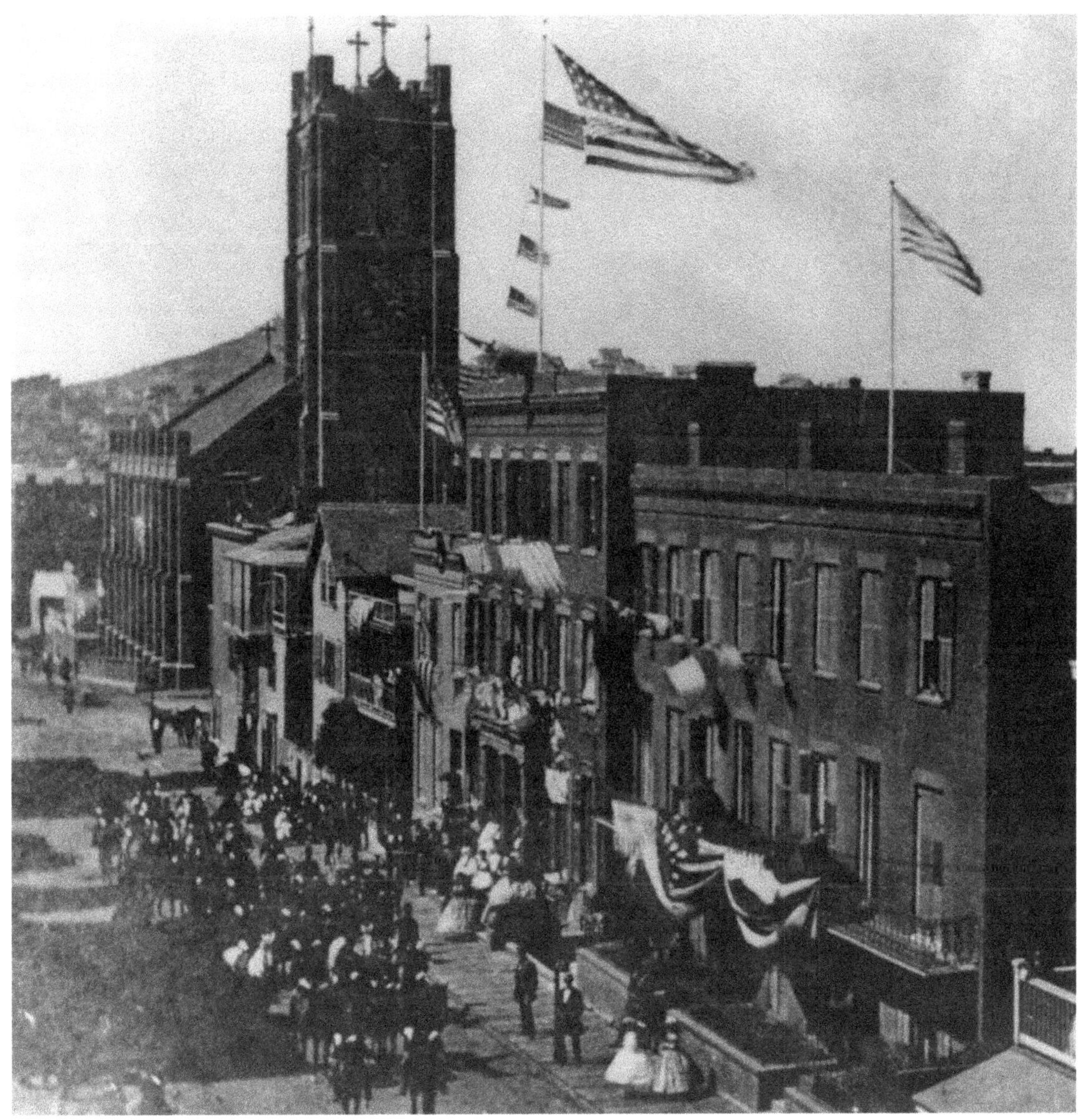

A Fourth of July parade in 1864 marches past Old St. Mary's Church on Dupont Street, now Chinatown's Grant Avenue. Built in 1853 and 1854 from imported Chinese granite and New England bricks—scarce materials in Gold Rush San Francisco—Old Saint Mary's was San Francisco's biggest building for a time. Brothels and other "un-Christian" indulgences surrounded the church into the twentieth century. Church leaders had hoped that the biblical command "Son, Observe the Time and Fly from Evil," prominently displayed on the front of the church clock, would resonate with neighborhood sinners, especially the prostitutes in the brothel located directly across the street, eye level with the clock tower. The early development of Telegraph Hill is visible in the background. The Bank of California opened the next day, July 5, 1864.

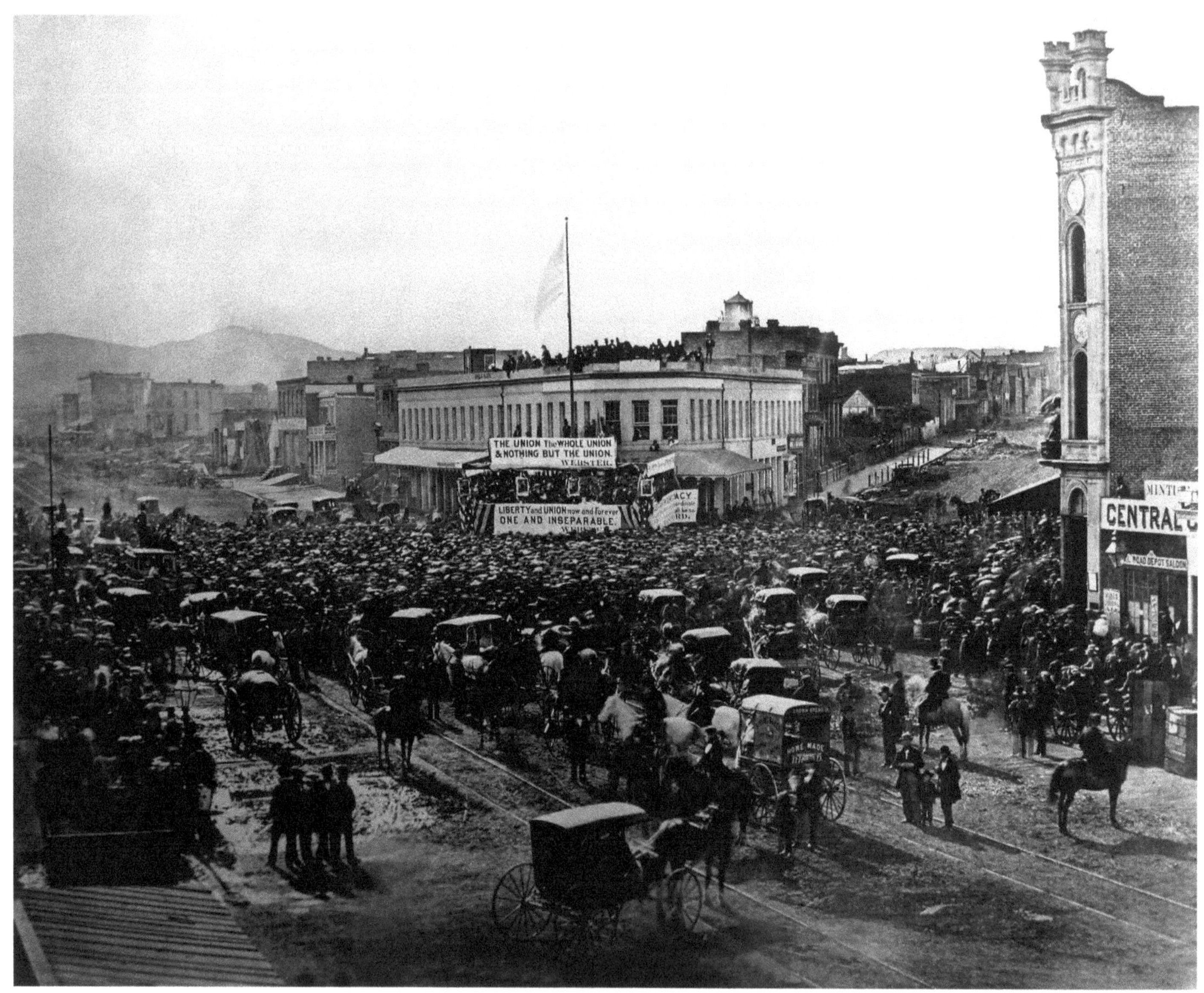

During the Civil War, rumors abounded that Confederate sympathizers would commit acts of sabotage at strategic San Francisco targets including Alcatraz, the Presidio, Fort Point, and San Francisco Mint, would seize outgoing ships filled with treasure, or would otherwise confiscate the city's wealth of gold, silver, and other natural resources for use by the Confederacy. In response, great efforts were taken by civic leaders to demonstrate California's loyalty to the Union, as evidenced by this pro-Union rally on February 22, 1861, at the intersection of Post, Montgomery, and Market streets. More San Franciscans came to show support for the Union that day than the number of San Franciscans who voted in the 1860 election.

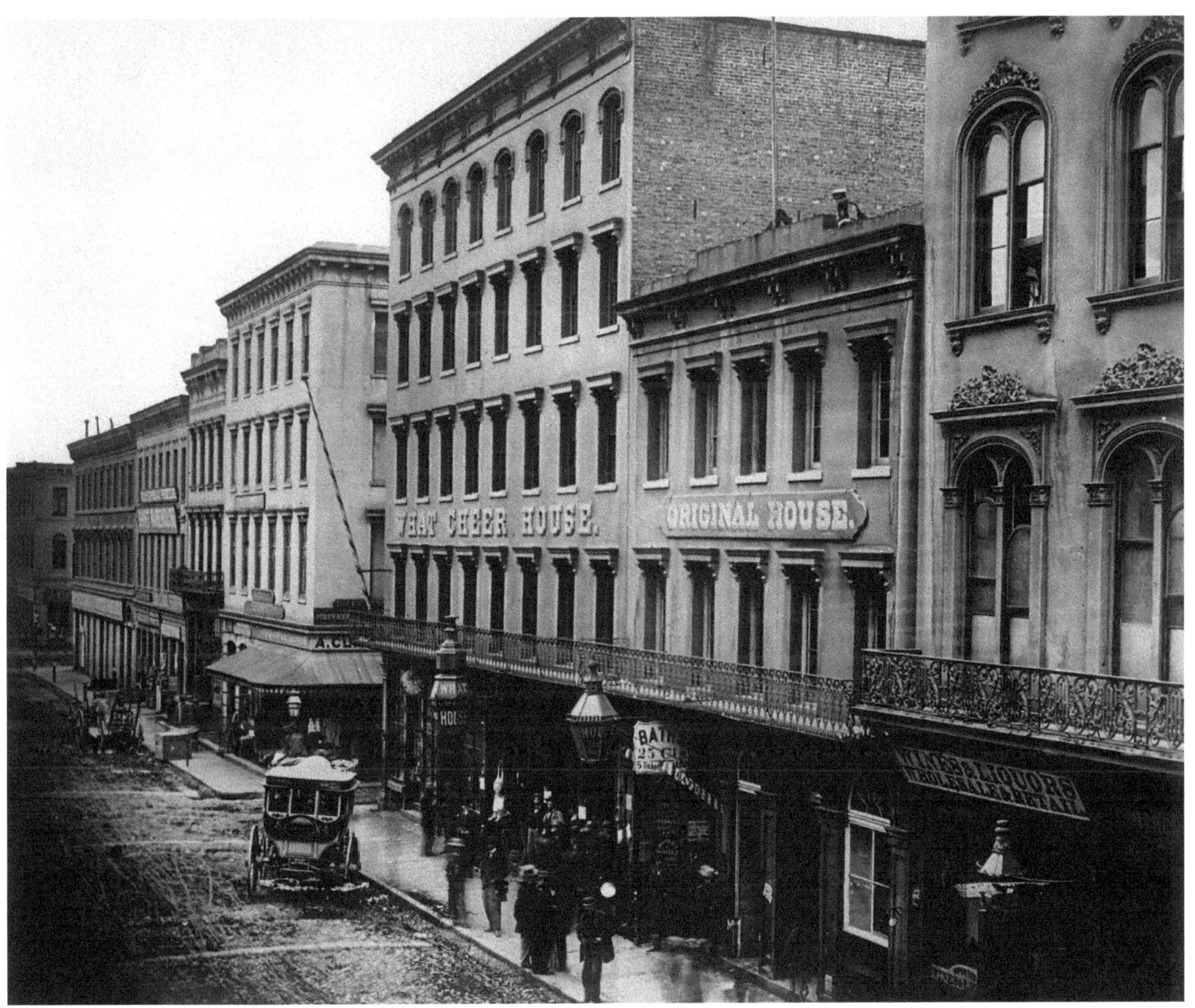

The famous hostelry, the What Cheer House on the south side of Sacramento, below Montgomery Street, is shown here in 1865. Founded in 1852 by R. B. Woodward, the hotel catered only to men, banned alcohol from its premises, and housed San Francisco's first museum and free library. It burned in the Great Earthquake of 1906. The site is now a California Registered Historical Landmark.

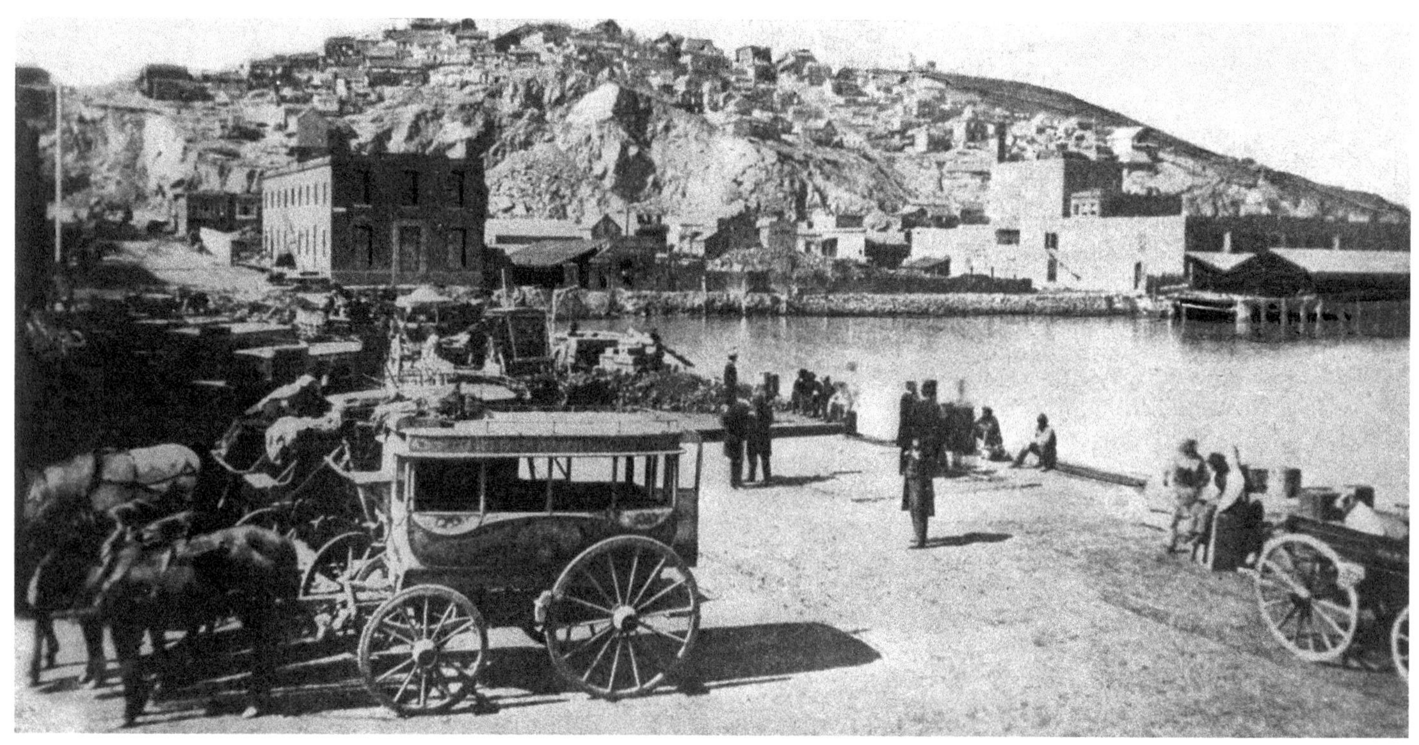

This photograph from 1865 shows San Francisco's old waterfront along the original San Francisco Bay shoreline on the northwest corner of Broadway and Front streets. In the background is Clark's Point Warehouse. Built by early pioneer William Clark in 1847 out of redwood trees from Corte Madera, Clark's Point served as San Francisco's first wharf and had a monopoly on waterfront port activities until after the Gold Rush.

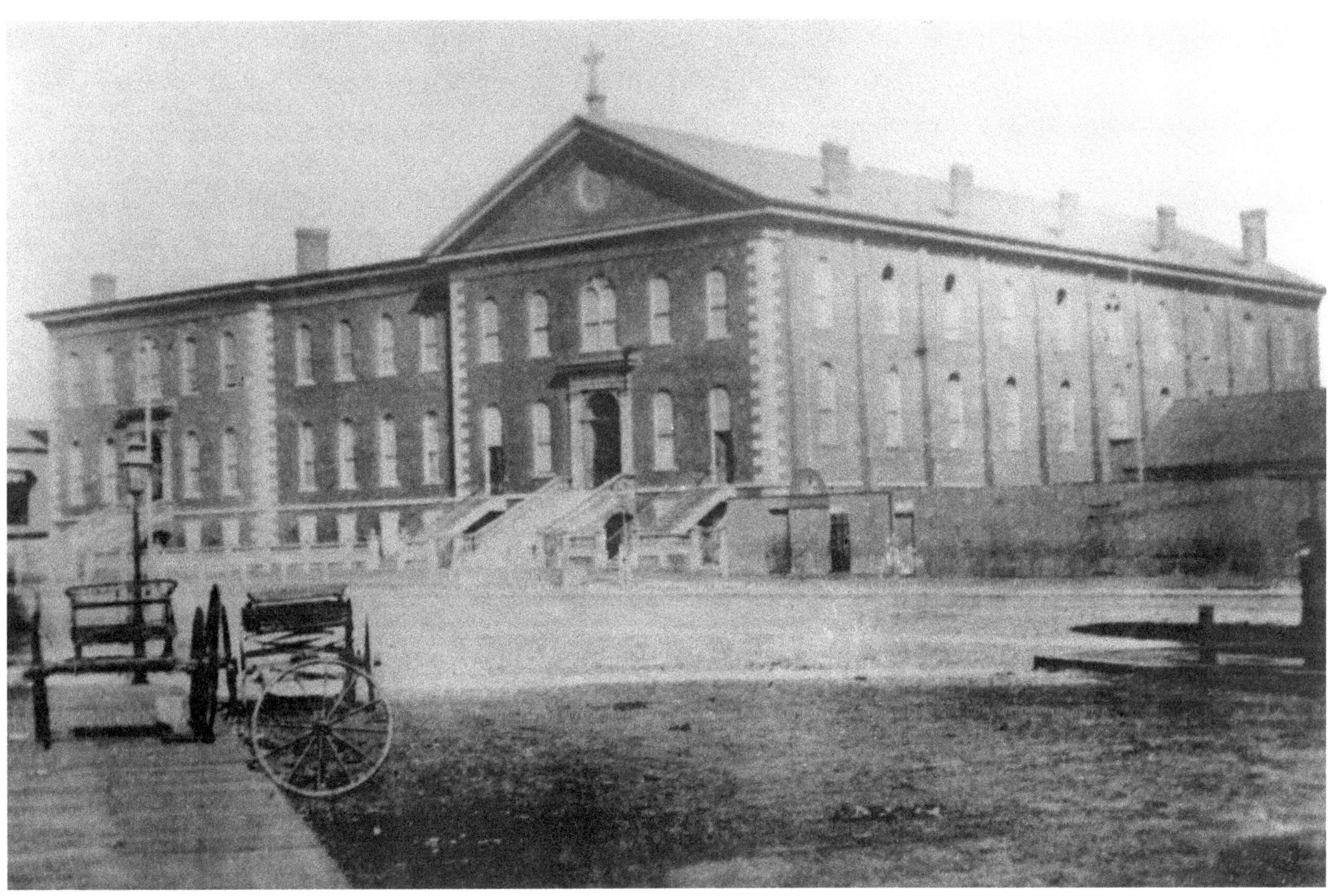

Shown here in 1865 is the second building of Saint Ignatius College along Market Street, San Francisco's first place of higher education. Sand dunes surrounded the first building of the college, constructed at this site in 1855 in what would become San Francisco's Financial District. A male-only institution for well over a century, the school offered a rigorous curriculum, which included Greek, Latin, history, geography, and elocution. The campus would change locations several times, and change its name to the University of San Francisco in 1930. The site later became home to the Emporium department store, and today is a Bloomingdale's.

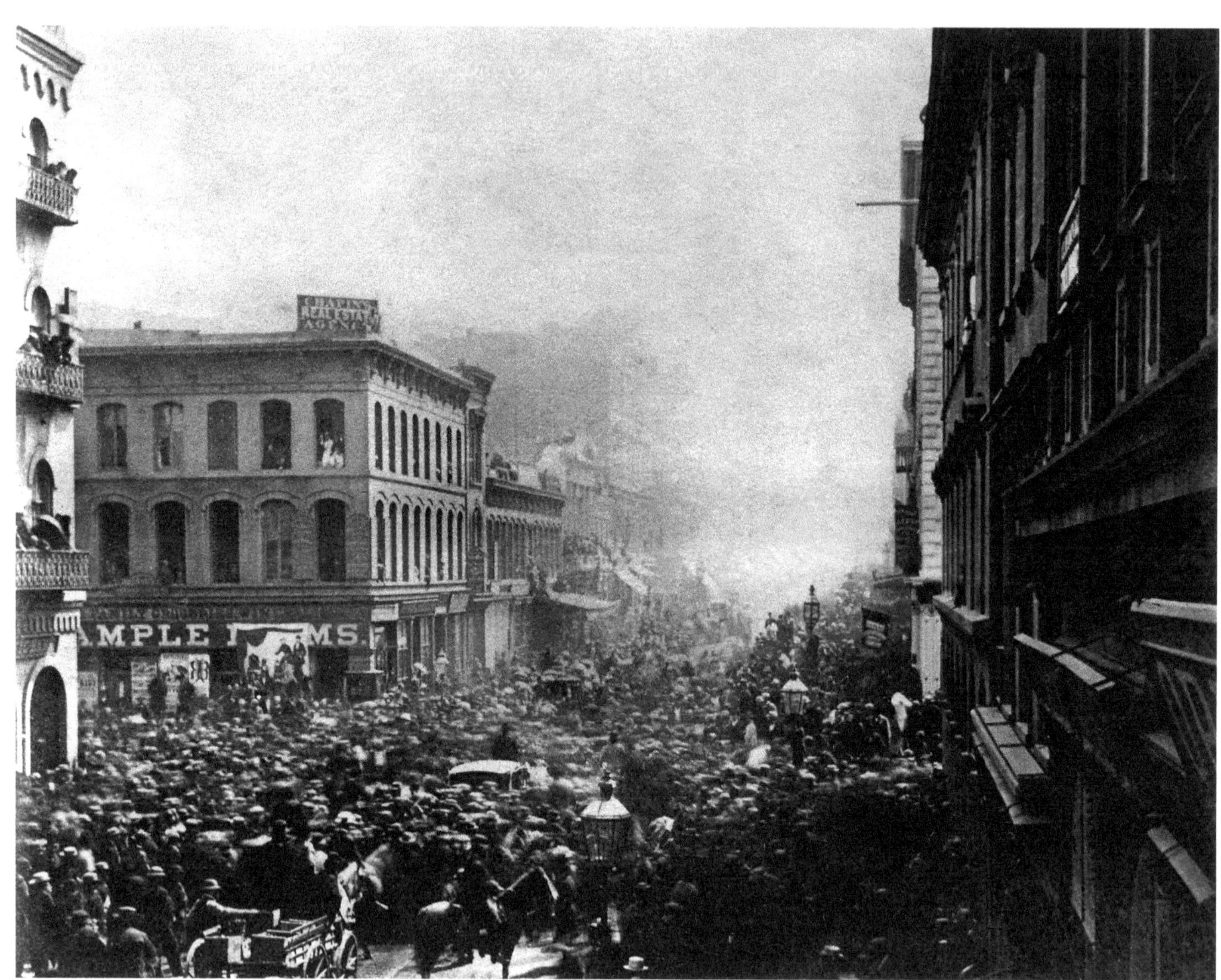

On Montgomery from California Street on September 11, 1867, A. M. Higgins marches south playing a hand organ to execute a wager he made regarding the results of the state election. The crowd contributed about $6,000 for the benefit of orphan asylums that day.

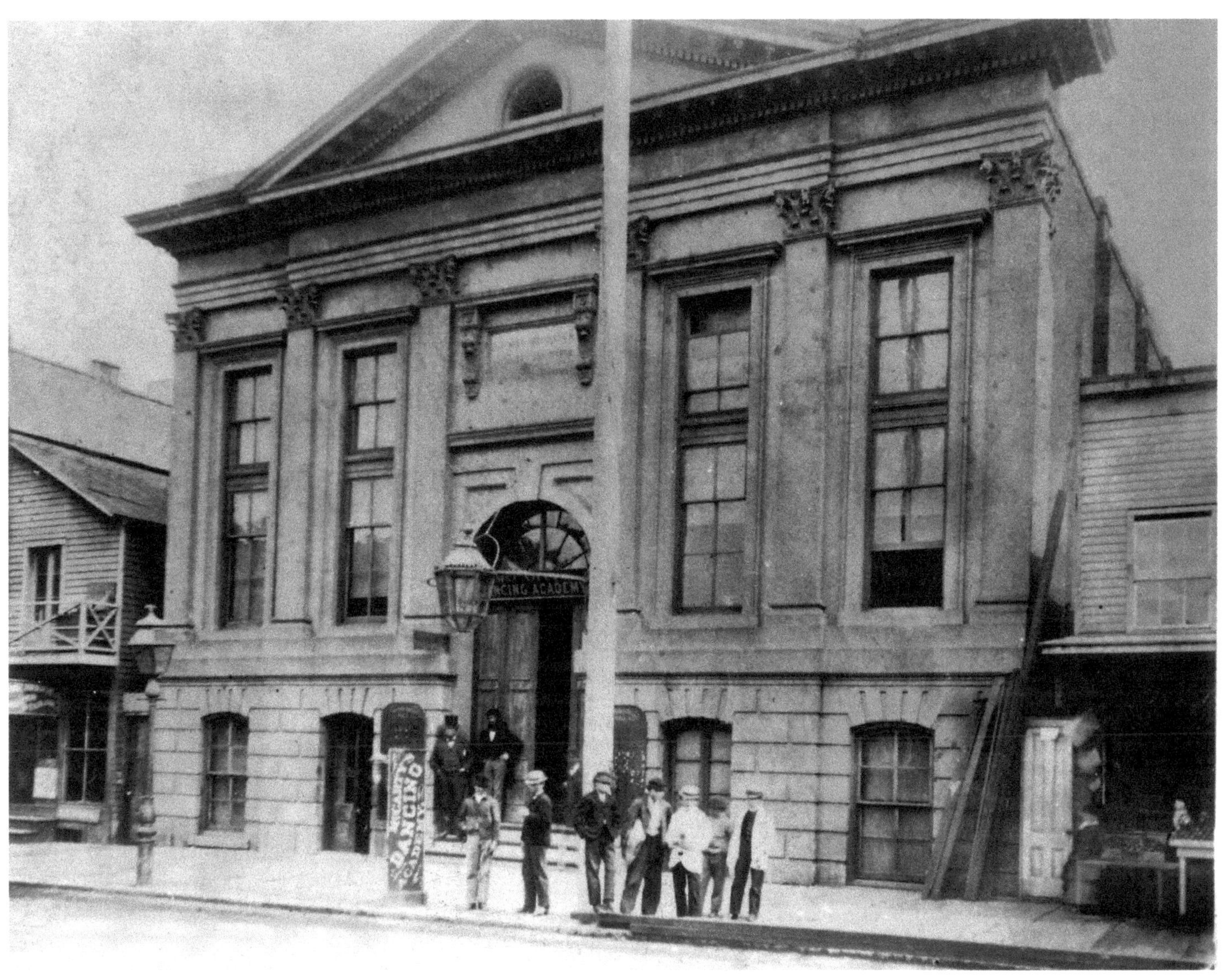

Dashaway Hall, seen here at Post Street near Dupont (present-day Grant) in 1869, was owned by the Dashaway Temperance Society, a group of women opposed to the consumption of alcoholic beverages. It is believed that the name of this group was based on the phrase "Dash Away the Cup." The site housed a number of significant public meetings in the late 1800s, including the California Woman's State Suffrage Convention in 1871, and the initial meeting of residents to advocate and raise funds for the San Francisco Public Library system in 1877.

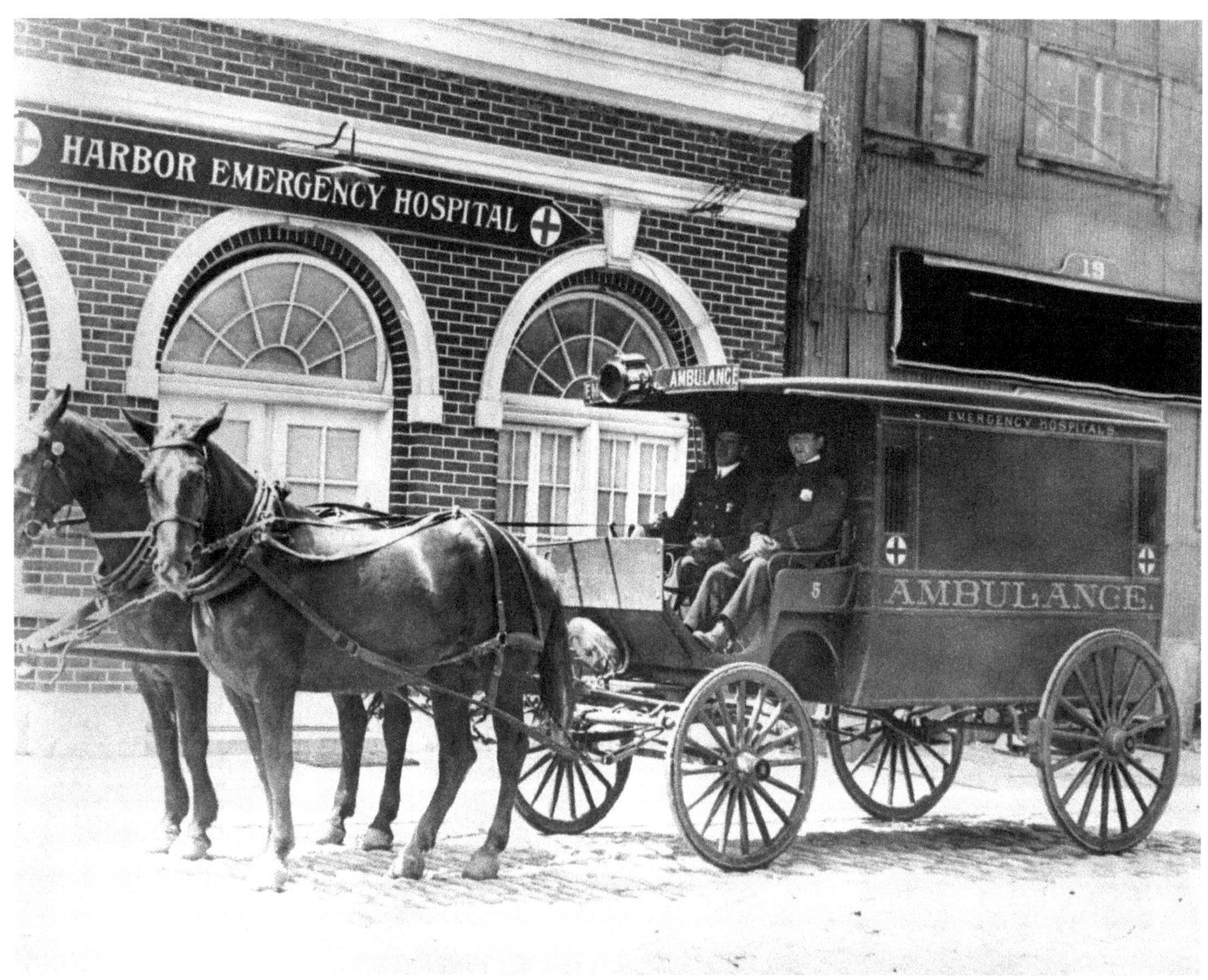

A horse-drawn ambulance waits outside Harbor Emergency Hospital in the late nineteenth century. After the Great Earthquake and fires of 1906, ambulances took injured citizens by the hundreds to this small downtown hospital, where steadfast medical personnel and volunteers worked swiftly to care for the wounded, while encircled by the blazing Financial District.

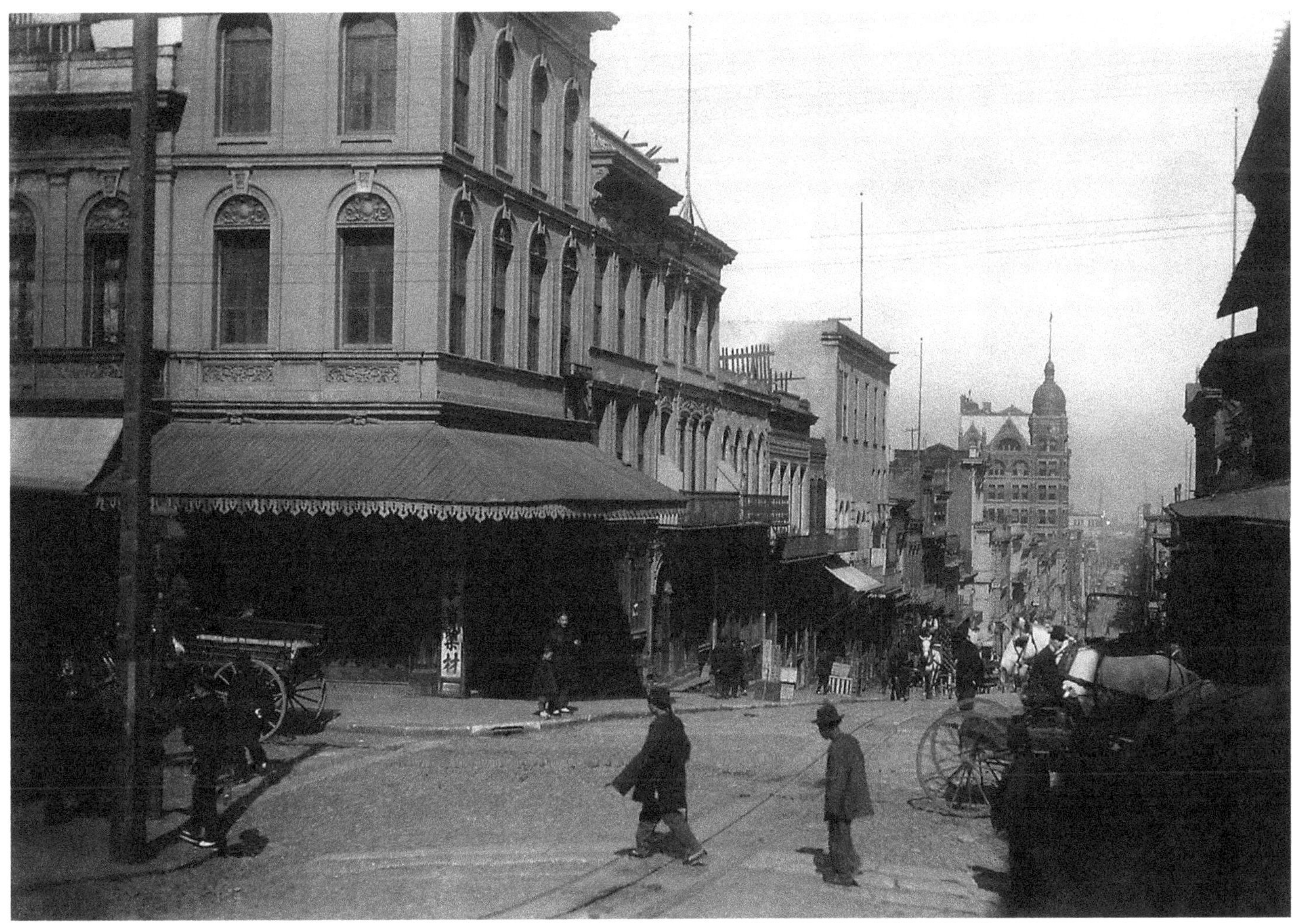

Today, San Francisco has North America's oldest and largest Chinatown, and is the largest base of Chinese activity outside mainland China. Chinatown is located in San Francisco's most coveted downtown real estate, bordered on the west by Nob Hill, on the east by the Financial District, and on the north by North Beach. The famous district originated in the 1850s. Tens of thousands of Chinese, mostly single men from the southern Chinese province of Guangdong, began to immigrate to San Francisco during the Gold Rush, seeking prosperity in the gold mines, and later to work on the building of the transcontinental railroad. Upon their arrival, the Chinese, whose presence and labor seemed to pose a threat, faced severe treatment. In the 1870s, San Francisco endured harsh economic times, and the hard-working Chinese became obvious scapegoats for the unemployed. The Chinese Exclusion Act of 1882, a law that reduced Chinese immigration to a trickle, was not repealed until World War II.

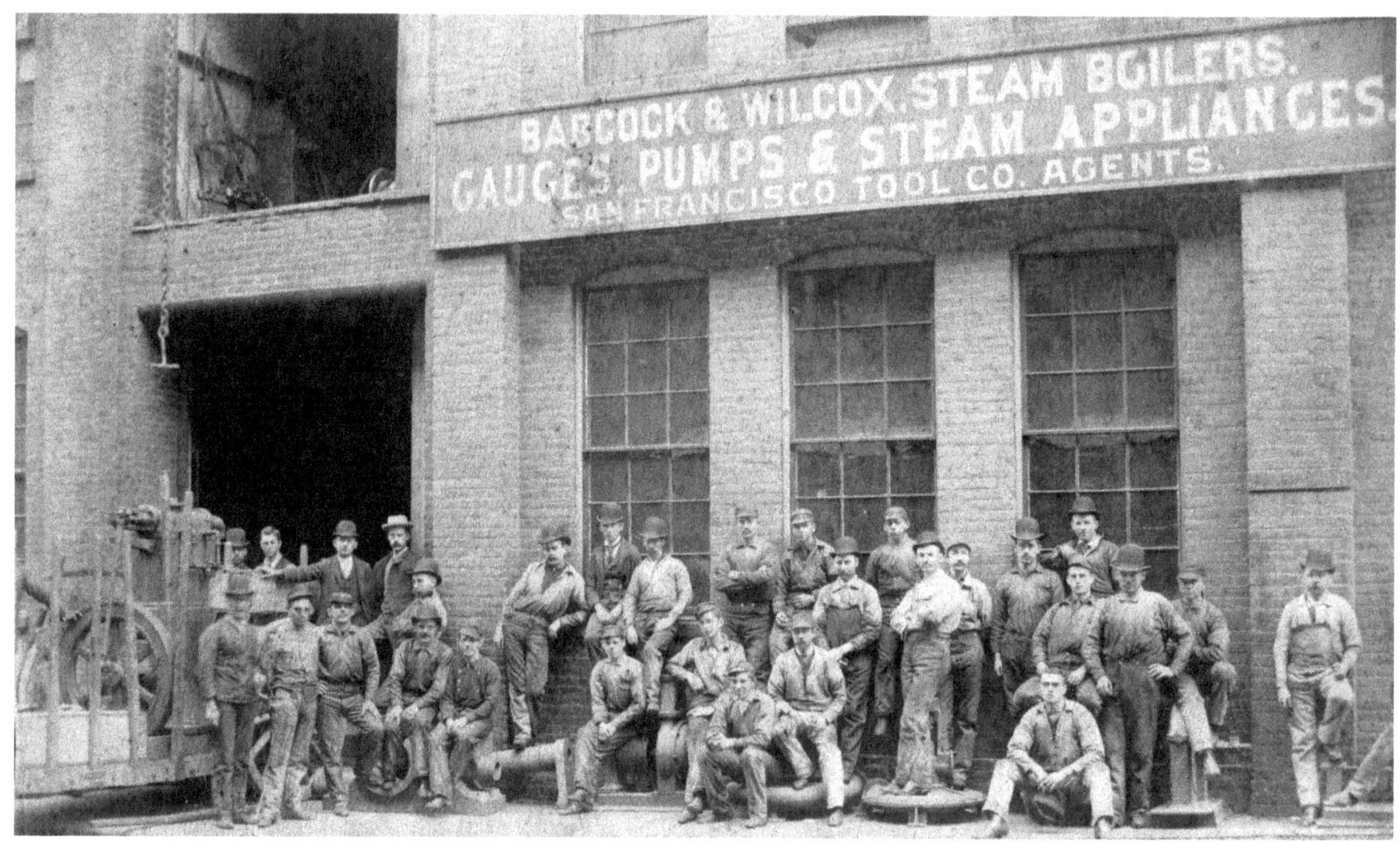

A group of employees proudly poses in front of the Babcock and Wilcox Building in the late 1800s. Founded in 1867 by Stephen Wilcox and George Babcock, the customer-minded company revolutionized the power generation industry with their water tube steam boilers, which made steam power safer in a variety of modes of transportation, and were the predecessor to modern high-temperature and pressure steam power plants. Babcock and Wilcox boilers were also used to heat many of the "modern homes" in San Francisco and other parts of the country starting in the nineteenth century. The company continues to build boilers today, employing more than 10,000 people.

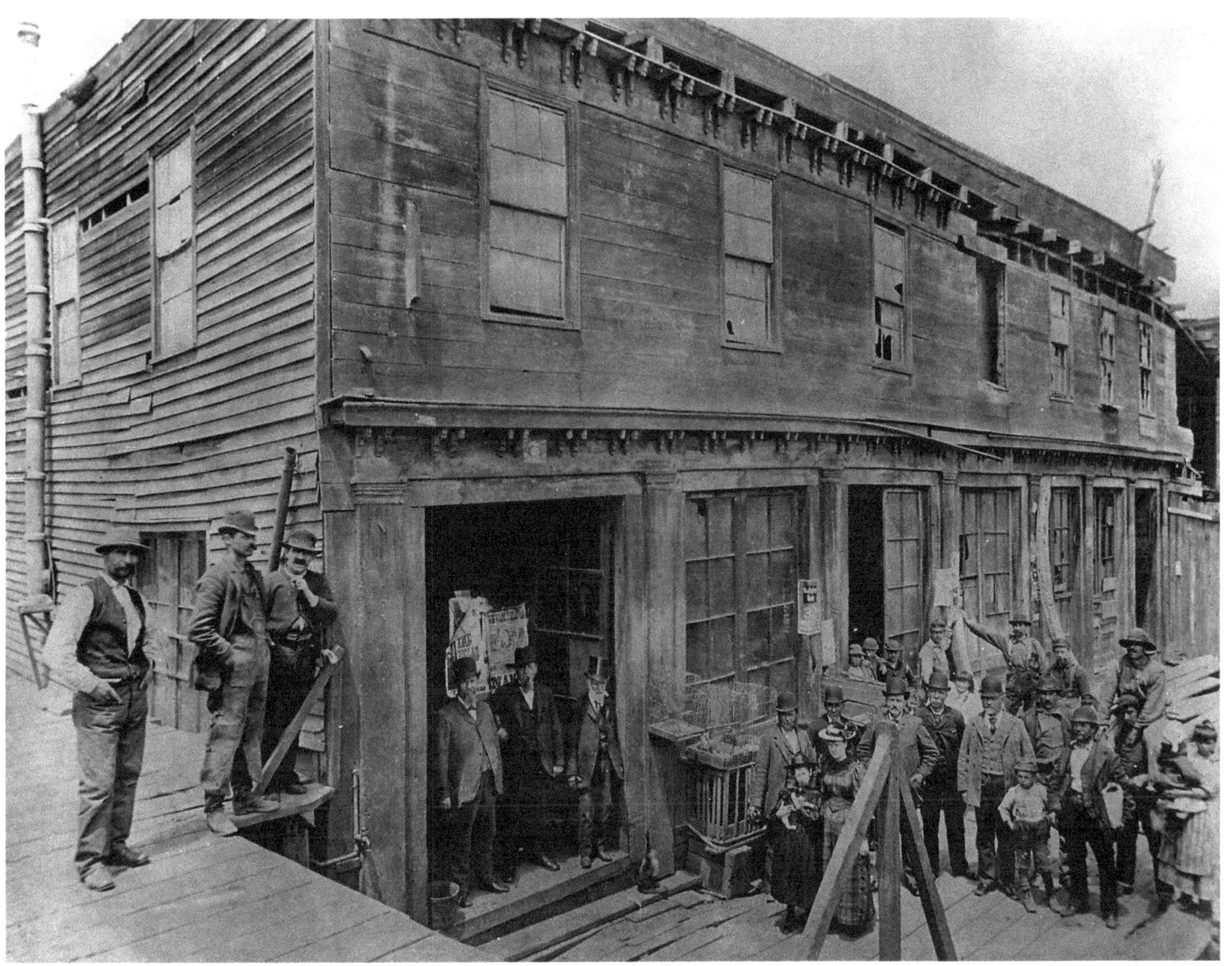

From its founding, San Francisco has always been a haven for eccentrics, mavericks, and curious individuals. Bob Warner was one such man who exemplified Old San Francisco's outlandish reputation. He opened Warner's Cobweb Palace in the 1850s, a kooky establishment situated at Meigg's Wharf on Francisco Street that was run by Warner for 40 years. The waterfront saloon and museum exhibited oddities and taxidermy from around the world, and a menagerie of live animals, including kangaroos, monkeys, and a trained parrot, legendary for its fondness for alcohol and ability to curse in four different languages. One of Warner's peculiarities was that he sincerely believed that spiders should never be killed, nor their web-building inhibited, and consequently cobwebs covered the building's grimy interior. One thousand portraits of named women adorned the walls of the arachnid-infested "palace."

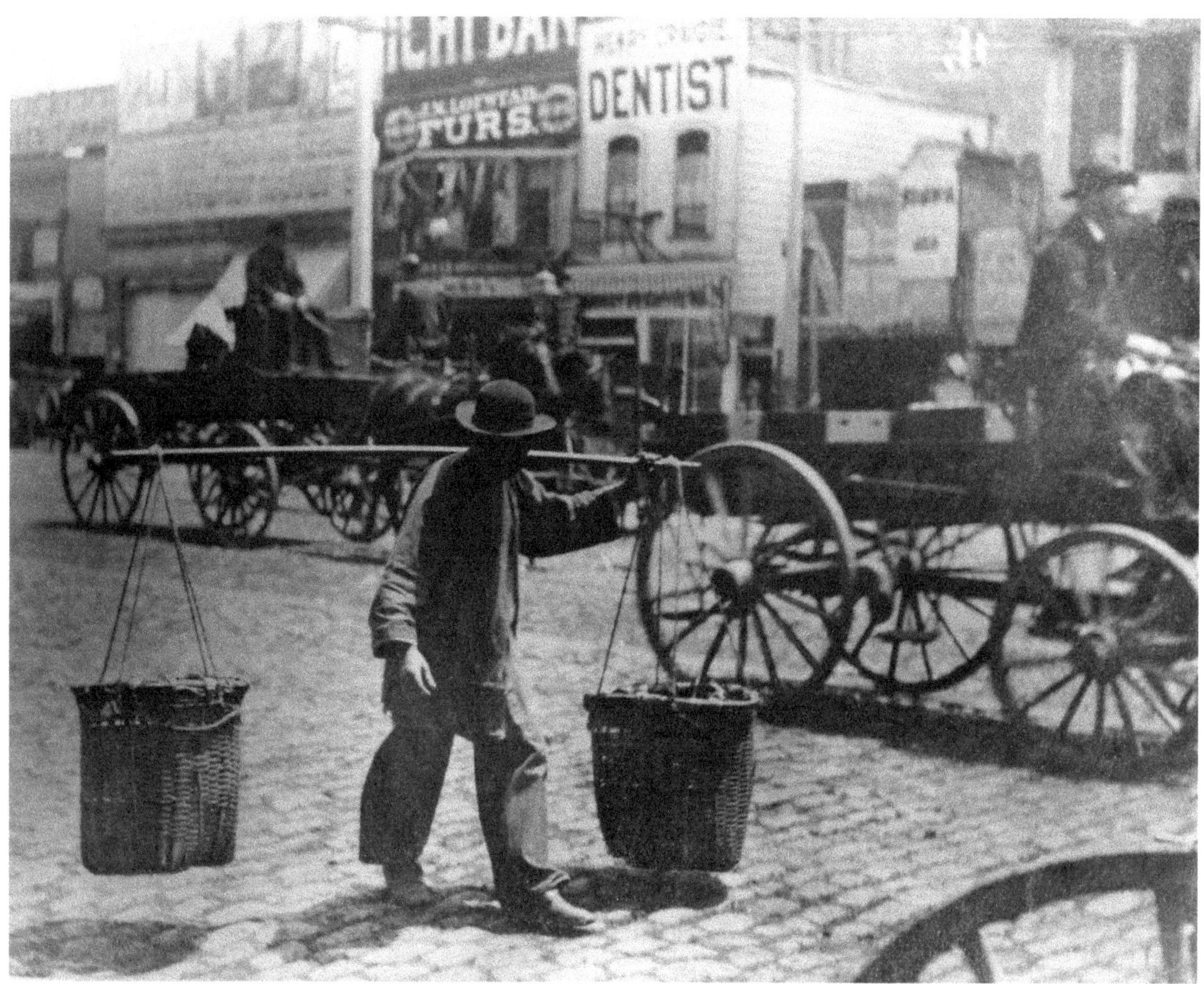

This Chinese peddler carries two large baskets of fresh food, most likely live chickens or fresh fish and vegetables, to sell to local residents in Chinatown in the late 1880s.

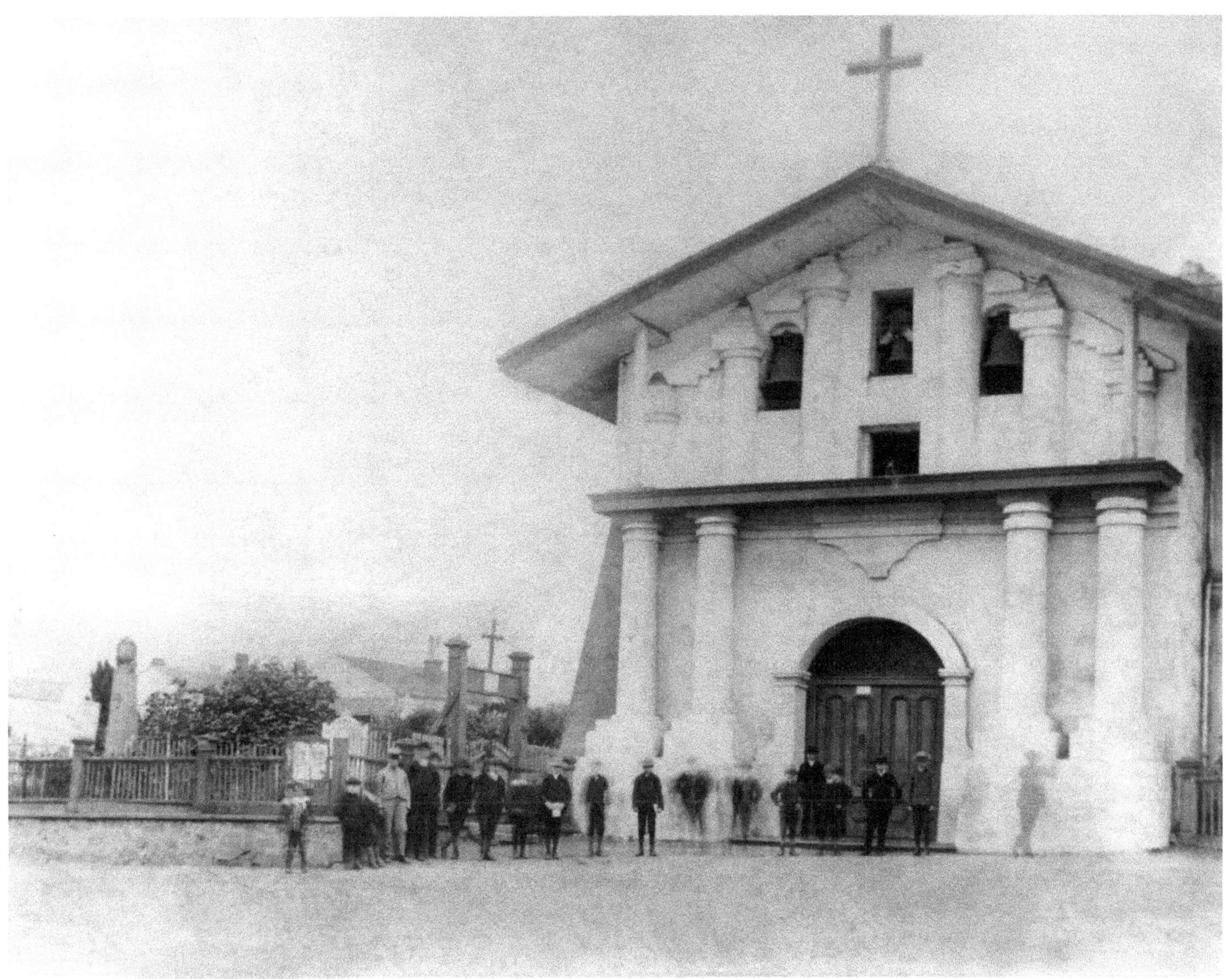

Mission Dolores, shown here in the late 1800s at 16th and Dolores streets, was founded by Father Junipero Serra as the 6th of 21 missions built during the Spanish Imperial rule of California in the eighteenth century, strategically placed so that each was no more than a day's horse ride apart as one traveled up the coast of California. Completed by Ohlone Indian workers in 1791, the church was built from 36,000 adobe bricks and has four-foot-thick adobe walls. During the Mission period, when Spain was trying to extend its empire in California and consolidate its territory, its goal was to Europeanize the neophyte Ohlone laborers and turn them into loyal Christian subjects of the Spanish crown. Mission Dolores is the oldest building in San Francisco, and contains San Francisco's oldest cemetery. It has survived several major earthquakes and is still an active church, serving the Mission and Castro districts.

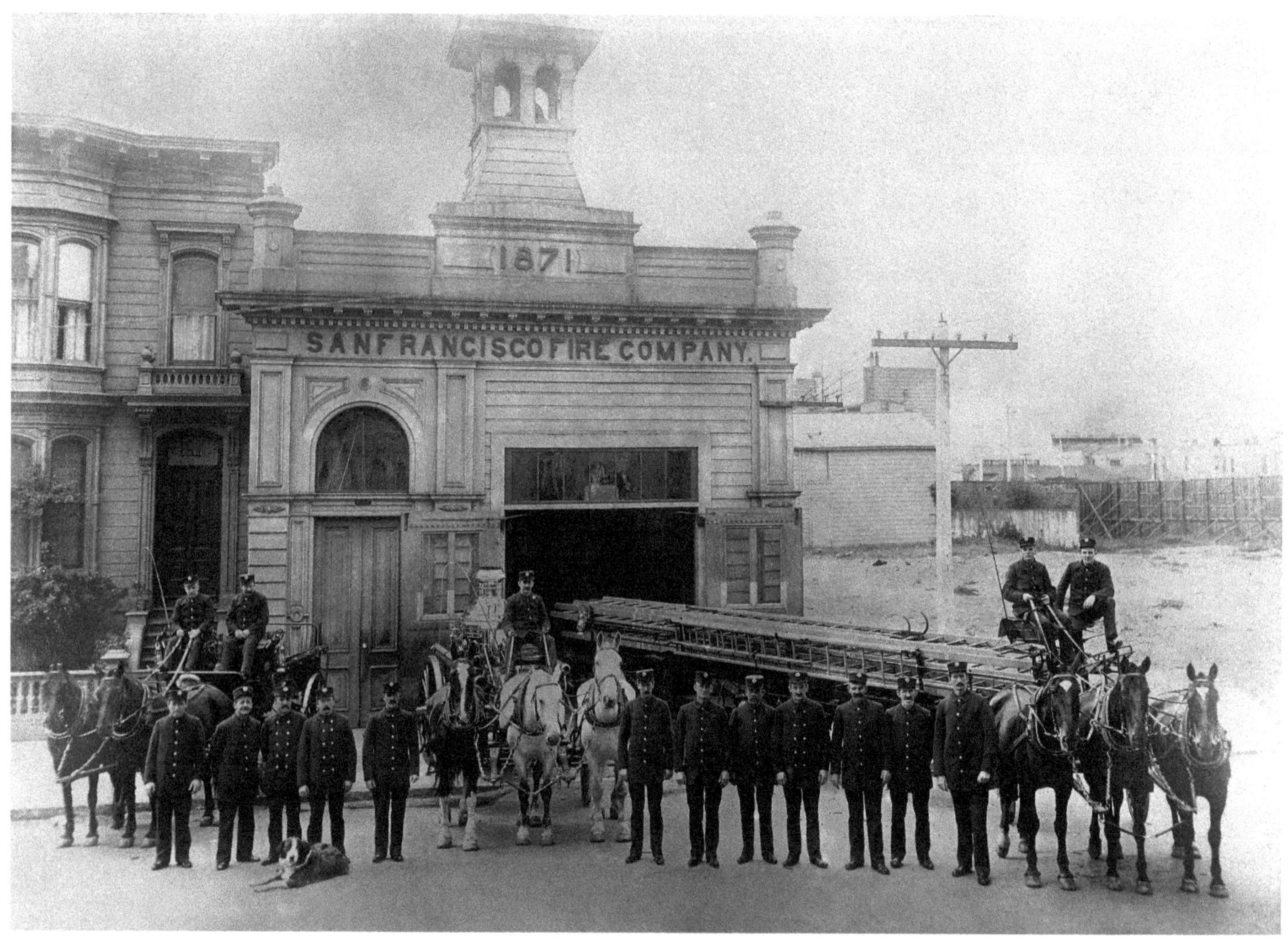

A group of firemen poses in front of the San Francisco Fire Company in 1871. After a number of major fires caused loss of life and property during the first several decades of San Francisco's history, in 1866 the existing volunteer fire department was formally reorganized as a paid professional department. In wake of the massive post-earthquake fire in 1906, the department saw massive growth in infrastructure and coverage of the city, which continues to this day. Horse-driven fire engines were used in San Francisco between 1863 and 1921. The ornate fire house in the background is typical of the structures erected in the decades following the Gold Rush, when fire company rivalries drove volunteer fire fighters to respond first to the ringing fire bell at City Hall, attempting to outdo the other companies.

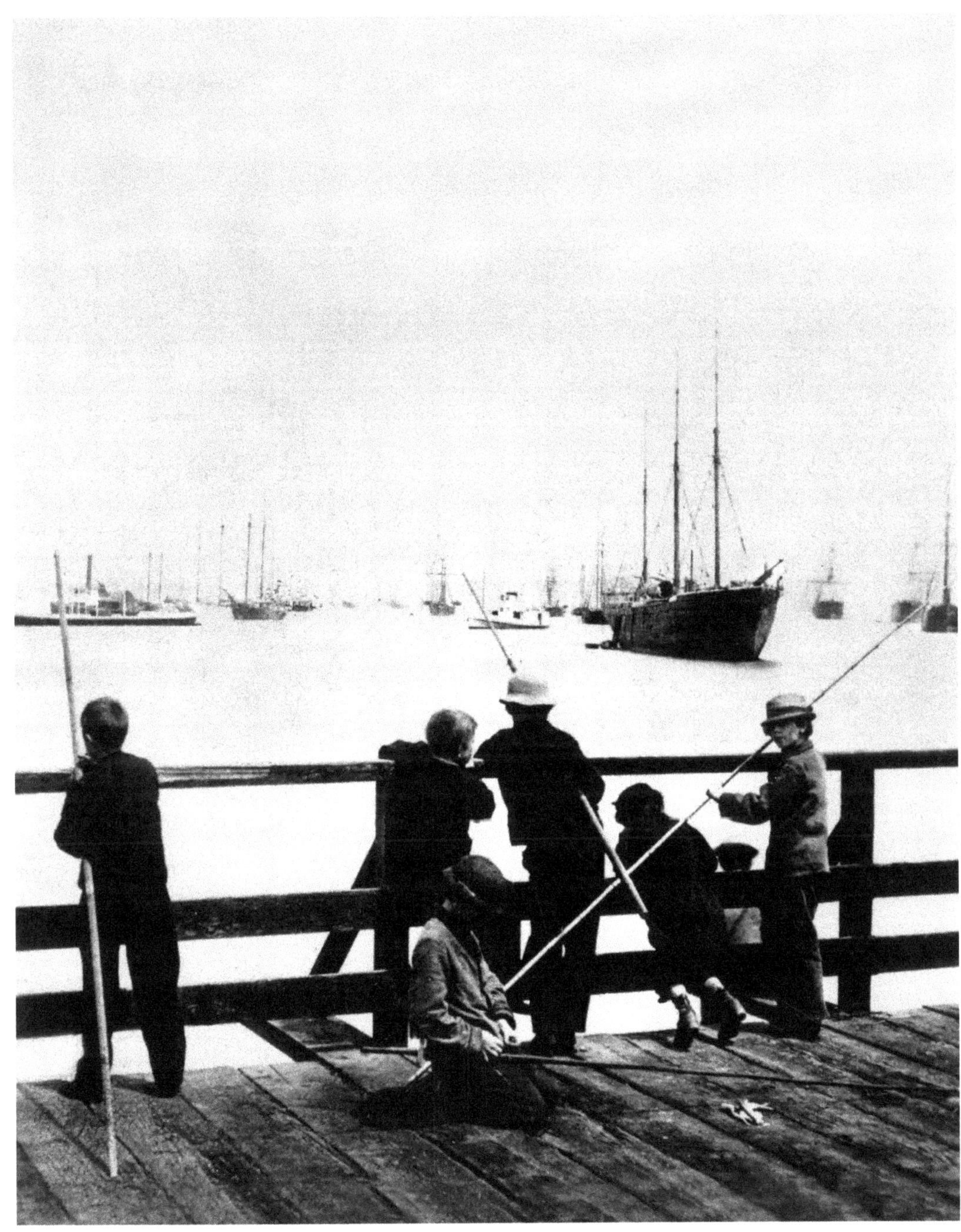

The fishermen in this 1871 photograph vie for smelt on Mission Bay Bridge, popularly known as "Long Bridge." The bridge, built in 1865 across Mission Bay, was traversed by horse-drawn carriages carrying people to Potrero Point in the south side of the bay—the location of several iron mills, a sugar refinery, slaughter houses, and the Hunter's Point dry docks. A streetcar route once crossed Long Bridge en route from North Beach to the Bay View racetrack. San Francisco once had numerous creeks, marshes, and bays that now exist only in legend, most of which were filled in during the rapid growth of the city in the nineteenth century. Mission Bay was a half-moon-shaped port in the inner San Francisco Bay. The southward curve of many streets south of Market, past 11th Street, arises from their tracing Mission Creek and Mission Bay, now filled in. Today, Mission Bay is one of San Francisco's fastest growing neighborhoods, with a new University of California San Francisco campus and many upscale condominiums.

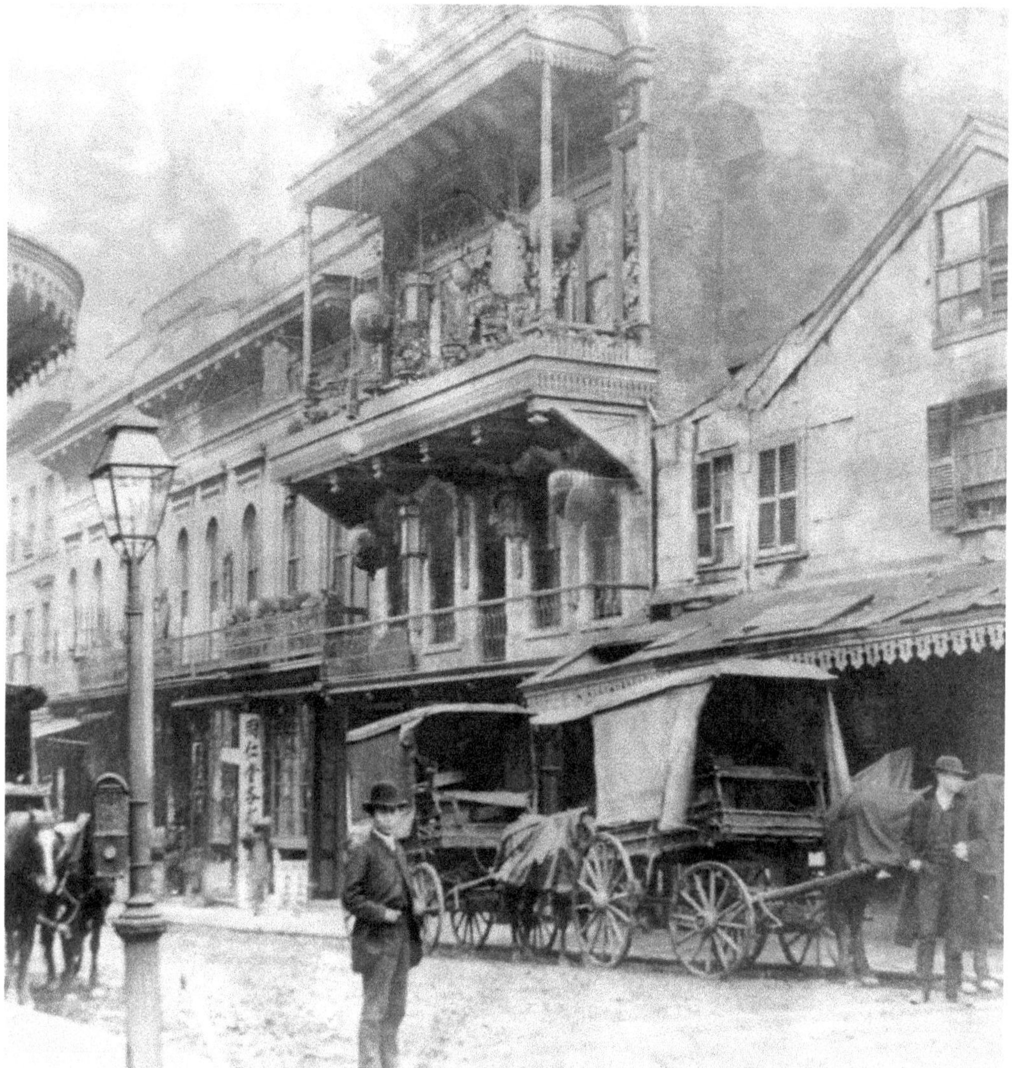

A view of Dupont Street in 1872, one of San Francisco's oldest streets. In 1845, when San Francisco was still the pueblo of Yerba Buena, the street was called Calle de la Fundacion, the Street of the Founding. The street was renamed Dupont Street after Samuel F. Dupont, Admiral of the U.S.S. *Portsmouth,* when California ceded to the Union. After the start of the Gold Rush and the establishment of Chinatown, Dupont Street became the district's main thoroughfare. It quickly earned a seamy reputation for its opium dens, brothels, and sing-sing girls. After the 1906 Earthquake and fire, it was renamed Grant Avenue, in honor of the 18th U.S. president. Many of the older residents of Chinatown still refer to Grant Street as "Du Pon Gai," Chinese for Dupont Street.

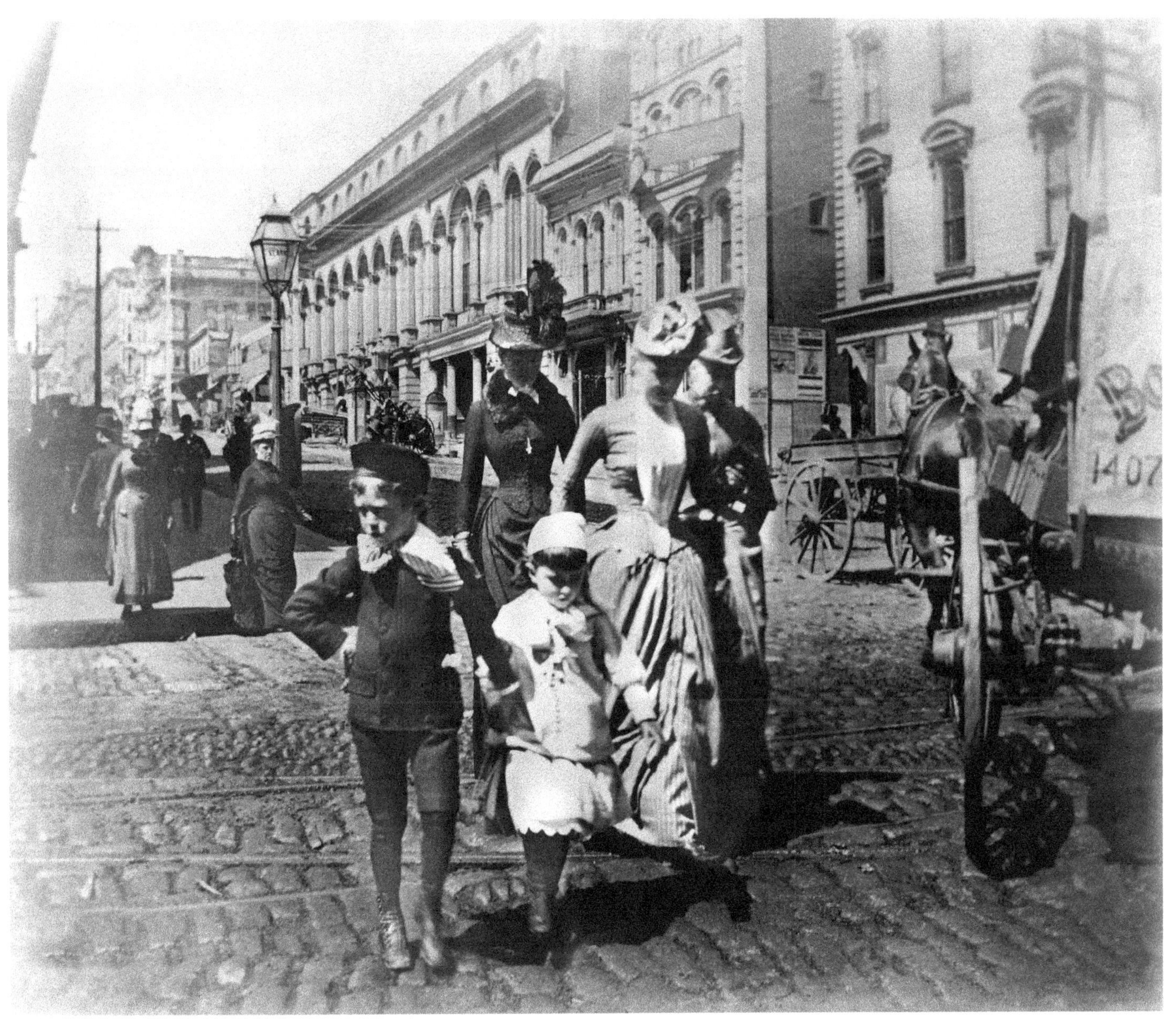

The family pictured here in 1877 is promenading down Bush Street, west of Kearny Street, to see a theatrical matinee at one of the downtown theaters.

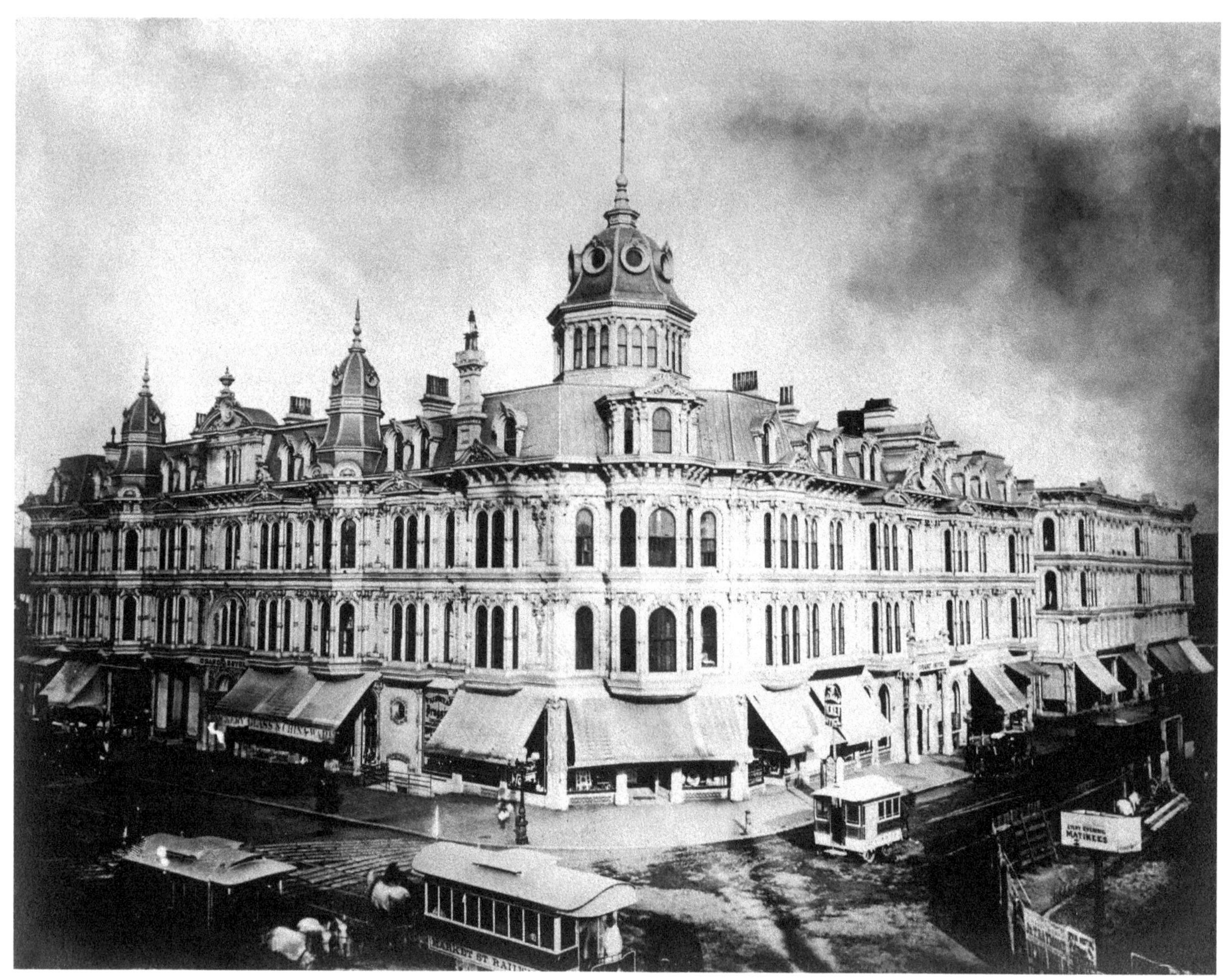

Pictured here in 1874 is the Grand Hotel, built by William Ralston, the "Silver King," a man whose impact on San Francisco was immense. Ralston built the Palace Hotel, the California Theatre, the Bank of California—and in the 1860s, for $2 million, the five-story Grand Hotel. When the Palace Hotel was complete, across New Montgomery Street from the Grand Hotel, a footbridge was constructed over the street to allow people to walk from one Ralston hotel to the other. The "Bridge of Sighs" was also used by wealthy businessmen (including Ralston) to surreptitiously meet their mistresses. Weeks before the Palace Hotel's opening, Ralston was informed that he had exhausted his corporate finances building the Palace, resulting in a public panic and a run on the Bank of California. The next day he was discovered floating in San Francisco Bay. Although the Grand Hotel is long gone, many of Ralston's other contributions to the city still stand.

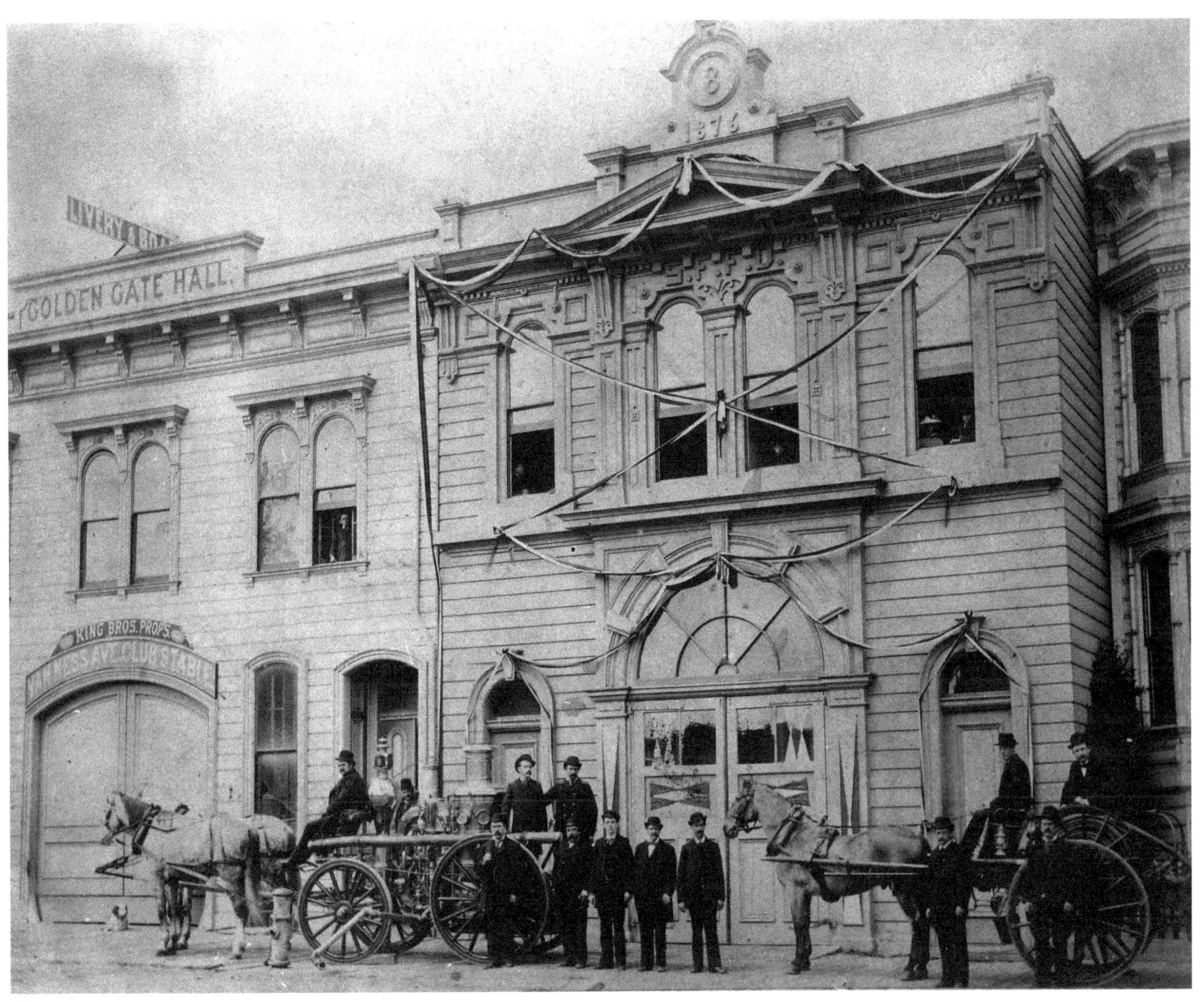

Members of the Veteran Firemen's Association were photographed in 1878 in front of the Number 8 Engine Company on Pacific Street (later Pacific Avenue), between Polk and Van Ness. Van Ness Avenue was the last stand for the fire following the 1906 earthquake, when fire fighters dynamited the whole boulevard, preventing its spread to the western part of the city.

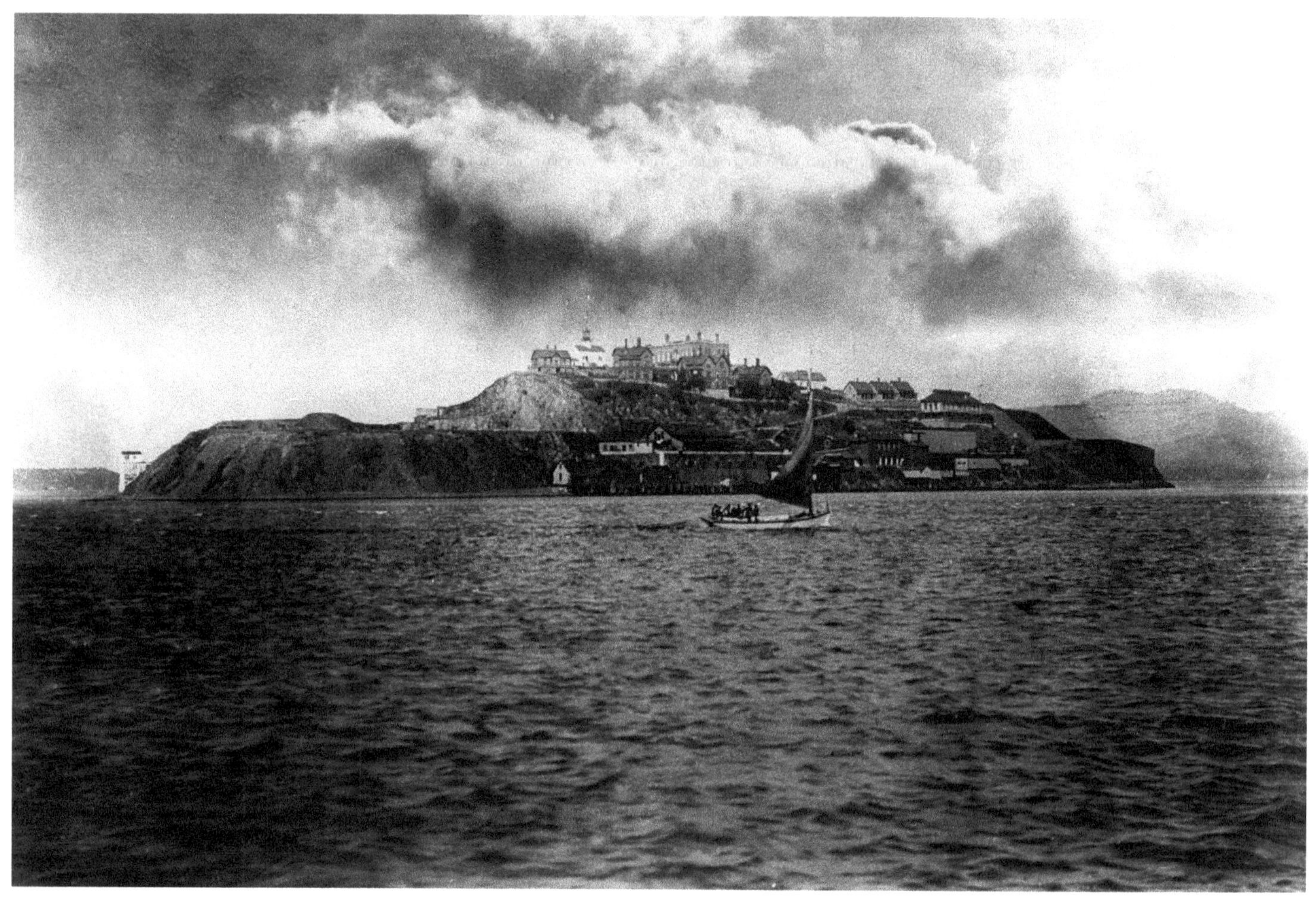

A view of Alcatraz Island in 1877 shows the fog bell on the southwest end. The island was referred to as La Isla de los Alcatraces, meaning Pelican Island, by Spanish explorer Juan Miguel de Ayala in the 1770s, the first European explorer to discover it. In the 1850s, the Coast Guard was contracted to build the West's first lighthouse here. Alcatraz Island became the Department of the Pacific's official military prison on August 27, 1861, imprisoning those whose loyalty to the Union was dubious, and foreshadowing the island's prison future.

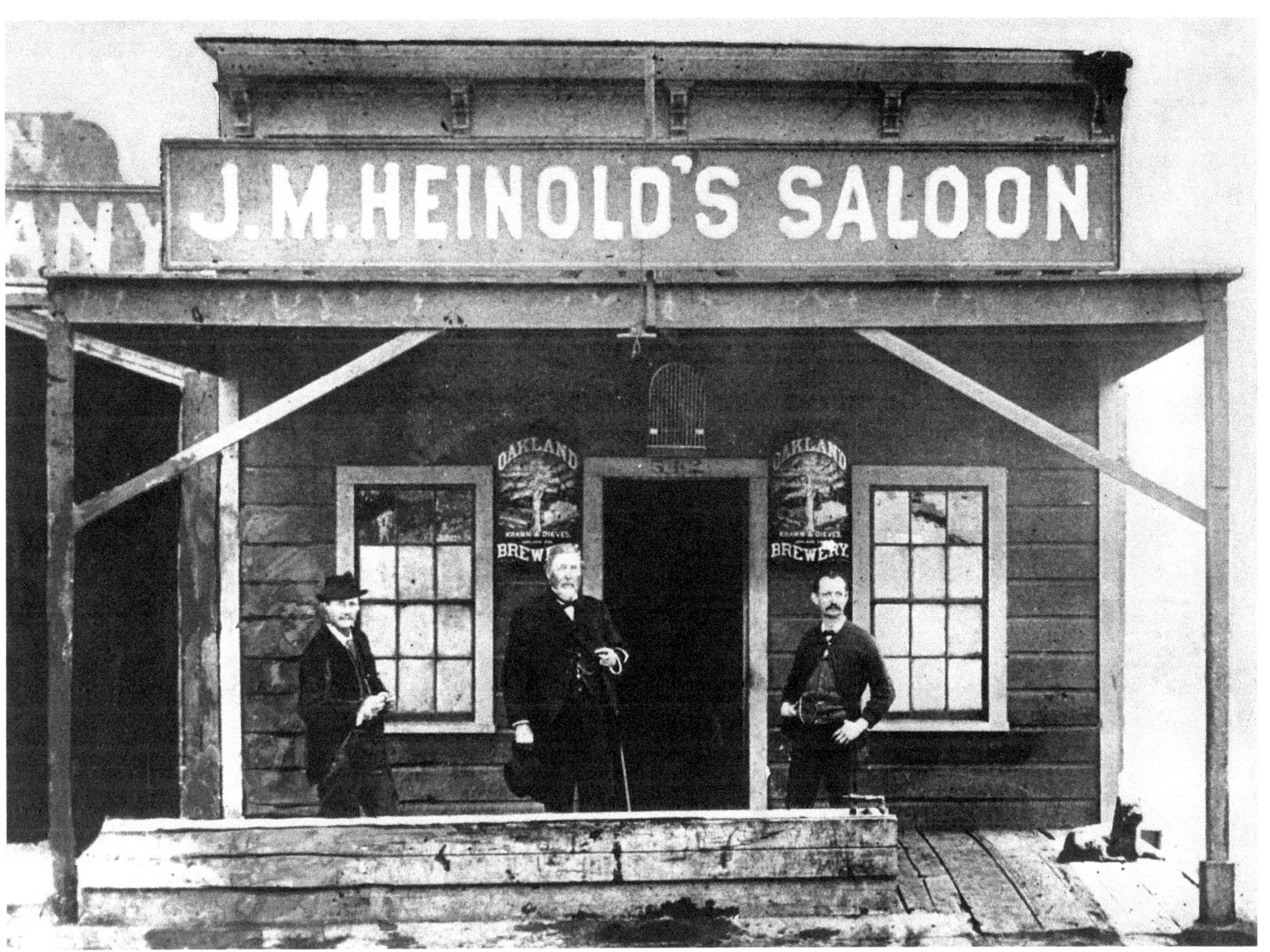

Across San Francisco Bay in Oakland, George Gibson, Alfred Burrell, and Jack Heinold stand in front of J. M. Heinold's Saloon in 1885. Built in 1880 out of the timber of an abandoned whaling ship, the structure was once used as a boarding house for oyster collectors, and was converted by Jack Heinold in 1883 into Heinold's Saloon for sailors and dock workers. The dive was renamed "J. M. Heinold's First and Last Chance" in the 1920s because for the first half of the twentieth century, the saloon was the "first and last chance" for workers commuting on the ferry to have a drink. Author and San Francisco native Jack London often patronized the saloon, and stories told by the sailors at the bar inspired London in his writing. The saloon itself is mentioned 17 times in his novels and the table where London wrote is still in use. President William H. Taft and Robert Louis Stevenson also frequented here.

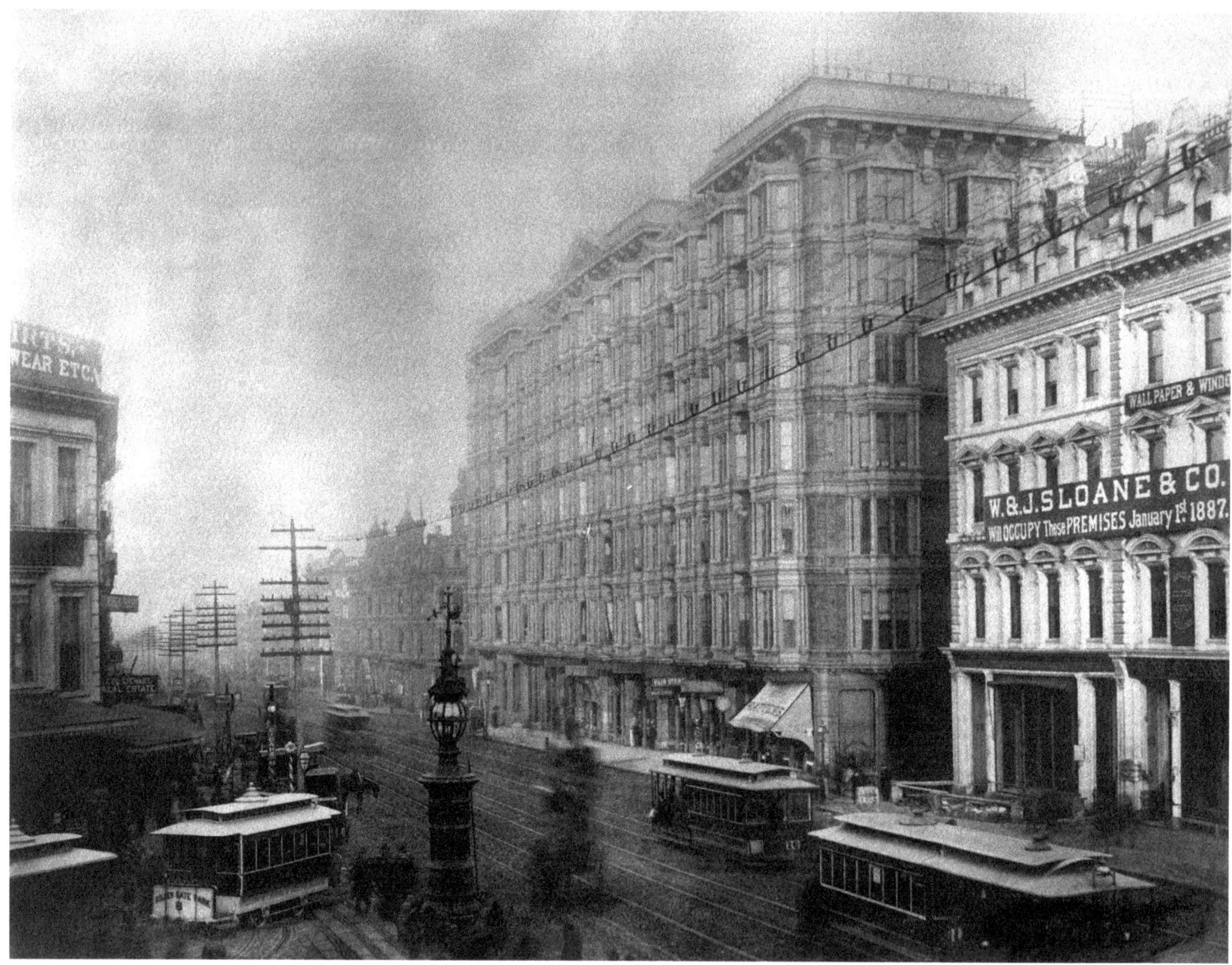

The Palace Hotel, shown here in 1886, financed in 1875 by William Ralston, had 800 rooms, reportedly cost over $6 million to construct, and towered over neighboring buildings. San Francisco had become quite sophisticated after the Gold Rush, and this elegant hotel, with its lavish interior, was thought of by wealthy San Franciscans as the most magnificent hotel in the world. Although the hotel survived the initial shock waves of the 1906 earthquake, the subsequent fires devastated the building. The night of the earthquake, the renowned tenor Enrico Caruso was staying here, and after the earthquake, he vowed never to return to San Francisco. Rebuilt in 1909, the new Palace Hotel hosted many significant events, most noteworthy among them President Woodrow Wilson's speech in 1919 to rally support for the Treaty of Versailles. Here President Warren G. Harding died, in 1923. The opening session of the United Nations was marked with a lavish banquet at the hotel in 1945. Other celebrity guests of the hotel included Amelia Earhart and Thomas Edison.

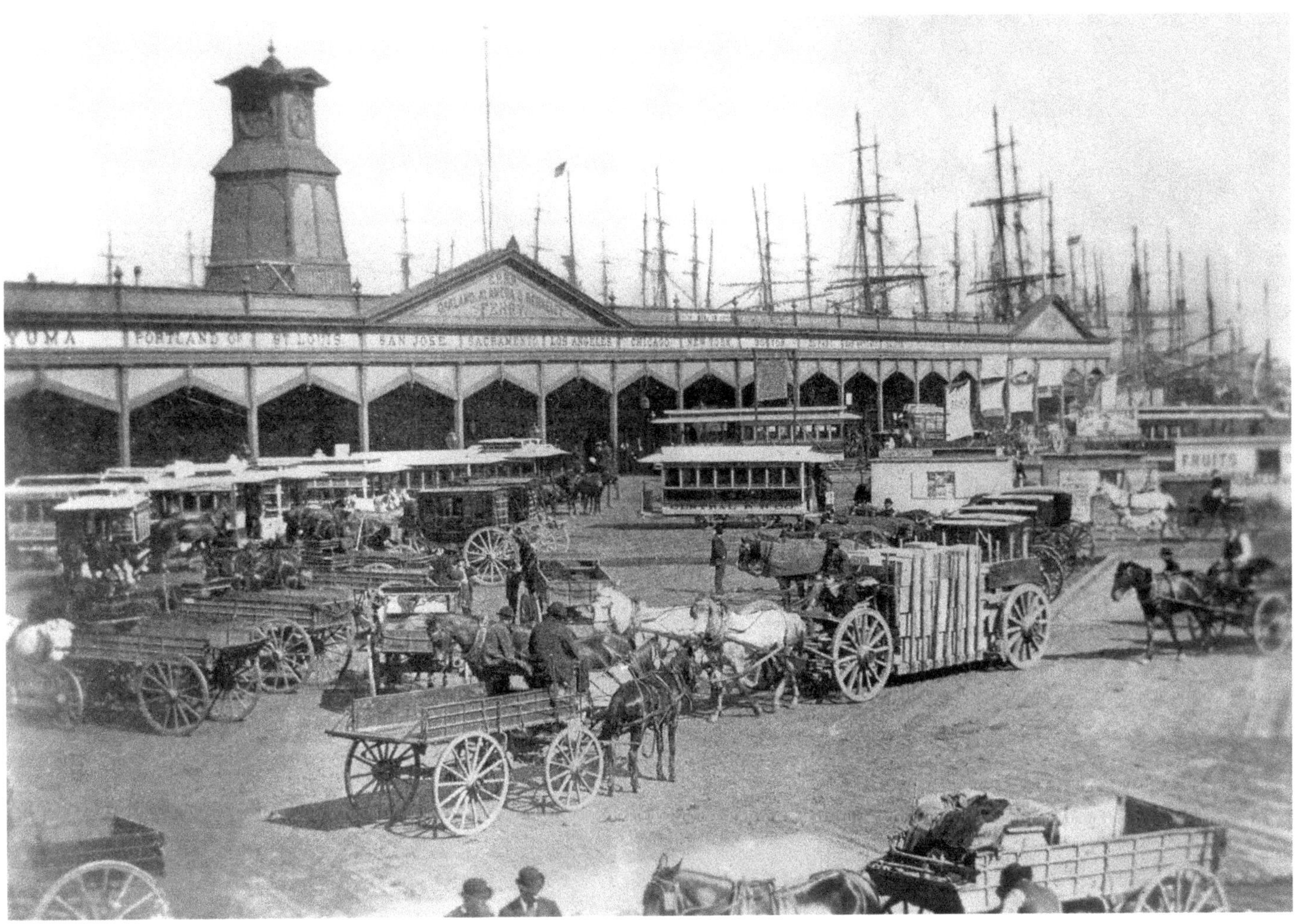

The Ferry Building has always been a bustling center of activity in downtown San Francisco. Originally called the Union Depot and then the Ferry House (seen here in 1886), the building, with its famous 235-foot clock tower modeled after the Giralda Tower of the Seville Cathedral, first opened in 1875 at the foot of Market Street. Horse cars and streetcars departed here to take people arriving in San Francisco by ferryboat to places throughout the city. At various points in its history, the area in front of the building has also served as a streetcar turnaround, a freeway, and today a busy roadway and antique streetcar route, along with a lively pedestrian plaza and farmer's market. The modern Ferry Building opened in 1898 as the depot for those arriving by boat from Marin County or the East Bay.

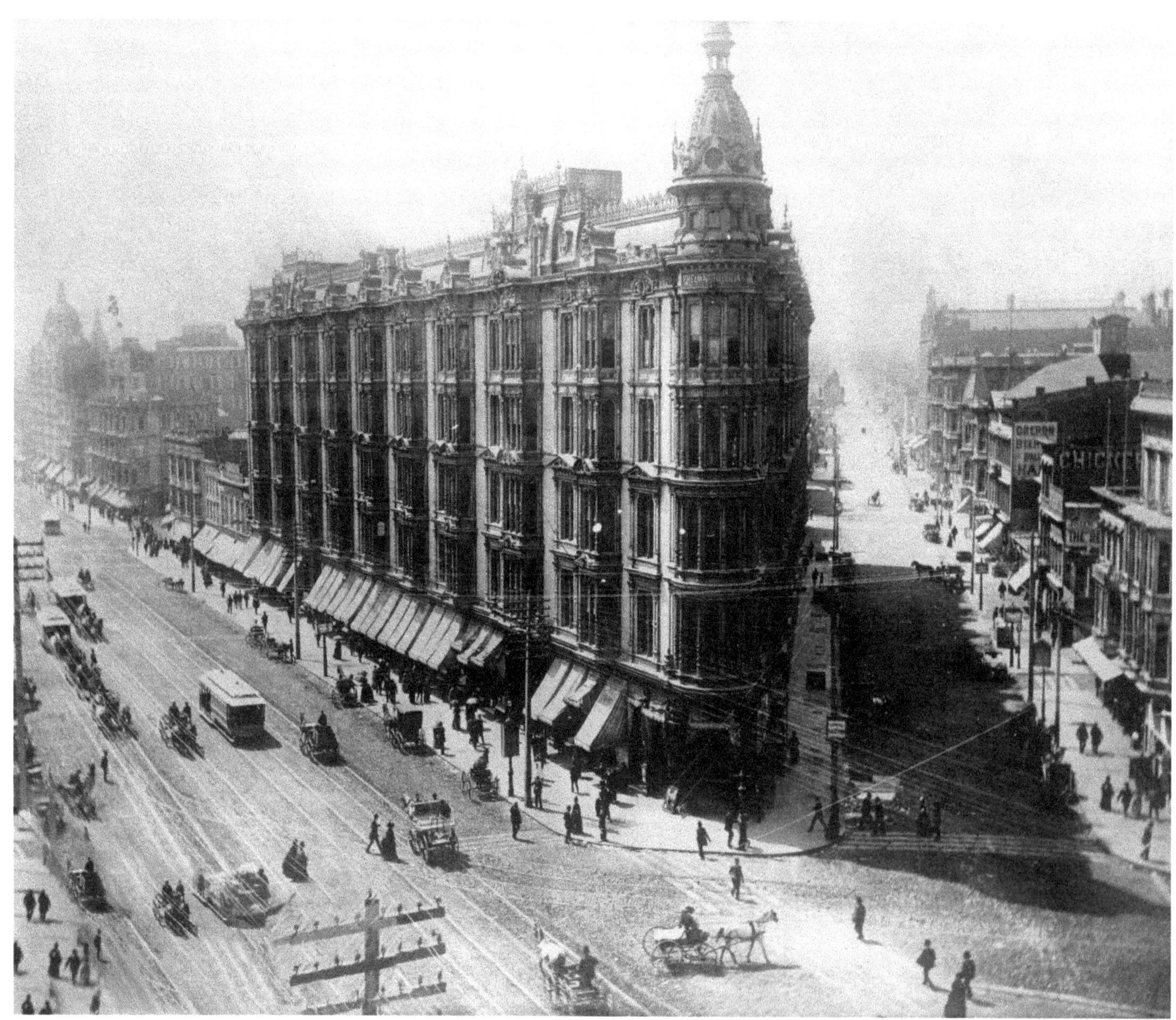

The original Phelan Building, at the intersection of Market and O'Farrell streets, is shown here in the late 1880s. The building was destroyed by fire after the 1906 earthquake, and rebuilt in 1908 by James Duvall Phelan, the former mayor of San Francisco and future U.S. senator. Today, the building houses major national retailers on the ground floor and basement, and small businesses in the offices above.

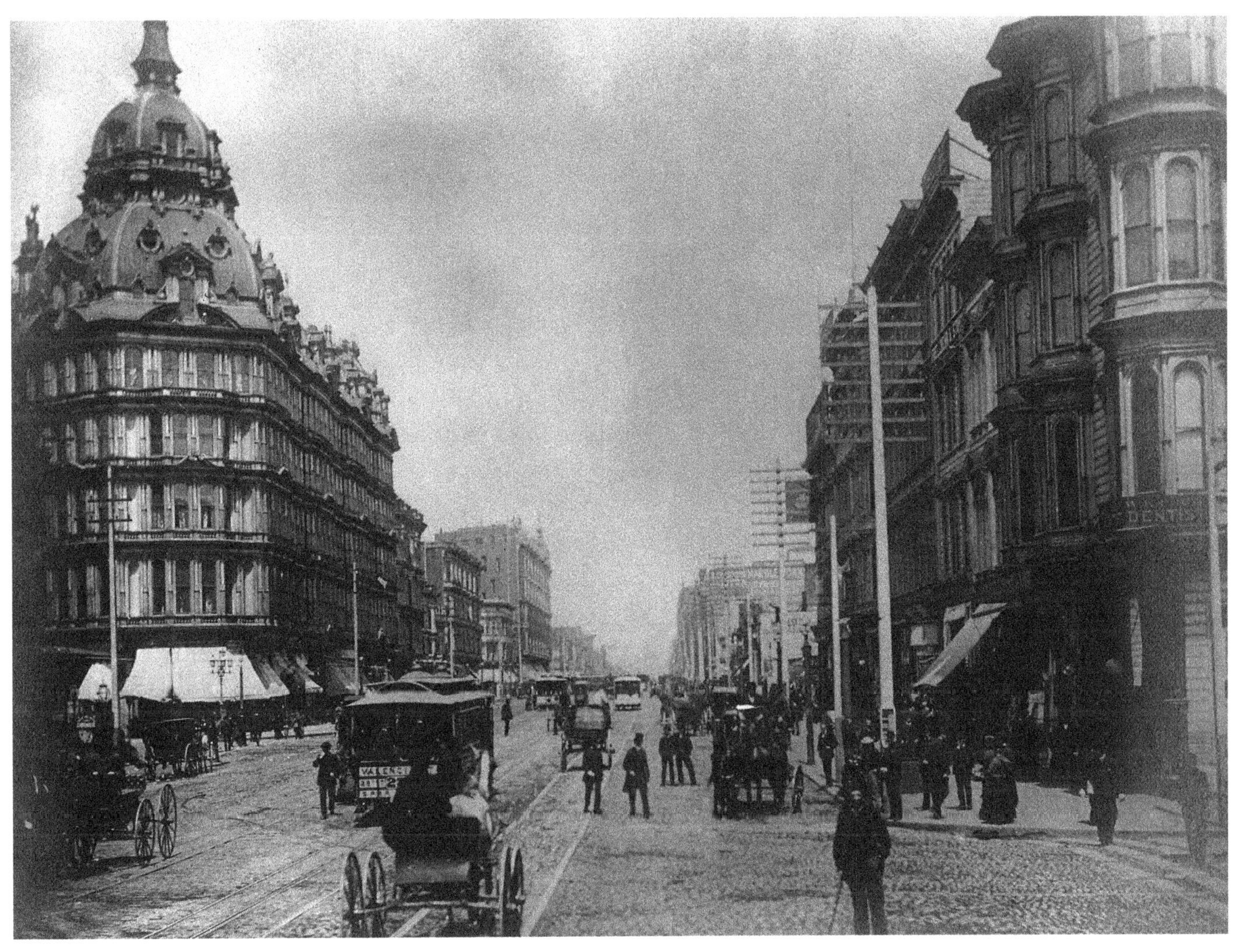

This view of Market Street in 1888, looking east from Powell Street, shows the massive Baldwin Hotel at left, along with a bustling scene of cable cars, carriages, and pedestrians.

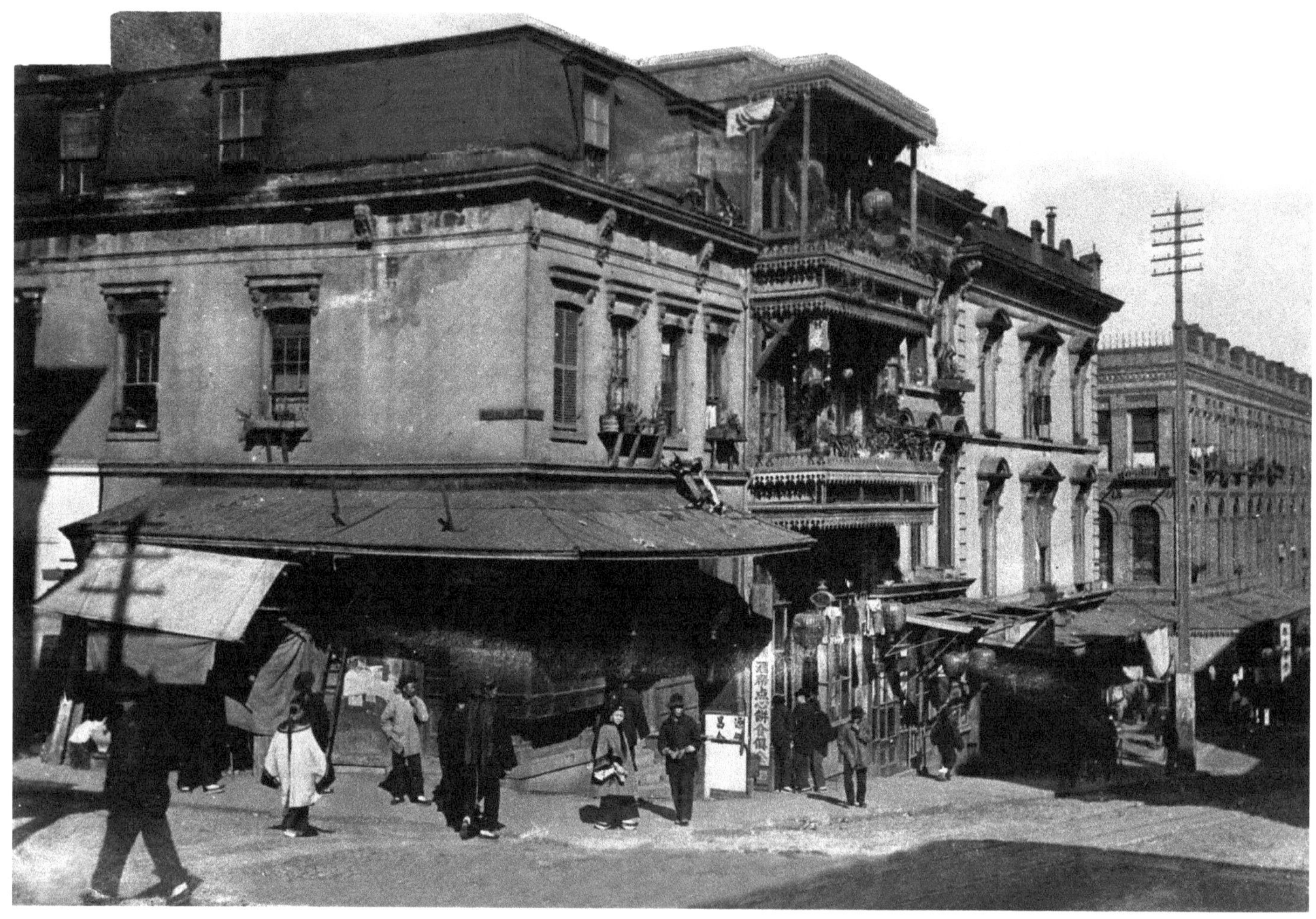

This Chinatown intersection at Waverly Place and Clay streets, shown in 1889, was the location of the city's first post office. The pagoda-style structures abundant in Chinatown today were not in evidence prior to the 1906 earthquake. The area is also known as "Tien Hau Mui Gai," after the Chinese Temple Tien Hau there.

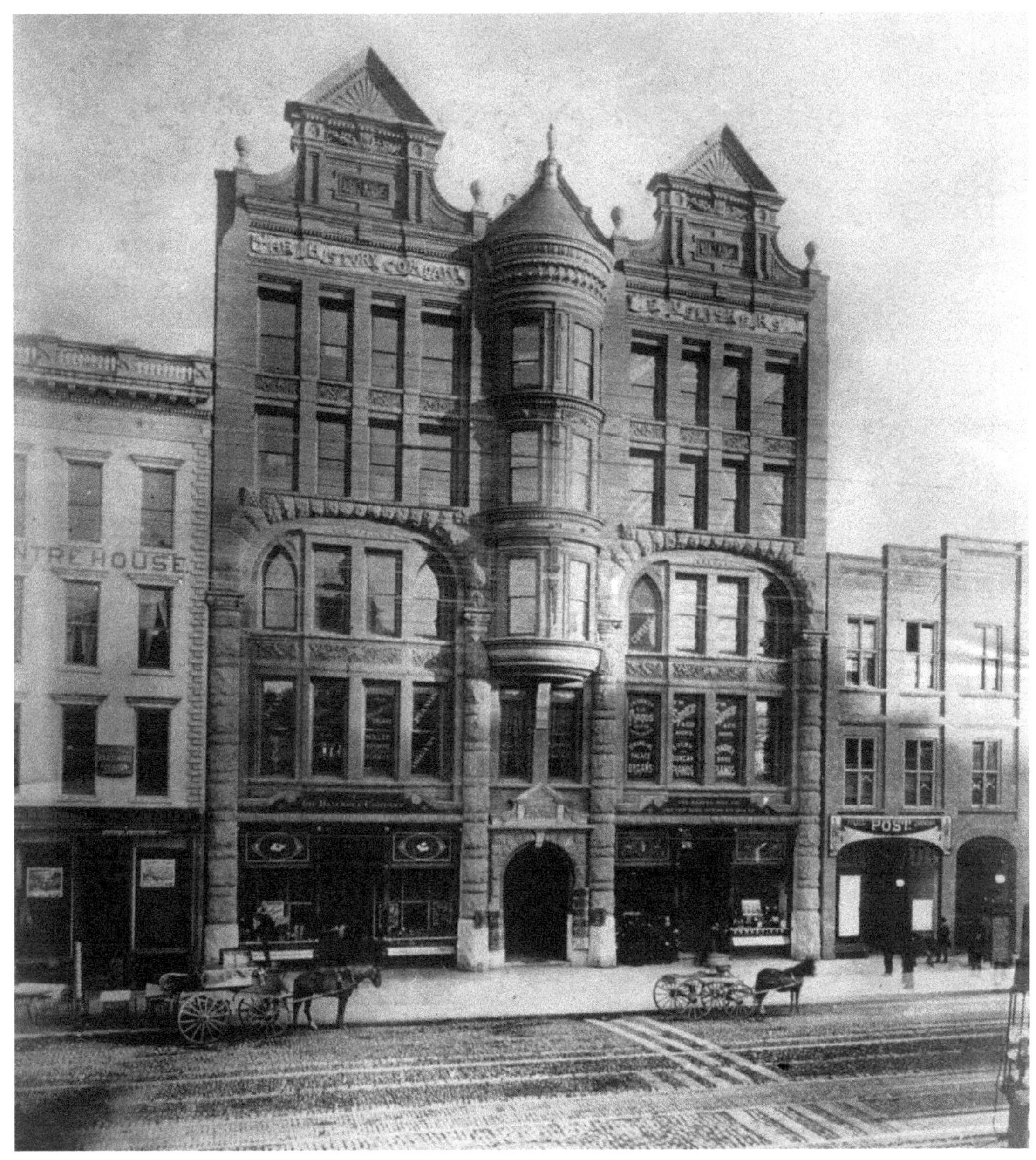

The H. H. Bancroft History Building at 723 Market Street, seen here in 1881, was built in 1871 by printer, publisher, historian, and book collector Hubert Howe Bancroft after he decided to write a history of the American West. The building also housed Bancroft's enormous book collection, eventually acquired by the University of California, Berkeley. In 1886, the building was nearly destroyed by fire and rebuilt at the same location. It is today a modernized building housing offices and first-floor retail establishments.

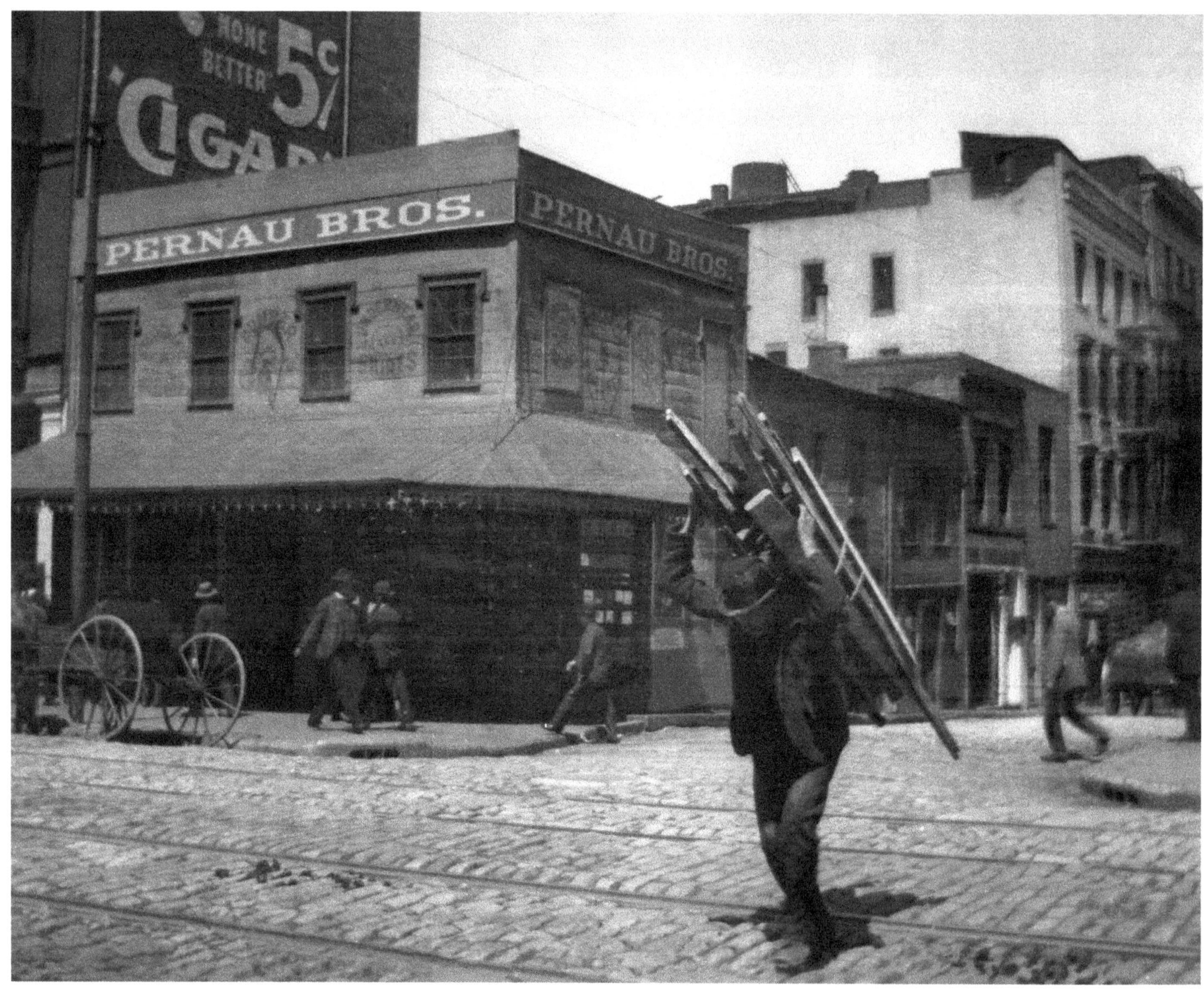

This photograph taken in 1896 on Kearny Street at the corner of Commercial Street shows a laborer hauling wood, with the stationery and printing company Pernau Bros. in the background. Wood choppers sold and delivered wood around the end of the nineteenth and beginning of the twentieth centuries because most homes burned wood for heating and cooking.

By the late nineteenth century, many large buildings stood in San Francisco's Financial District, as seen in this photo from the 1890s on Bush Street, east of Montgomery Street. Many would exist only until 1906.

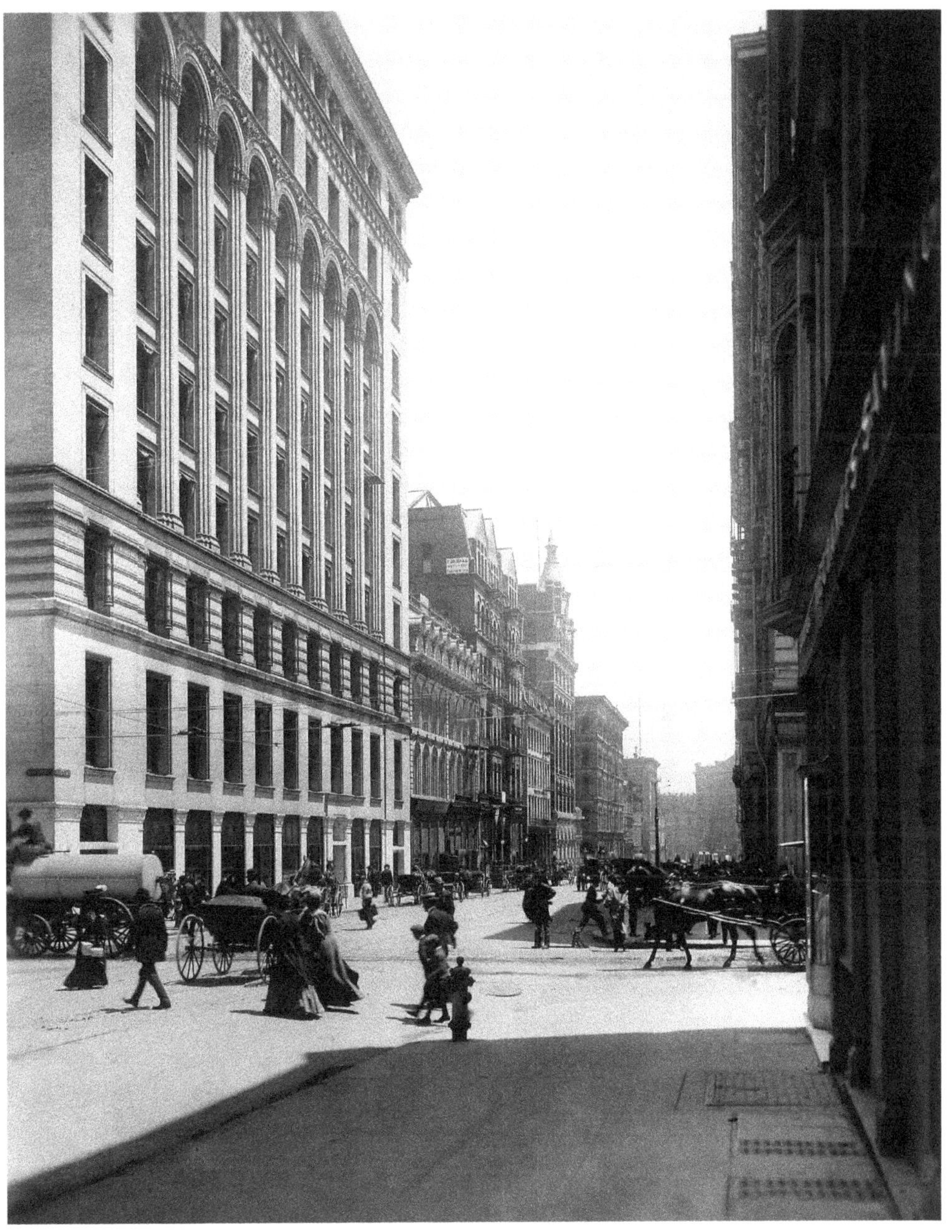

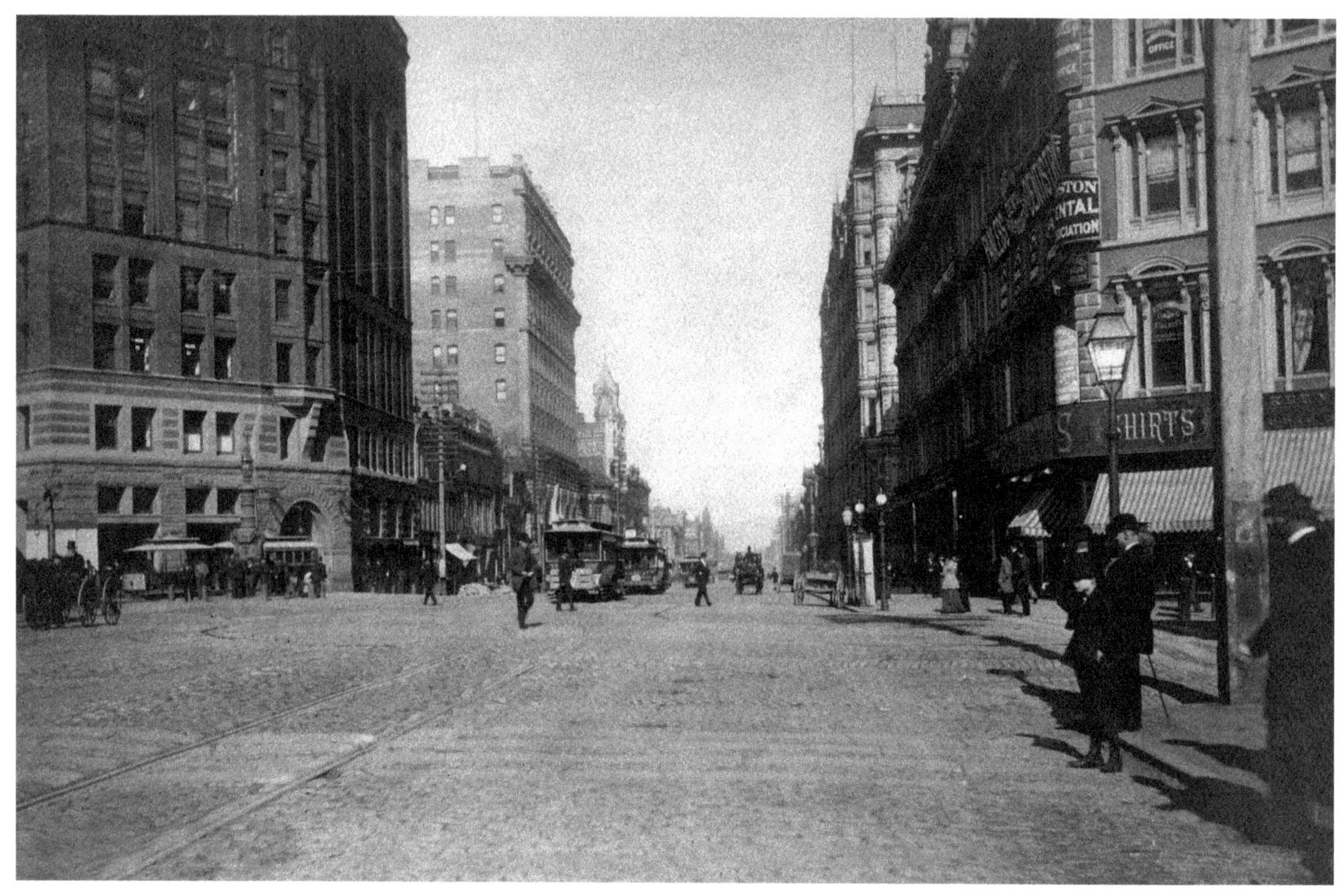

During the 1890s, the intersection of Market, Third, Kearny, and Geary streets became known as "Newspaper Row." When it was built in 1889 to house the *San Francisco Chronicle,* the 10-story Chronicle Building, shown at left in 1892, was the tallest building in San Francisco. After it was completed, William Randolph Hearst, publisher of the *San Francisco Examiner,* moved across the street. In 1895, the 19-story Call Building was built across Market Street from the other two to become headquarters of the *San Francisco Call,* another rival newspaper, owned by Claus Spreckels. The Chronicle and Call buildings were among few in the area to survive the 1906 earthquake.

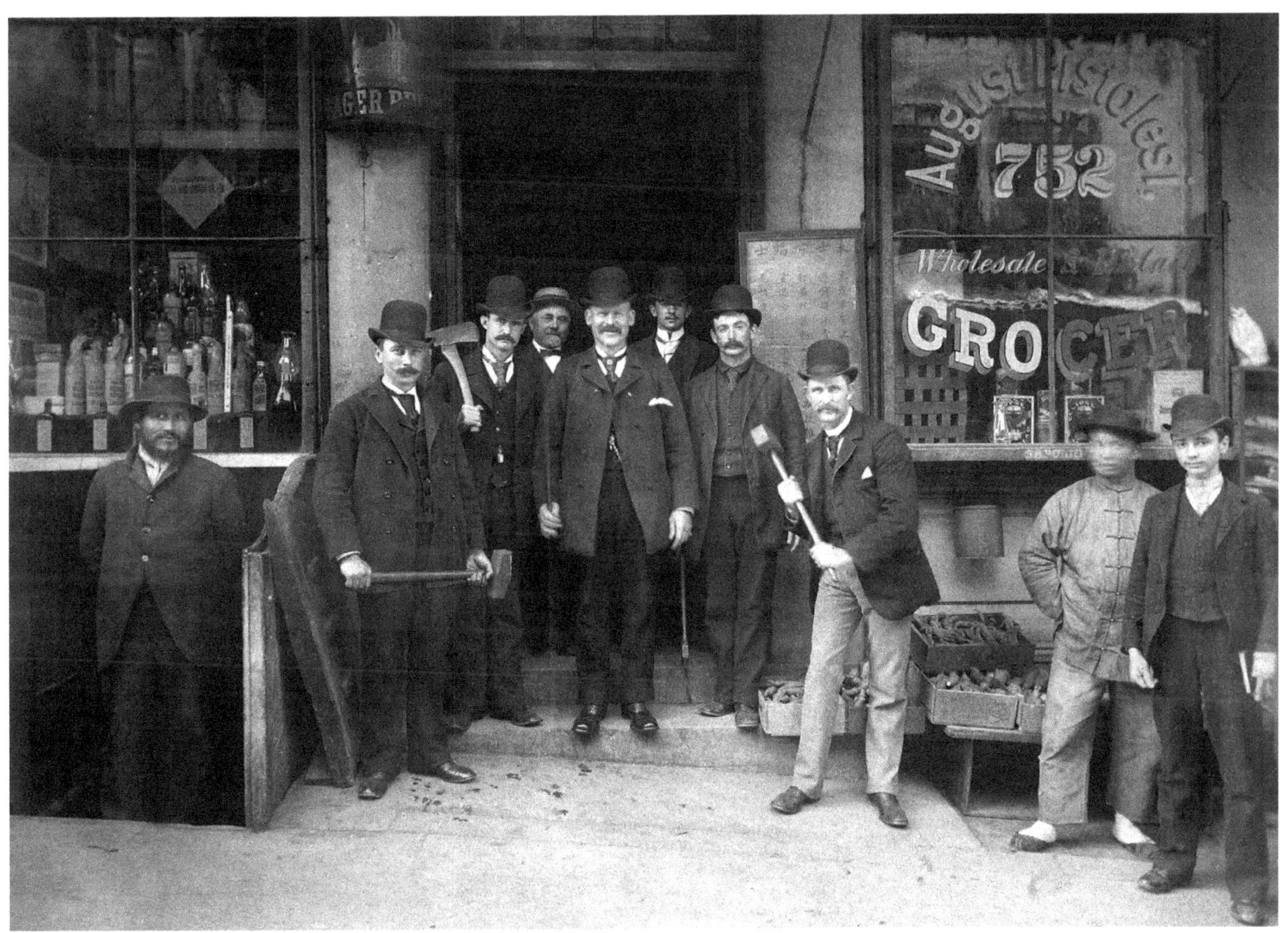

In 1881, the San Francisco Police Department formed a special Chinatown Squad to patrol and investigate the Chinatown area, for years plagued by gambling halls, brothels, opium dens, and street fights between rival tongs. Members, led by Sergeant William Price (fifth from the left), pose in 1895 with sledge hammers and axes in front of August Pistolesi's grocery at 752 Washington Street.

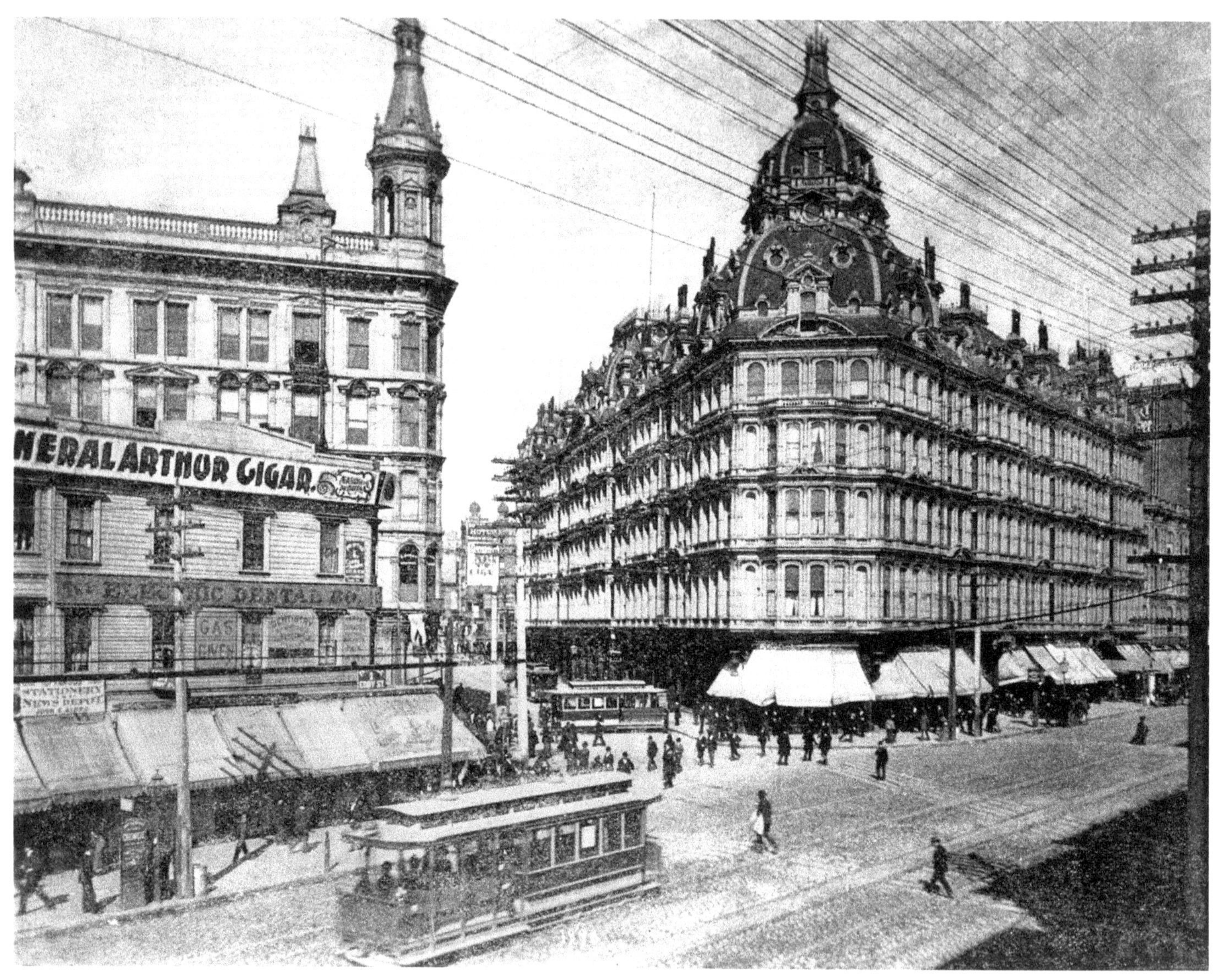

With his sizable fortune amassed from silver mines in Nevada, "Lucky" Baldwin opened the Baldwin Hotel at the corner of Powell and Market in 1877 at a cost of $800,000. The Baldwin Hotel with the enclosed Baldwin Theatre, shown here in 1896, was considered to be one of the grandest hotels west of New York, and it certainly rivaled the nearby Palace Hotel in elegance. It burned in a disastrous fire on November 23, 1898, which exposed the flaws in San Francisco's hydrant system (to have even more disastrous consequences in 1906). It was replaced in 1904 by the James Flood Building, which to this day overlooks the cable car turnaround.

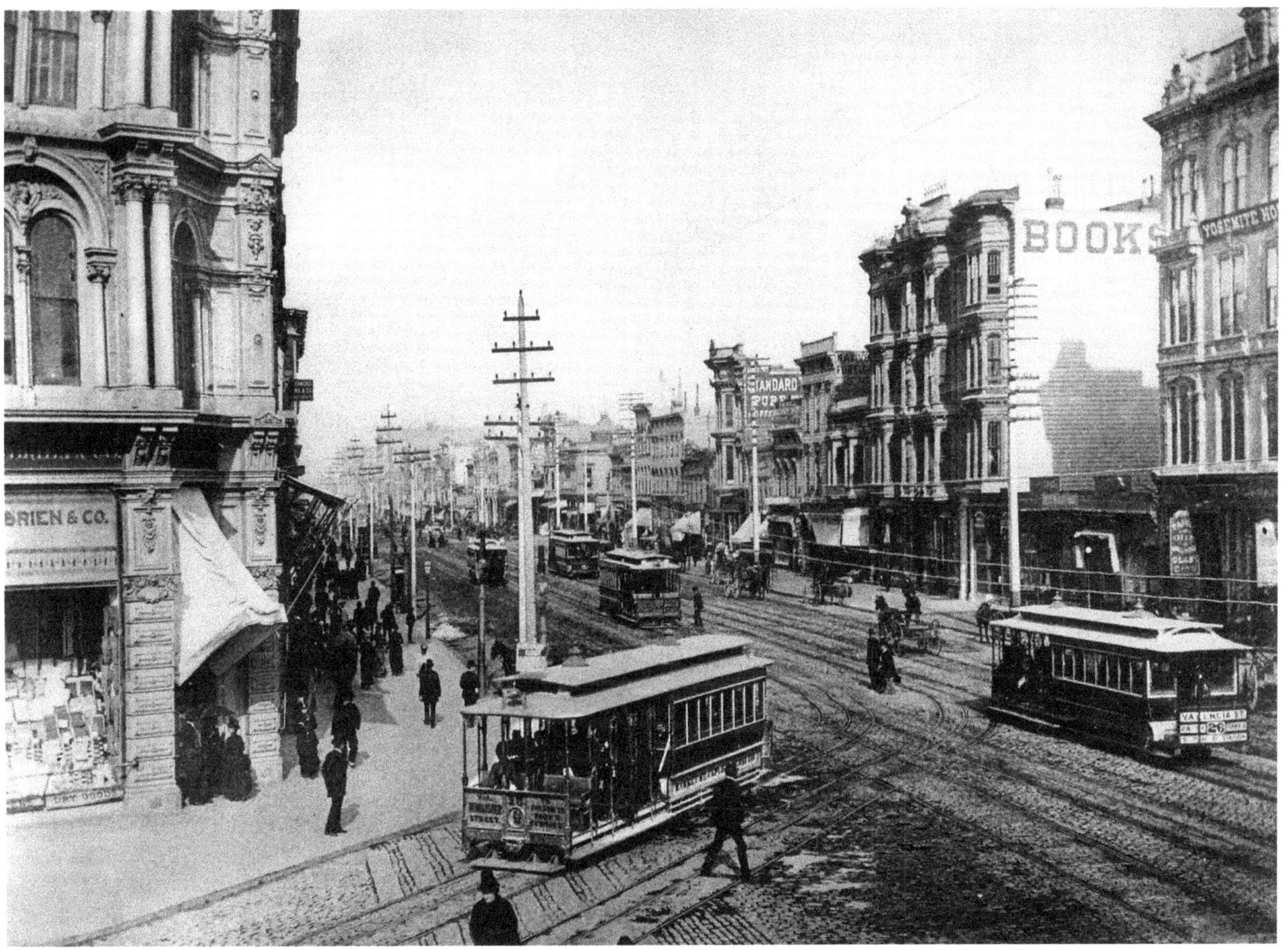

Cable cars operated by United Railroads make the turn from Market onto McAllister Street to head to the western neighborhoods in 1897. The company was anxious for years to convert the McAllister Street cable car line, as well as lines it operated on Valencia, Hayes, Castro, and Haight streets, to electric lines, but residents protested stringing wire above Market Street. The company tried to bribe the mayor and the board of supervisors to no avail. After the 1906 earthquake, the company claimed the cable car lines were damaged and strung "temporary" wires. Vigorous protests from the McAllister Street Improvement Club to restore cable car service went unheard, and the electric line operated until the conversion to buses in 1948. Today, trolley buses ply the route. Adjacent the intersection but not visible is the Hibernia Bank building, built in 1892 by architect Albert Pissis (later the James Flood Building), which withstood the 1906 earthquake and today stands as a San Francisco Historic Landmark, though in disrepair.

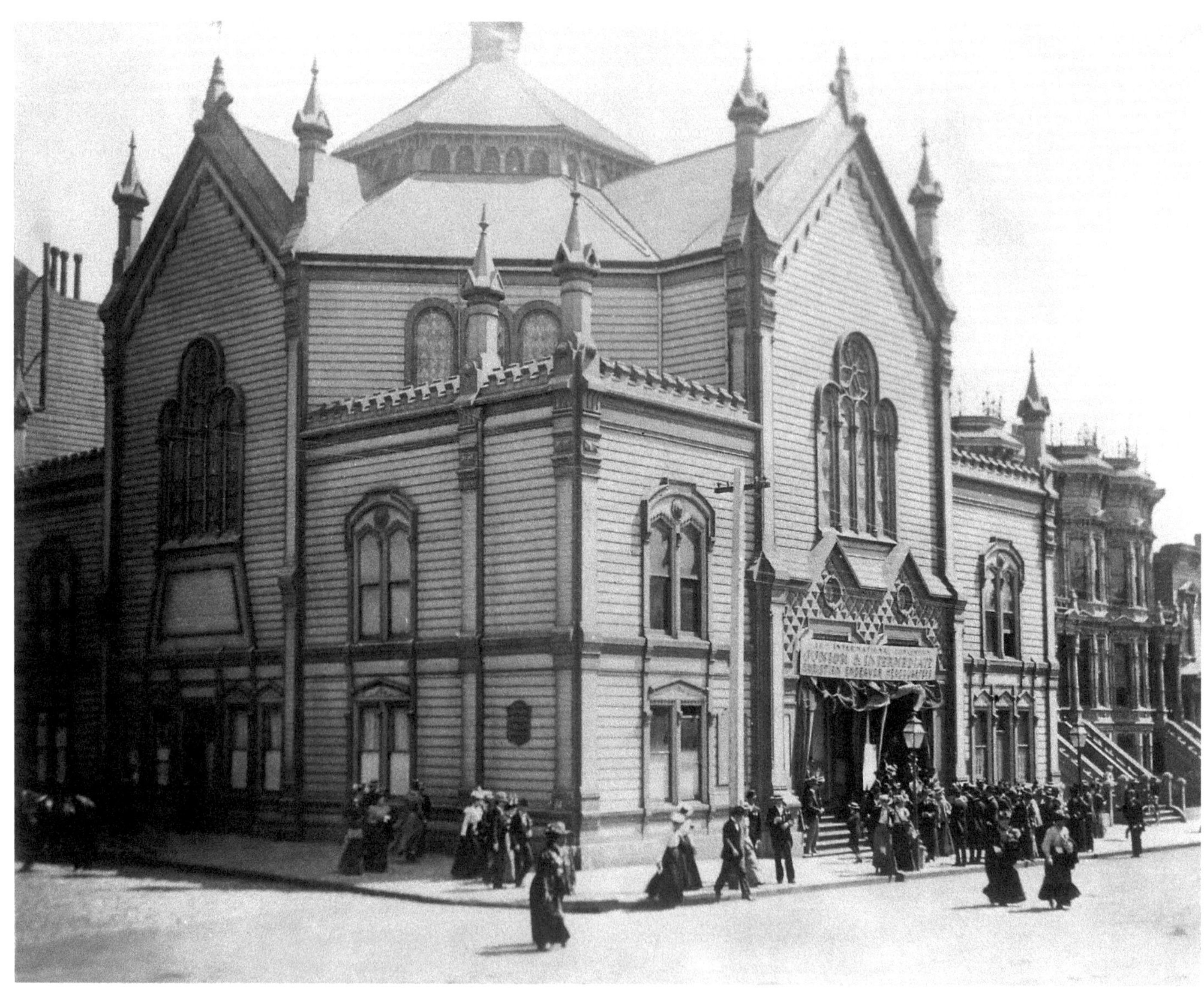

Trinity (also known as United) Presbyterian Church, seen here in 1897, opened in 1892 at the corner of 23rd and Capp streets in the Mission District. The Romanesque-style revival building was designed by famous architects of the day, George W. Percy and Frederick F. Hamilton. Today the church is a National Historic Landmark.

Market Street at Mason Street in 1898. The Baldwin Hotel is at left in the distance.

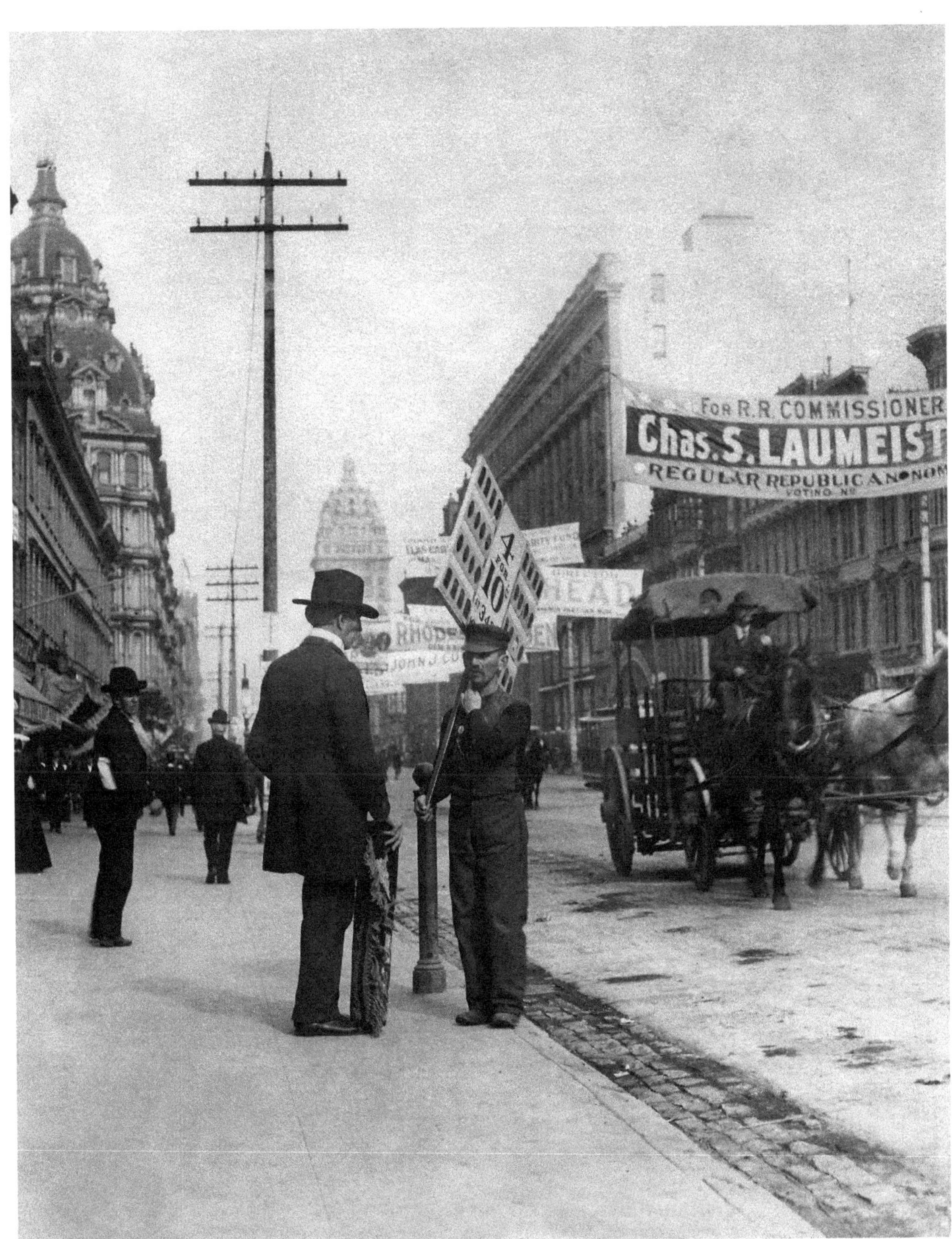

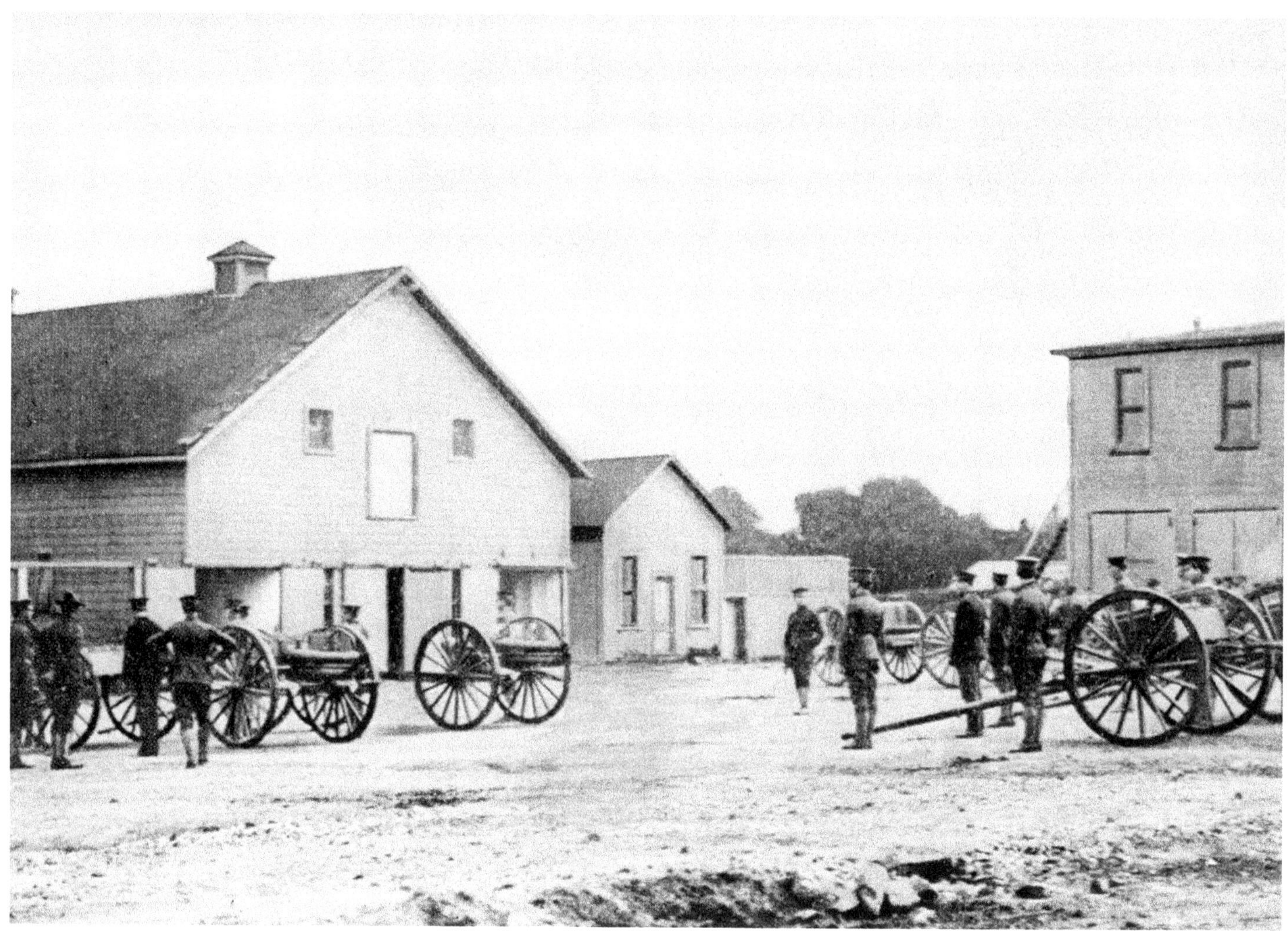

This late-nineteenth-century postcard shows an artillery drill in the San Francisco Presidio. A Spanish Imperial outpost from 1776 to 1821, and later owned by Mexico until 1846, the Presidio became the most crucial U.S. Army headquarters on the Pacific Coast from 1846 until 1994, when it became part of the Golden Gate National Recreation Area. It is now cared for by the National Park Service. San Franciscans today can live in the Presidio in the former homes and barracks of officers and soldiers.

OUT OF THE ASHES

(1900–1919)

Buoyant optimism marked the initial years of the 1900s in San Francisco. In the half century since the Gold Rush, San Francisco metamorphosed from a sleepy trading town to the so-called Paris of the West—once a small hamlet with fewer than 700 people in the 1840s, San Francisco's population had swelled to around 400,000 by the early 1900s to make it the ninth largest city in the nation. San Francisco had persevered through a depression in the late nineteenth century and emerged prosperous, though this period of euphoria was short-lived.

Disaster struck at 5:12 A.M. on April 18, 1906, when the San Andreas Fault ruptured. The city suffered the largest earthquake the country had yet seen, estimated as high as 8.3 on the Richter scale. What the earthquake and aftershocks did not reduce to rubble, the fires that followed destroyed, as separate blazes converged into one massive inferno, ultimately destroying over 500 city blocks with firemen helpless to extinguish them. Rendering homeless two-thirds of the population, the earthquake and subsequent fires were the most significant event in San Francisco's history, and one of the nation's worst urban disasters.

In the smoldering ruins, San Franciscans immediately began a massive rebuilding project. Like the phoenix, rising from the ashes of death, San Francisco was rebuilt as a world-class city, perhaps even more spectacular than before, and proclaimed itself open for business. Within several years, almost 20,000 new buildings were added to its streets. It is this resilience, in part, that has given San Francisco its unique persona.

In these early years of the new century, San Francisco was also at the forefront of great social and scientific innovation. In 1911, women were given the right to vote in California, almost a decade before American women as a group. In 1915, the city consecrated its new beaux-arts city hall in the civic center, touted as even more magnificent than the capitol building in Washington, D.C. That same year, the first bicoastal telephone conversation took place when Alexander Graham Bell in New York spoke to Thomas Watson in San Francisco. After nearly a decade of rapid rebuilding, the city made its debut in the Panama Pacific International Exposition of 1915. The exposition officially signified the completion of the Panama Canal, which substantially shortened the voyage to San Francisco from the East, but more than anything else it was a tribute to the old city lost in the quake and a celebration of its rebirth, recovery, and endurance.

On November 11, 1918, with the end of the First World War, returning soldiers marched down Market Street in a victory parade, and the great city looked toward a new era of peace and prosperity.

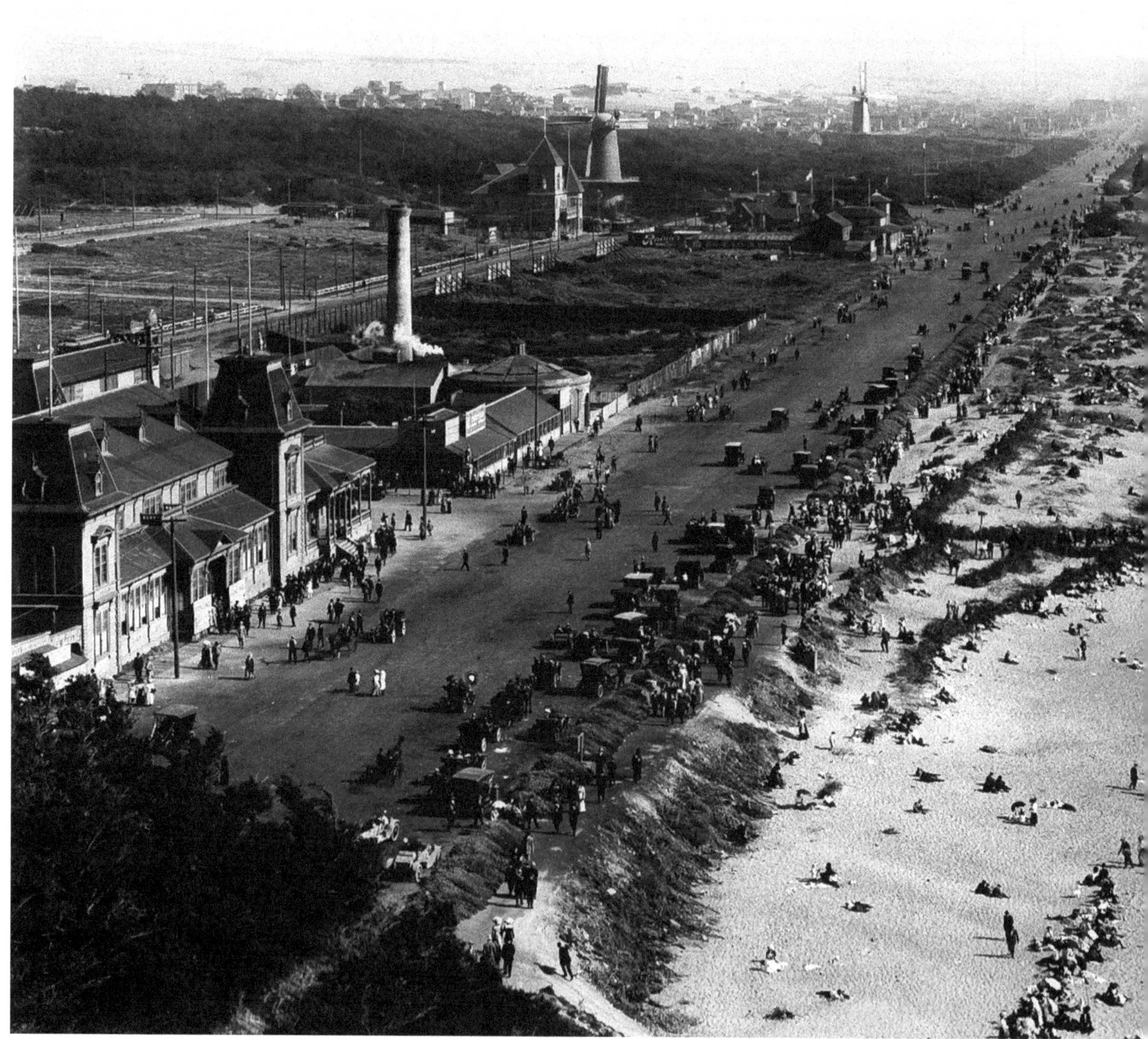

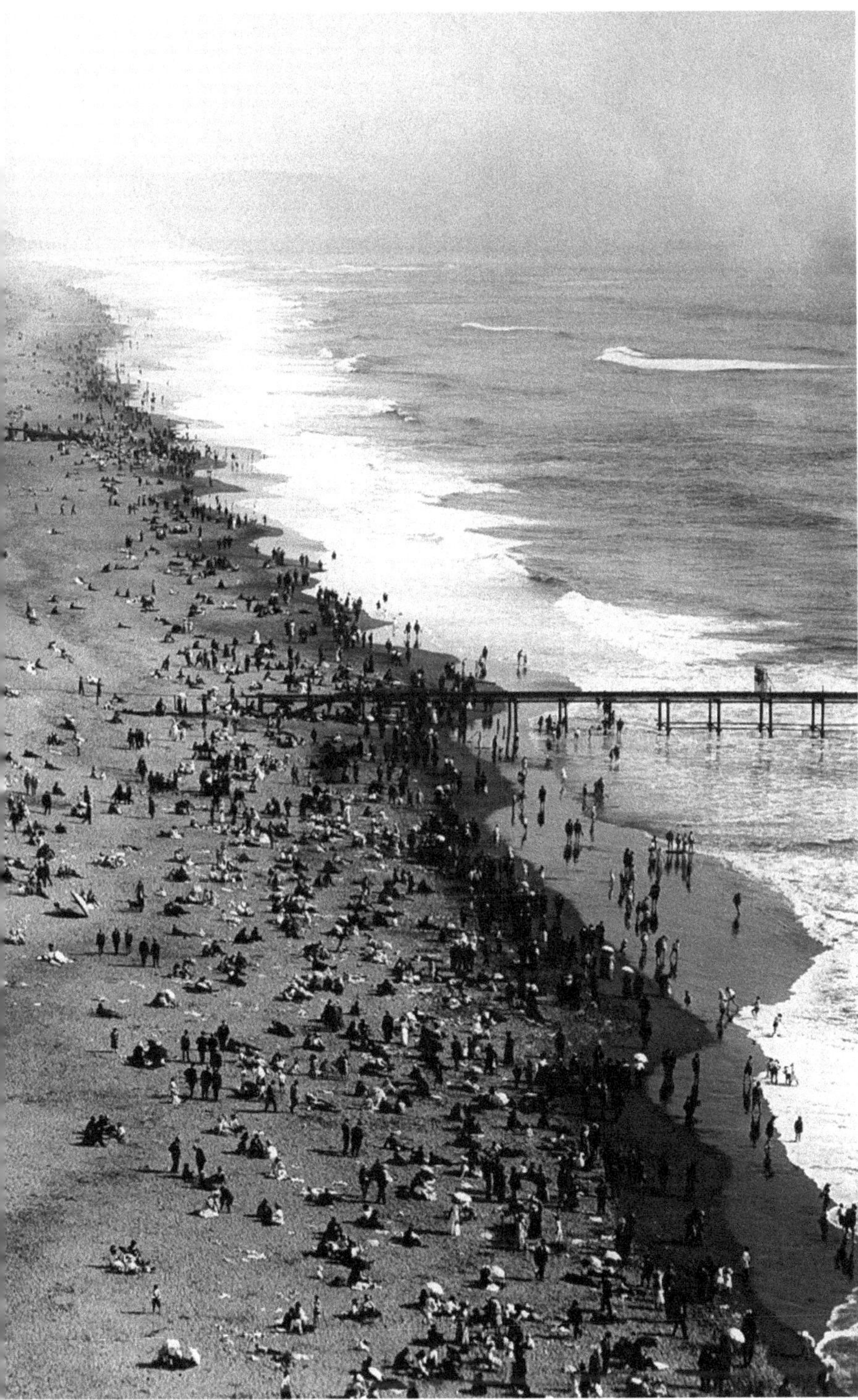

Crowds gather at Ocean Beach on the Pacific Coast in San Francisco in the early 1900s near the site of the historic Cliff House and Sutro Baths. Formerly referred to as "the outside lands," the area was developed by Adolph Sutro as a resort in the late nineteenth century. Tourists not scared away by the frequent fog and wind can still dine at the historic house and walk among the ghostly ruins of the baths.

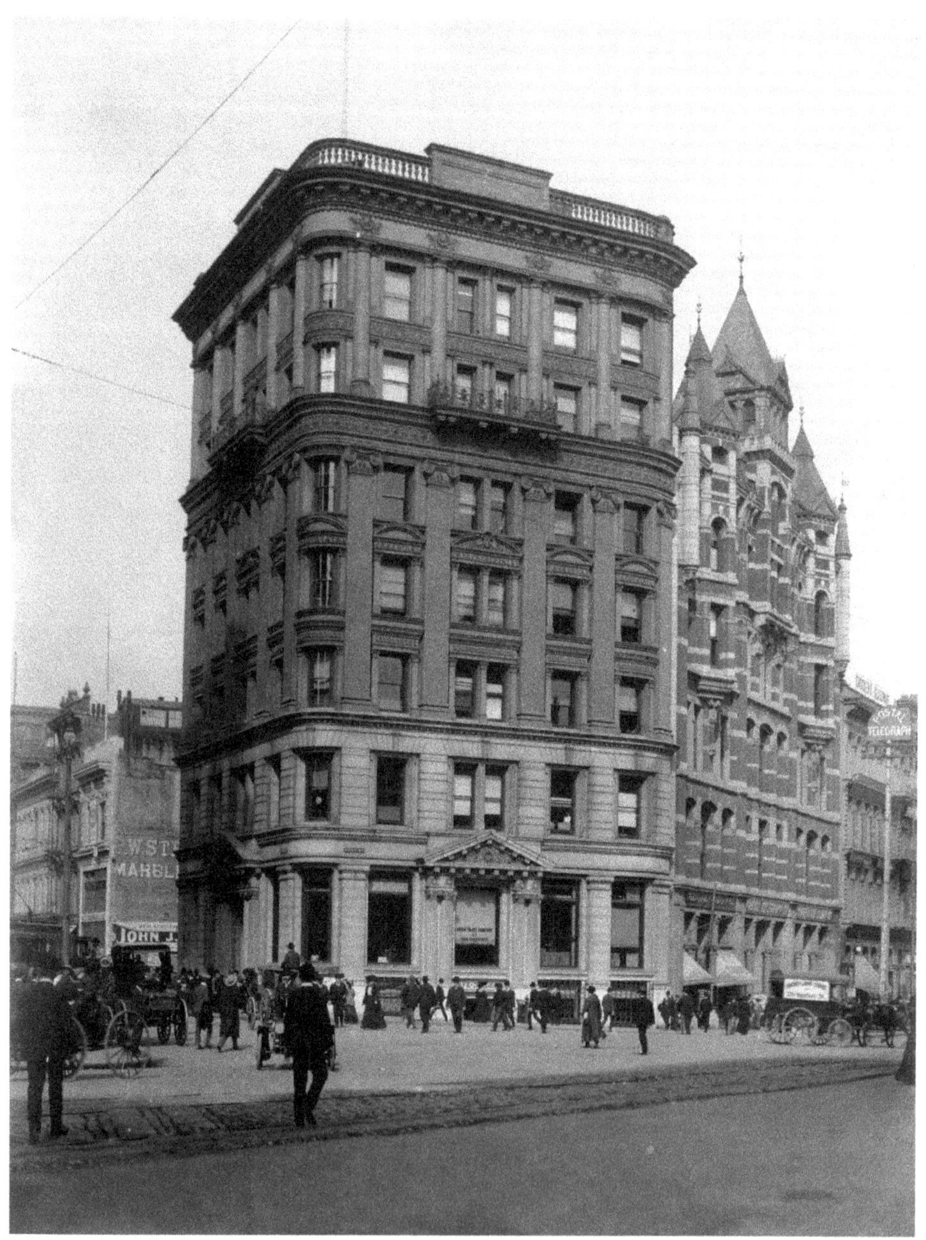

The Union Trust Building, shown here in 1903, was located at Market and Montgomery streets. Designed by celebrated architect Clinton Day, the bank was completed in 1894. In 1924, Wells Fargo merged with the Union Trust Company to become Wells Fargo Bank and Union Trust Company, later renamed Wells Fargo Bank.

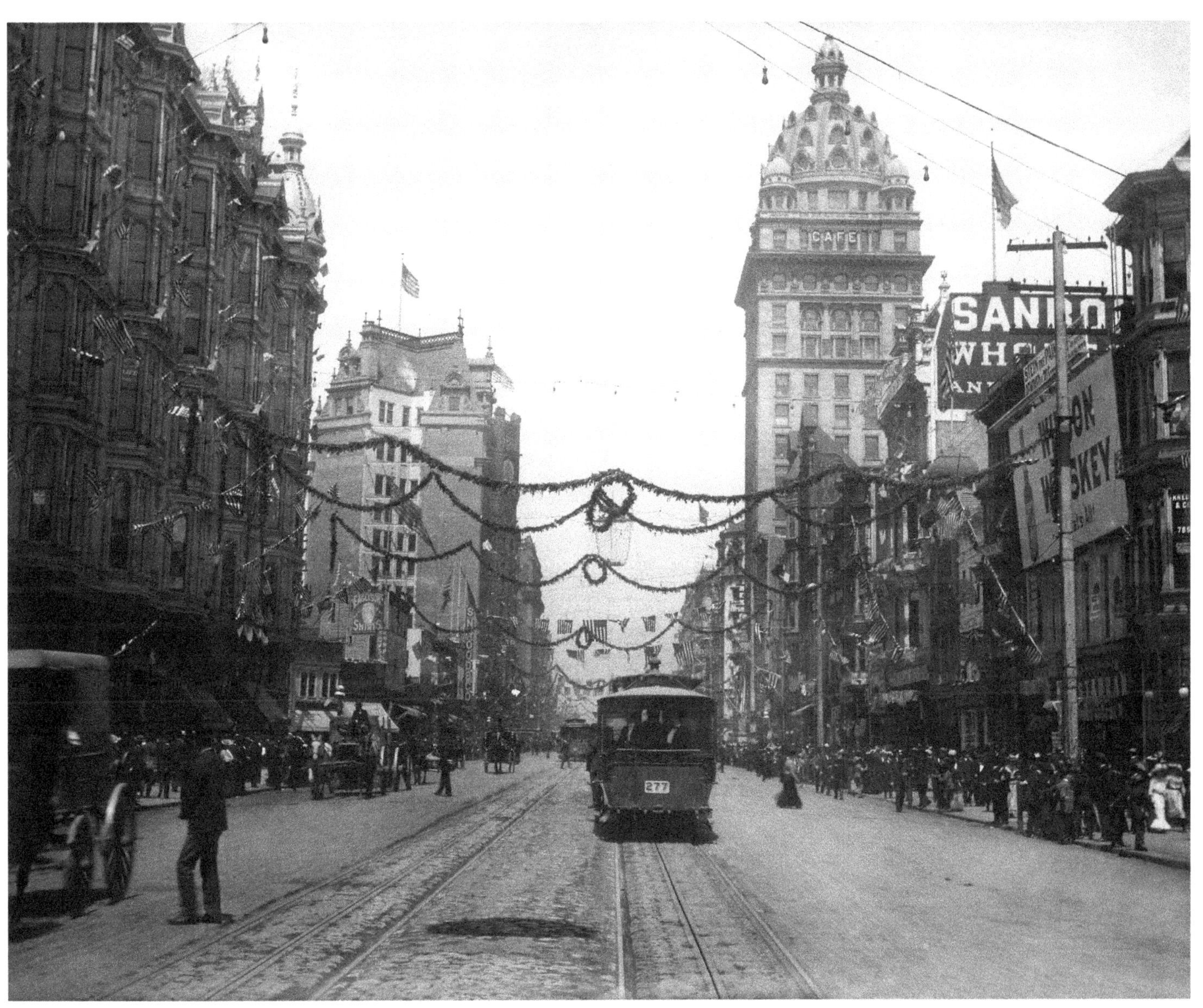

Market Street was decorated for the holiday season each year, as shown in this Christmas Day photograph from 1903. The 19-story Call Building is at right.

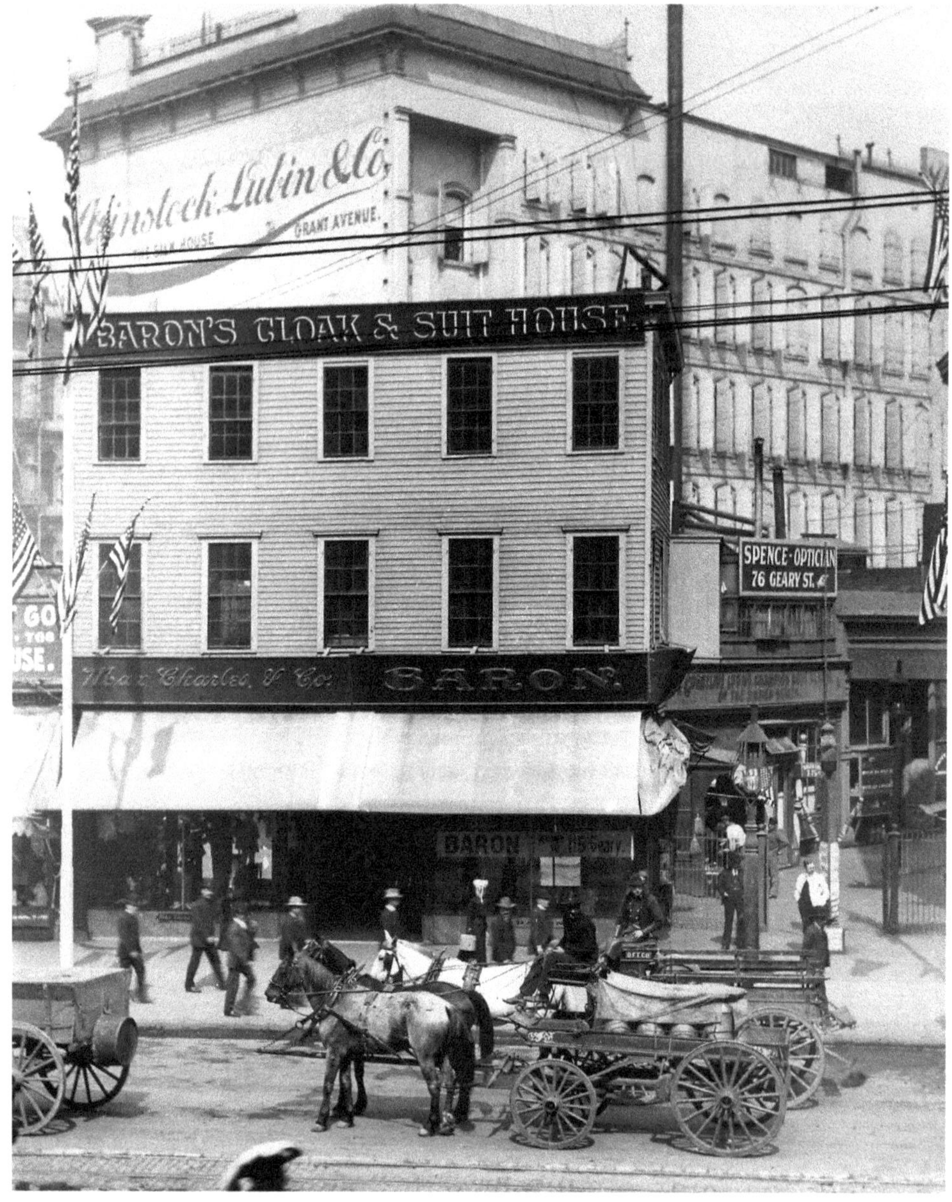

As far back as the Gold Rush, San Francisco had many small streets and alleys in the vicinity of Market Street and south. One such alley, shown here in 1904, was Brook Alley, to be found on the north side of Market Street between Grant Avenue and Kearny Street. The alley no longer exists, replaced as many were by modern construction.

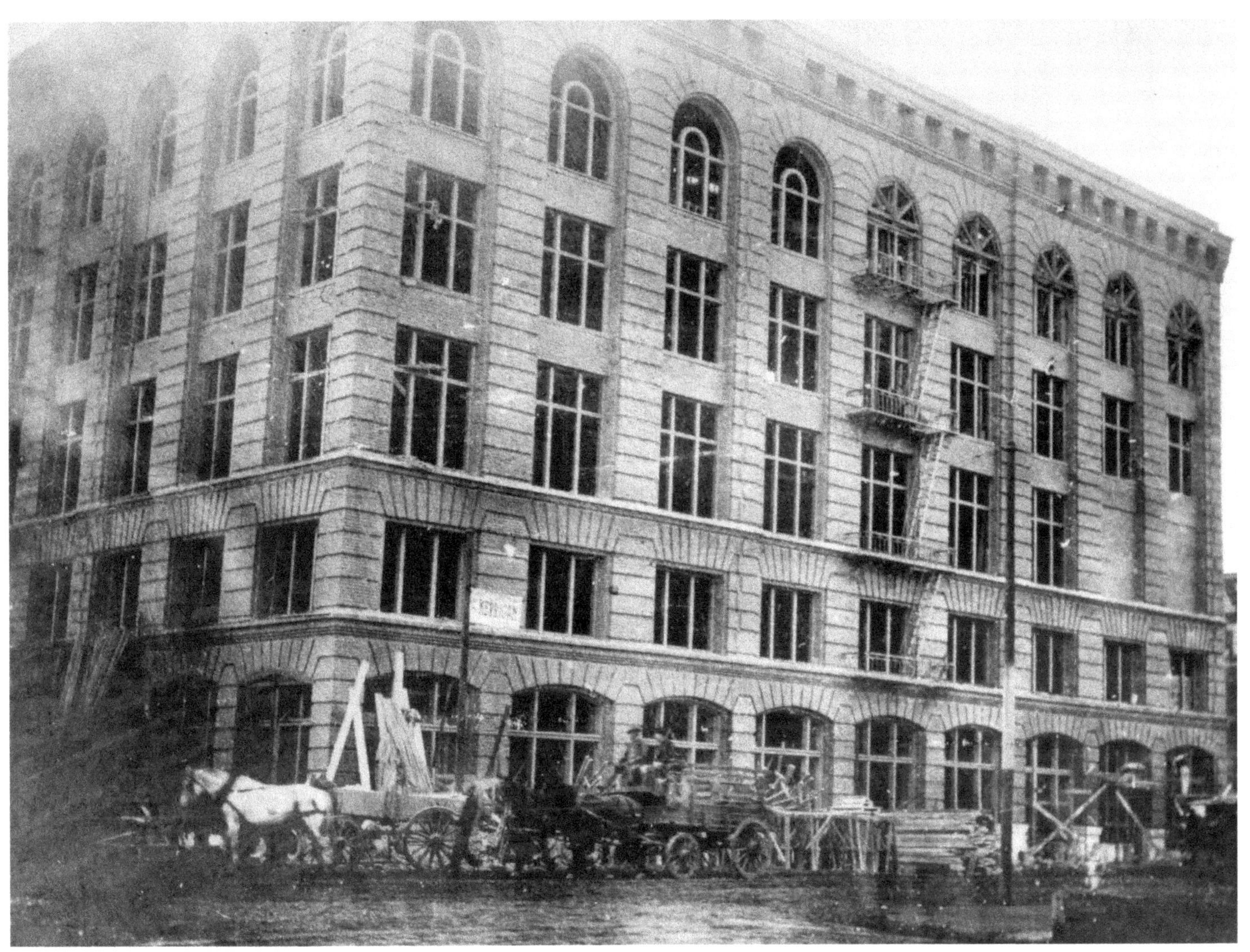

Construction of the Folgers Coffee building at 101 Howard Street at Spear Street in the SoMa neighborhood is in progress November 26, 1904. Its founder, Jim Folger, came from Nantucket to San Francisco with his brothers during the Gold Rush and started the business, helping to popularize a beverage up to that time sold exclusively as a luxury item for the wealthy. This roasting plant, built to accommodate rapidly increasing demand, survived the Earthquake and served as the company's headquarters for many years. The SoMa area was home to many rival coffee companies, including Hills Bros., MJB, and Schilling. For generations, commuters arriving at the Ferry Building would be welcomed by the strong aroma of roasting coffee beans. Folgers was purchased by Procter & Gamble in 1963, and operations were soon relocated to the Midwest. Over time, its chief rivals also were purchased by national manufacturers, and the scent of locally roasted coffee no longer treats residents and officeworkers. Today, the building houses offices, with a bronze plaque reading "The Folgers Coffee Company" mounted on the exterior.

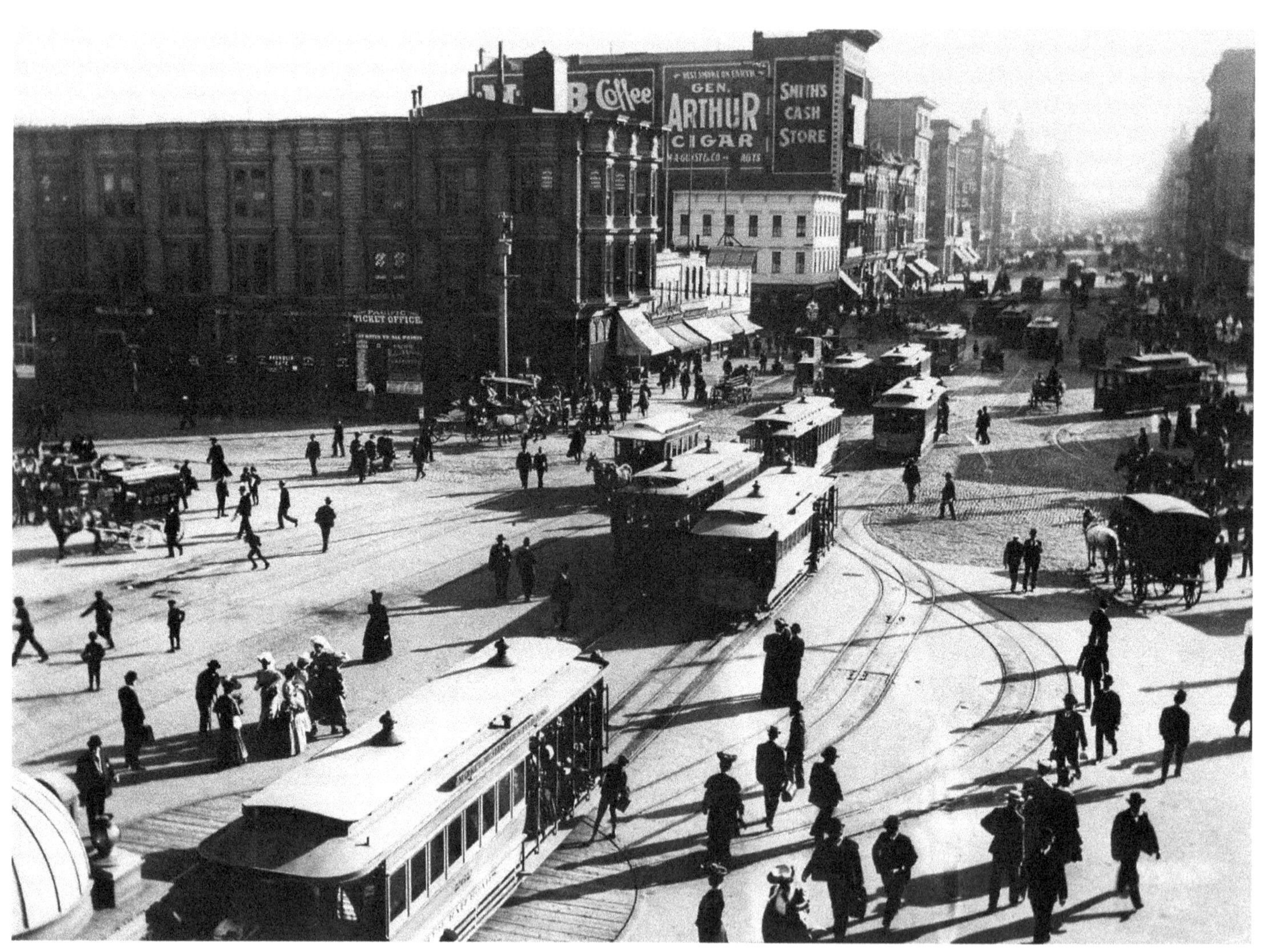

Market Street looking west from the Ferry Building in 1905, at the height of San Francisco's cable car era. The earthquake and fire of 1906 provided the impetus for replacing the cable cars with electric streetcars.

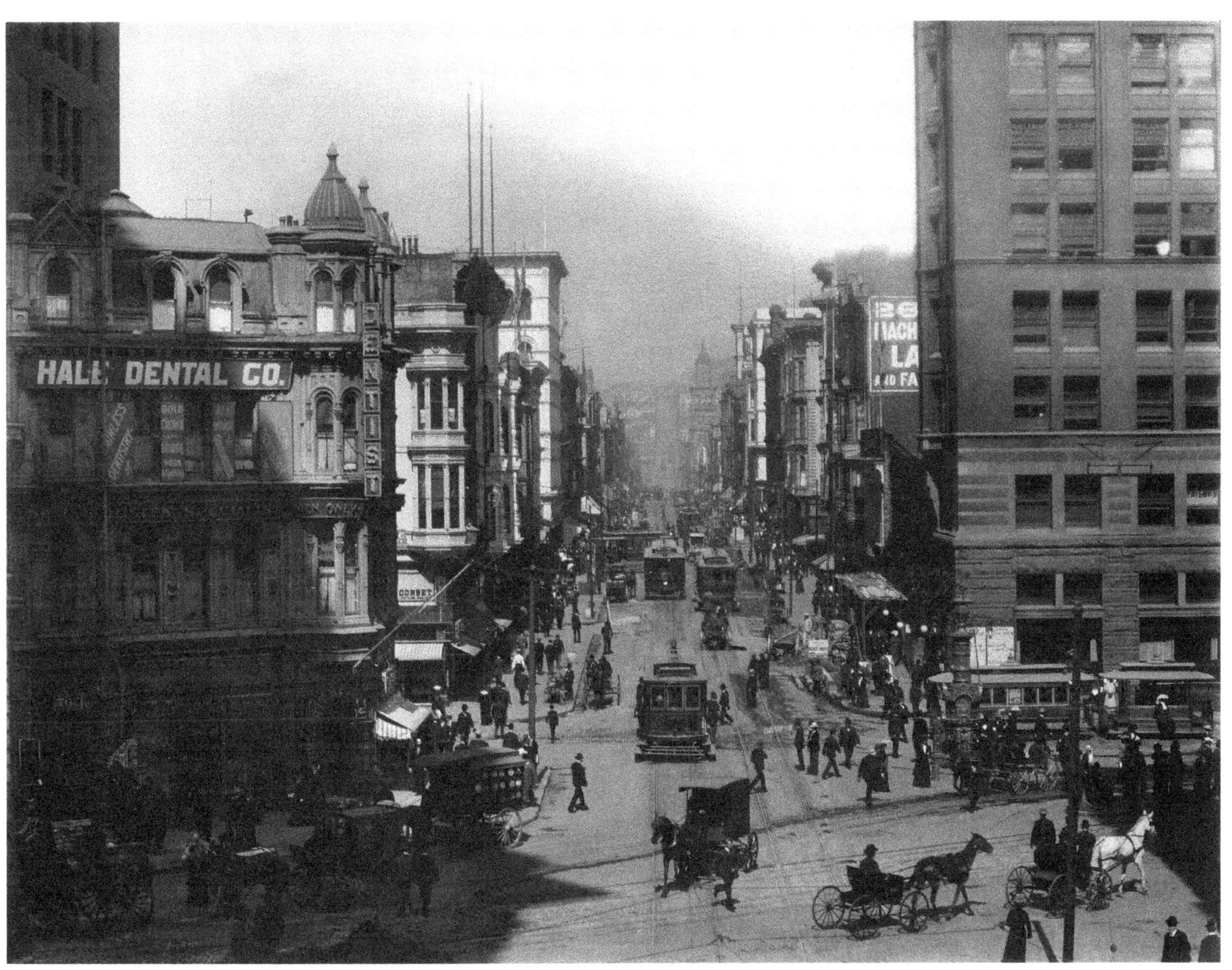

Named after General Stephen W. Kearny, veteran of the War of 1812, Kearny Street, shown here looking north from Market Street in 1905, was a busy thoroughfare for pedestrians and vehicles. During the Barbary Coast era, Kearny Street between Pacific and Broadway further north earned the reputation as "Devil's Acre." Lotta's Fountain can be seen at lower-right.

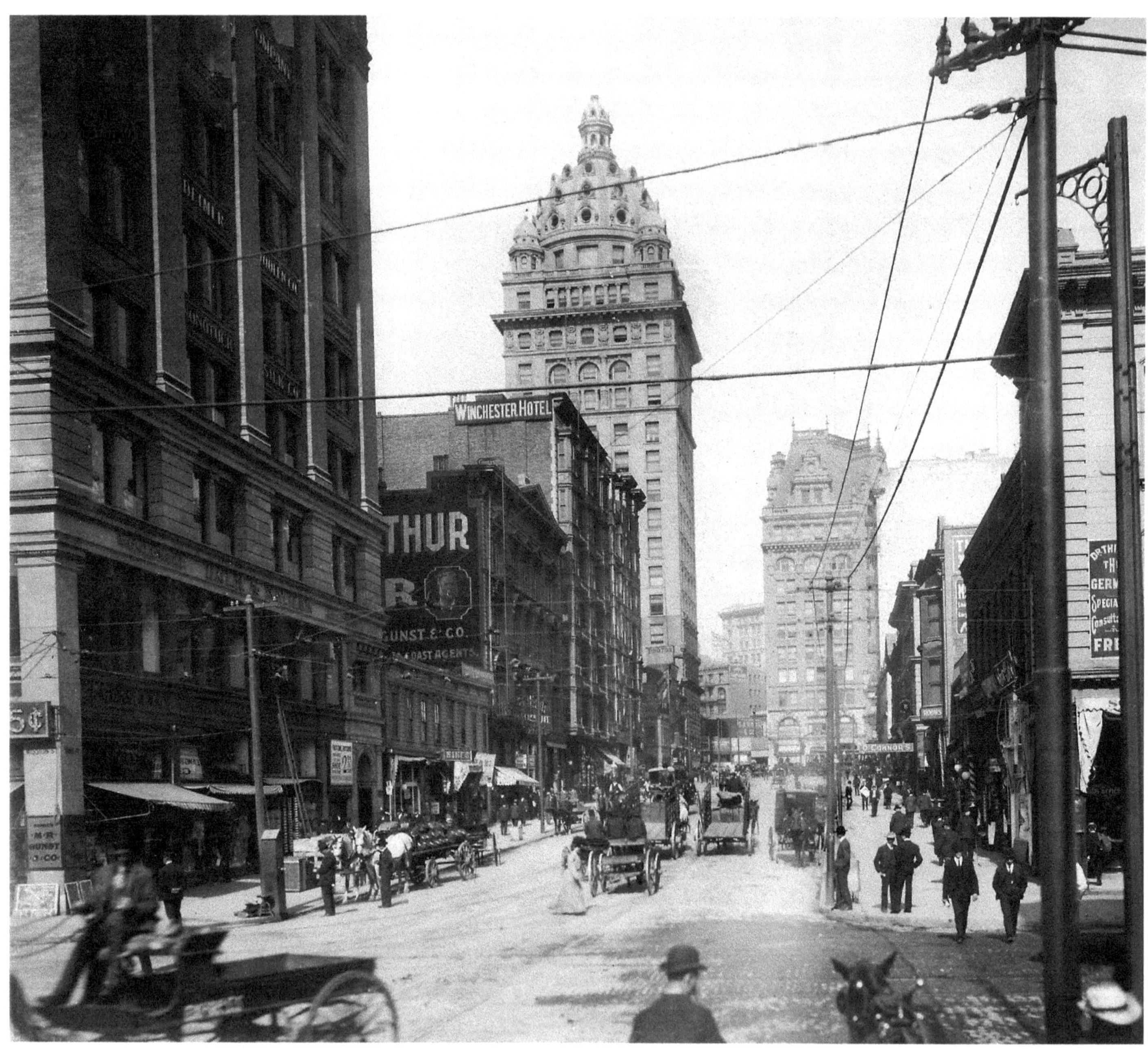

Third Street was a bustling thoroughfare in 1905 and led to the Call Building at Market Street in the distance. The Call Building stands today much changed, while most of the scene in the foreground perished.

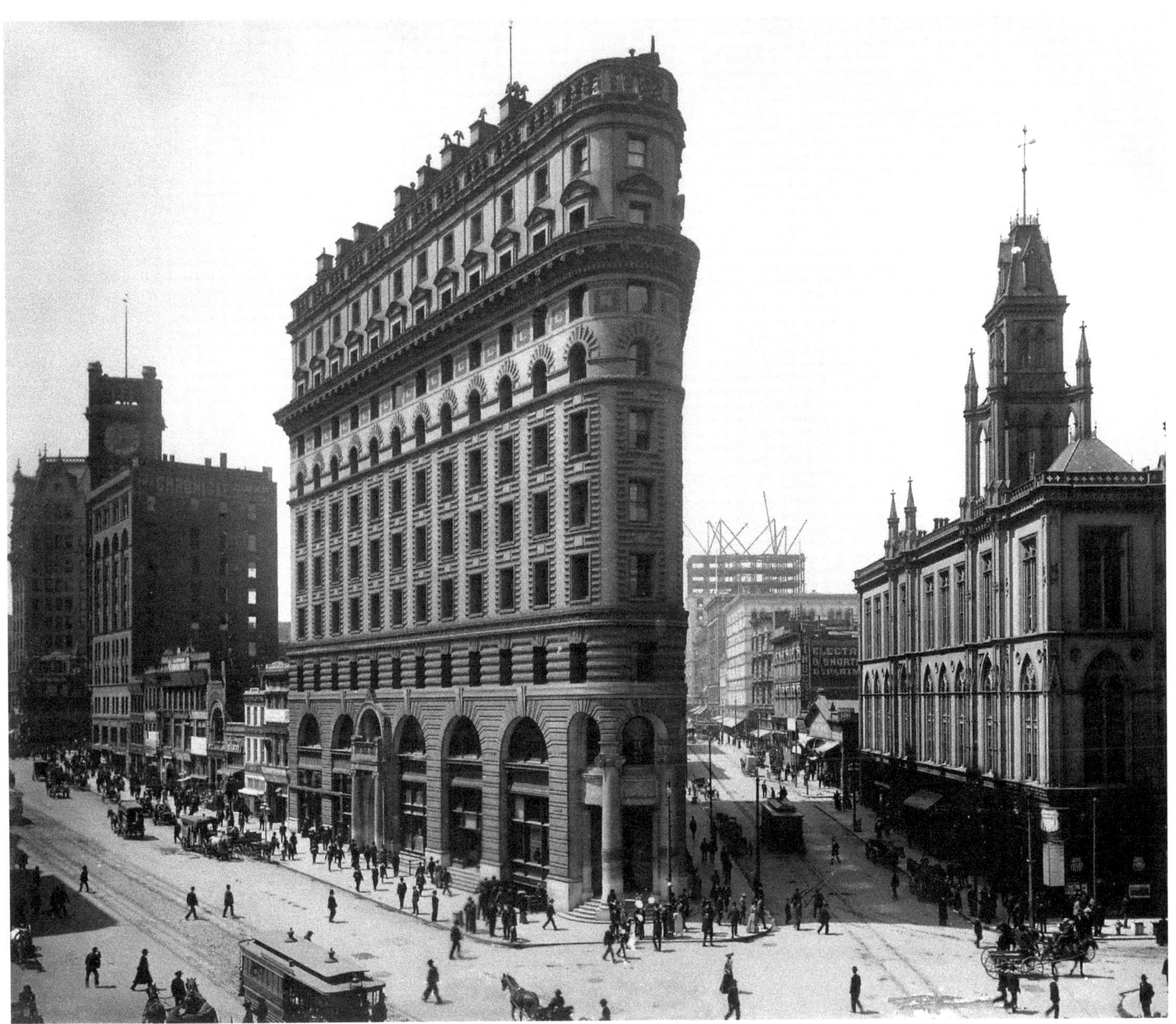

The Crocker Building, built in 1892 by noted architect Arthur Page Brown, to honor railroad baron Charles Crocker after his death in 1888, stands at the heart of the Financial District at Market and Post streets in this view from April 21, 1905. The Crocker Building survived the Earthquake and fire but was demolished in 1960 and replaced with the McKesson Building. A Bay Area Rapid Transit (BART) station is now located near the site.

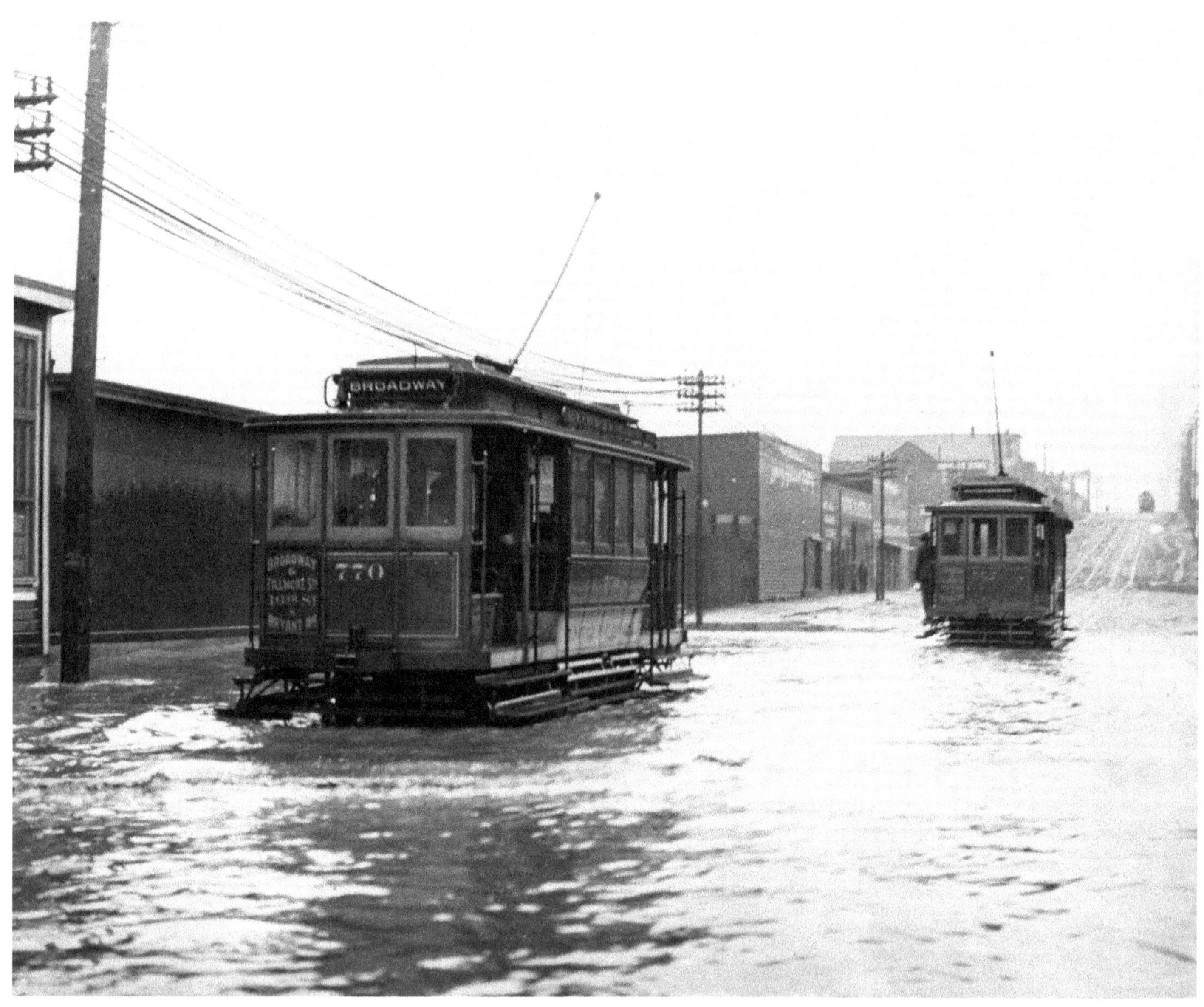

Electric streetcars drive through a 1905 flood on 16th and Folsom streets.

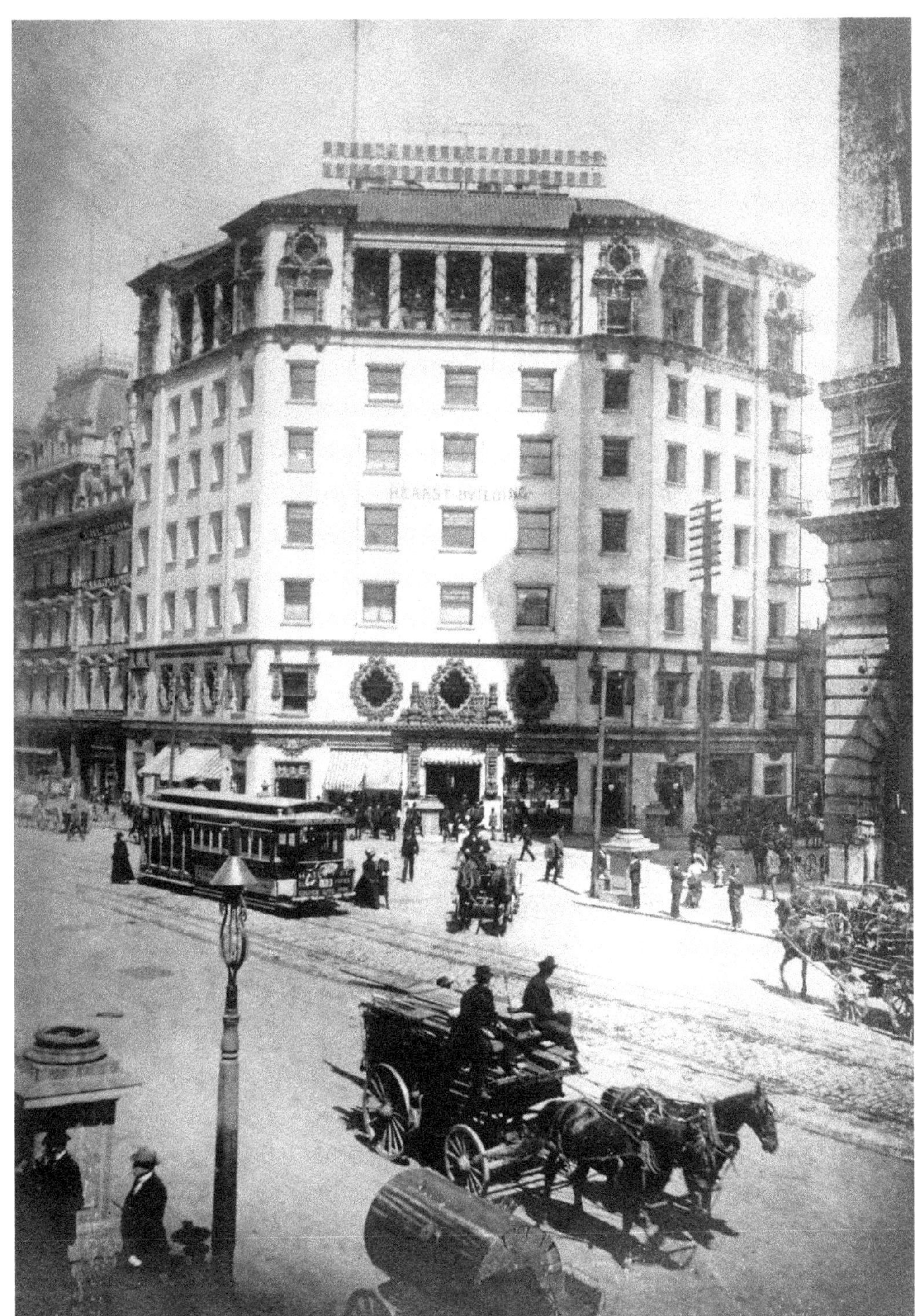

The Hearst Building, shown here in 1905 on "Newspaper Row" at 3rd and Market, housed the *San Francisco Examiner,* the newspaper founded by William Randolph Hearst, up until the late 1960s, when the Examiner formed a joint operating agreement with the rival Chronicle and began to share offices and publishing facilities at 5th and Mission. The Hearst Building was gutted by fire after the 1906 earthquake, but rebuilt in 1909 by Phoebe Hearst. In 1937, it was lavishly remodeled in its current baroque style by architect Julia Morgan. Today, small businesses occupy the building.

The History Building on Market Street, which housed H. H. Bancroft's Western American history book collection and his library with tens of thousands of other books, was rebuilt after the older Bancroft structure was partially destroyed by an 1886 fire. It was one of few libraries in the city to escape total destruction during the 1906 earthquake and fires.

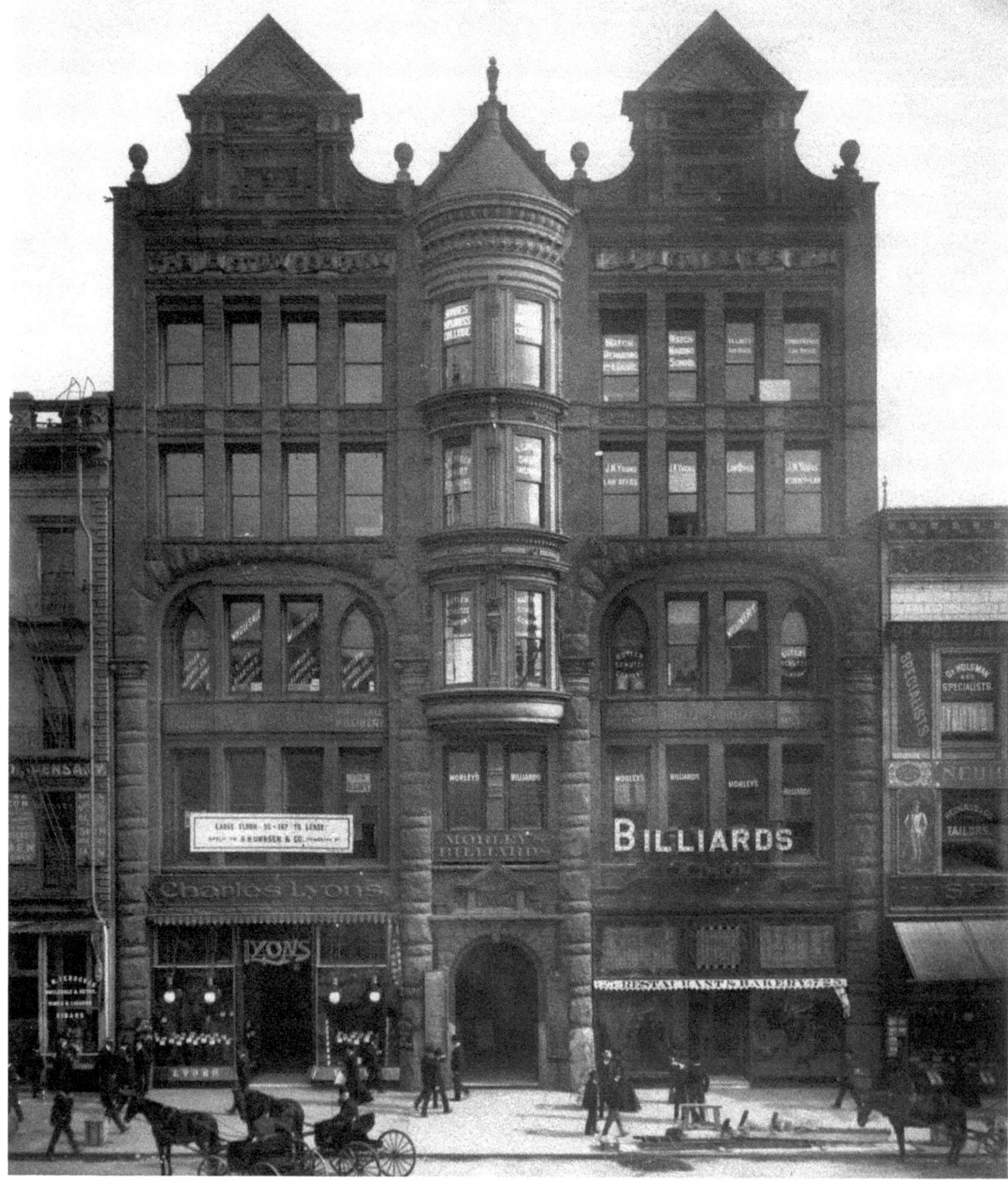

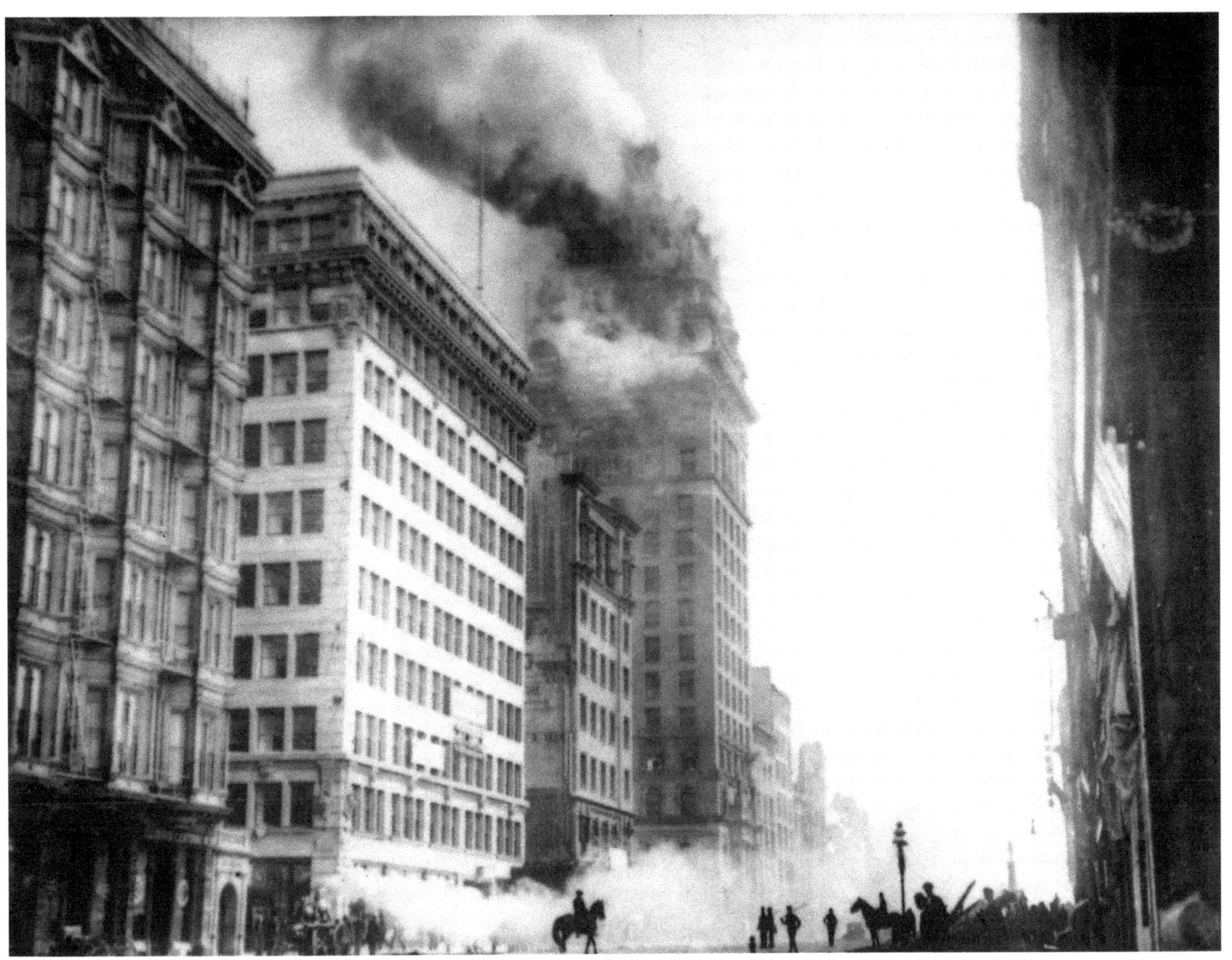

The Call Building burns as downtown San Francisco turns into an inferno after the earthquake of April 18, 1906. Also known as the Call-Spreckels Building, the Call Building was built in 1898 by the Reid brothers. The 315-foot-tall San Francisco landmark, with its signature dome roof, remained the tallest structure west of the Mississippi for many years. It survived the trauma of the earthquake and fires with some bruises and still stands at Market and 3rd streets today, renamed Central Tower.

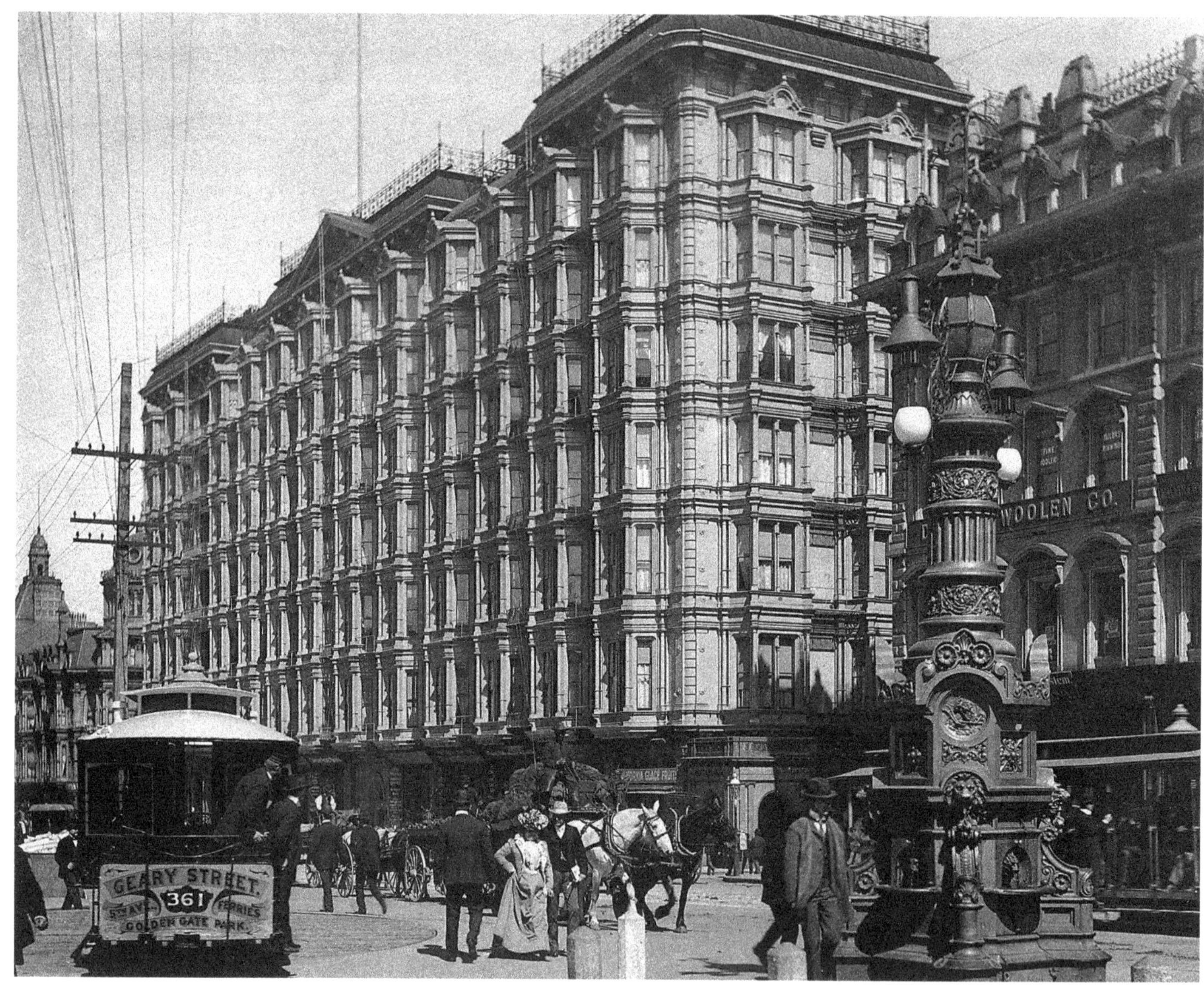

The Palace Hotel and Lotta's Fountain in 1906, at the intersection of Market where Geary and Kearny unite. The beautiful fountain was famed actress Lotta Crabtree's gift to the city in 1875. One of the few structures to remain standing in the Financial District after the 1906 earthquake, Lotta's Fountain served as a meeting spot for San Franciscans during and after the disaster. Every April 18th, at 5:12 A.M., thousands of San Franciscans convene at Lotta's Fountain to commemorate the anniversary of the earthquake, including a few centenarian survivors of the quake itself.

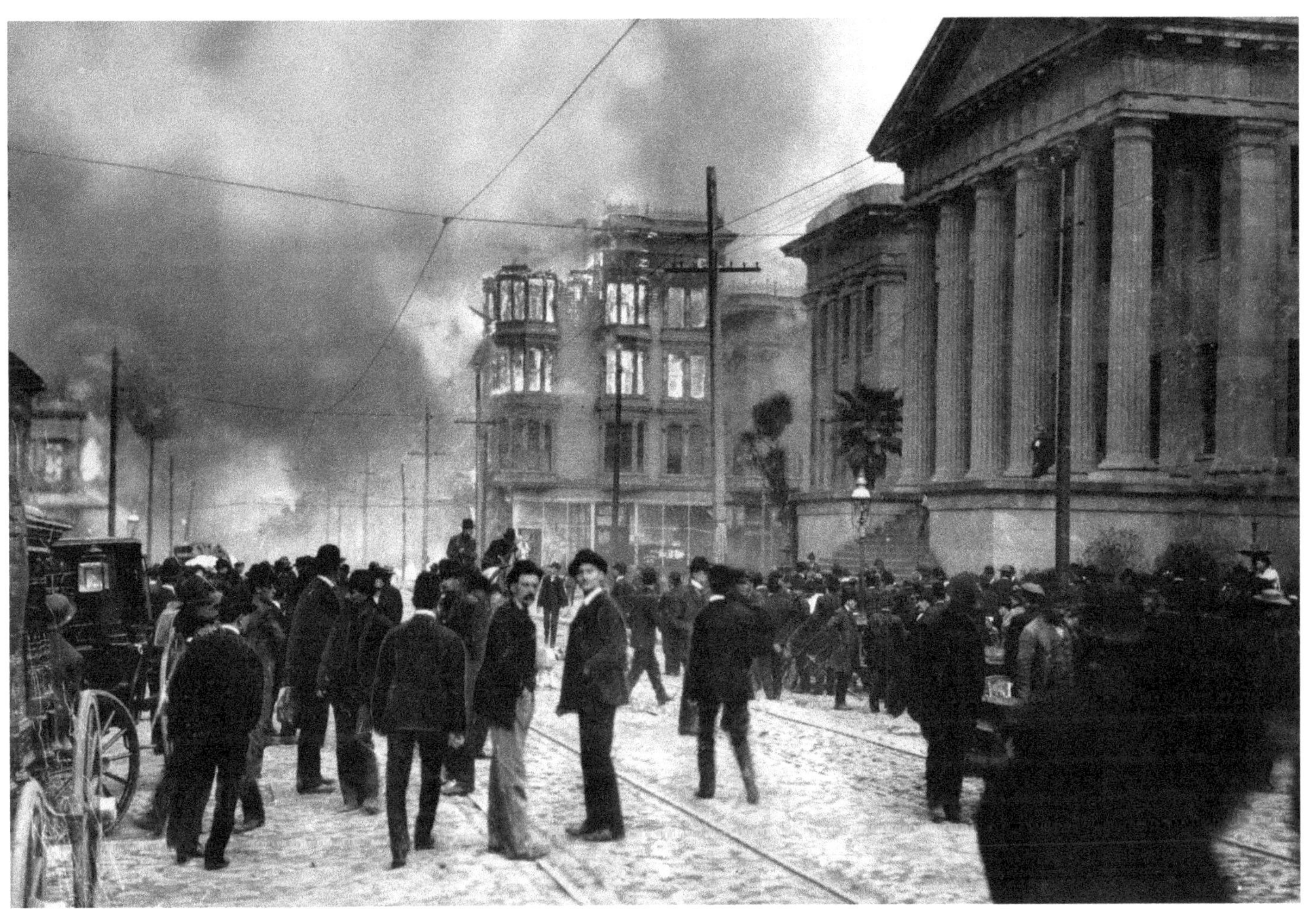

Shown here in 1906, crowds gather in front of the U.S. Mint, at 5th and Mission streets to watch a tenement burn at the site of the present-day Chronicle Building. The director of the Mint stands at rooftop observing the destruction. The horse-drawn hearses at left were used to evacuate personal belongings and ill dwellers. The U.S. Mint withstood the seismic jolts and fire following the earthquake, thanks to its structural fortitude, and the $200 million inside were kept safe. Mint operations were transferred to a new San Francisco Mint on Duboce Street in 1937, but the Old Mint still stands and is being prepared to reopen as a museum of San Francisco history.

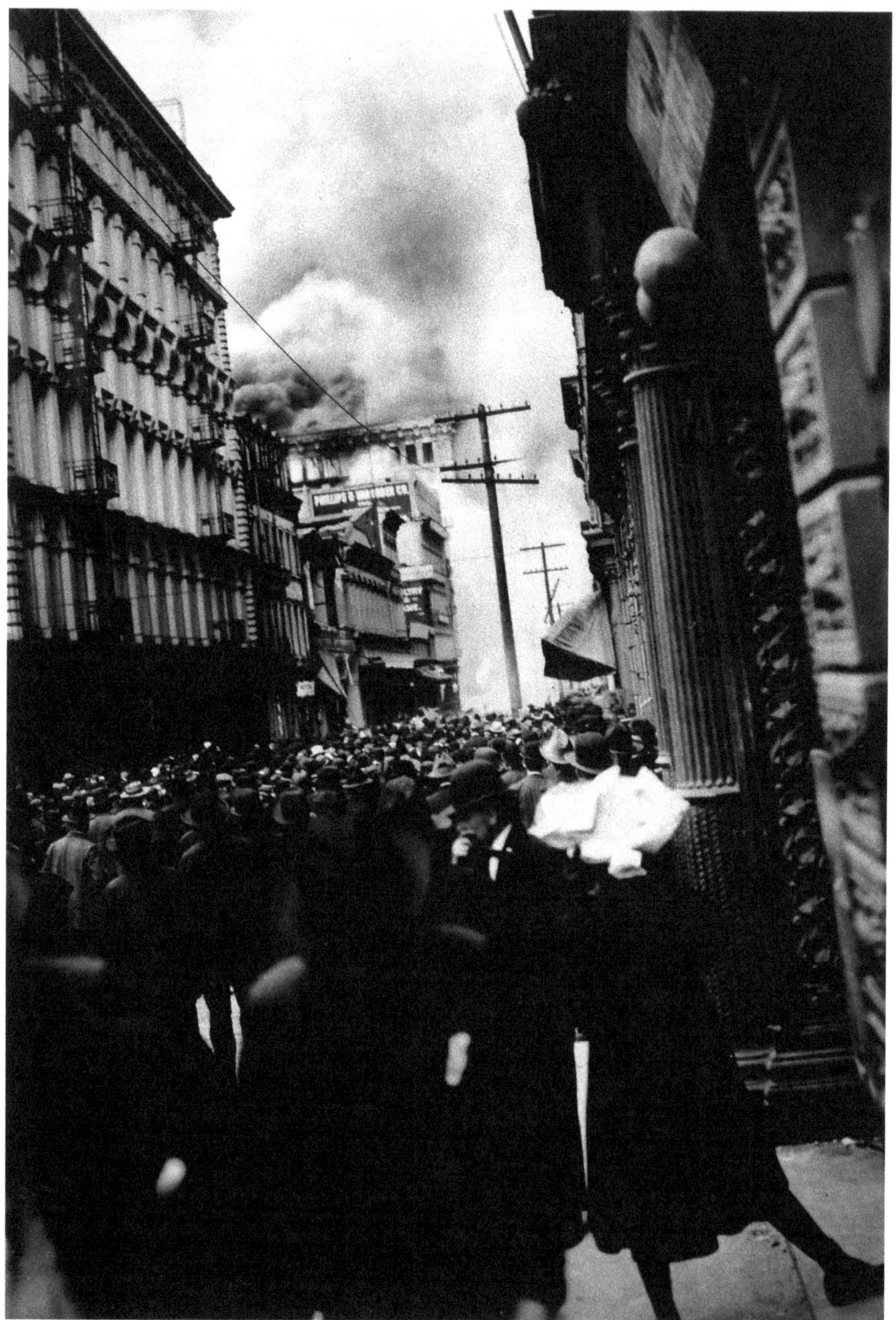

Chinatown was leveled during the earthquake and subsequent fires of 1906. At the time, most Chinese people in the city were bachelors, partly due to restrictive immigration laws that prohibited bringing families into the country. Because the fires of 1906 destroyed most of San Francisco's birth records, Chinese-born men living in San Francisco were allowed to claim American citizenship, and in some cases have their families join them.

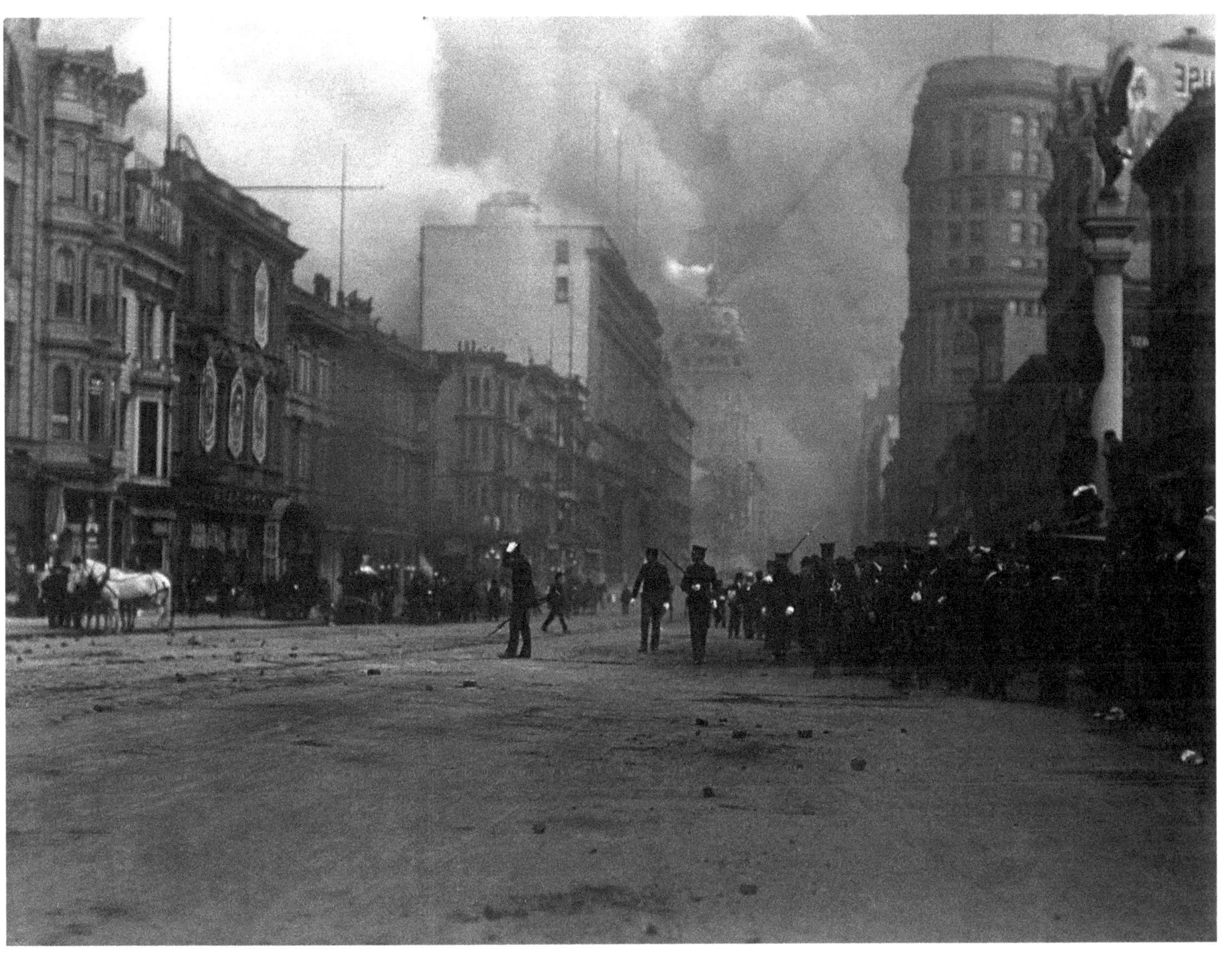

Buildings burn on Market Street in the fires that razed downtown. The fires burned for three days and did far more damage than the earthquake itself. The earthquake knocked out transportation and telephone lines, as well as water mains, rendering efforts to extinguish the flames futile. Of a population of 400,000, over 250,000 were left homeless, and 28,000 buildings went up in flames. More than $500 million of damage occurred (about $50 billion in today's currency). The 1906 earthquake was the first disaster of this magnitude to be captured by photography. People all over the world saw the devastation that befell the city.

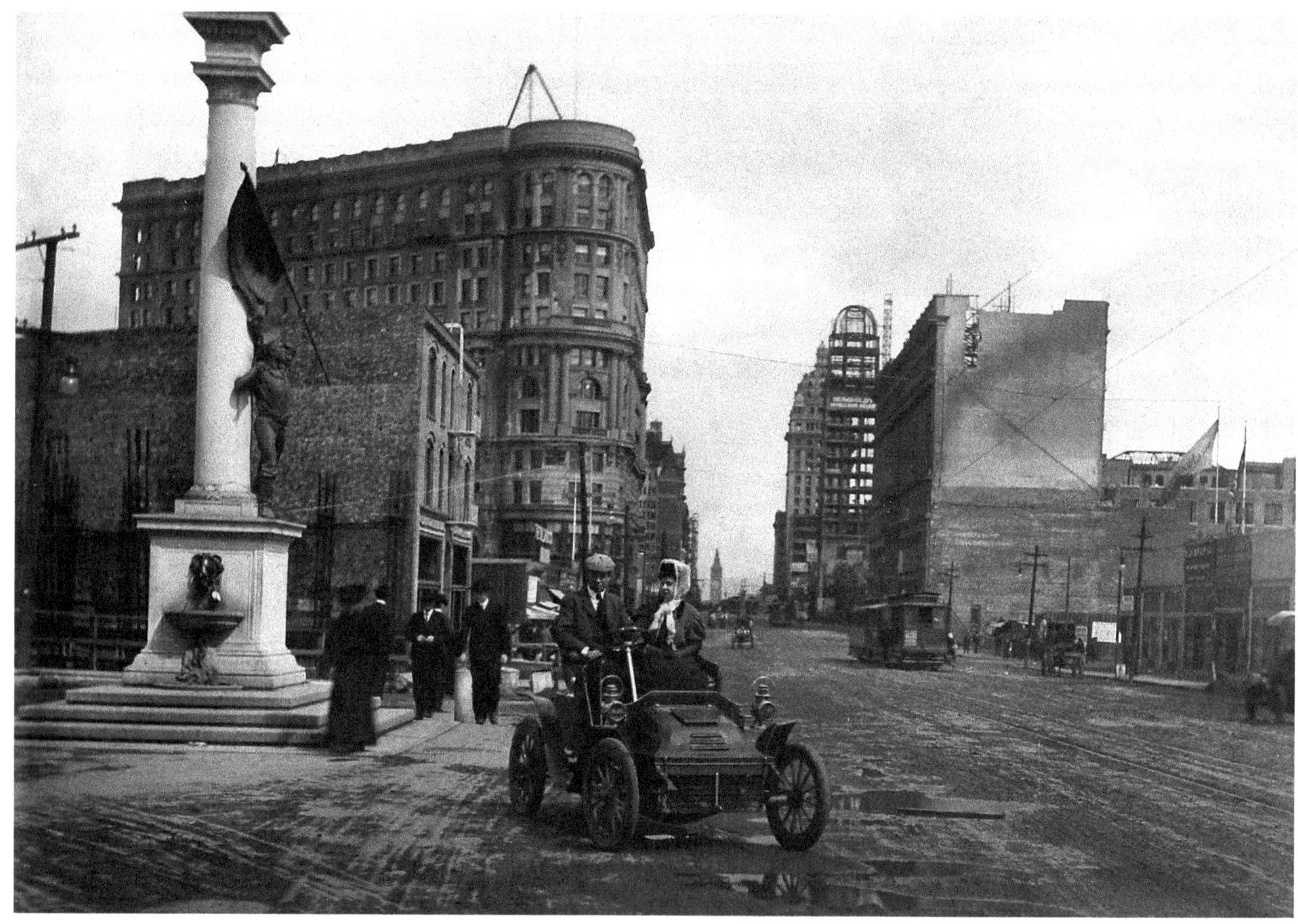

Onlookers driving down Market Street survey the devastated city after the earthquake and fires in 1906. Although the official death toll was less than 400, researchers believe that more than 3,000 people perished, and that the casualty rate was deliberately played down to protect real estate prices and encourage investors to finance rebuilding. Many sacrosanct San Franciscans believed that San Francisco was destroyed because of its "sinfulness," and made efforts afterward to make it more refined and virtuous.

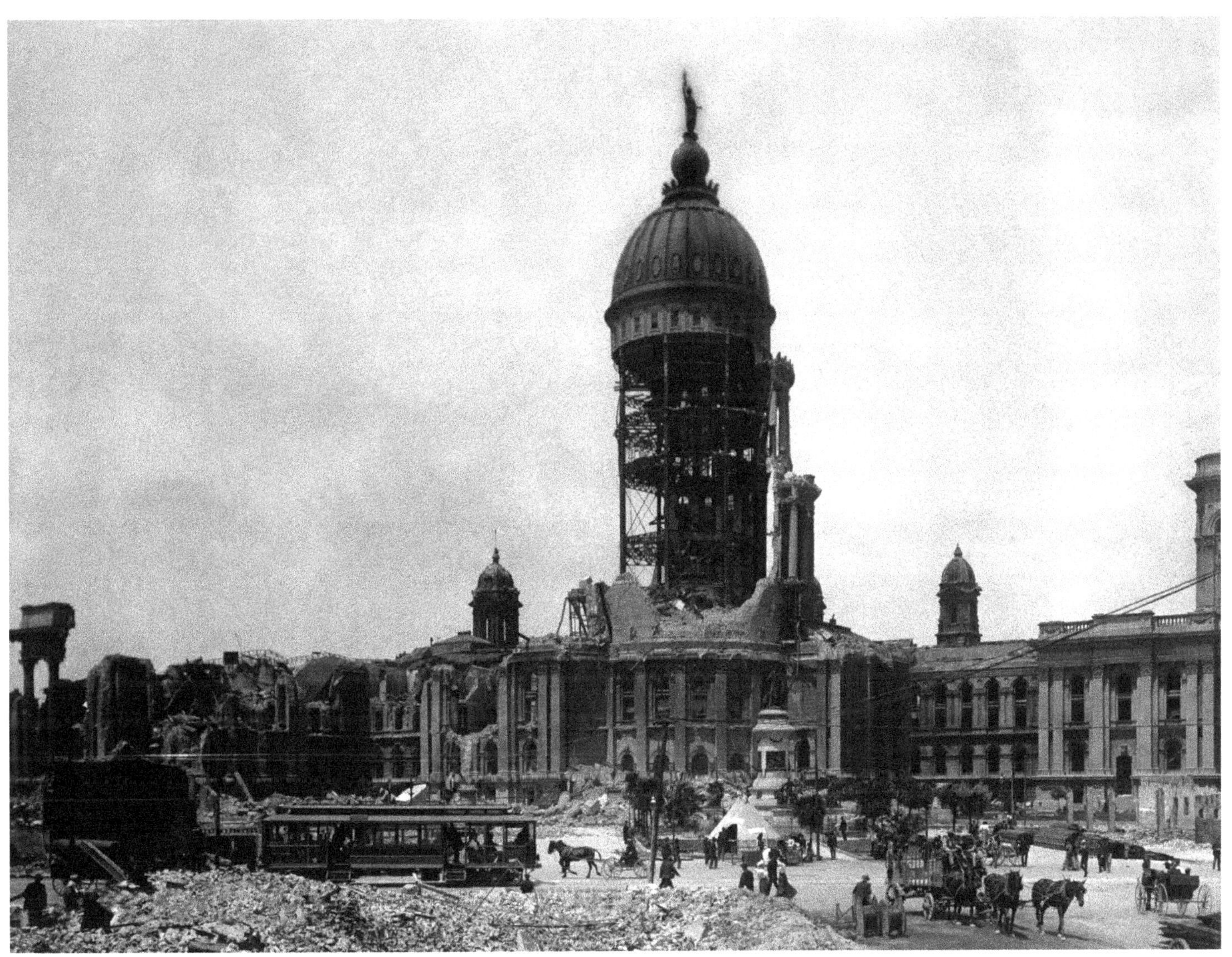

In ruins after the earthquake and fire was San Francisco's City Hall, at the corner of Larkin and Grove. The lavish building, completed in 1899 after 27 years of construction, crumbled to the shaking ground in less than 30 seconds. Only the skeletal dome remained.

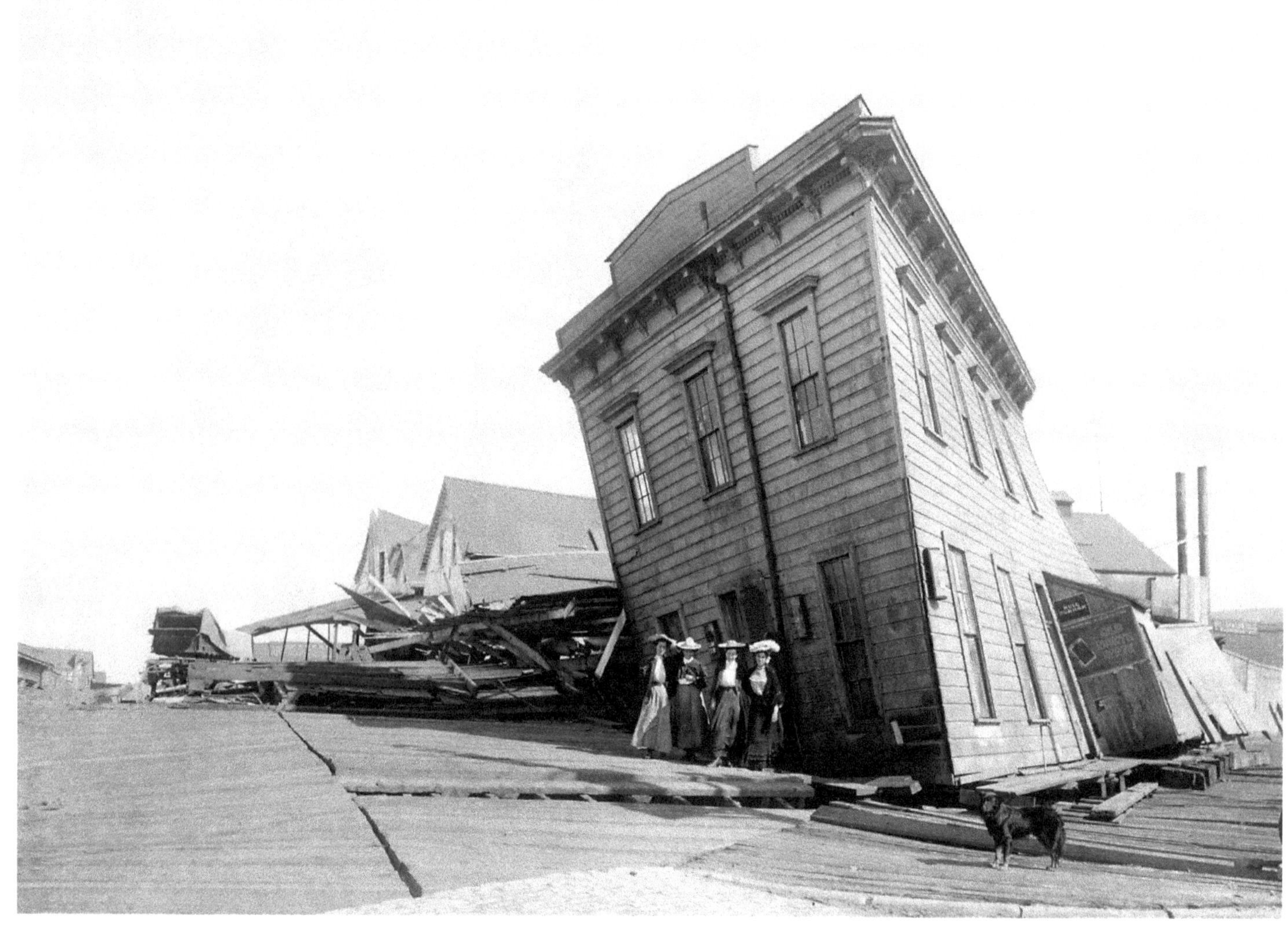

Four women survey the obliteration in front of a leaning building on the waterfront. After the earthquake, San Francisco parks were turned into refugee camps. Even where housing remained standing, cooking inside was outlawed for weeks, owing to the hazard of broken gas and water lines.

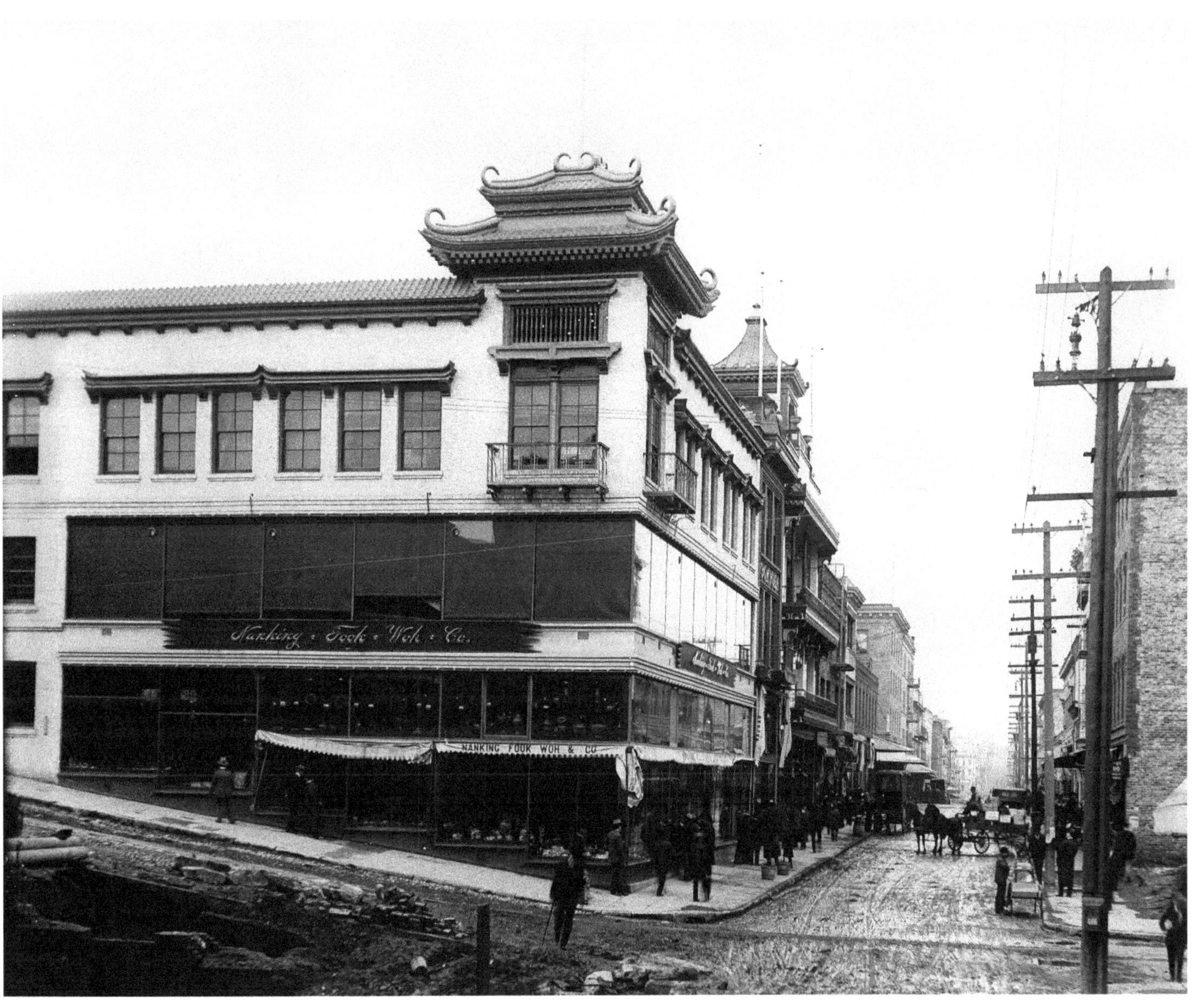

Nanking Fouk Woh & Co., an importer of Chinese merchandise, stood on the corner of Dupont (now Grant Avenue) and Sacramento streets in Chinatown.

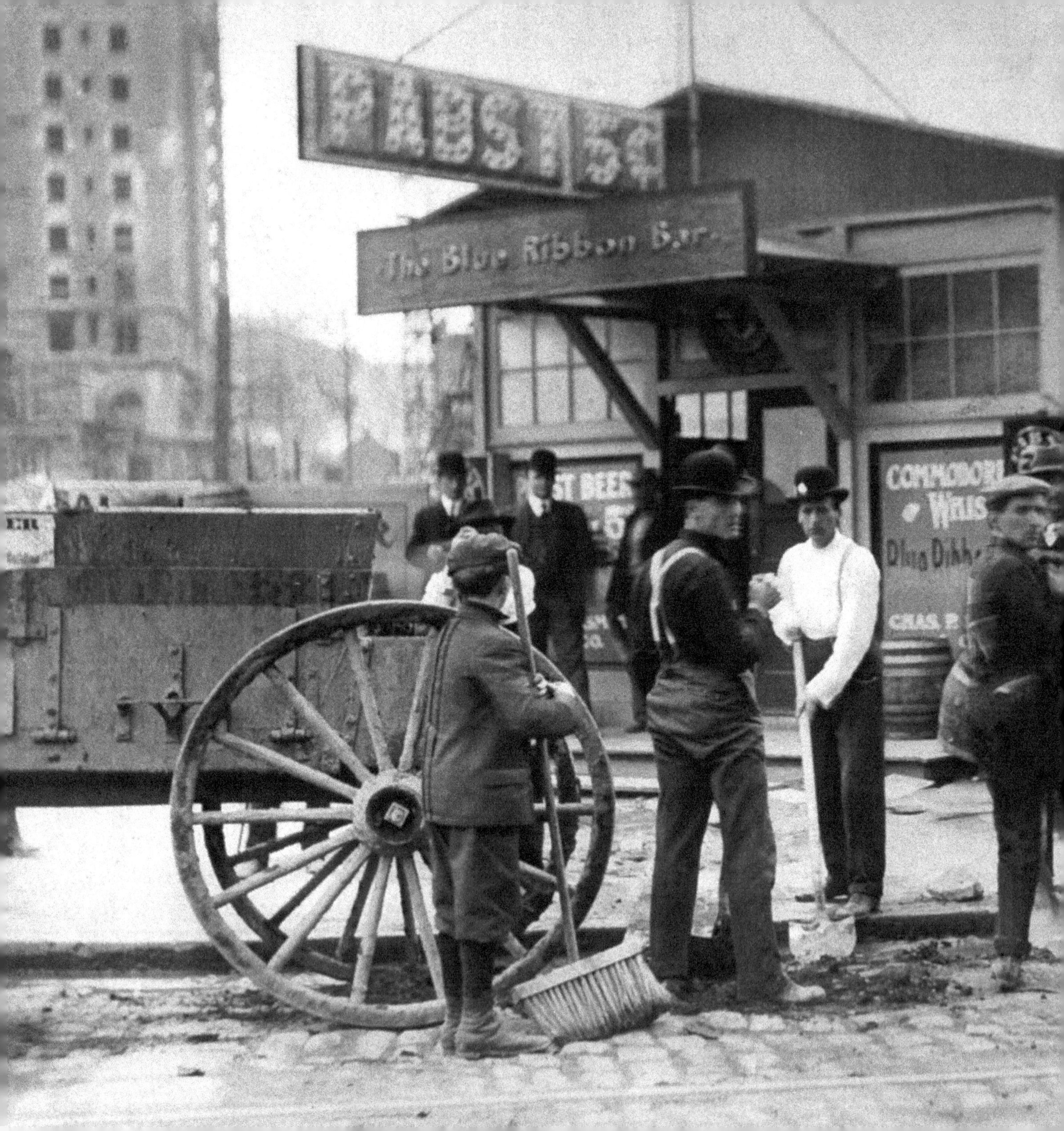
The Blue Ribbon Bar.

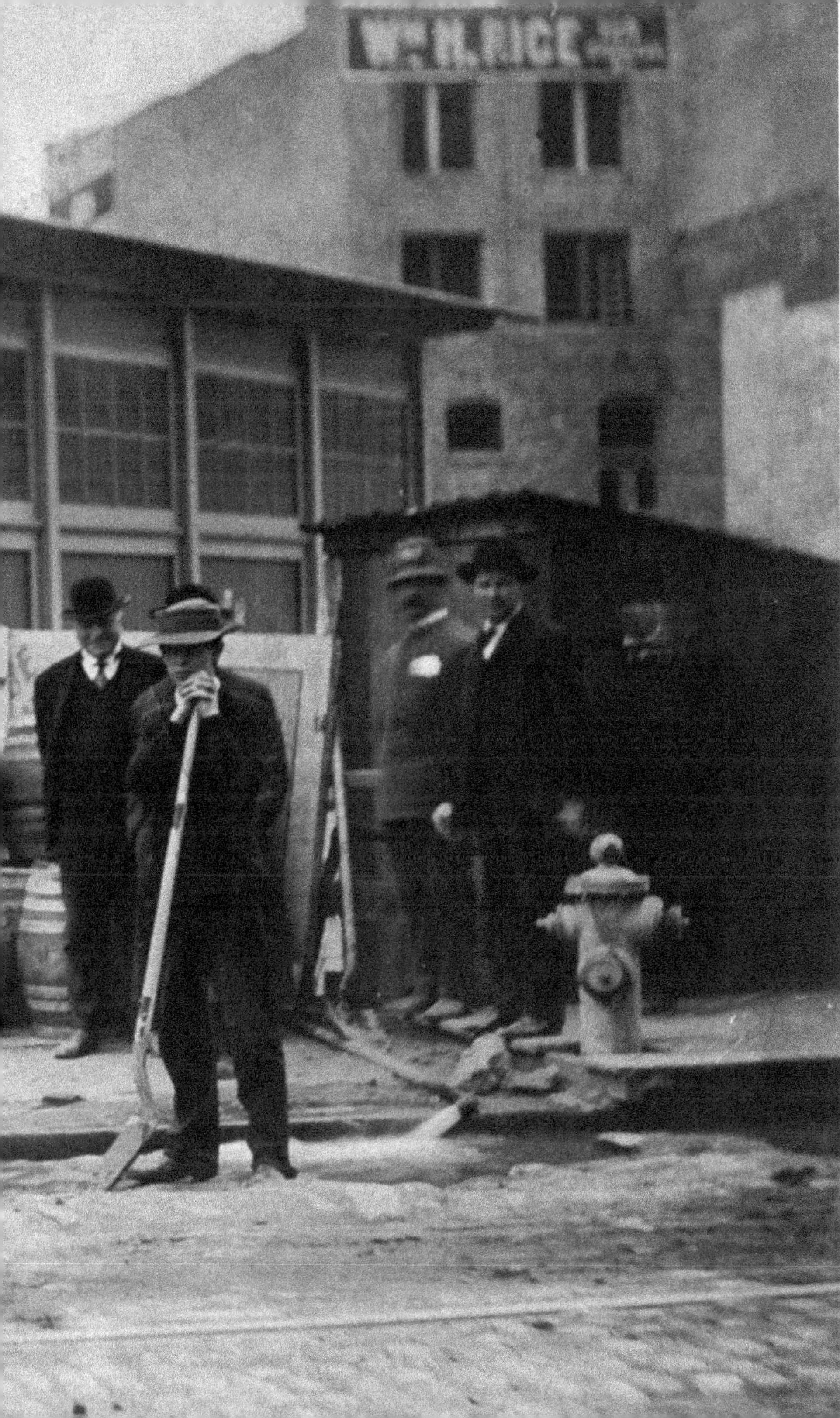

Men and boys, some with brooms and shovels, are seen standing outside a bar on O'Farrell Street after the earthquake. Many people dug through the wreckage looking for souvenirs or canned food. Because of lawlessness following the disaster, San Francisco Mayor Eugene Schmitz issued a shoot-to-kill decree to discourage looters, resulting in a few additional deaths.

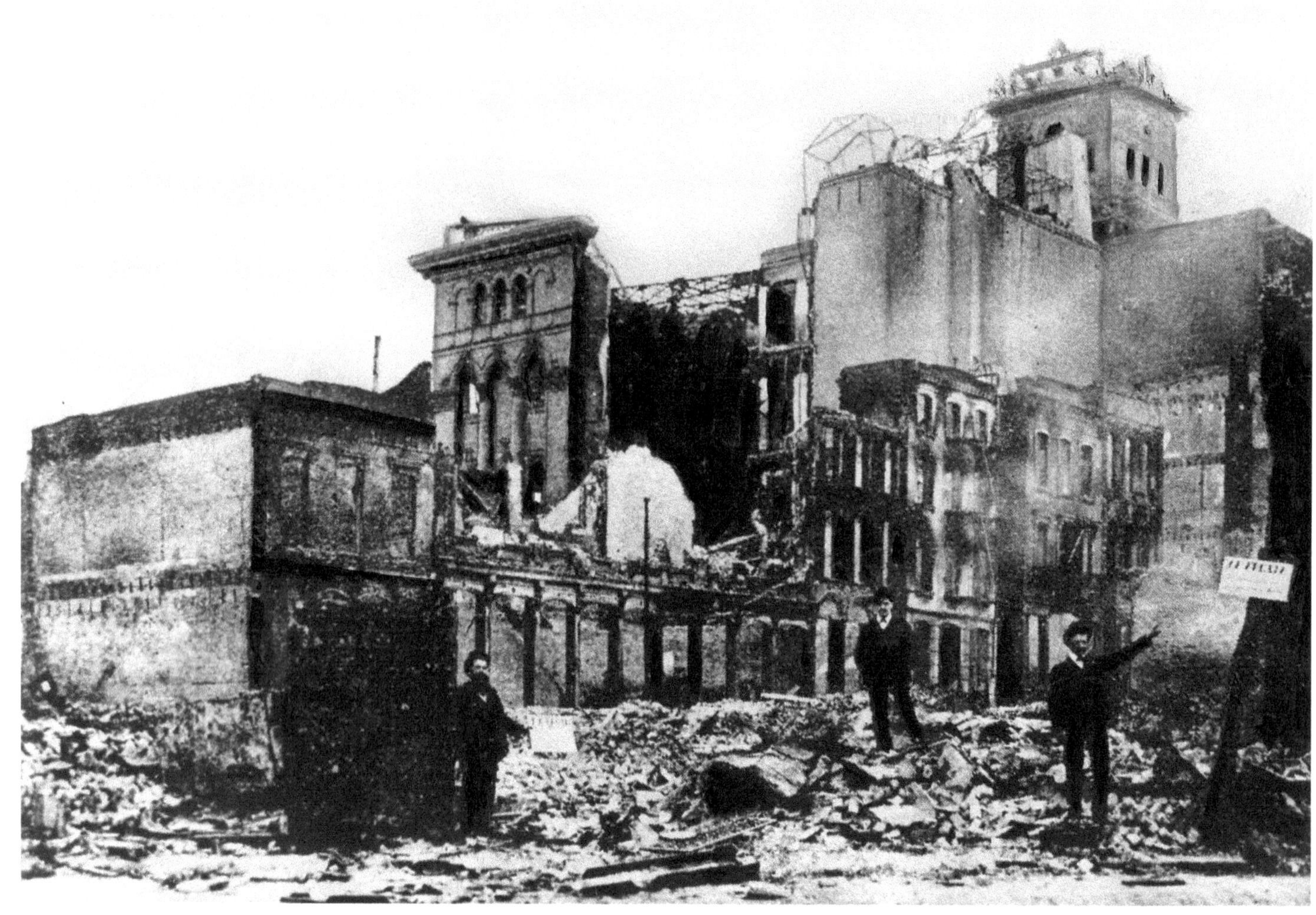

A. P. Giannini, the son of Italian immigrants, was distraught by how poorly he saw banks serving the community in the late nineteenth century. In 1904 he opened the Bank of Italy in an old saloon in North Beach. His bank provided outstanding service, attracting immigrants and other clientele who otherwise would never have set foot in a bank, and was one of few banks that would lend money to immigrants. After the 1906 earthquake and fires, the Bank of Italy building at the corner of Columbus and Washington in North Beach was in ruins, as seen here April 19, 1906. Giannini saved the future of his company when he filled a borrowed wagon from his vaults, covered the stash with fruits and vegetables, and fled to safety.

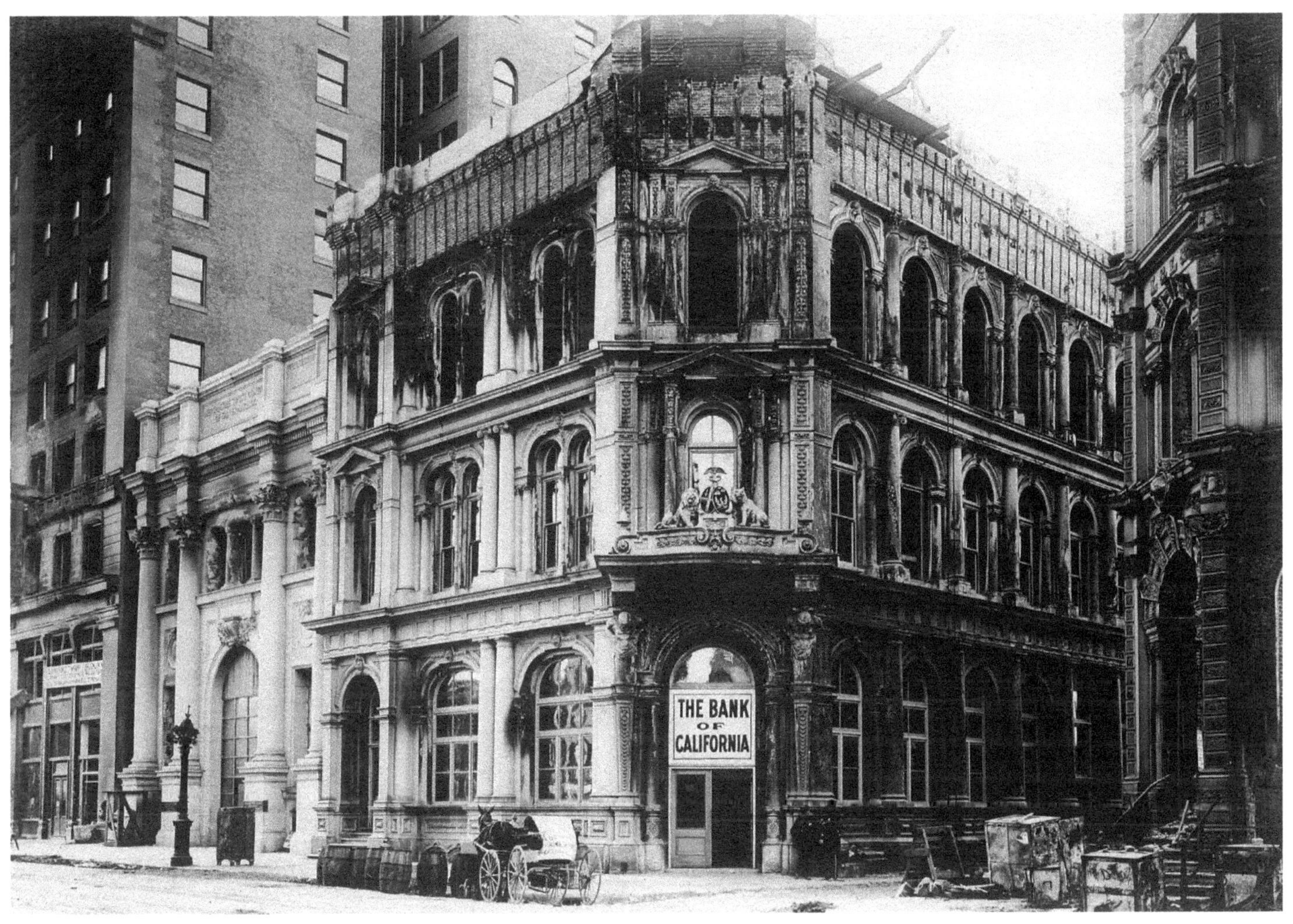

Founded by William Ralston on July 5, 1864, the Bank of California, located on the northeast corner of California and Sansome streets, was the first commercial bank in the western United States, and played an instrumental role in western growth. The ornate building, seen in this 1906 picture, was destroyed in the earthquake. In 1908, the bank was rebuilt at 400 California Street, and is now a San Francisco Historic Landmark. In 1996, the Bank of California and Union Bank merged to form the Union Bank of California.

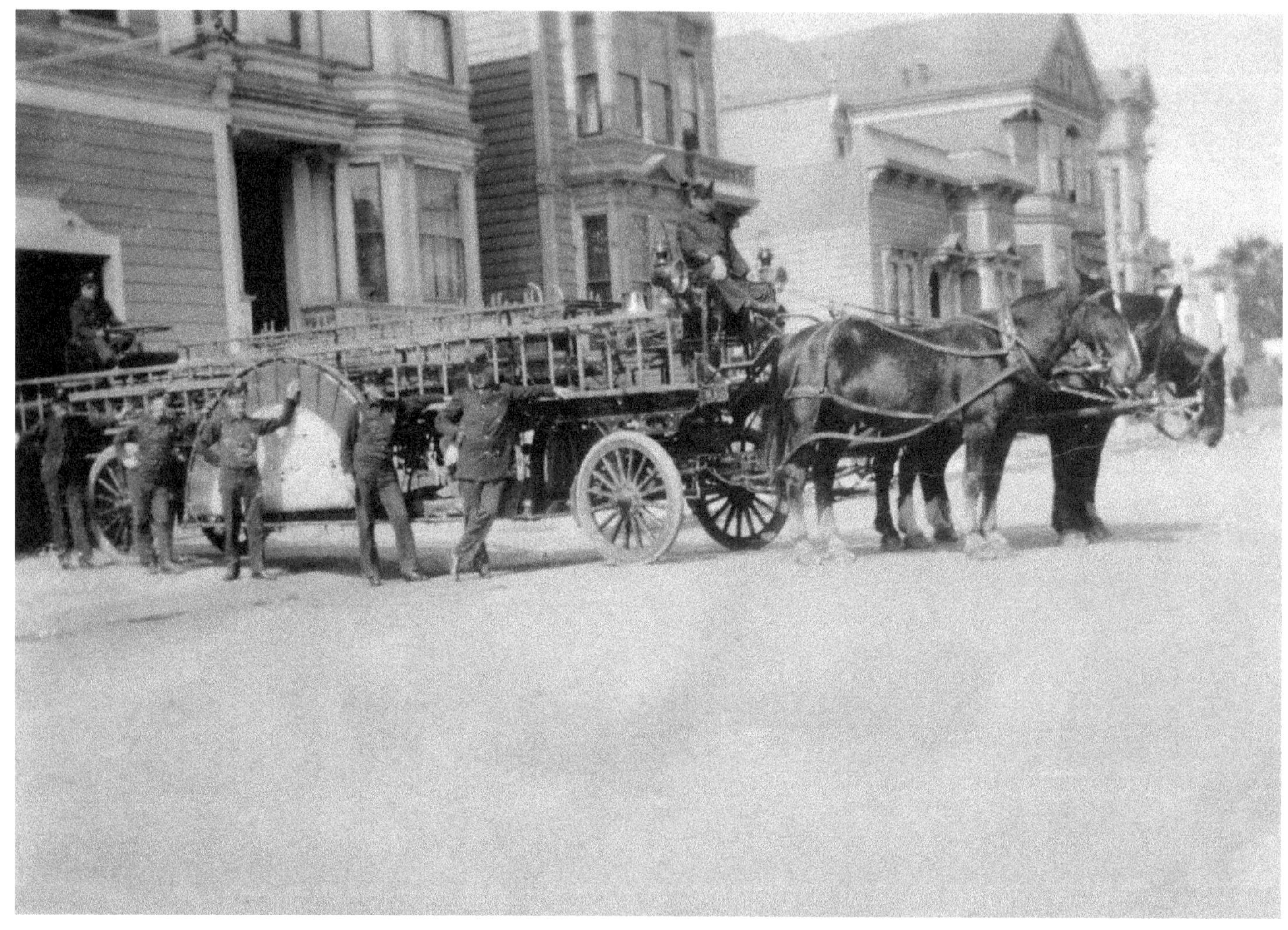

After the 1906 calamity, San Franciscans grew extremely fire-conscious. Starting in 1909, the city financed a unique high-pressure water-supply system from a ten-million-gallon reservoir resting on Twin Peaks, along with many other subsidiary and auxiliary satellite pumping stations. Shown here is the San Francisco Fire Department—Truck Company Number 9—located at 1374 Utah St., a few years after these improvements to the system.

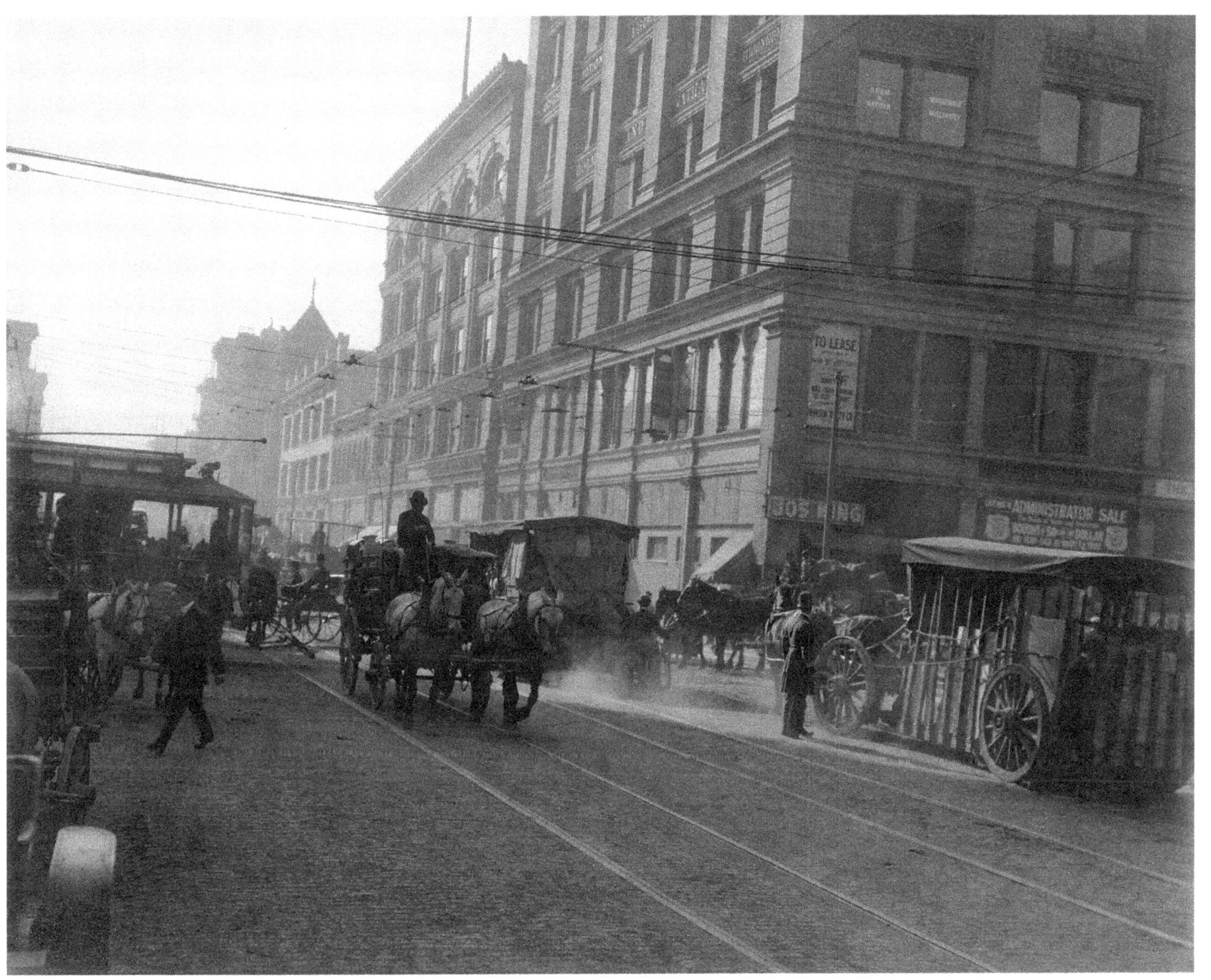

This 1909 photograph of Mission Street, west of Third Street, shows how soon San Franciscans rebuilt their city after the 1906 earthquake. The part of Mission Street that was not destroyed was turned into a tent city to house victims. Yerba Buena Gardens currently rests on this site.

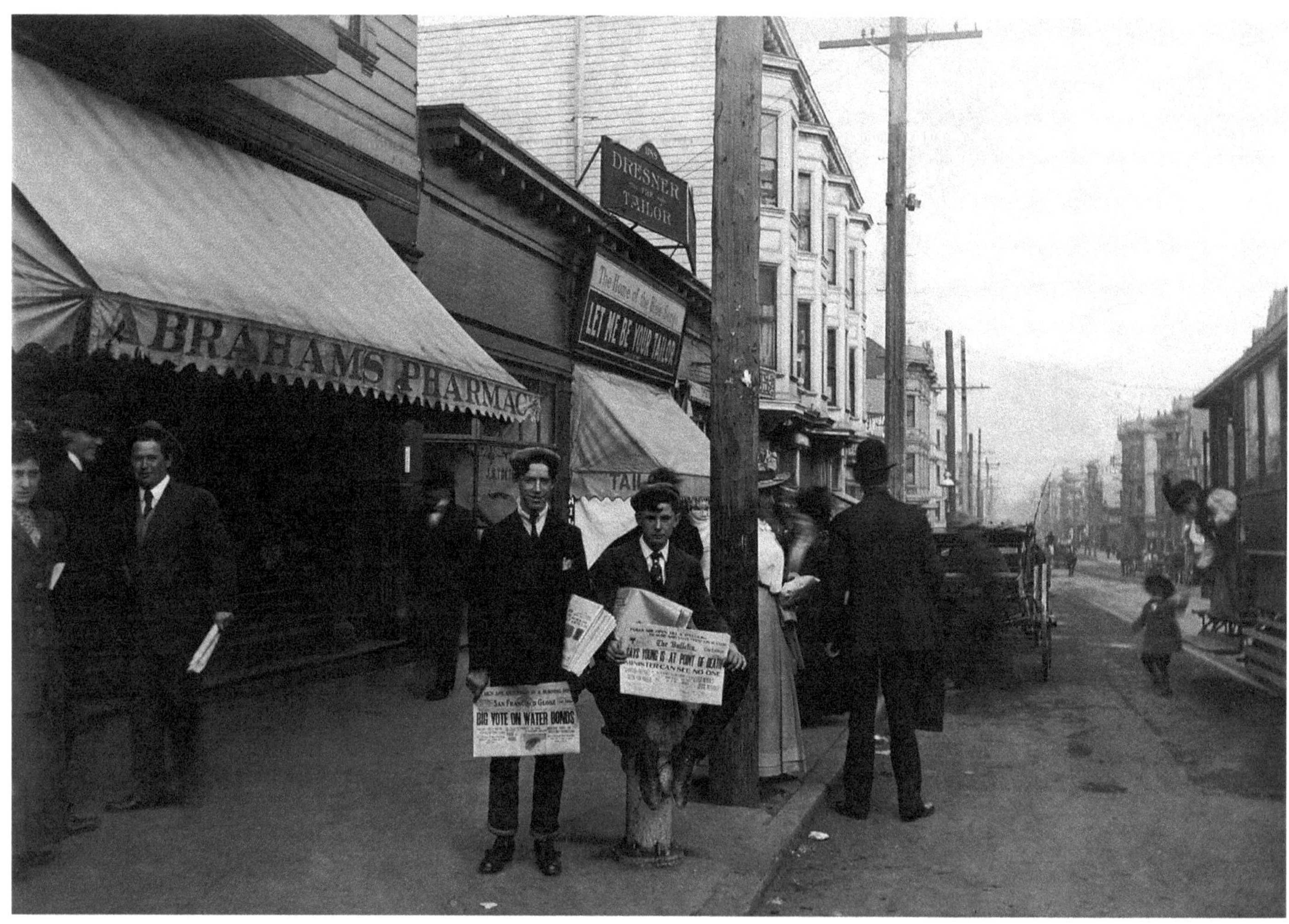

Pete Rielly and Eddie Campi sell newspapers in 1909 in front of Abraham's pharmacy at 1198 McAllister Street in the heart of the Fillmore district. The Fillmore had at various times been a Jewish, Irish, Scandinavian, and Black neighborhood. Today, a public housing project occupies the site shown.

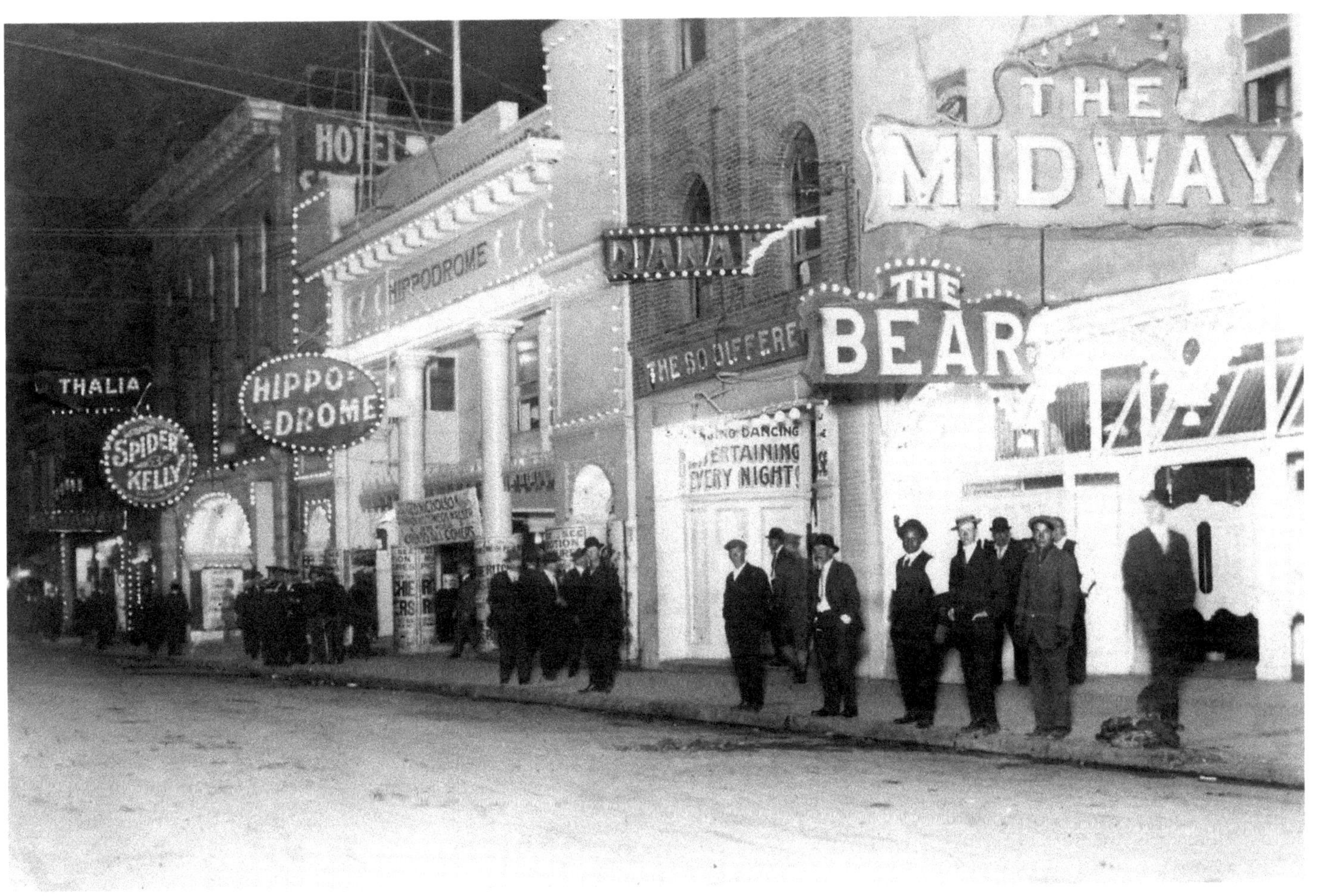

This 1909 photo shows nightclubs on Pacific Street in the Barbary Coast district. The Barbary Coast of San Francisco, named after the pirate-infested west coast of Africa, was a seedy district known for crime, saloons, prostitution, gambling halls, bordellos, and opium dens. It was also infamous for "Shanghaiing," the practice of the nineteenth century in which unwary victims were beaten, deceived, or drugged and kidnapped to work aboard ships headed to far-off ports, like Shanghai. Destroyed in the great earthquake and fires, the area failed to recover its pre-1906 debauched reputation, especially after the Red Light Abatement Act closed down brothels in the area in 1917. The former Barbary Coast is now part of the trendy Jackson Square district.

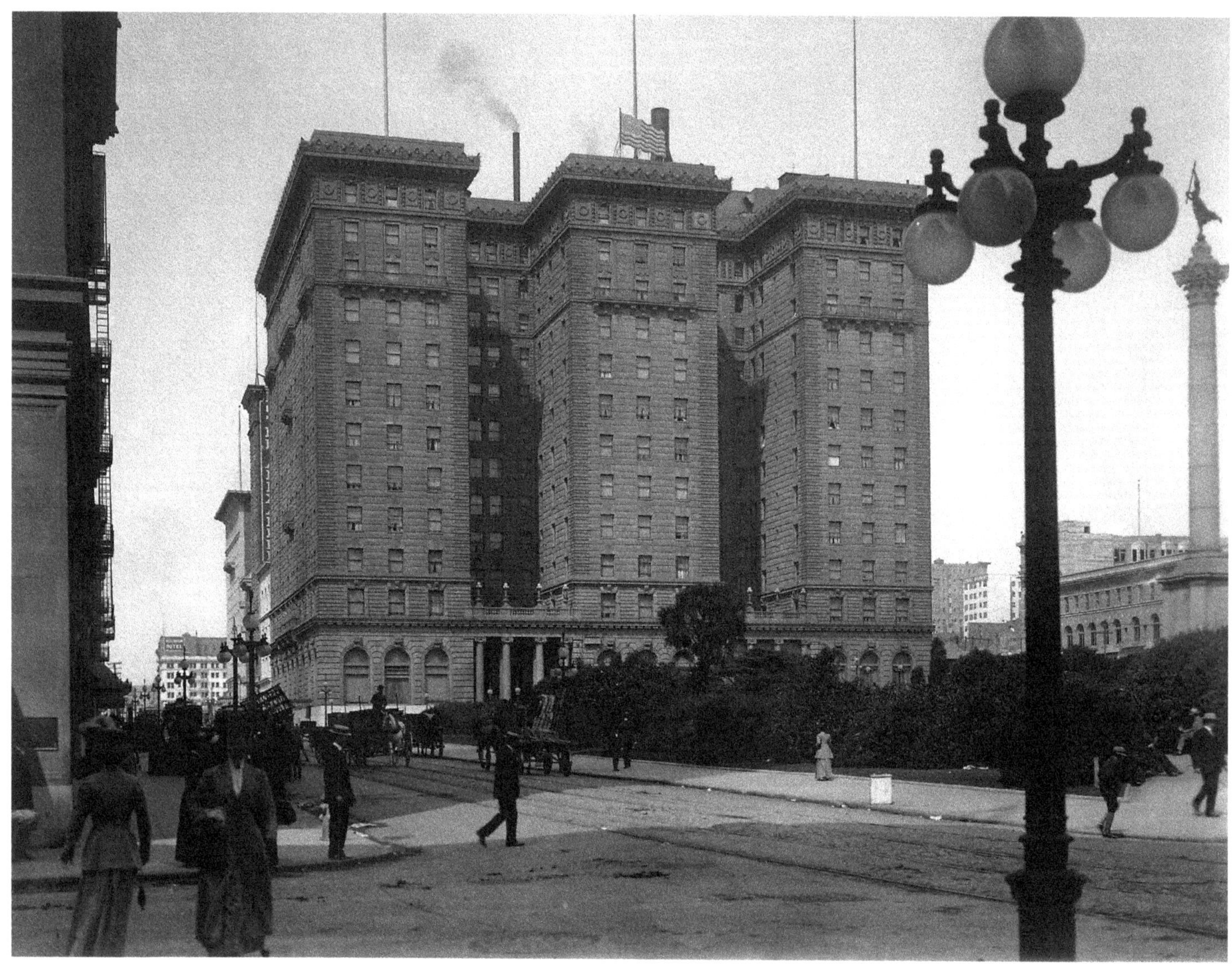

Shown here is the regal St. Francis Hotel facing Union Square at Powell and Geary in the early 1900s. The St. Francis, modeled after Europe's grandest hotels, opened March 21, 1904, and prided itself on being one of the most modern hotels in the nation. Early on, it became a gathering point for the literary, artistic, and social life of the city. For more than a century, people have planned to "meet at the clock" in the hotel's lobby, which has become emblematic of the hotel's endurance. When the earthquake and fires reduced most of Union Square to ruins, the St. Francis was one of few buildings to remain standing. Actor John Barrymore stayed here the night of the earthquake, and legendary opera singer Enrico Caruso, who had performed as Don Jose in *Carmen* at the Grand Opera the evening before, ate breakfast at the hotel's cafe that morning with a warm towel enveloping his sensitive throat. In 1921, the famous scandal involving silent film star "Fatty" Arbuckle and starlet Virginia Rappe took place here. Today, the hotel looks the same in the front, but has added a modern high-rise in the back.

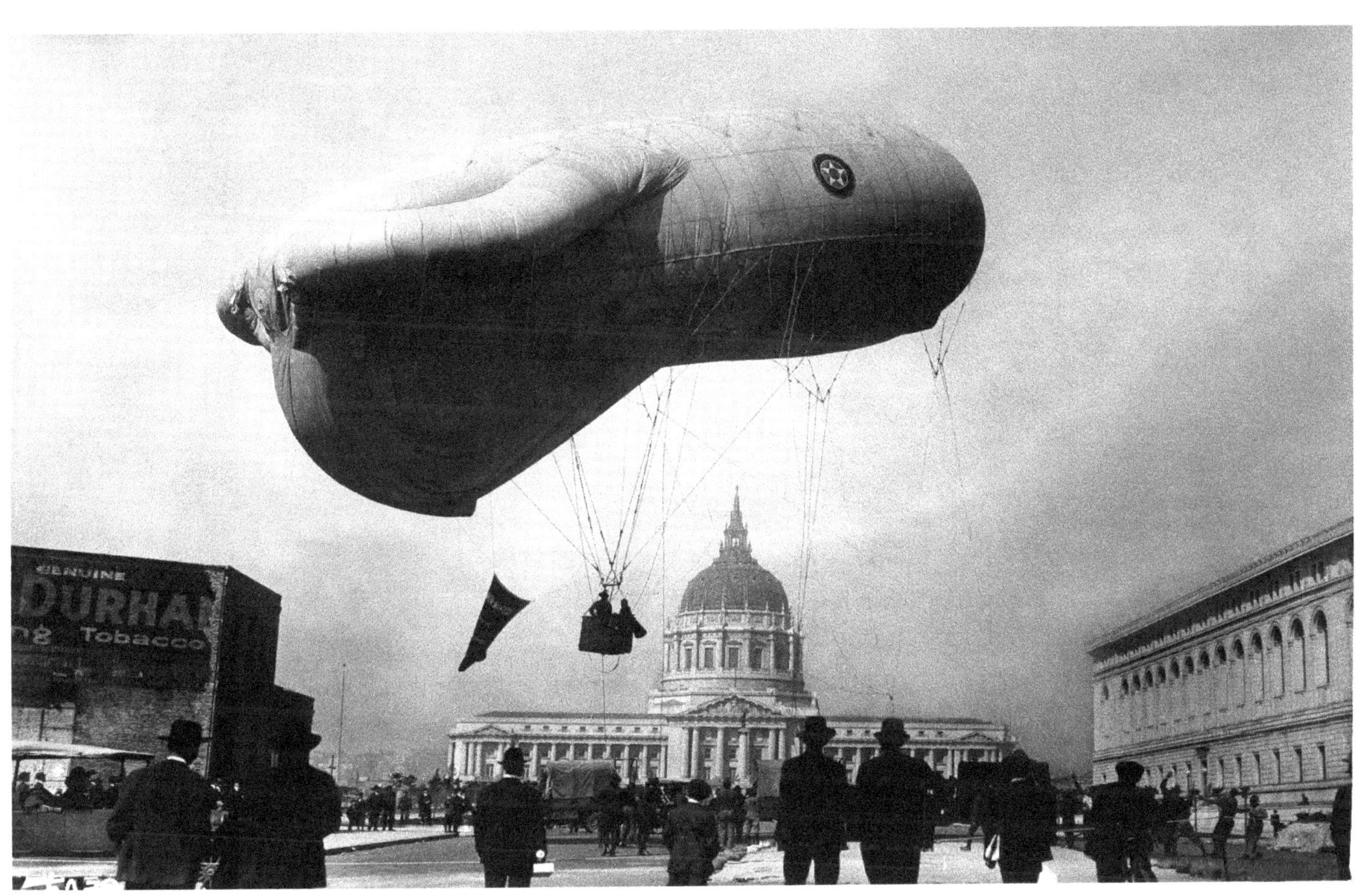

Spectators watch a hot air balloon float over the Civic Center in the late 1910s. By 1915, San Francisco's new beaux-arts city hall opened in the civic center as part of the nationwide "City Beautiful" movement, part of the Progressive Reform movement of the late nineteenth and early twentieth centuries, which believed that through the beautification of cities, the economic and moral decay of poor inner cities would be alleviated, resulting in civic virtue and social harmony. Its 307.5-foot-high dome, modeled after Les Invalides in Paris, is the 5th largest in the world, more than a foot taller than the nation's capitol building in Washington, D.C. The 500,000-square-foot stately monument consumes two city blocks.

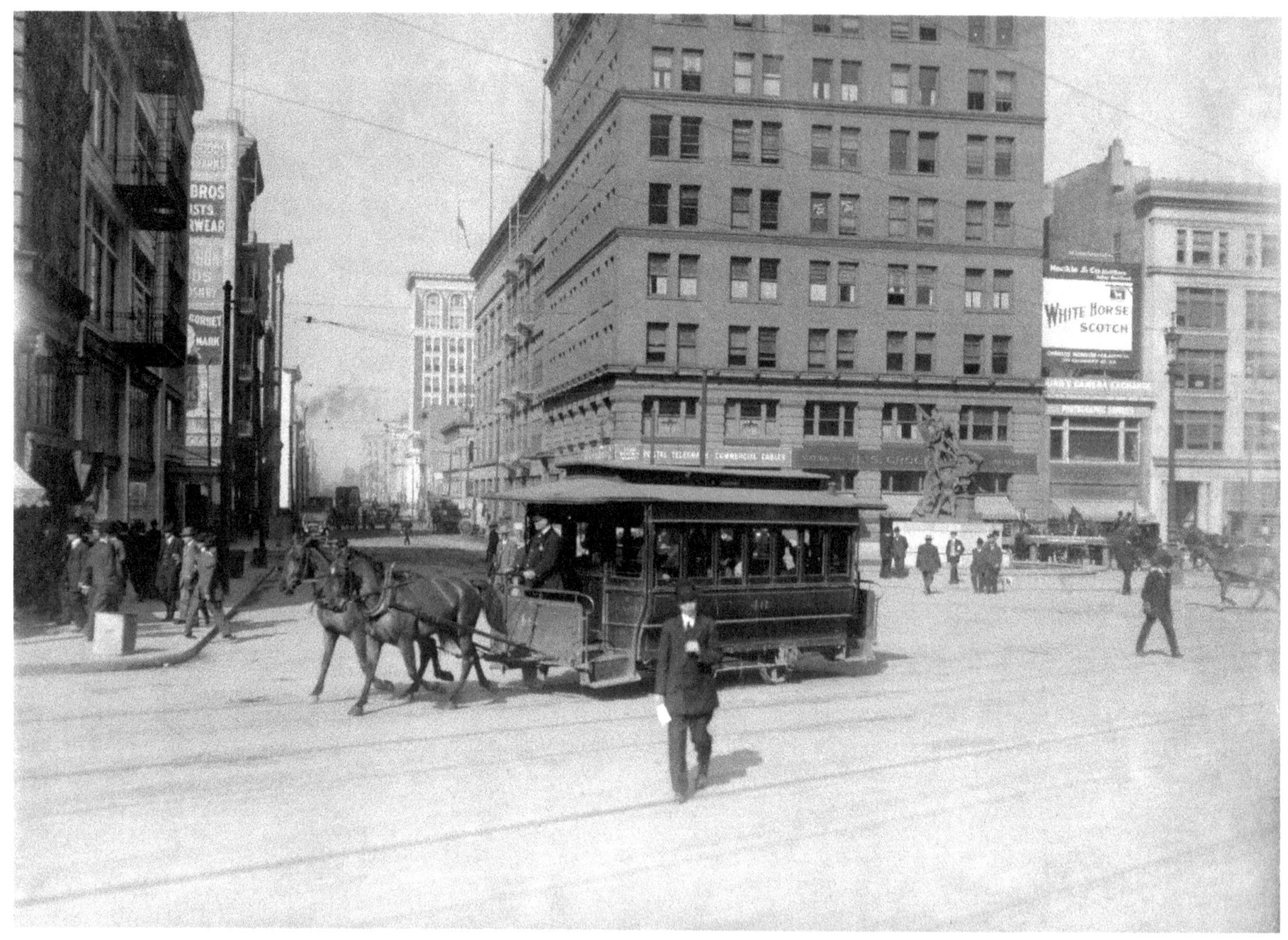

A horse-car stops at Market and Battery streets in 1912. Horses have been hugely important in San Francisco's history, especially before the introduction of the cable car in the 1870s. Even with the variety of modern transportation available at the time, San Franciscans in the early twentieth century still relied on horse-driven vehicles. After the 1906 earthquake and fires, horse-drawn wagons delivered building supplies and removed debris. Thousands of horses were fatally overworked in rebuilding the city.

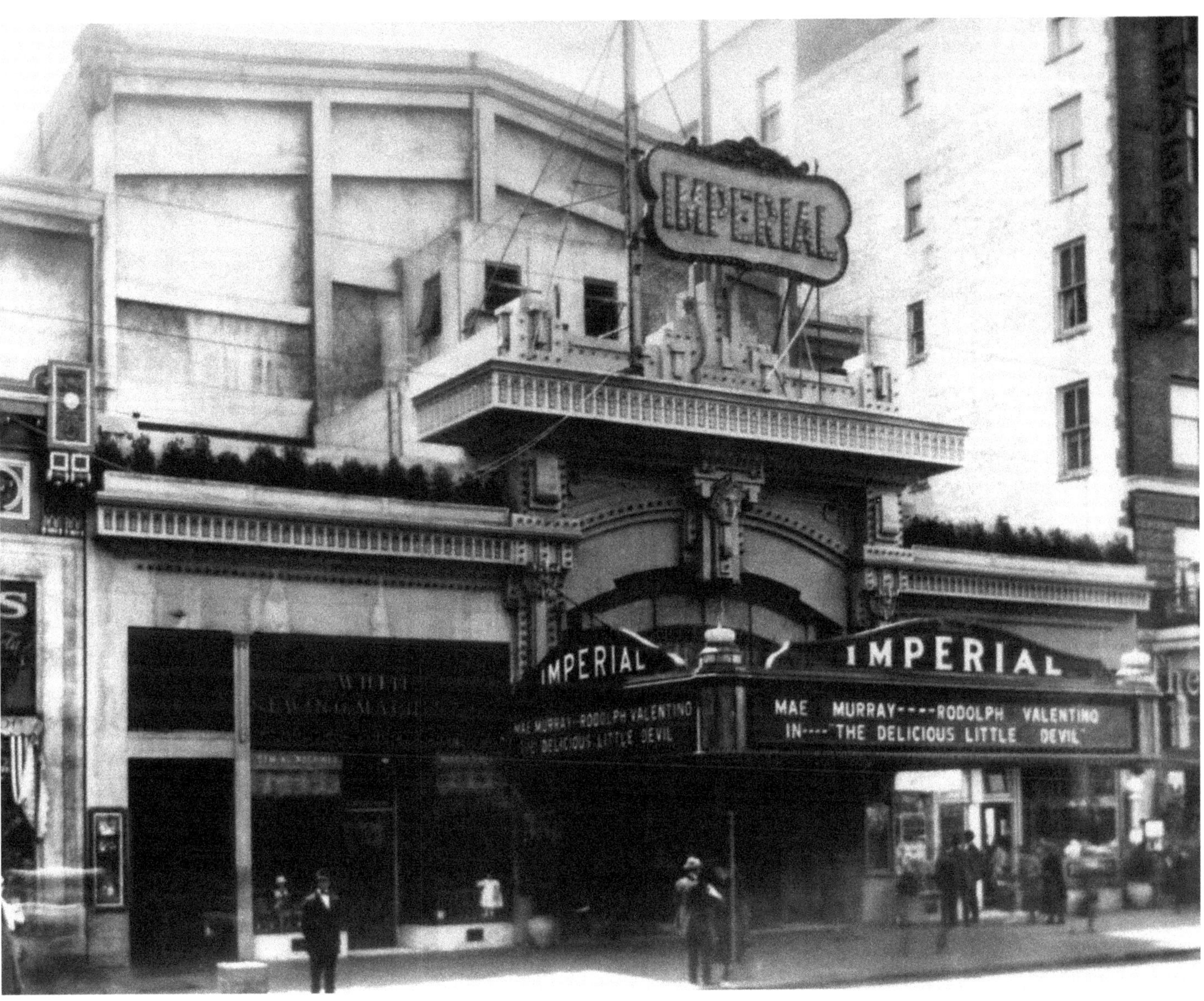

The Imperial Theatre, pictured here in 1919, opened in December 1912 on Market Street. It was one of the most popular entertainment spots of the day. It was renamed the Premiere in 1929, then United Artist Theatre in 1931. In 1972, it became Market Street Cinema, and today features "adult" entertainment.

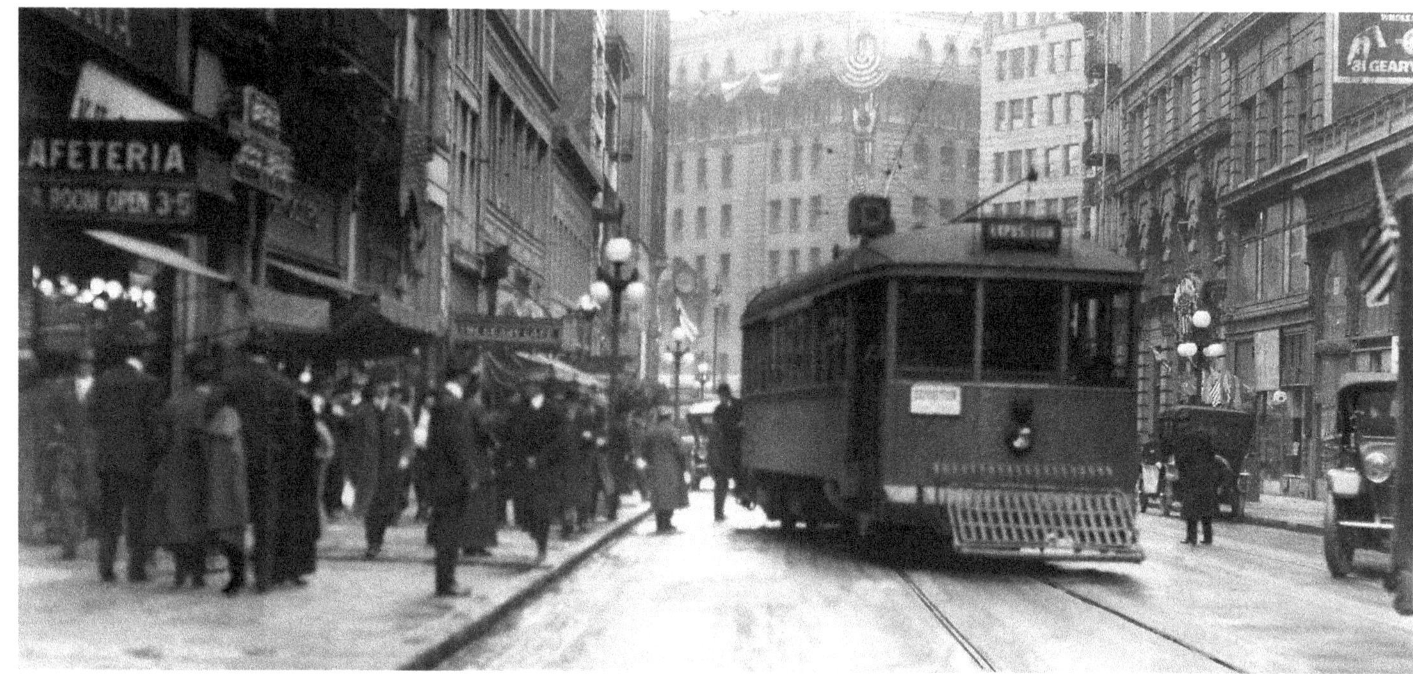

A streetcar on the D Geary–Van Ness Line, operated by the San Francisco Municipal Railway (MUNI), begins its outbound run in 1920. MUNI merged with its rival Market Street Railway in 1944 to form the basis of today's MUNI transit system. The D Line ran from the Ferry Building to the Presidio via Market, Geary, Van Ness, Union, Steiner, and Greenwich streets. The route was discontinued and replaced by buses in 1950, one of many conversions of streetcar and cable car lines to bus lines throughout the city. By the late 1950s, all but 5 streetcar lines and 3 cable car lines had been withdrawn.

The Party Moves Underground

(1920–1929)

San Francisco entered the 1920s proud and confident. The decade of jazz and flappers was a paradoxical one, with innocence wedded to extravagance, avant-garde as much as it was conservative. Trends throughout the country became magnified to extremes in San Francisco's cultural lens, and as always, the city's population carried on in a grandiose and exceptional style. A sudden departure from the traditional and familiar to new technologies and ways of living marked the era. Many Americans experienced unprecedented prosperity and optimism for the future, while others experienced profound resistance, fear, and apprehension.

San Franciscans, whose spirited history was fueled on alcohol, were less than accommodating to the passage in 1920 of the 18th Amendment prohibiting the manufacture and sale of alcohol. While the country went dry, San Francisco, with notoriously more bars per capita than any other American city, moved the party underground, often to one of many North Beach speakeasies. More than a few family restaurants were known to have brewed their own illegal wines, furtively serving them in coffee cups to patrons.

Many of San Francisco's magnificent movie houses thrived in this decade—the Alexandria, the Coliseum, the Coronet—most of them today no longer in operation. At this time, the city also started to develop its "outer lands" in the west—the Richmond and Sunset districts—as improved streetcar links to downtown spawned rapid housing construction. But just as San Francisco again reached euphoric heights not seen since before the disaster of 1906, the city would be tested, this time in step with the rest of the nation.

Early one Indian summer day, soon to be known as Black Thursday, the Stock Market crashed. In San Francisco, traders at the Pacific Stock Exchange exploded into full panic. Fortunes amassed over lifetimes vanished instantly, and some people committed suicide. The decade that began with a roar ended with a whimper, and the decade of the Great Depression began.

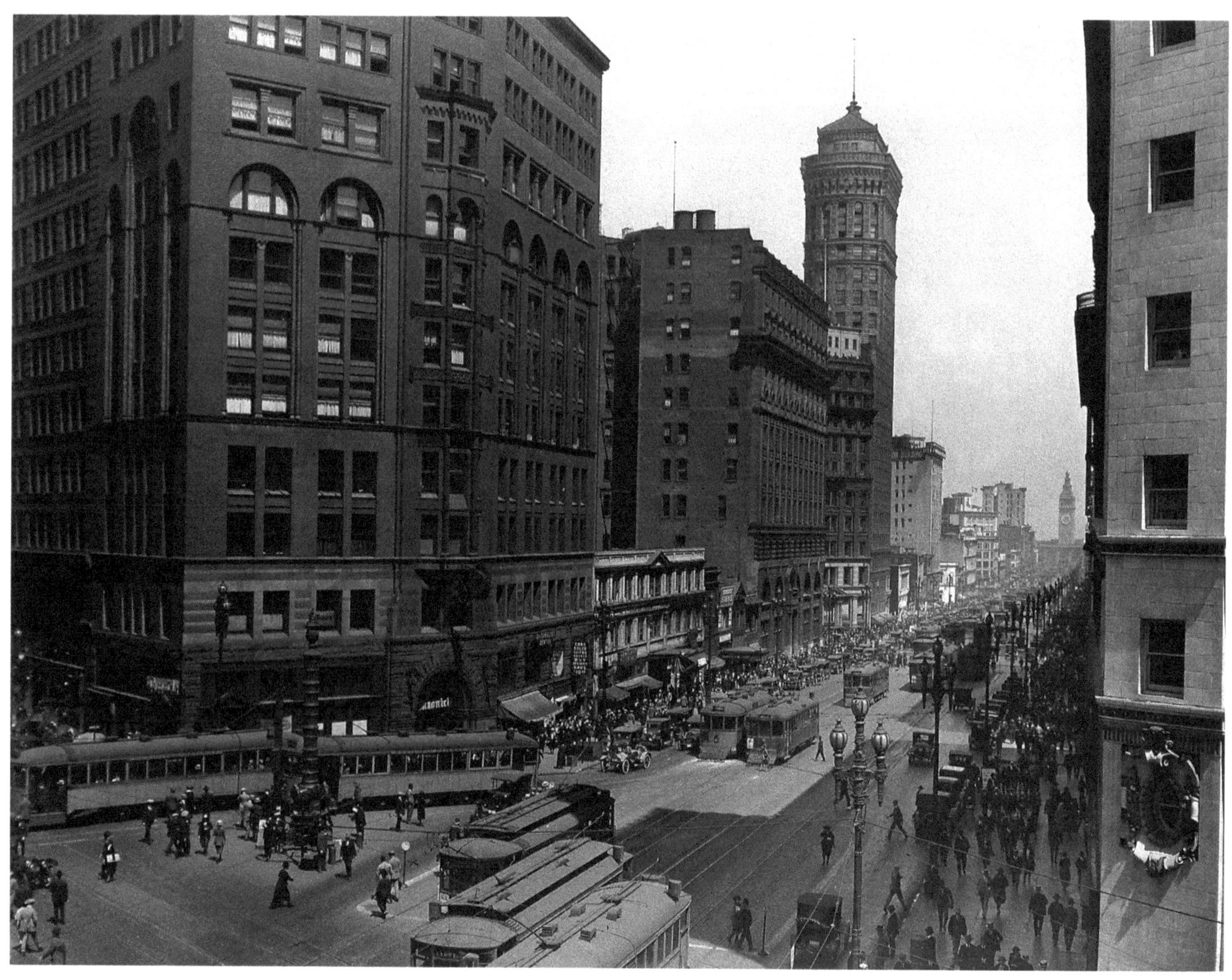

Streetcars crowded Market Street during the 1920s, as seen in this photograph looking east from Third Street. In the lower left of the picture is Lotta's Fountain. Over the two decades following the 1906 earthquake and fires, the buildings on Market Street were rebuilt, and many resembled their pre-earthquake antecedents.

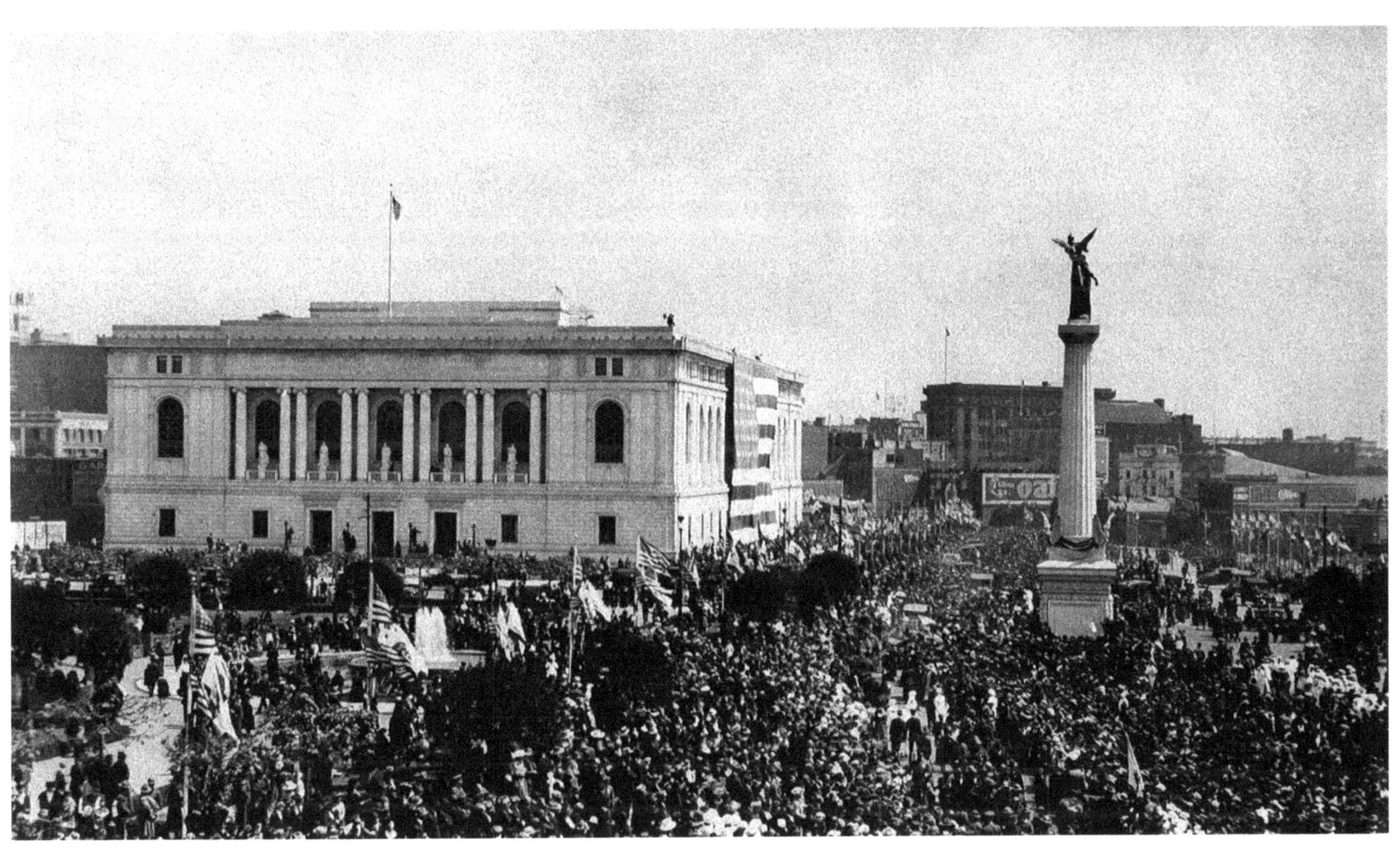

Crowds of people gather in the 1920s in the Civic Center Plaza across from the San Francisco Public Library. The grand central staircase at this 1917 beaux arts–style public library was a reminder of the one in nearby City Hall. In 1996, following the construction of a new public library at Larkin and Fulton streets, the former library facility was redesigned to accommodate the Asian Art Museum of San Francisco. The Civic Center Plaza has been the location of numerous festivities, rallies, and demonstrations every year since its founding.

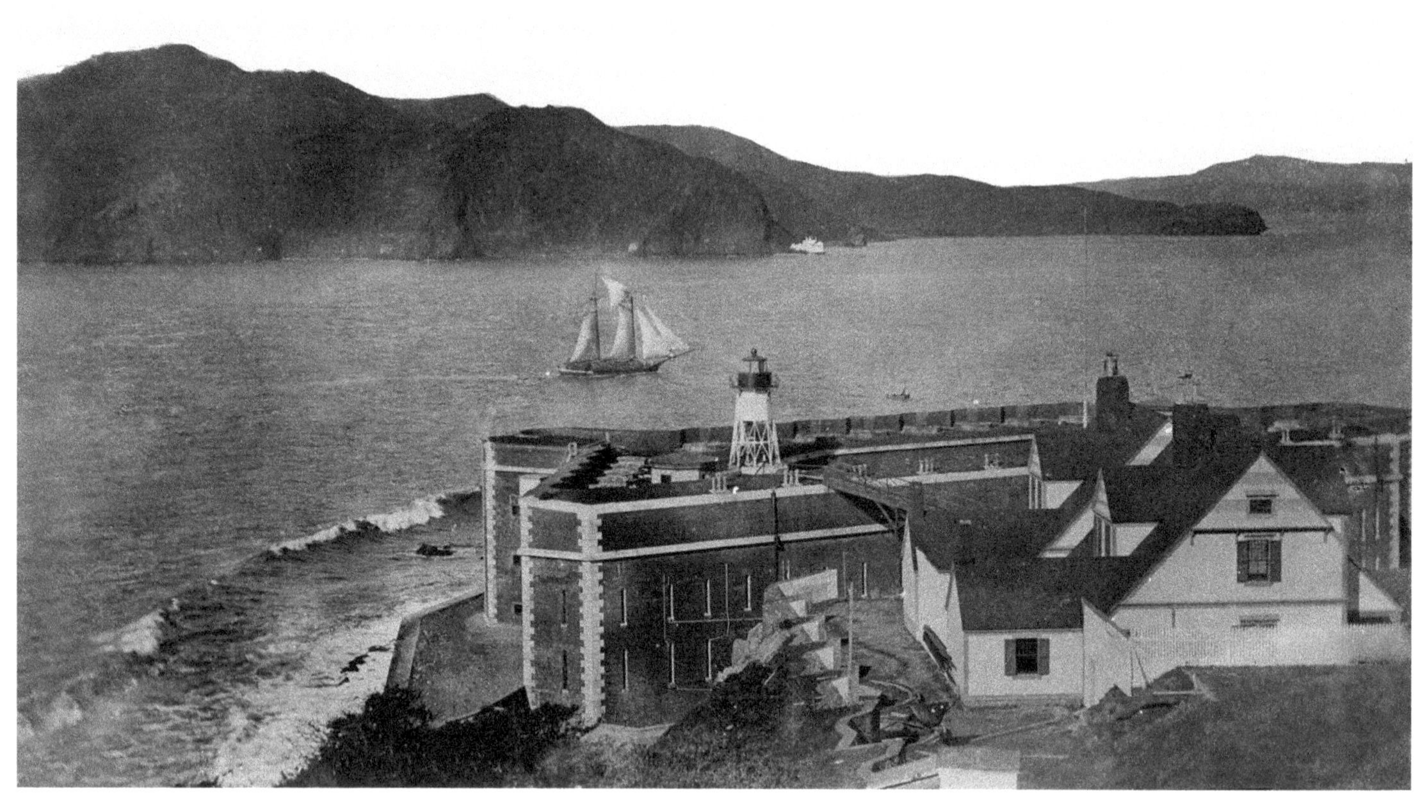

Fort Point. Situated at the mouth of the Golden Gate, this Civil War–era fortress protected San Francisco Bay from Confederate attack during the Civil War and foreign attack afterward. Its seven-foot-thick walls and multi-tiered casemated construction were state of the art when construction started in 1853. When construction on the Golden Gate Bridge began in the 1930s, city officials planned to demolish the historic fort, but the bridge's chief engineer, Joseph Strauss, reconfigured the bridge's design to save it. Alfred Hitchcock fans know Fort Point as the place where Jimmy Stewart saved Kim Novak from drowning in the frigid Pacific waters in the film *Vertigo.* Fort Point is now a protected National Historic Site, and visitors can admire its arched casemates and brick masonry as guides in Civil War–period costume bring the fort's military history to life.

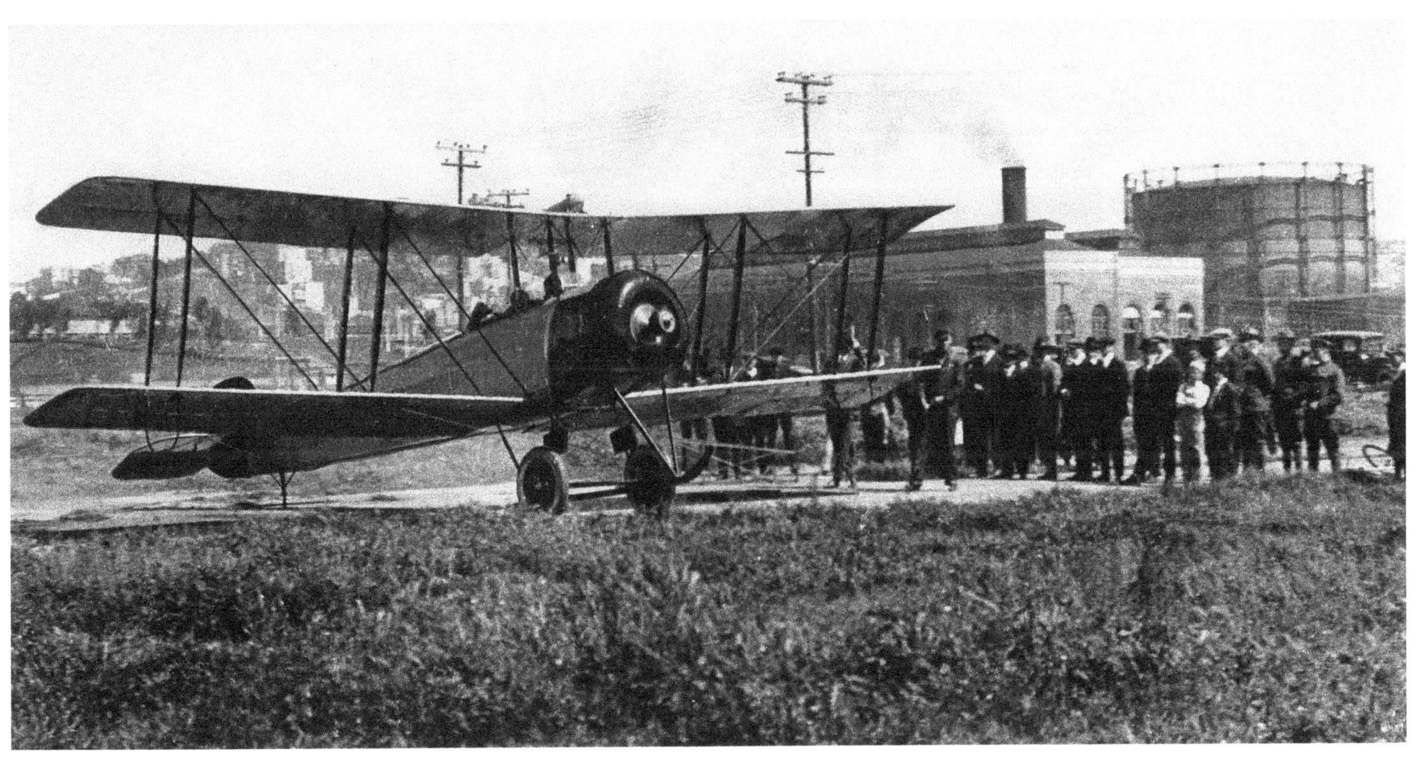

Crissy Field, seen here in the mid 1920s, at that time called Mills Field, was the first San Francisco airport, built in 1921 on the site of the former auto racetrack from the 1915 Panama-Pacific International Exposition. Civilian air operations were transferred to the present location south of San Francisco in the late 1920s. In 1936, the military ceased major flight operations, using the grounds as an assembly area for troop mobilization, although helicopter flights and light aircraft continued to use the field on occasion. Crissy Field, as part of the Presidio, was managed by the U.S. Army until 1994, when along with the rest of the Presidio it became part of the Golden Gate National Recreation Area. After a number of years of restoration, Crissy Field reopened in 2001 to widespread acclaim.

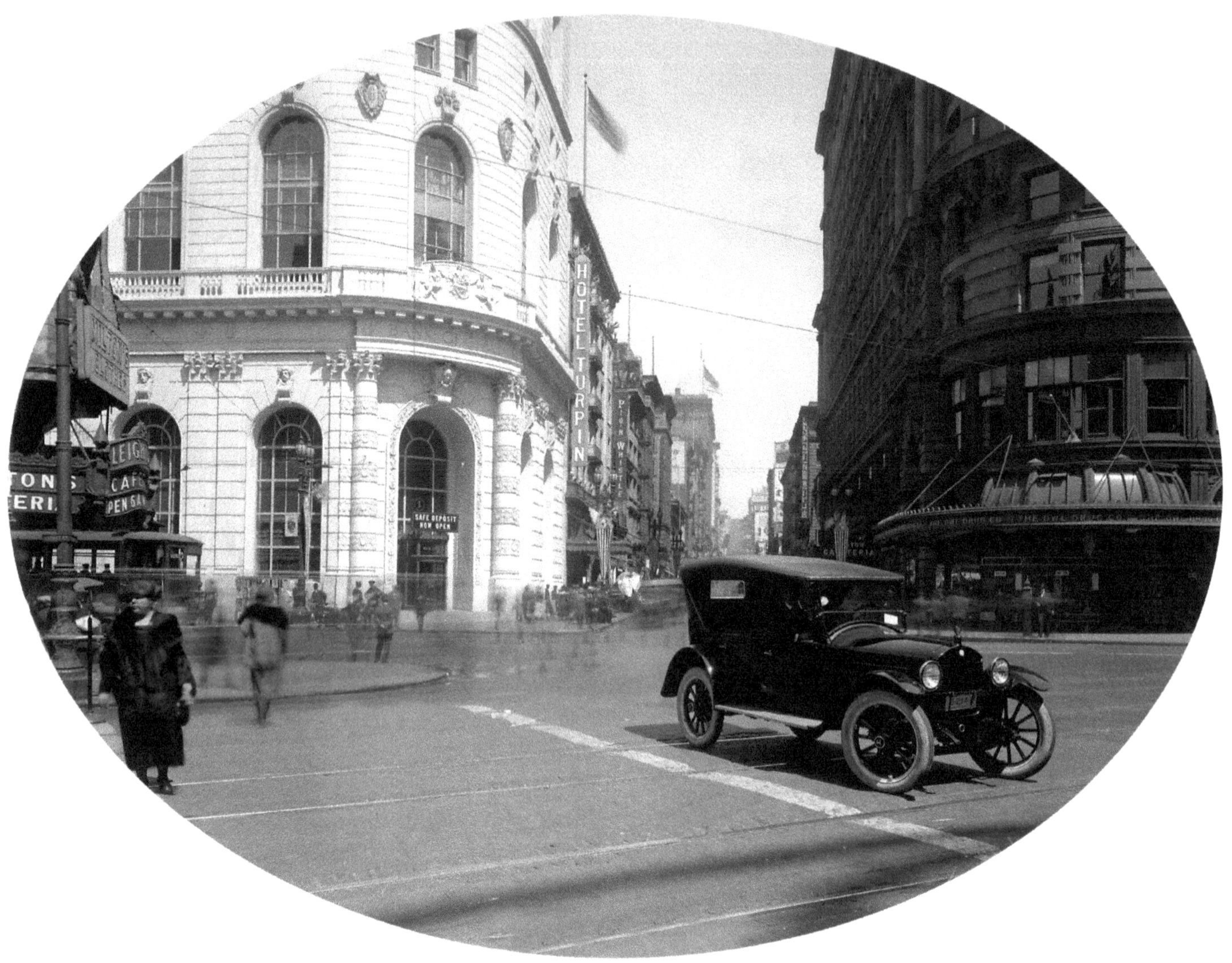

After the 1906 earthquake, the Bank of Italy re-opened (shown here in the 1920s at Market Street), and founder A. P. Giannini played a pivotal role in rebuilding the city by giving loans and setting up immediate banking from a wooden plank atop several barrels in North Beach. In 1928, the Bank of Italy became the Bank of America, the largest commercial bank in America and the third largest company in the world.

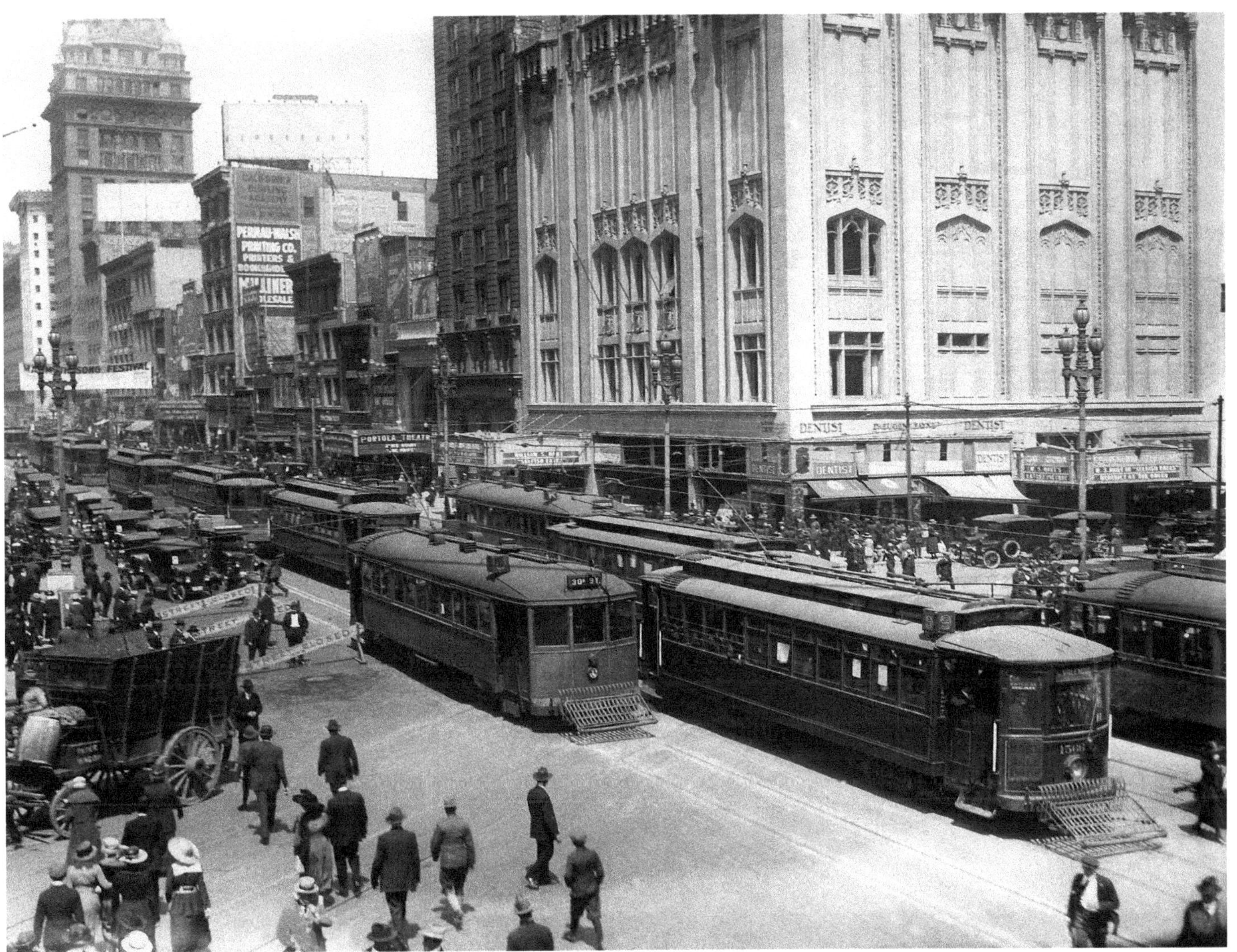

Market Street was jammed with electric streetcars throughout the 1920s and 1930s, as shown here at Market and 4th streets. People at the time were able to travel by streetcar throughout the city for a nickel. Two sets of tracks ran in each direction on Market Street, the inner ones operated by Market Street Railway, the outer by MUNI. Today, only the inner tracks remain, serviced by MUNI's F Market historic streetcar line.

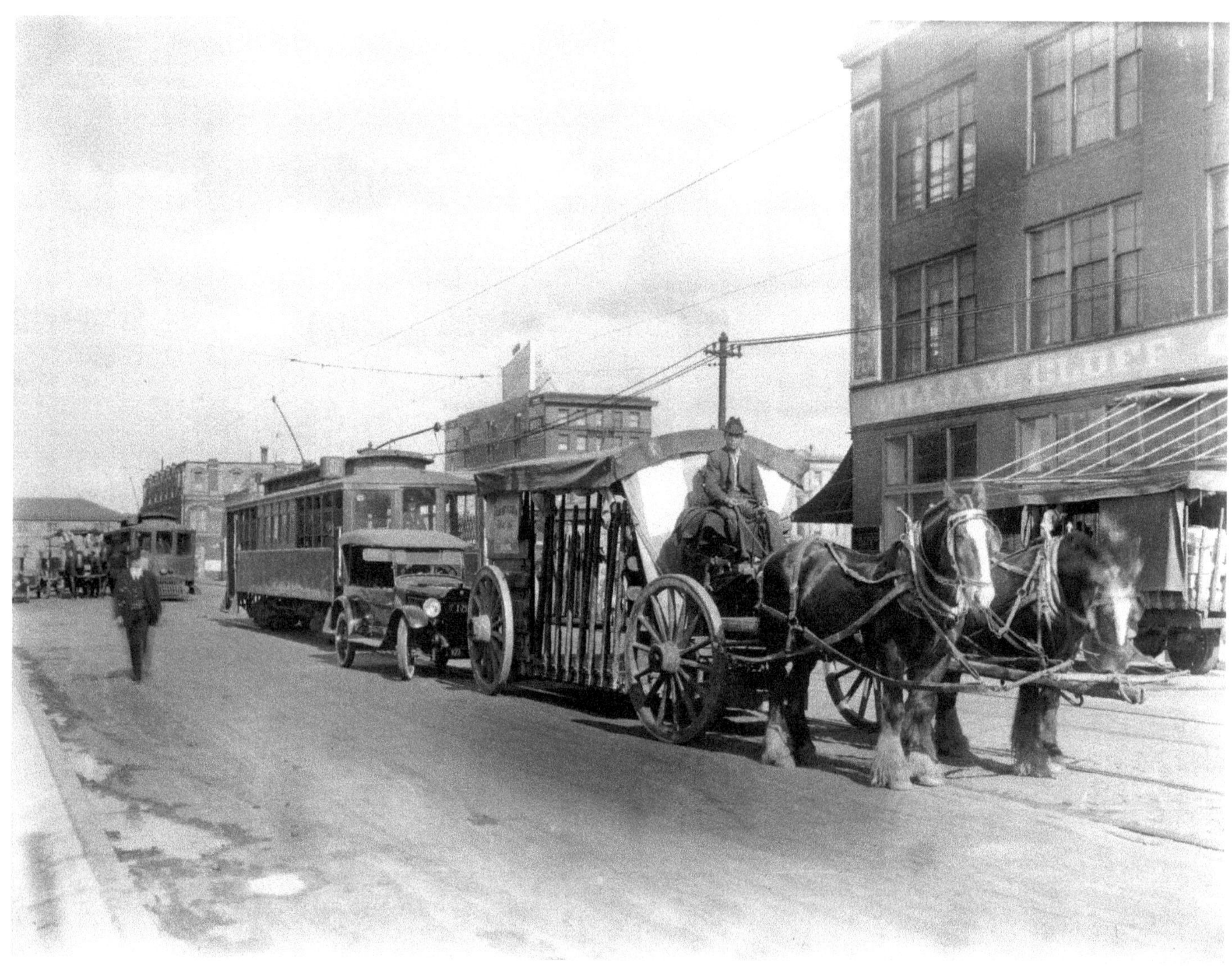

Despite the widespread use of electric streetcars and the increasing number of automobiles and trucks in San Francisco in the 1920s, many businesses still used age-old forms of transportation, including the McNab and Smith Company with its horse-drawn wagon here at Spear and Mission streets. This is now the site of several high-rise office and residential buildings, as well as Rincon Center, formerly a central U.S. Post Office and now a residential tower and popular lunchtime food court.

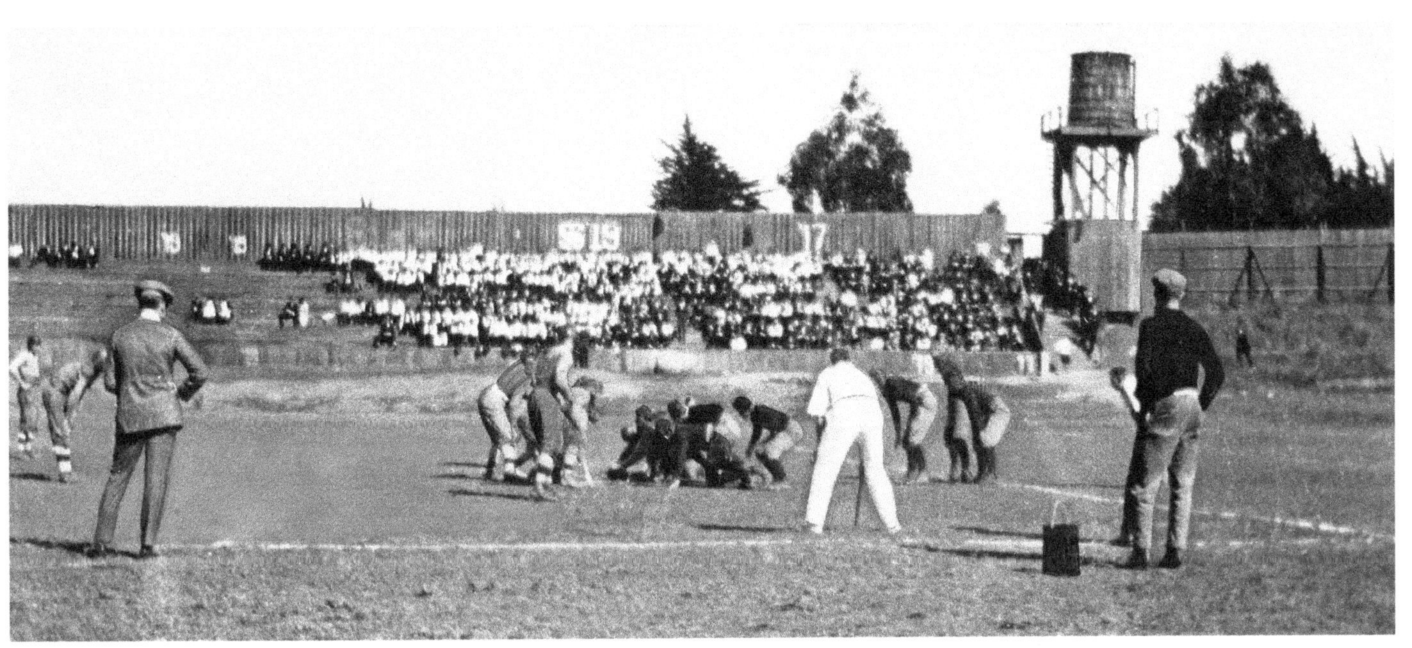

St. Ignatius College, the antecedent of the University of San Francisco, was founded in 1855 by an Italian immigrant priest, Father Anthony Maraschi, and its first location was on Market Street between 4th and 5th streets. By 1920, the school had relocated, and St. Ignatius Field was an important part of the campus. In 1927, the University of San Francisco moved to its current Fulton Street location.

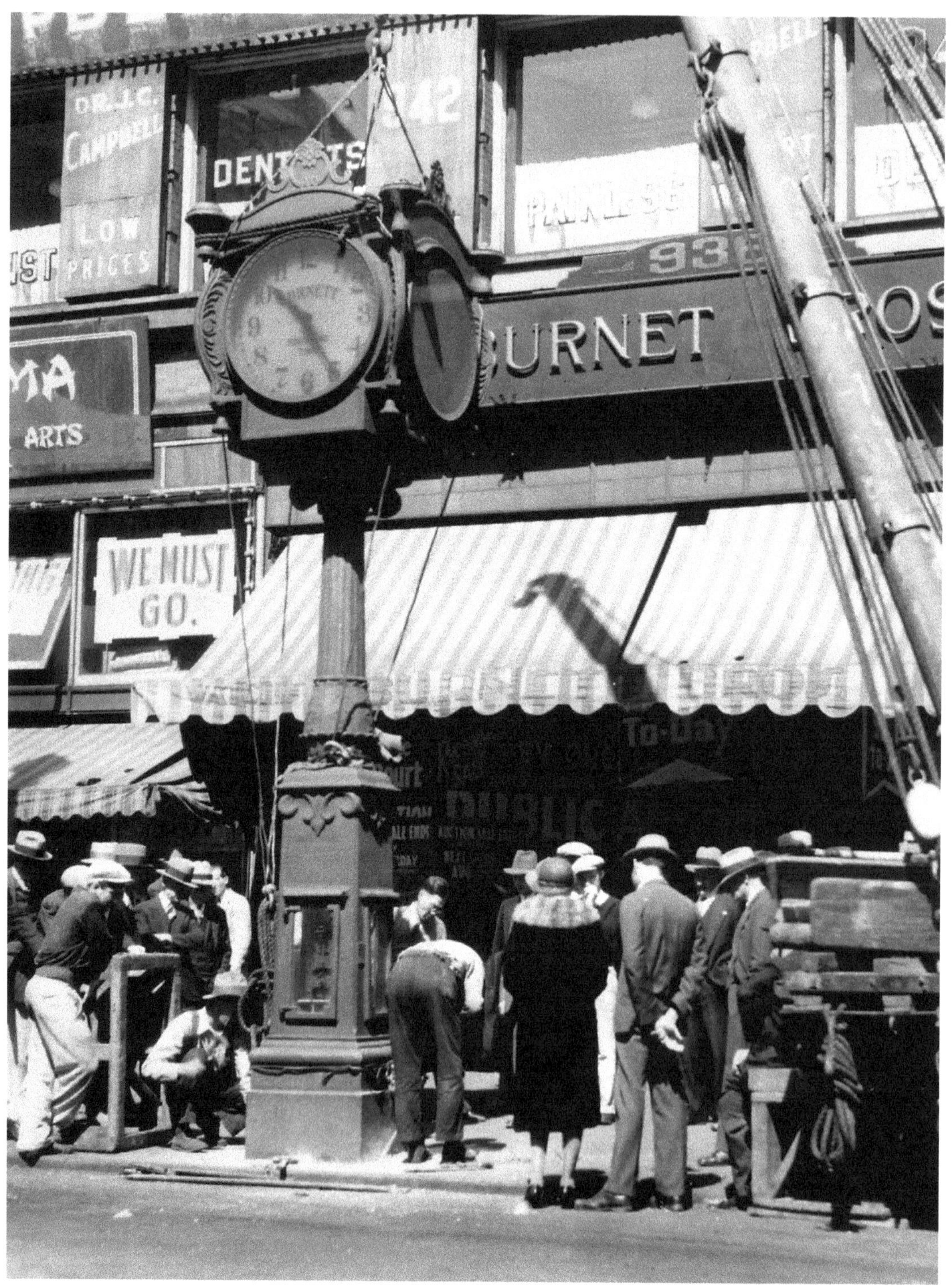

The Alibi Clock in this 1920s photograph, built by E. Howard of Boston in 1914, originally stood in front of Burnett Brothers Jewelry Store on Market Street. The clock became nationally known after it appeared in photographs taken during the San Francisco Preparedness Day Parade on July 22, 1916, when a bomb killed ten bystanders. In 1932, the clock was moved to Simon's Jeweler, in Vallejo, California, and when Simon's closed in 1984, the clock was purchased by the City of Vallejo, moved down the street, overhauled, and restored.

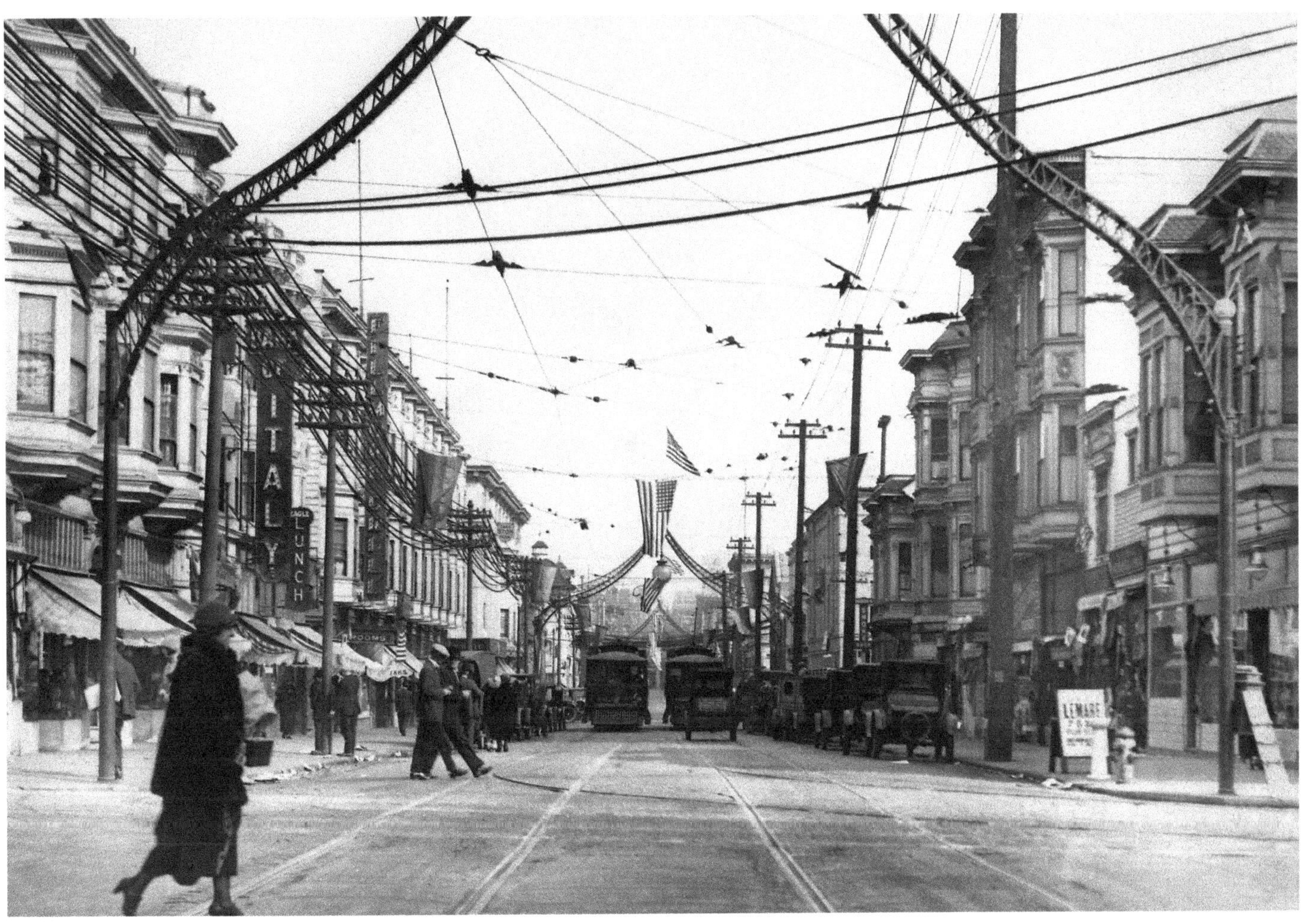

Lower Fillmore Street was a major shopping street in the ethnically diverse Western Addition, which was lined with many neighborhood family-owned businesses. Near the corner of Fillmore Street at McAllister, shown here in 1919, were several Jewish bakeries and kosher markets. At left is a branch of the Bank of Italy.

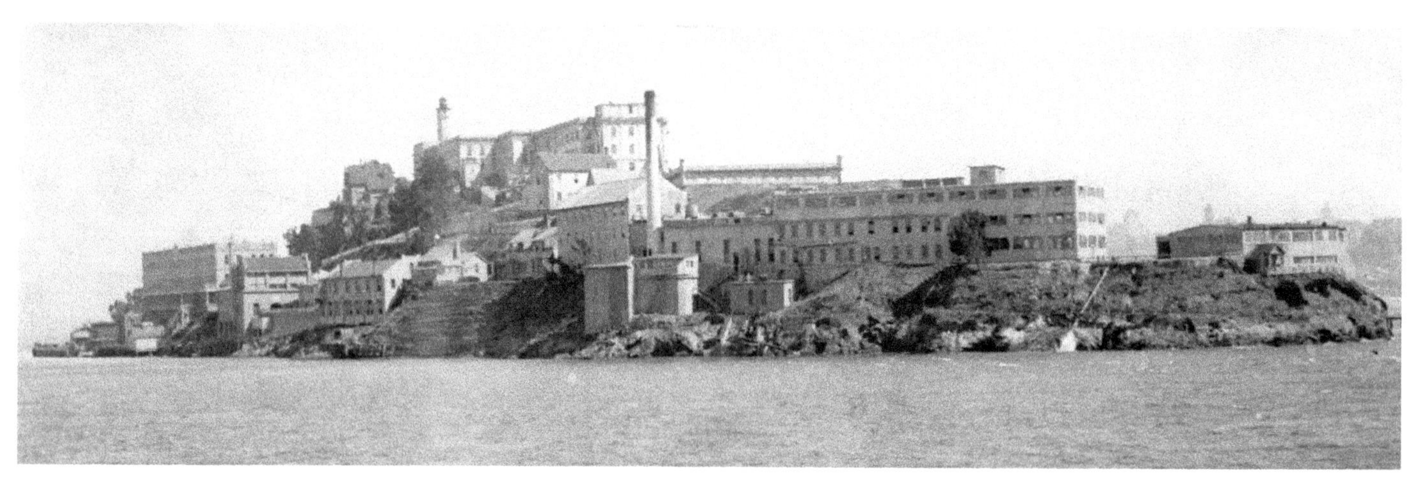

Alcatraz Island, shown here in the 1920s, was originally a military installation and prison, from Gold Rush times until 1933. Recognized for its potential as an inescapable locale in the middle of the bay, in 1934 the island became the home of the famous federal prison, frequently depicted in film and literature, and jailing notorious criminals such as Al Capone, and Robert Stroud, the "Birdman" of Alcatraz. From then on, many simply referred to the island and the prison itself as "the Rock."

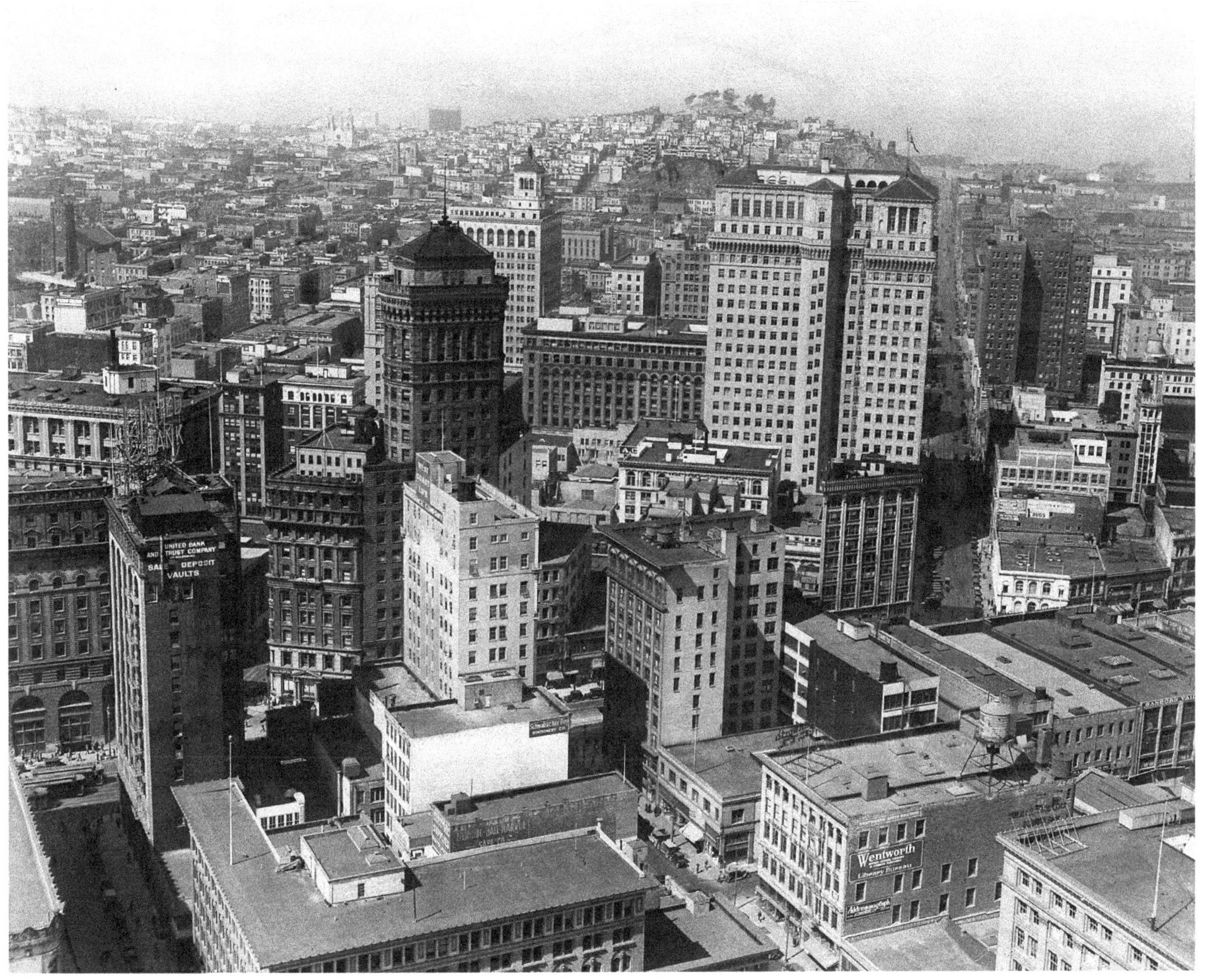

This aerial view of downtown San Francisco, taken on March 18, 1925, atop the flagpole of the new 26-story Pacific Telephone and Telegraph Company building on New Montgomery Street, shows the vast breadth of rebuilding and growth in San Francisco in the two decades after the 1906 earthquake. By 1925, the population of San Francisco had grown to 550,000, making San Francisco the tenth largest city in the U.S.

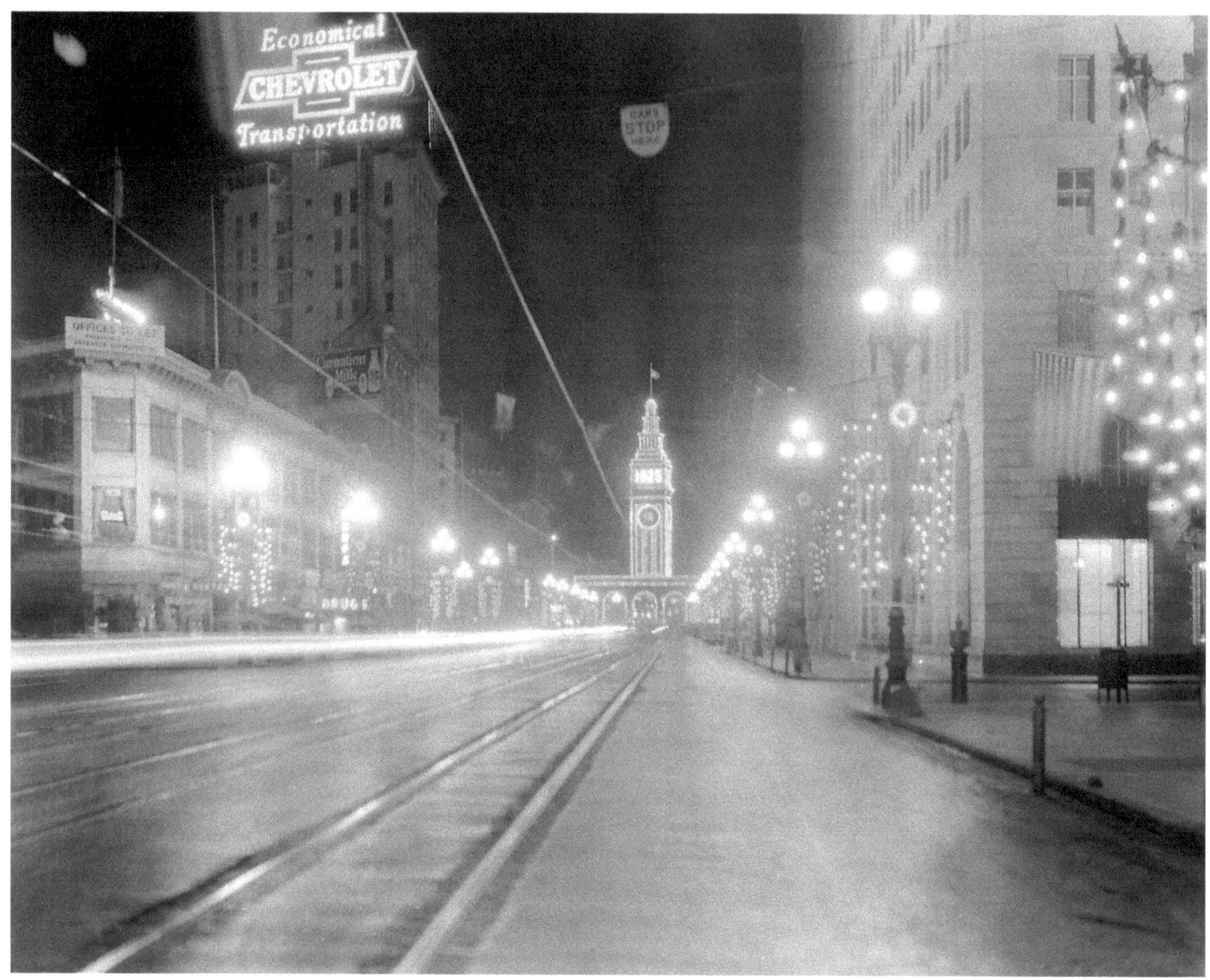

At center is the Ferry Building on September 10, 1925, from Market Street during the Diamond Jubilee, the 75th anniversary of the admission of California to the Union and the founding of San Francisco. Souvenir half-dollar coins featuring a gold miner on one side and the California state bear on the other were issued to commemorate the occasion. The Ferry Building's sturdy steel-framed structure kept it standing through both the 1906 and 1989 earthquakes.

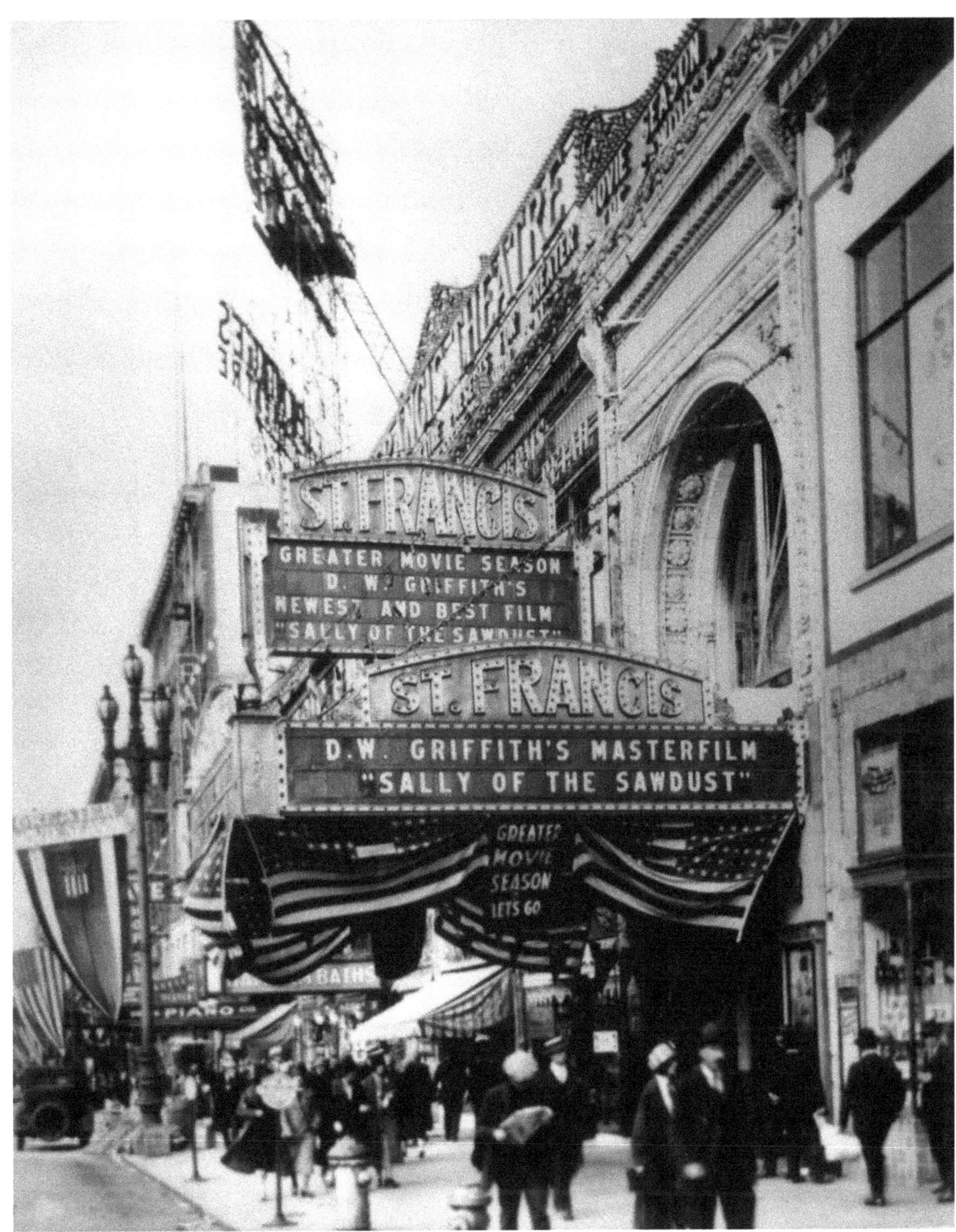

Built in 1910 as the Empress Theatre, renamed the Strand in 1917, and finally renamed the St. Francis in 1925, this Market Street theater had more than 1,400 seats. In 1968, the theater was split into two, with the downstairs screen remaining the St. Francis, and the upstairs facility renamed the Baronet. The theater closed in 2001.

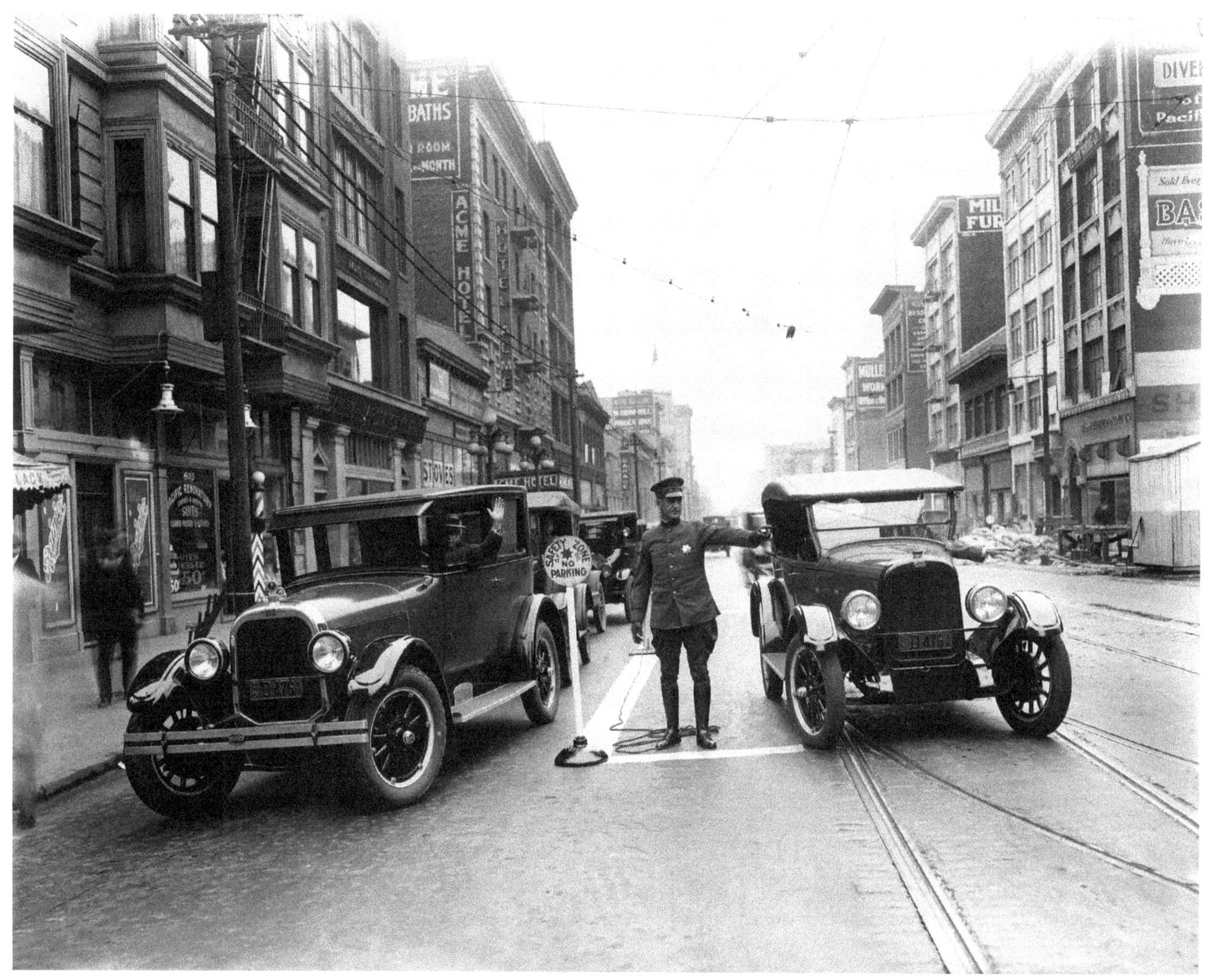

A policeman is directing traffic at Mission and 4th streets in 1925. By the 1920s, automobiles were seen throughout the city. Visible are the Acme Hotel at 819 Mission Street and Gille Show Print Company across the street at 818 Mission Street.

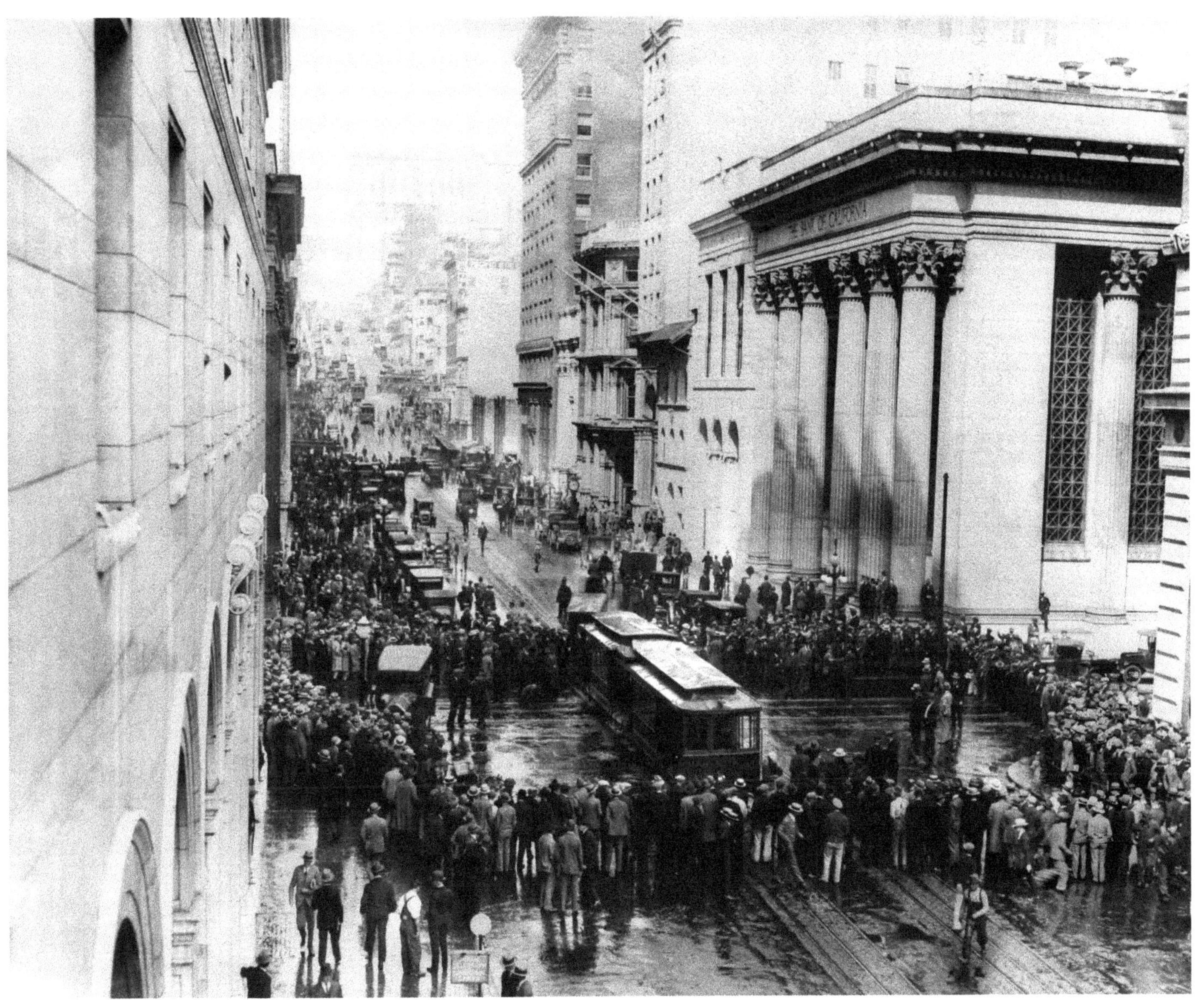

A group of people gathers around a cable car at Sansome and California streets on May 7, 1926. The first cable car ran down Clay Street on August 2, 1873. At the height of the cable car years, there were eight different cable car companies, 600 cable cars, and over 100 miles of track. The California Street cable car continued to operate independently until 1952, when it became part of the San Francisco Municipal Railway (MUNI). In 1964, the cable car system was designated a National Historic Landmark. At right is the Bank of California Building.

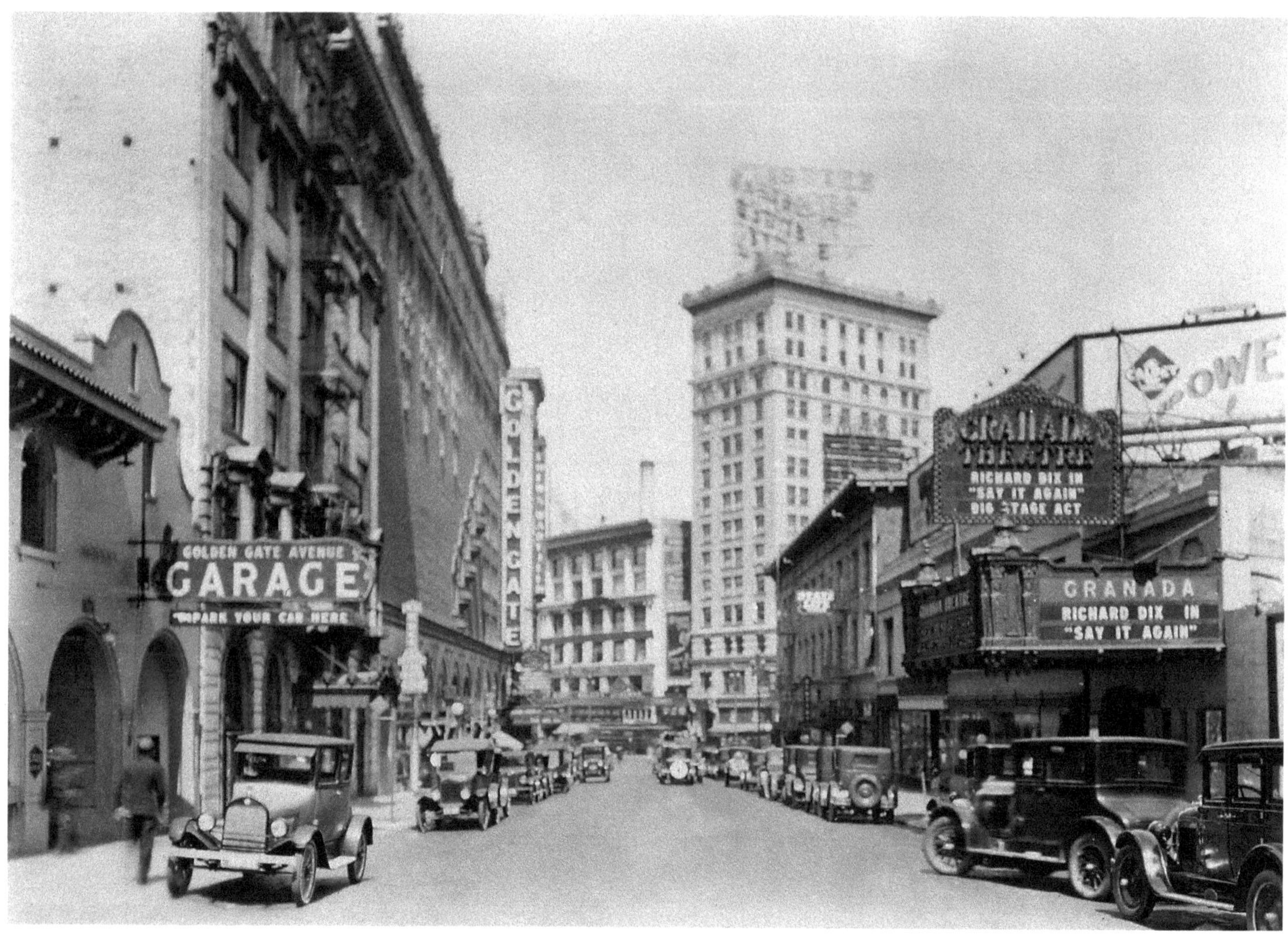

Several theaters lined Golden Gate Avenue in the 1920s. Golden Gate Theatre, built in 1922 and shown at left in 1926, had more than 2,800 seats and was used for both vaudeville performances and movies. Today it is one of San Francisco's largest live theater venues, and is especially popular for its staging of traveling musical productions.

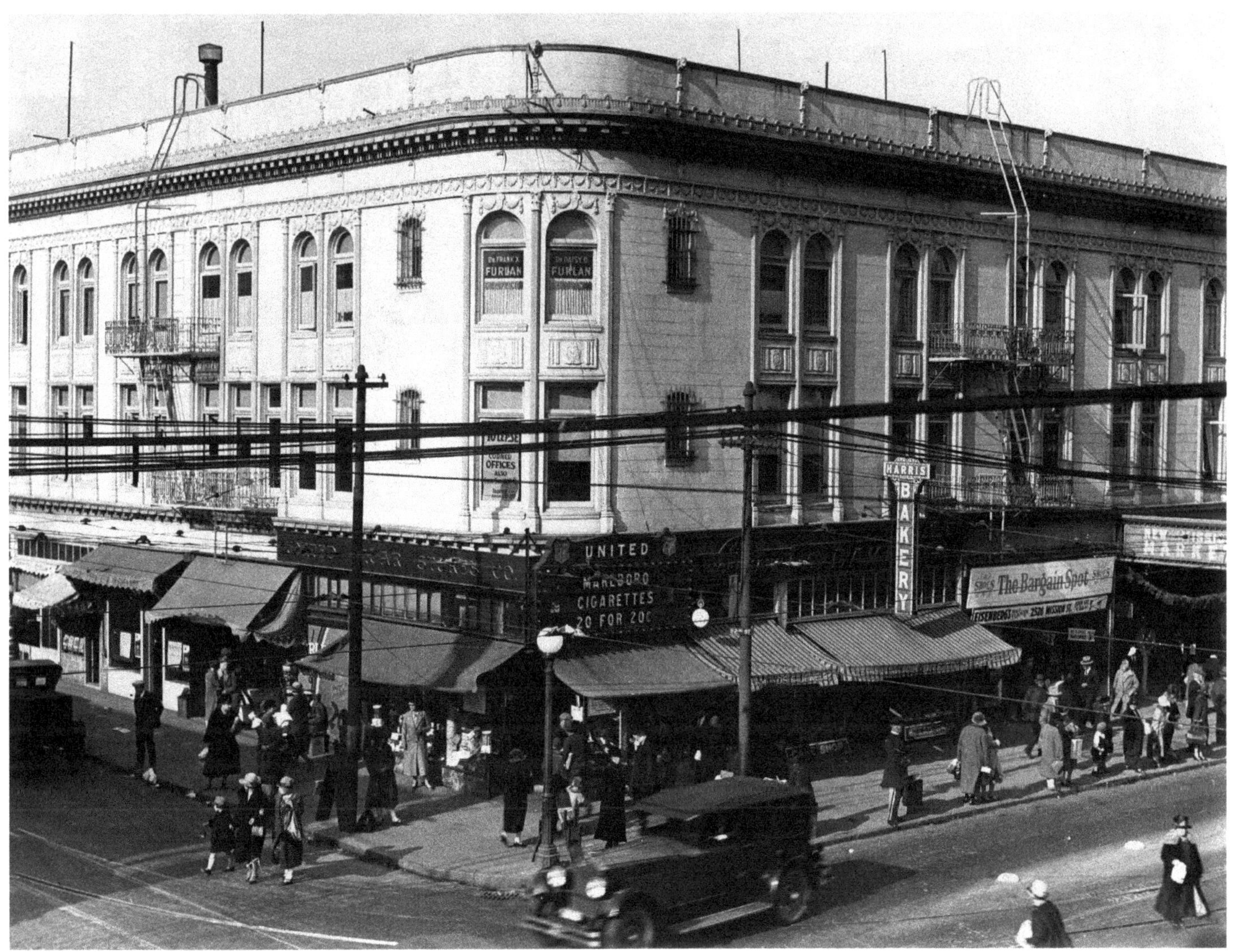

The Mission District has had a multitude of ethnic flavors for the past century. In the nineteenth and early twentieth centuries, the area was home to many Jews as well as Irish, German, and other European immigrants. After the 1906 earthquake and fires, many displaced people and businesses relocated to the Mission, and Mission Street became a main thoroughfare. The two ethnic groups that remained in the area were the Irish, who had been forced to leave their South of Market homes, and the Italians, who had left North Beach. The intersection of Mission and 22nd Street shown here on December 11, 1926, was in the heart of the Mission. Italian-owned and Irish-owned businesses helped turn the Mission into a blue-collar working-class neighborhood. Beginning in the 1940s, the Mission became home to many Mexican immigrants. Beatniks attracted to the cheap rents in the Mission moved into the area in the 1960s, and since the 1980s and 1990s, with the influx into San Francisco of thousands of Central and South Americans, the Mission has become the center of Hispanic activities in the city. Others who chose to live in the Mission in the 1990s were young people involved in the dot. com explosion. Today, the Mission is multi-ethnic, although Mission near 22nd Street maintains its Hispanic flavor.

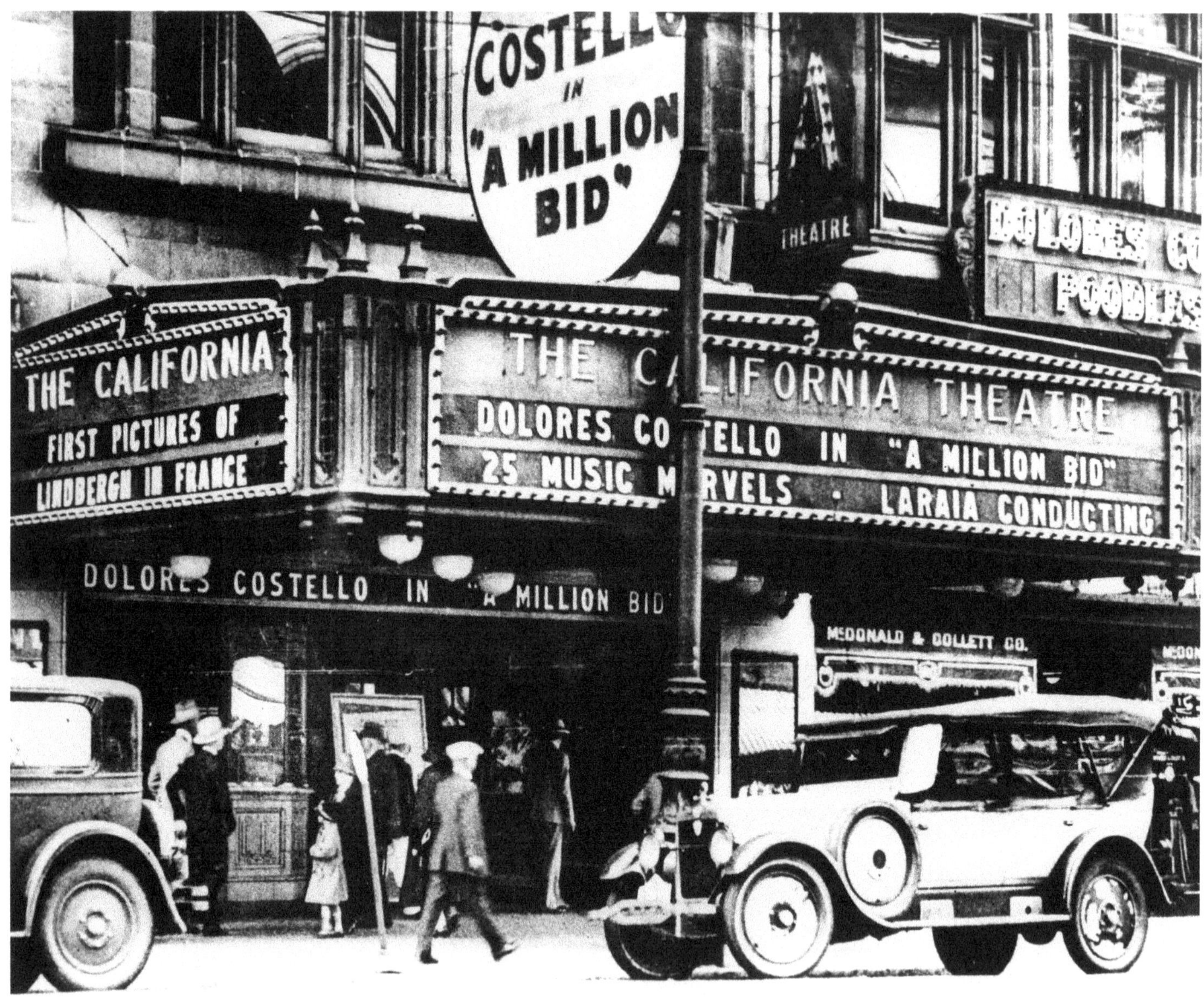

The California Theatre in August 1927. The original California Theatre, built by William Ralston in 1869 at 4th and Market streets, stood here until 1888. Rebuilt in 1917 in Gothic style, the theater had 2,135 seats, most of them in the balcony. It was renamed the State in 1941 and was shut down in 1954. In 1961, the building was razed to make room for the Roos-Atkins clothing store, which went out of business in 1976.

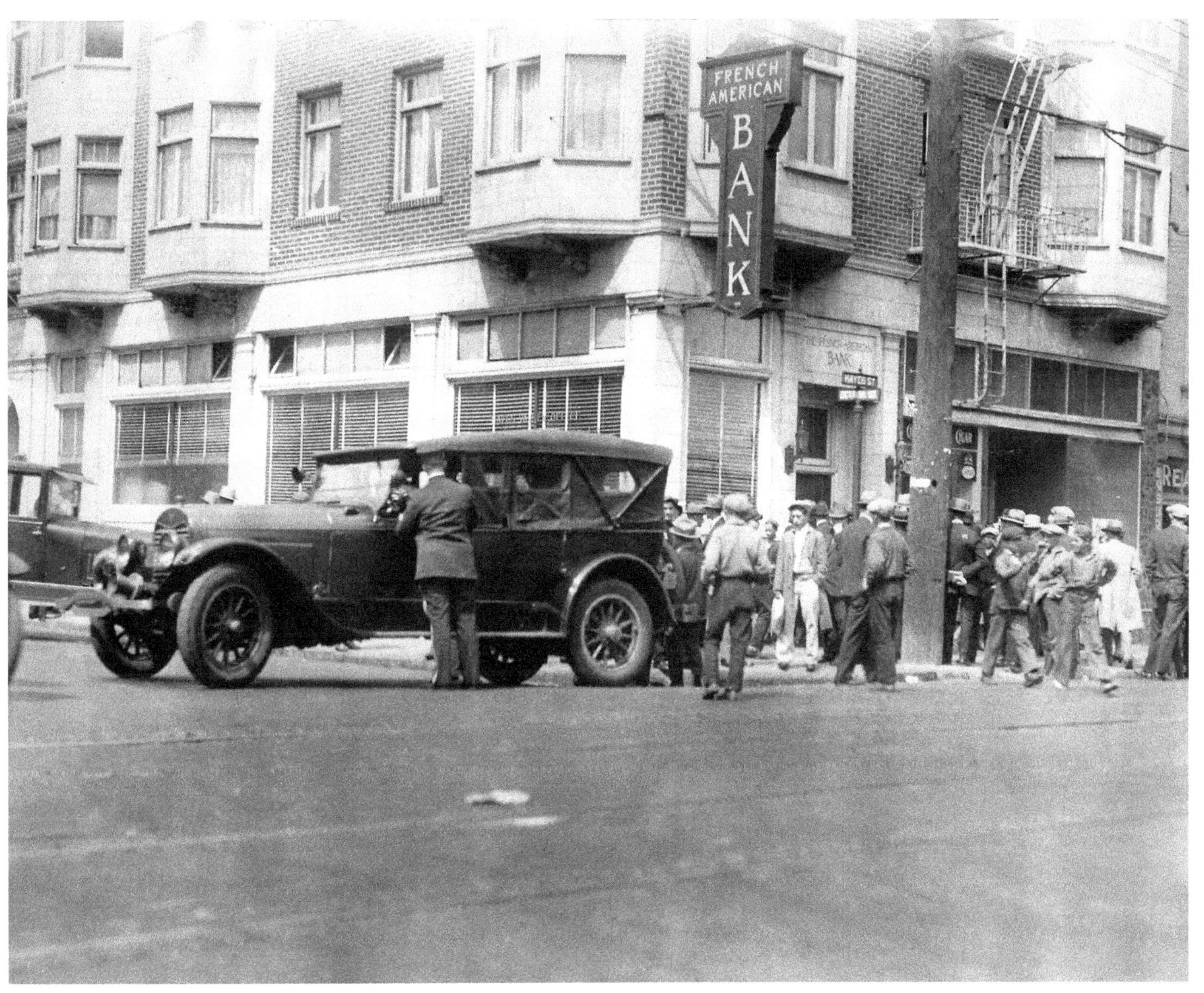

A crowd of people waits outside the French American Bank at Hayes and Octavia streets on August 6, 1927, as the bank is being held up by robbers.

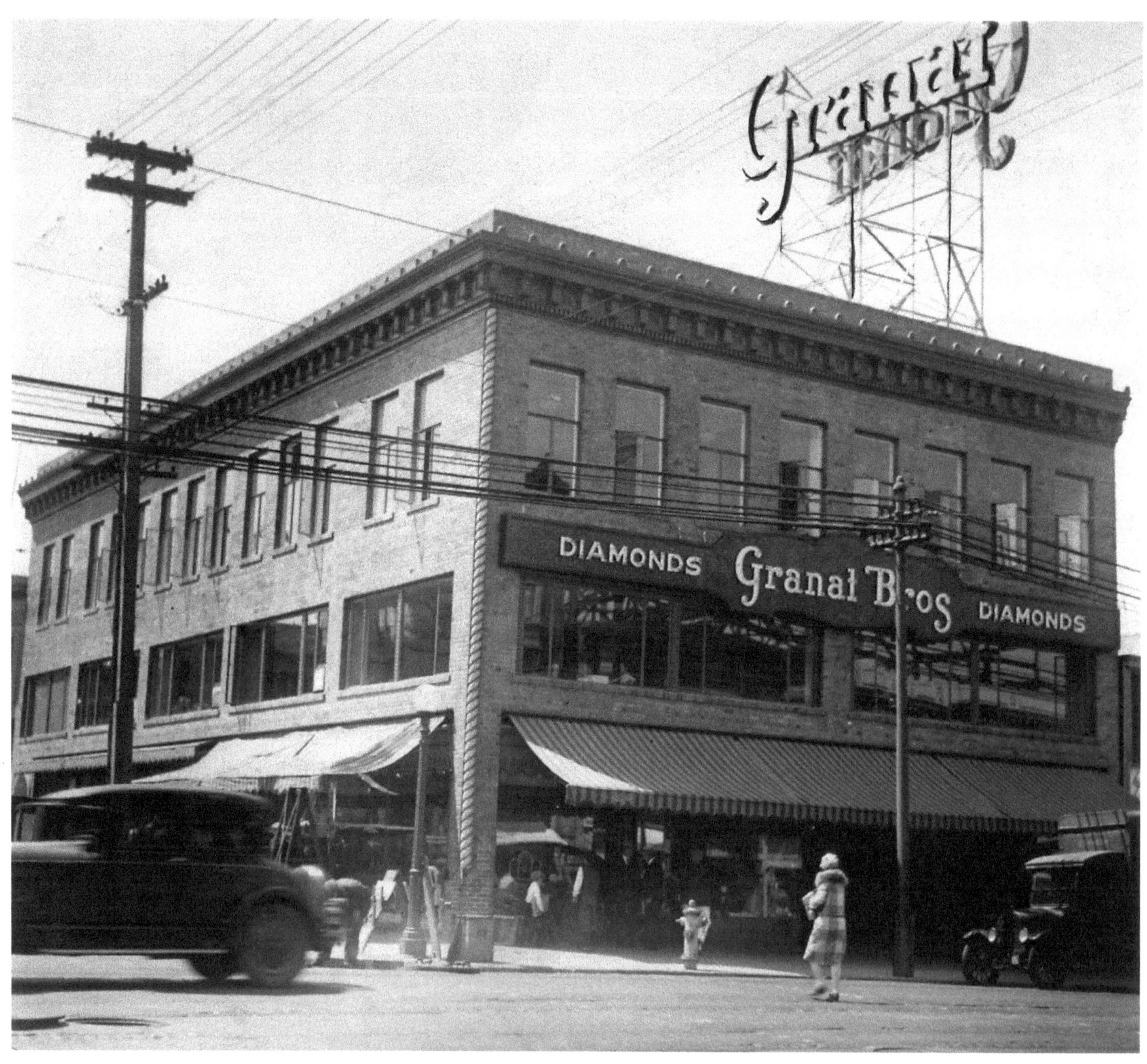

Granat Bros., pictured here on August 11, 1927, at 20th and Mission streets, was one of the most popular San Francisco jewelers for decades, and later at its store at Geary Street and Grant Avenue.

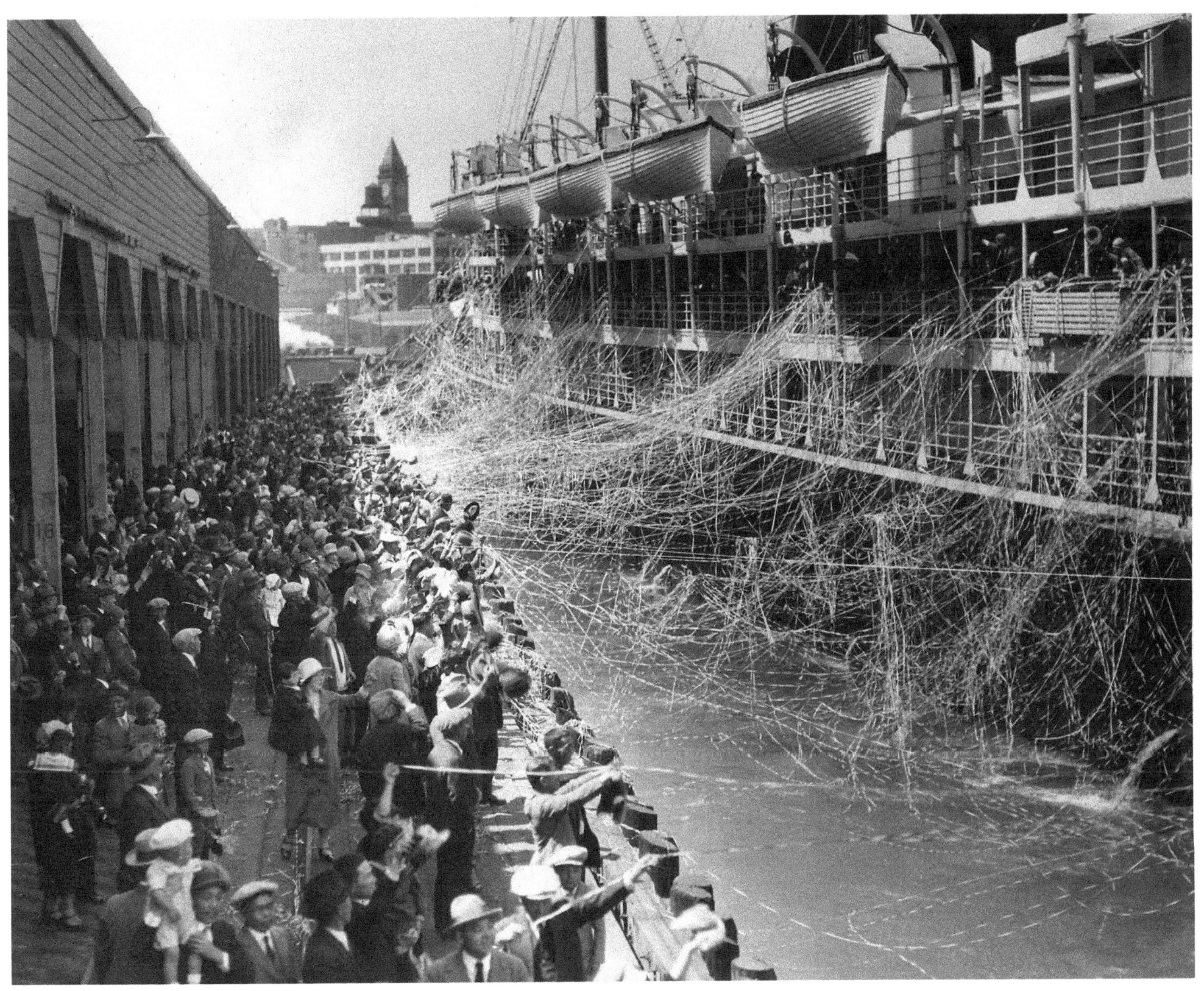

Spectators say farewell to the Japanese N.Y.K. liner *Siberia Maru,* shown here leaving the Port of San Francisco on August 30, 1927. The ship was sunk by the U.S. Navy during World War II.

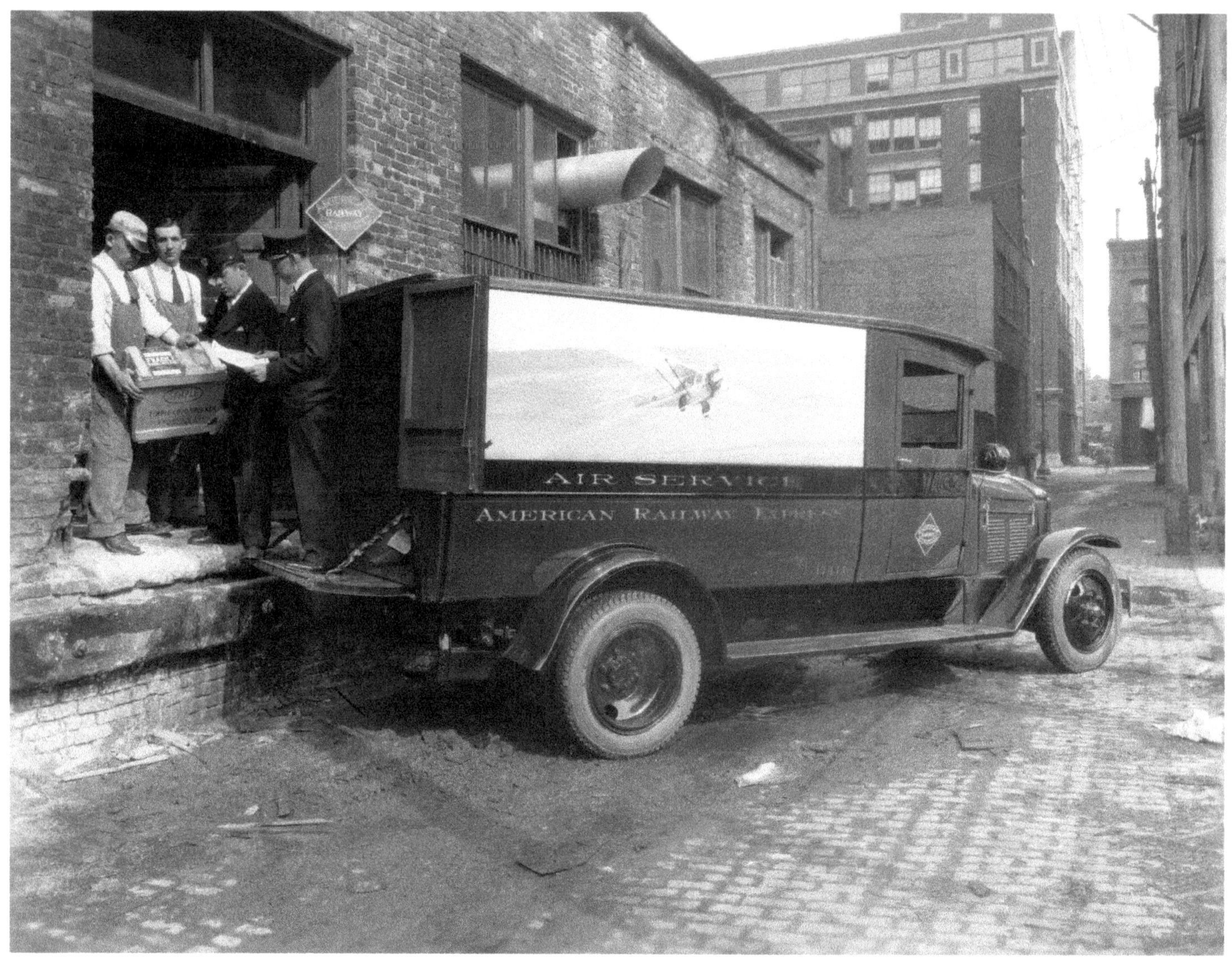

Four men load an American Railway Express truck on September 19, 1927. During World War I, at the direction of the federal government, American Railway Express Agency became a national express organization as seven separate companies were consolidated. The company's name was changed to Railway Express Agency in 1929. After numerous mergers, acquisitions, and name changes over the next several decades, the company filed for bankruptcy in 1975.

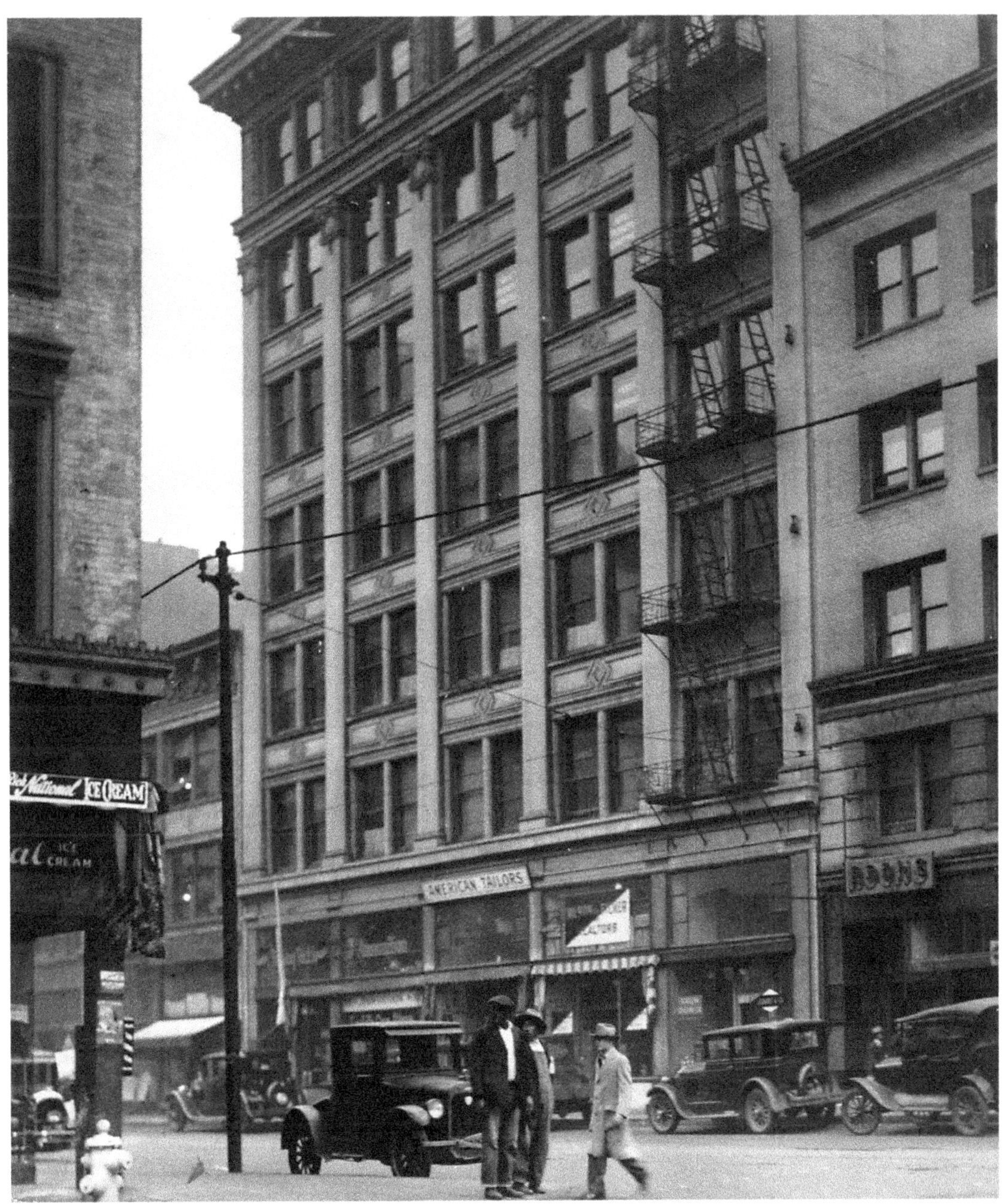

The McLeran Building, pictured here in November 1927, was located at 333 Kearny Street in the Financial District. The building stands today and houses ground floor retail, though most of the now run-down building is vacant.

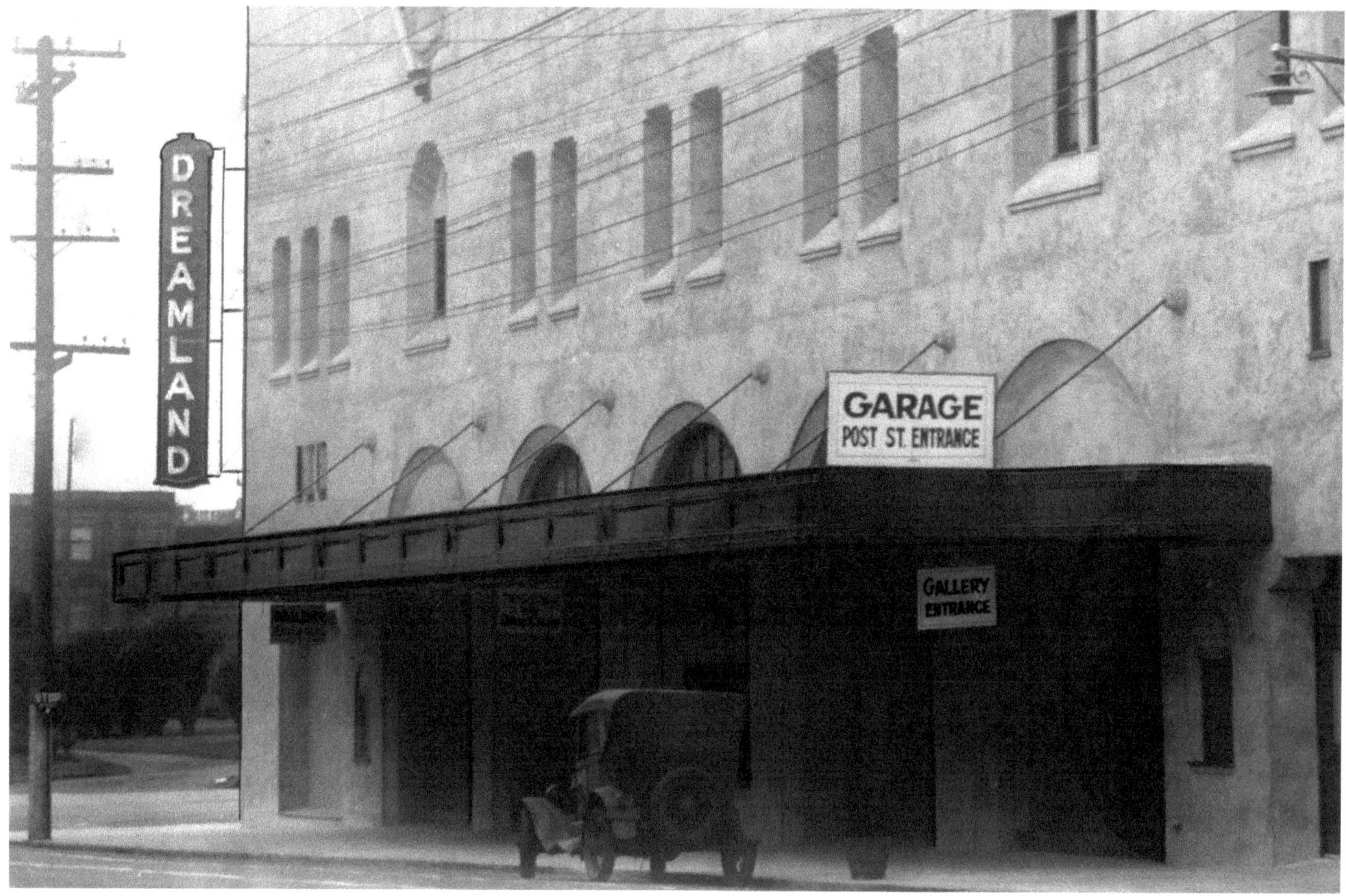

This photograph, taken on July 14, 1928, shows the exterior of the Dreamland Auditorium at Post and Steiner streets in the Fillmore district. The boxing, sumo wrestling, and dancing showcased at Dreamland consistently lured large crowds. It eventually became Winterland, an indoor ice-skating rink, in the 1940s. By 1971, Winterland became exclusively a music venue, run by Bill Graham and accommodating an audience of up to 5,400 people. When Graham's nearby Fillmore Auditorium could not provide enough seats, often the musical acts would divide their time between the two auditoriums. The most popular acts of the 1960s and 1970s played at Winterland, including Jefferson Airplane, the Rolling Stones, the Grateful Dead, the Ramones, Bob Dylan, the Sex Pistols, and Jimi Hendrix. Winterland closed after an all-night Grateful Dead concert on New Year's Eve 1978, and today on the site stand apartments.

The San Francisco Curb Exchange at 350 Bush Street, shown here on January 28, 1929, shortly after opening, was located in the Miller and Pflueger–designed building where the San Francisco Mining Exchange operated between 1923 and 1928. The Curb Exchange operated until it moved in 1938, after merging with the San Francisco Stock Exchange, and the Chamber of Commerce became the next tenant. The building has been vacant for more than 25 years. Developers have proposed a 19-story office tower, in a design that incorporates the historic Exchange building.

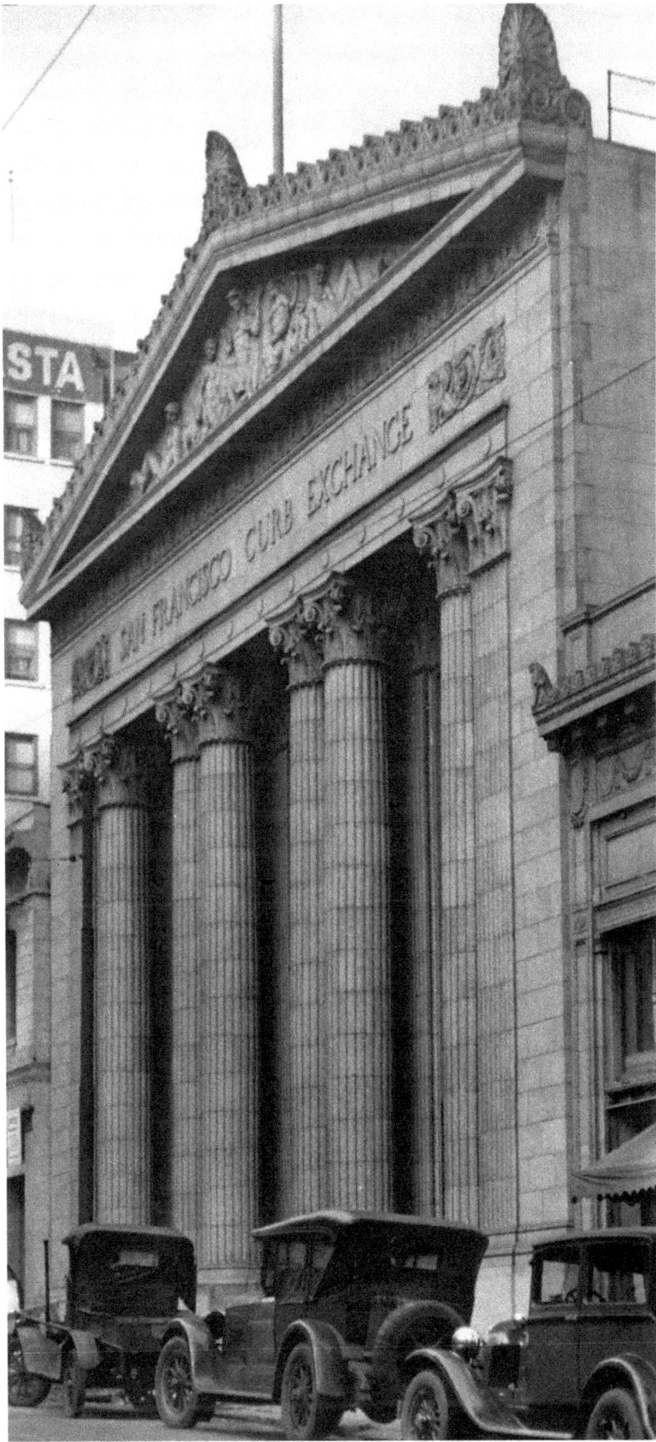

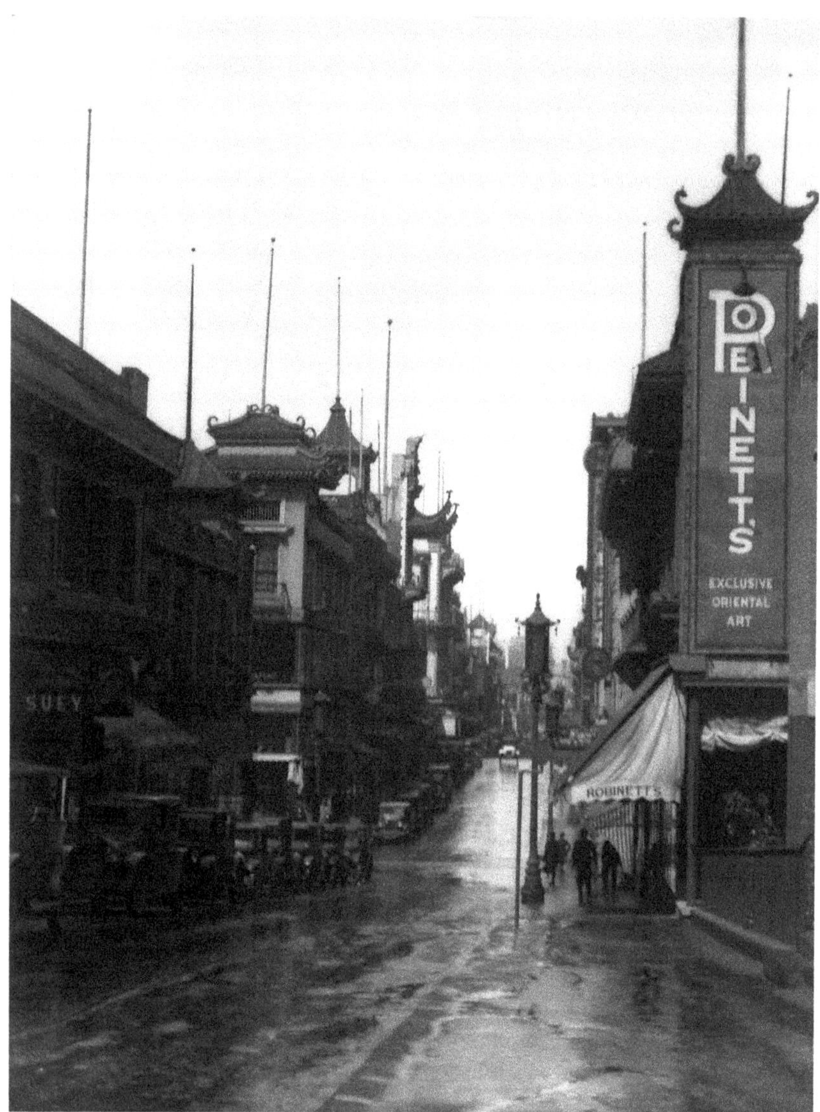

Chinatown in the late 1920s. City planners attempted to prevent its re-establishment after 1906 to claim the prime locale as an addition to the Financial District. Many proposed relocating the Chinese community to the mud flats in Hunters Point in southern San Francisco, or other undesirable vicinities, but these efforts were thwarted, in part with help from the Chinese government and American enterprises. Chinatown was rebuilt on its former grounds with rigid building codes and structures made from concrete or brick, and as a compromise, the new Chinatown was sanitized from its formerly seedy reputation and catered more to Western tourism and family life. Shown here is the more contrived "oriental" façade, with its colorful pagodas, curled eaves, dragon motifs, and cornices meant to attract tourists.

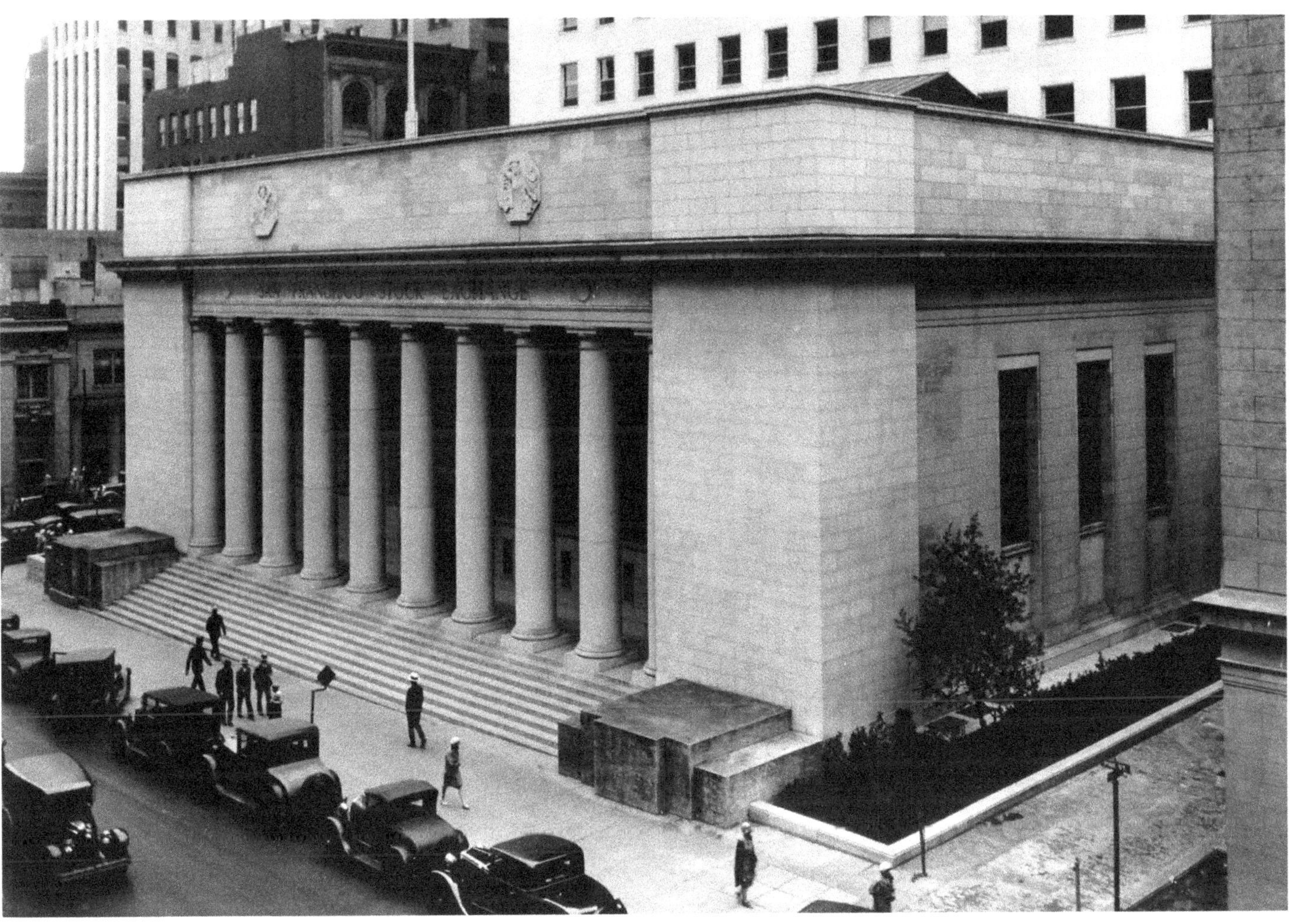

This picture shows the exterior of the Stock Exchange at Sansome and Pine in the late 1920s. The institution was founded in 1882 as the San Francisco Stock and Bond Exchange, and later became the Pacific Coast Stock Exchange. In 2002, the Exchange closed its doors and sold the building to private developers. It is now a trendy downtown gym, where active San Franciscans socialize in locker rooms that were formerly Exchange vaults.

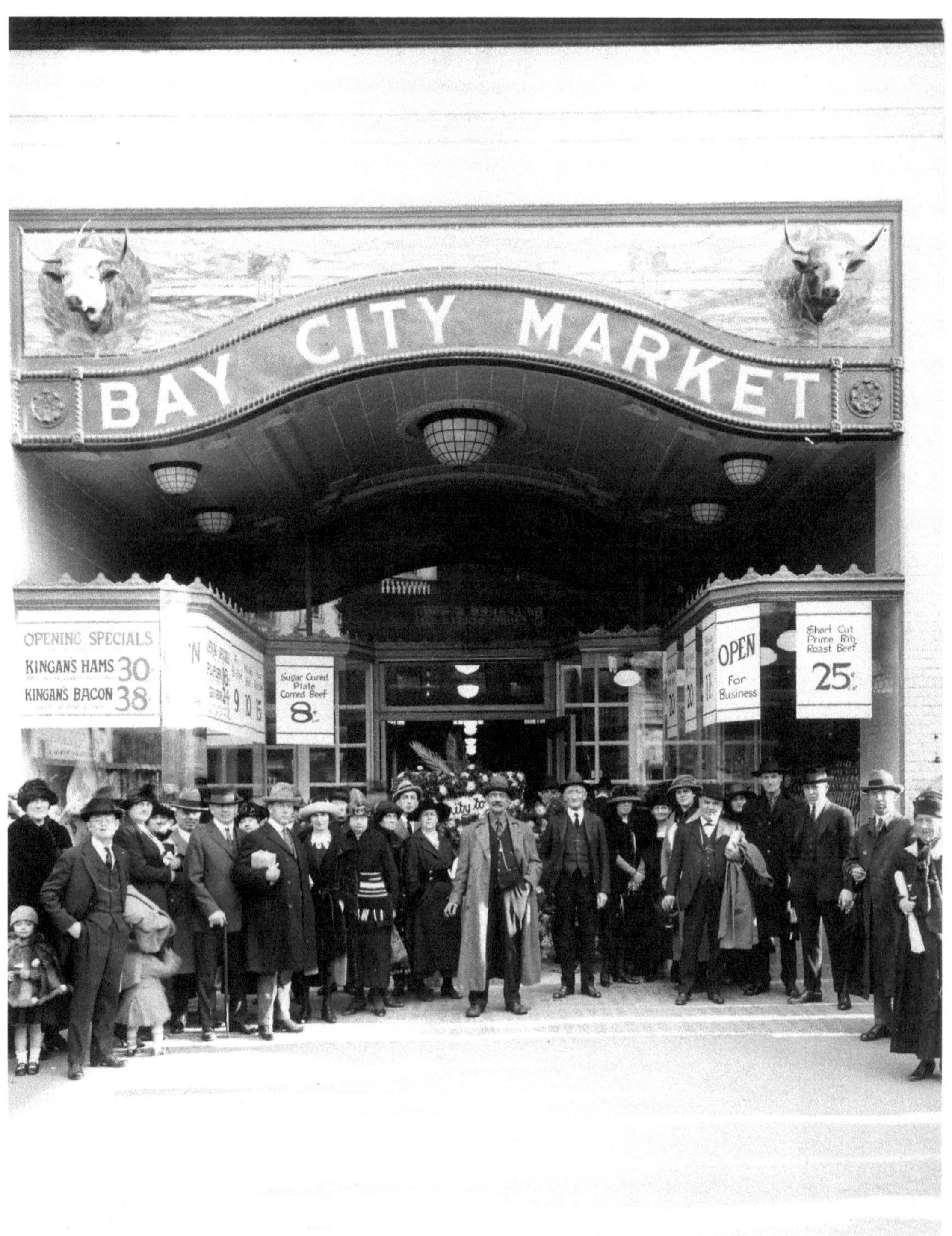

A crowd of people stands outside the Bay City Market in the 1930s during the Great Depression. Special prices on chicken and other food are posted on signs in the front windows.

Bridge to the Future

(1930–1939)

During the thirties, San Francisco plunged into the Great Depression along with the rest of the nation. San Franciscans were forced to make an abrupt shift, from the lifestyles they led in the bountiful twenties to a frugal existence that allowed for none of the extravagances of the previous decade. Bread lines and soup kitchens suddenly became ubiquitous on San Francisco streets. Yet while the Great Depression was a dark moment in the city's history, San Franciscans had overcome adversity before. People pursued their lives as best they could. In many ways, entertainment was more accessible to the general public now, with a plethora of cheap diversions throughout the city, such as Playland at the Beach, vaudevilles, theaters, and parks.

President Frankin D. Roosevelt's New Deal used government spending on a large scale to alleviate unemployment across the country, which in San Francisco meant significant new construction projects. Among them were the Bay Bridge and Golden Gate Bridge, completed in 1936 and 1937, to become beloved landmarks and transform how people lived and worked, at last linking San Francisco to the East Bay and Marin County.

In 1934, a four-day general strike among sailors along the San Francisco Embarcadero led to the 83-day West Coast Longshore Strike and the unionization of western ports. Also in 1934, Alcatraz began operating as a maximum-security federal prison. In 1936, Herb Caen, soon to be known as "Mr. San Francisco," started writing a column for the *San Francisco Chronicle.* The completion of Coit Tower on Telegraph Hill became a welcome addition to the San Francisco skyline. The 1930s ended as San Francisco hosted a world's fair on newly built Treasure Island, called the Golden Gate International Exposition, which welcomed 17 million visitors.

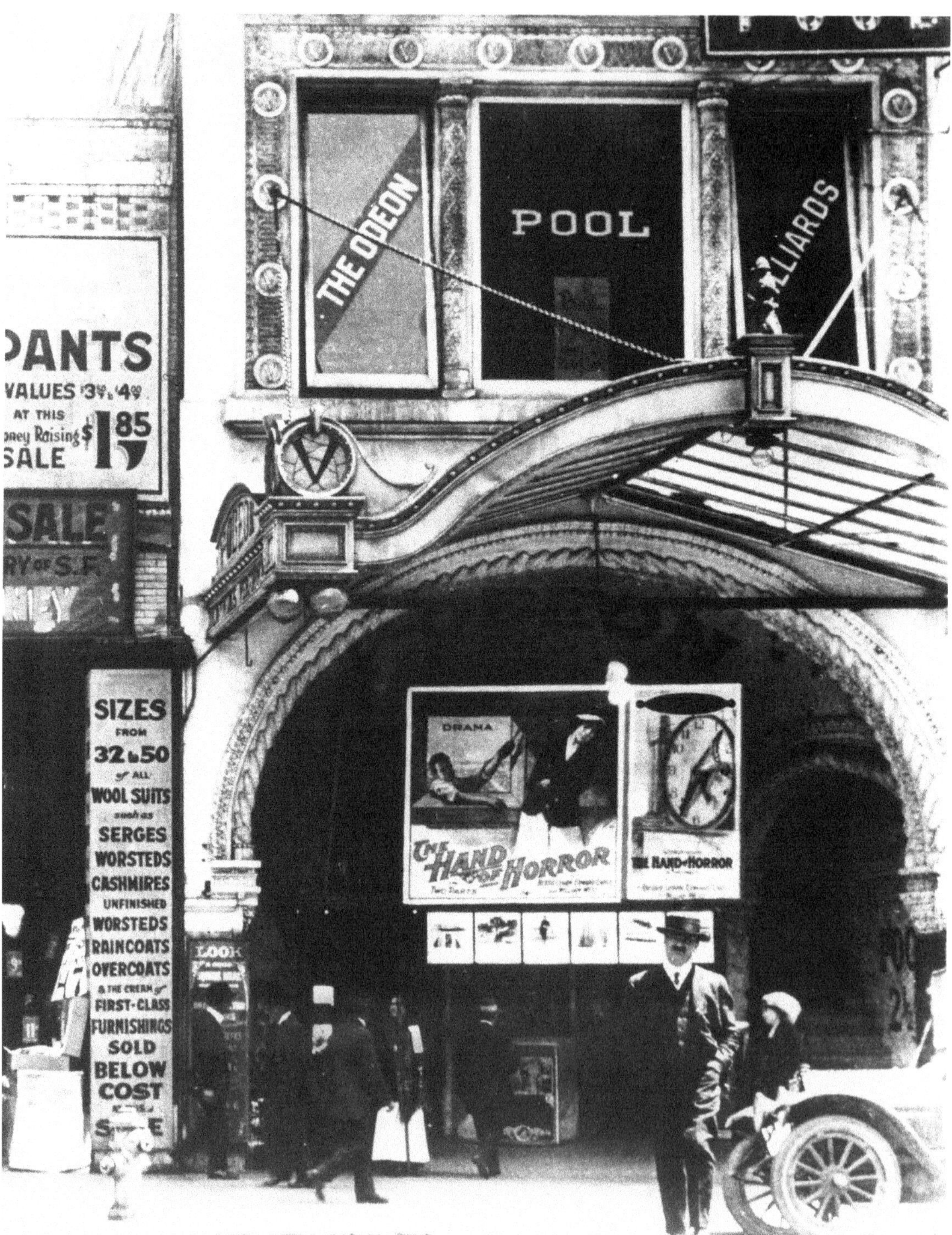

The Odeon Theatre, shown here, was built in 1914 on the south side of Market Street between Third and Fourth streets where the Cineograph once stood. The Odeon was one of numerous theaters built before World War II on this stretch of Market Street, known for decades as "The Great White Way of San Francisco." During the Depression, San Franciscans escaped their worries and paid a few cents to see a movie in this and the city's many movie houses, which were very successful in those days. The Odeon eventually closed and was replaced with the Metropolitan Market.

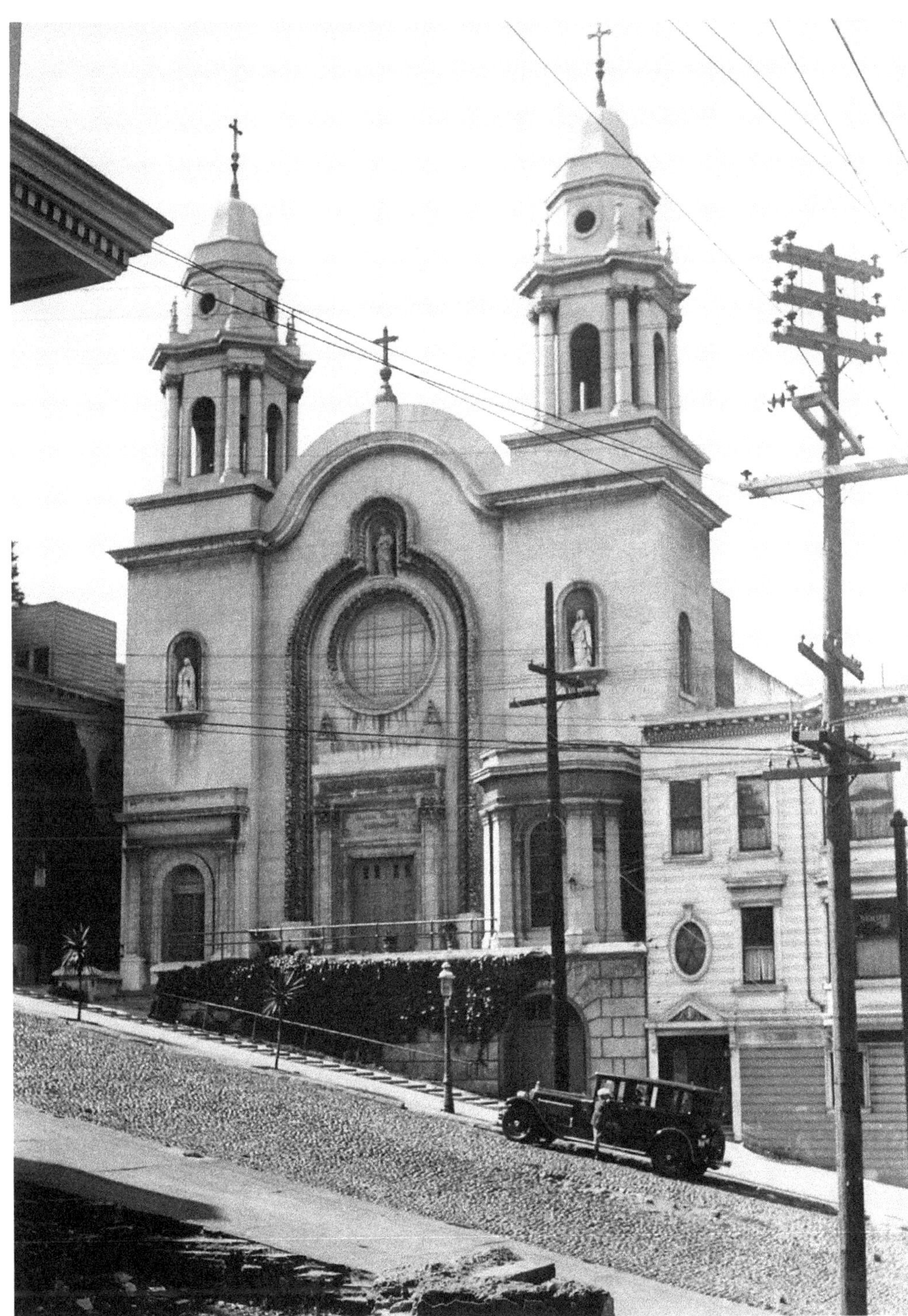

Shown here in the early 1930s is Nuestra Senora de Guadalupe, a Spanish Mission–style church constructed in 1906 and rebuilt in 1912 from reinforced concrete. This Historic Landmark, at 906 Broadway between Mason and Taylor streets, has mostly ethnic Chinese congregants.

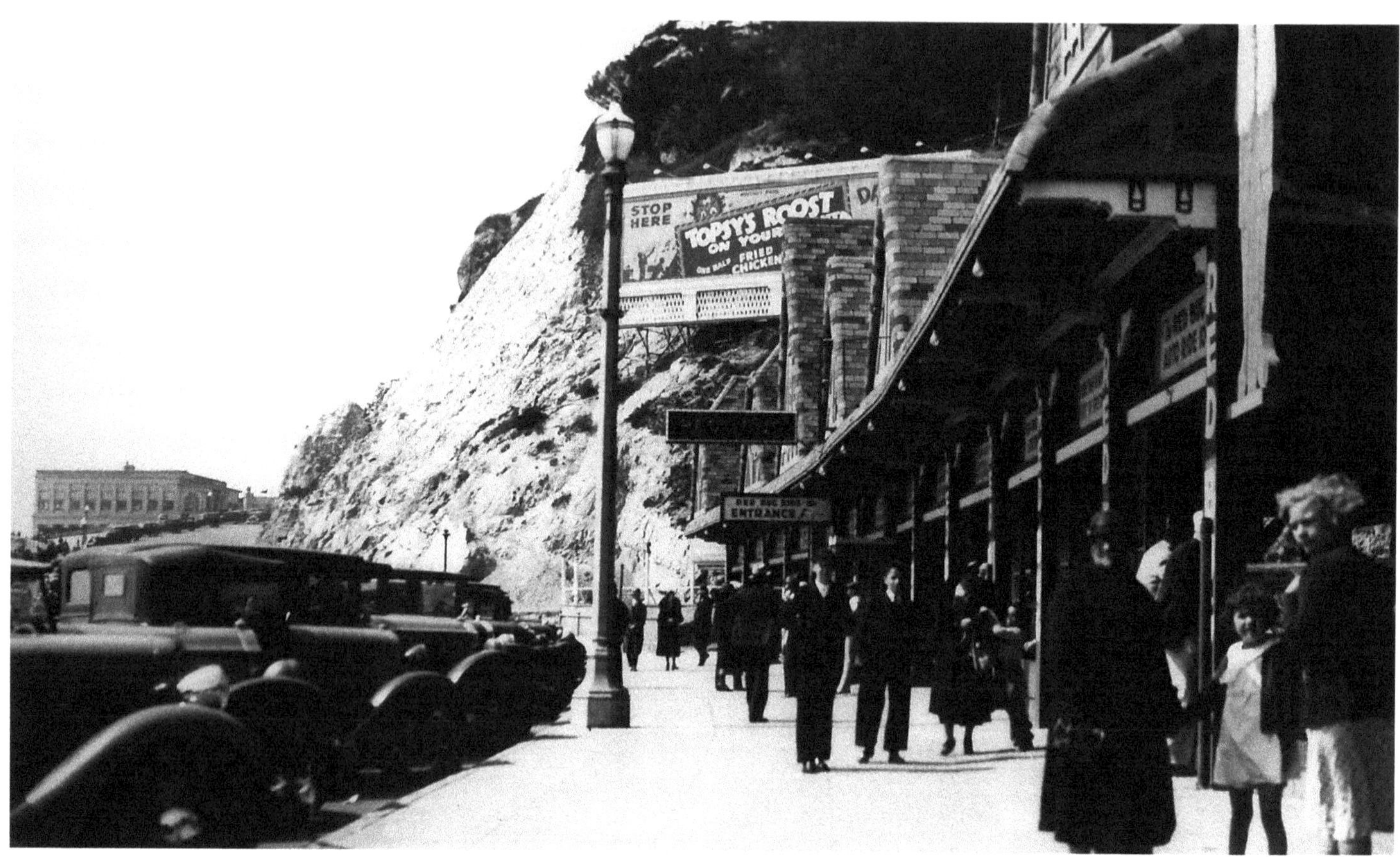

Ocean Beach, shown in this 1930 photograph along the Pacific Ocean on the western shores of San Francisco, developed in the late nineteenth century as a resort featuring the Cliff House and Sutro Baths. Trains took people from downtown San Francisco through the then-undeveloped western end of the city, still known as the "outside lands." Several generations of San Franciscans flocked to Playland at the Beach, the amusement park built along Ocean Beach, and known as the Coney Island of the West from the time the park was built in 1928 until it was closed down in 1972. Major development near Ocean Beach continued into the 1920s and 1930s, when the Great Highway was constructed, and the Richmond and Sunset districts expanded out to the beach.

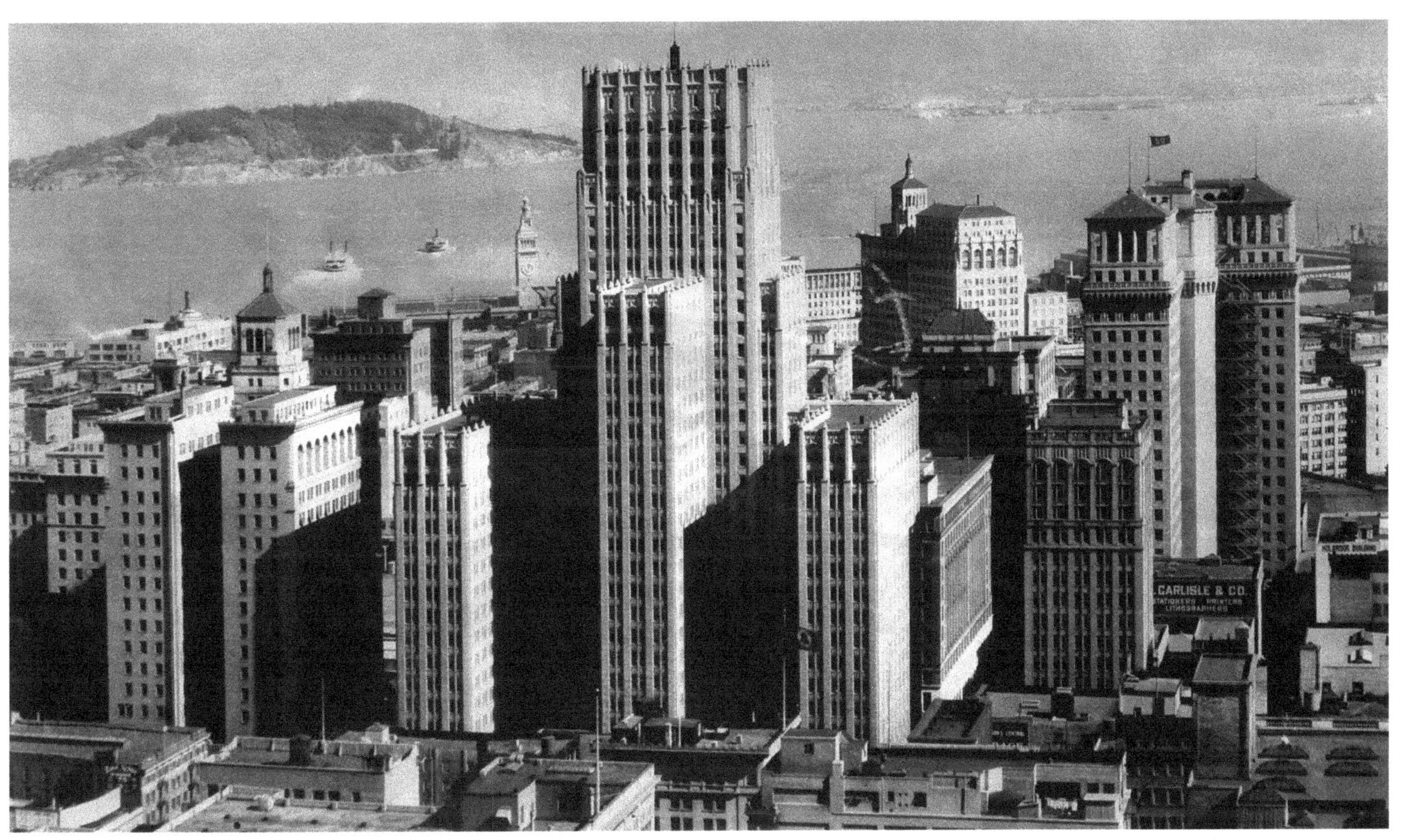

This view, taken from Nob Hill by telephoto lens on March 8, 1930, shows the rapidly developing downtown skyline. The Financial Center, the Russ Building, the Matson Building, PG&E, and others are visible, with Goat Island and the East Bay shore in the background. The island was known as Yerba Buena Island from 1850 to 1895, and from 1931 through today.

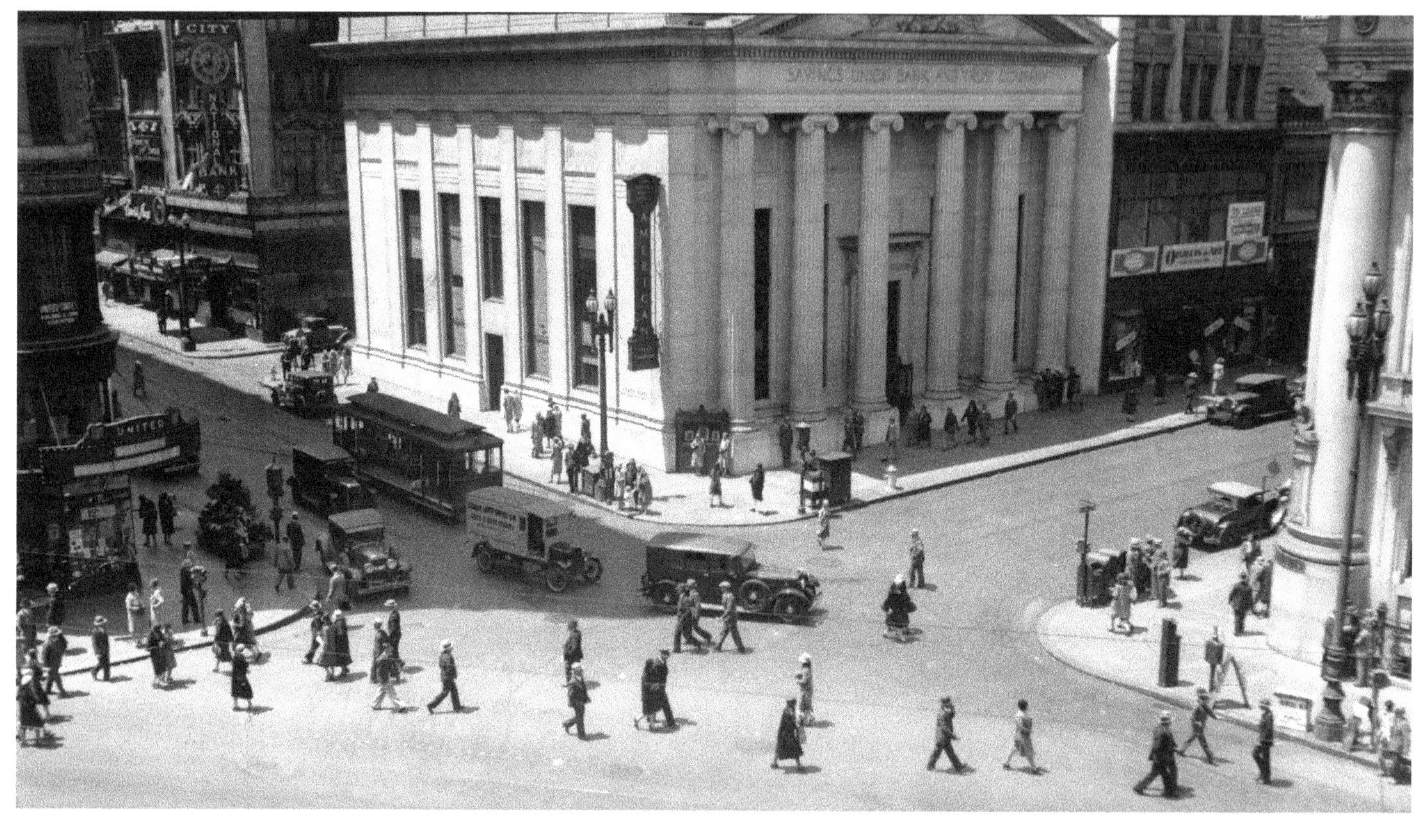

The Savings Union Bank and Trust Company, shown here on May 21, 1930, stood at 1 Grant Avenue at the corner of O'Farrell Street. The ornately pillared bank once housed the Bankers Club on the top floor. Although the bank merged decades ago, the building remains and is occupied by retailer Emporio Armani.

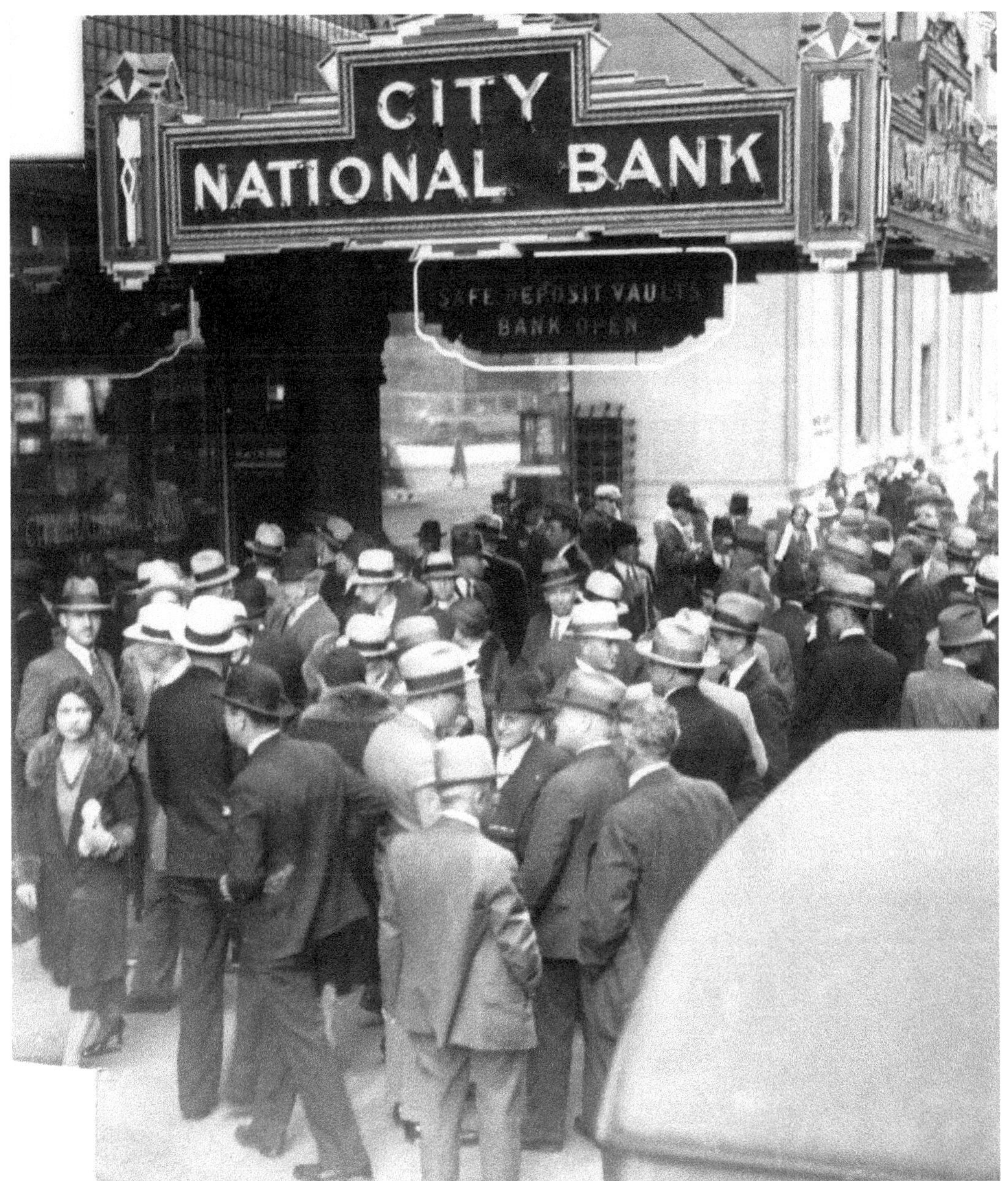

Crowds assemble in front of City National Bank to watch the excitement on January 29, 1931, as a hold-up scene unfolds inside.

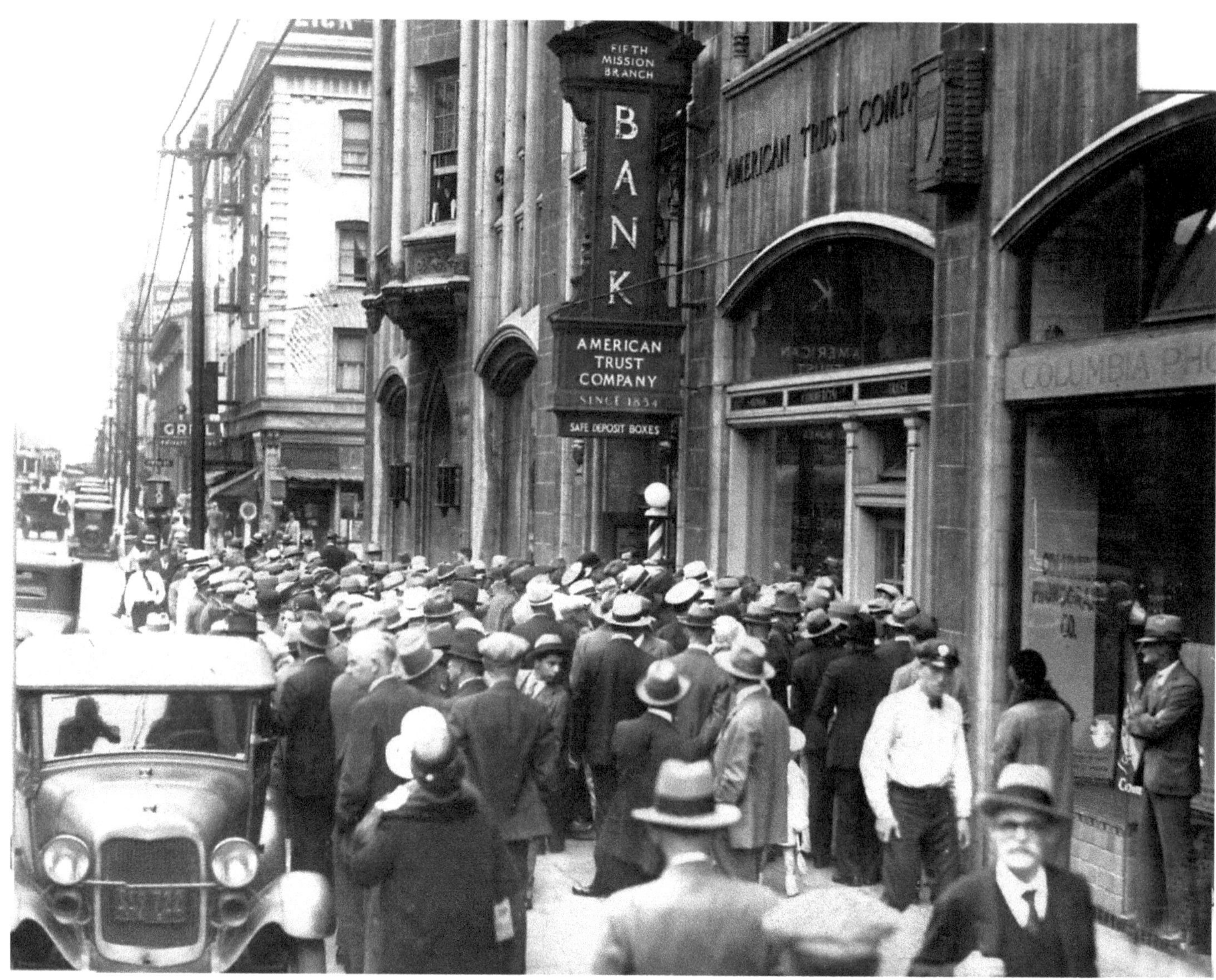

Crowds gather on May 14, 1931, during the depression in front of the American Trust Company, a large northern California retail bank and the second oldest financial institution in California. In 1960, American Trust merged with Wells Fargo Bank to form the Wells Fargo Bank American Trust Company, renamed Wells Fargo Bank again in 1962.

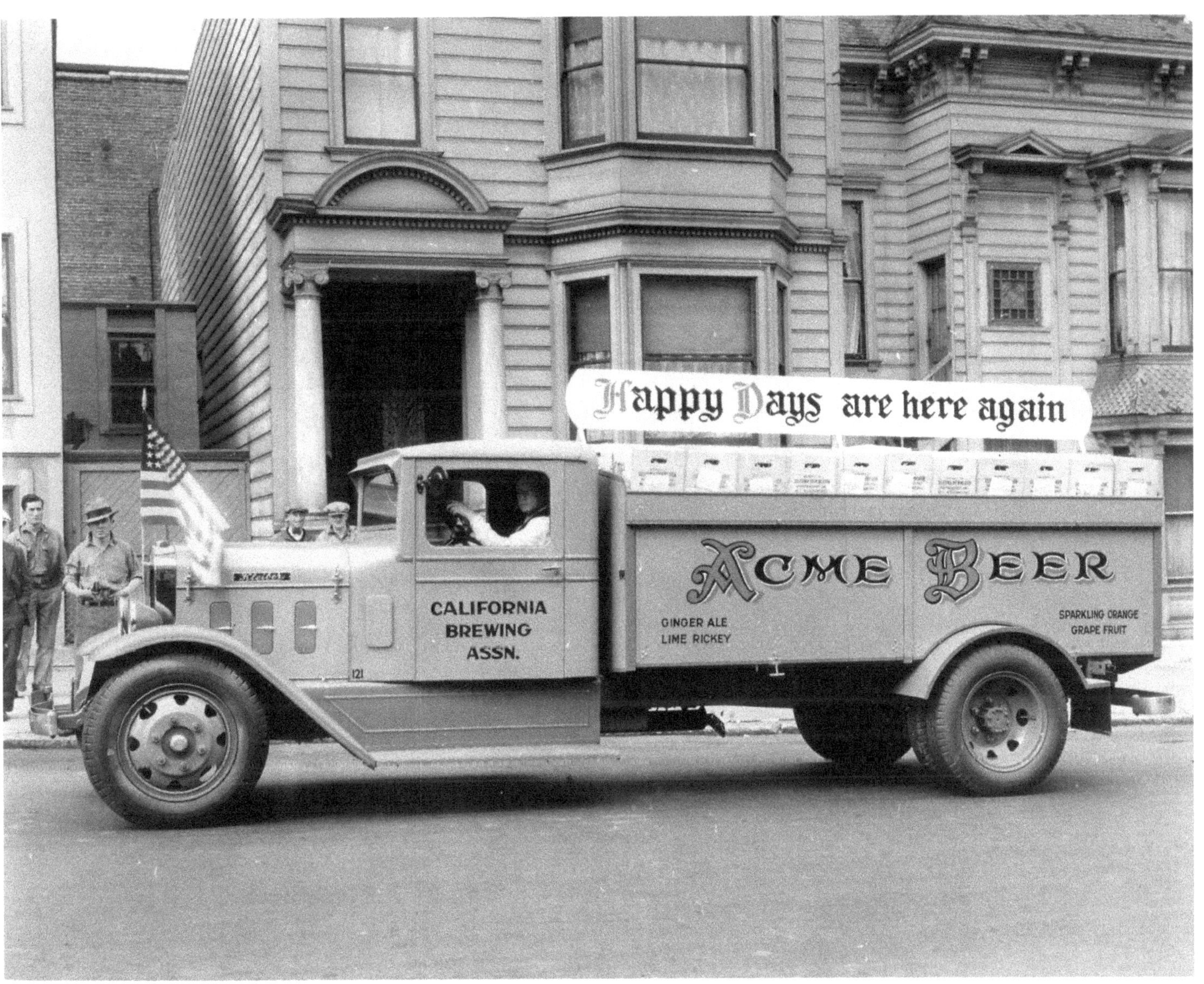

This photo shows an Acme delivery truck in 1933, displaying the New Deal–era slogan "Happy Days are here again." During Prohibition, Acme Beer continued brewing a less than satisfactory light beer, which the company sarcastically endorsed as "a delightful beverage containing less than 1/2 of 1% alcohol." When Prohibition was repealed in 1933, the Acme Beer Company aggressively and proactively advertised in newspapers, billboards, and over the radio, helping to make its beer one of the most popular in the West.

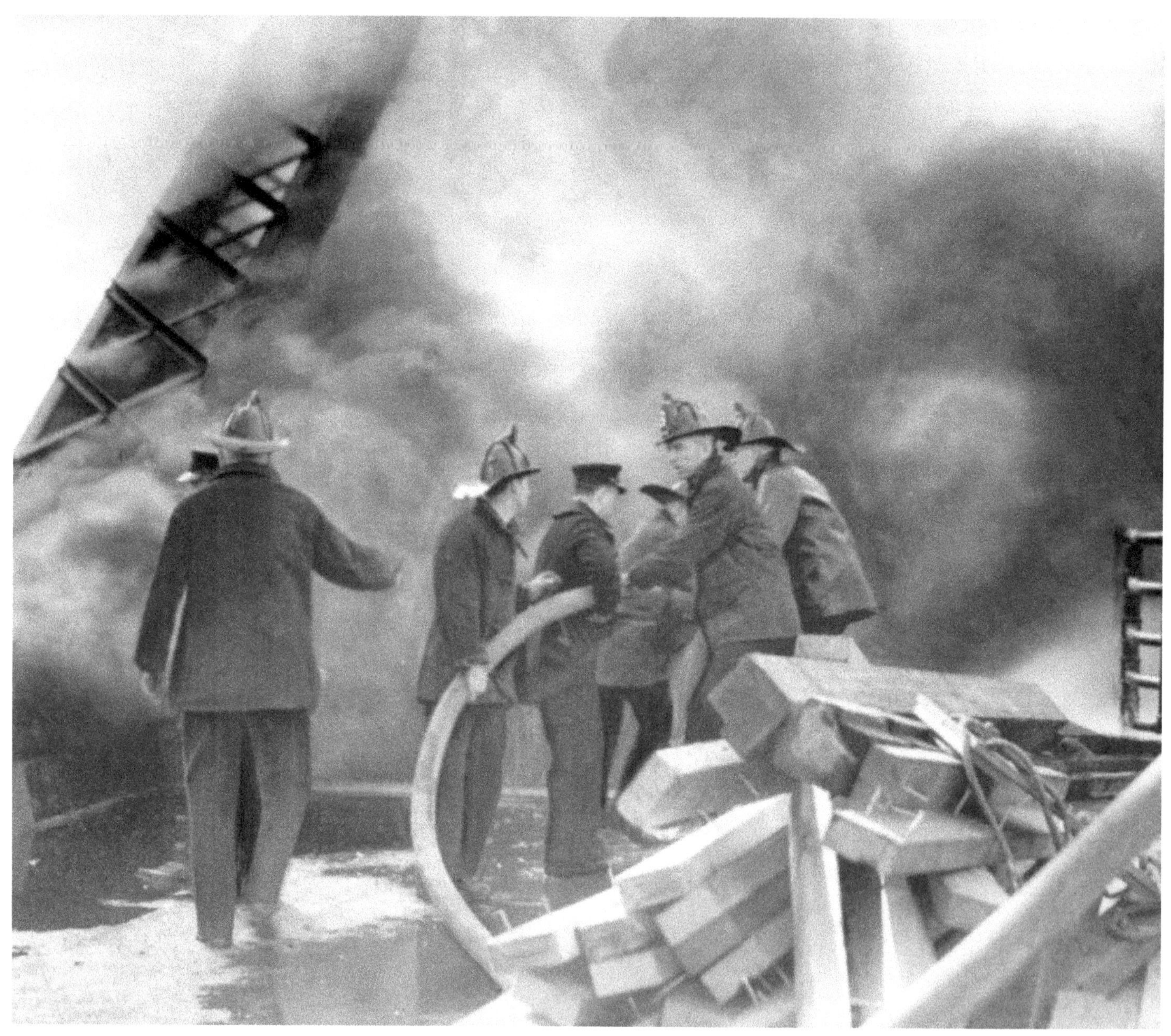

On April 13, 1933, San Francisco fire fighters extinguish a fire on the Third Street Bridge a month before its formal opening. Fortunately, the fire did not do much damage.

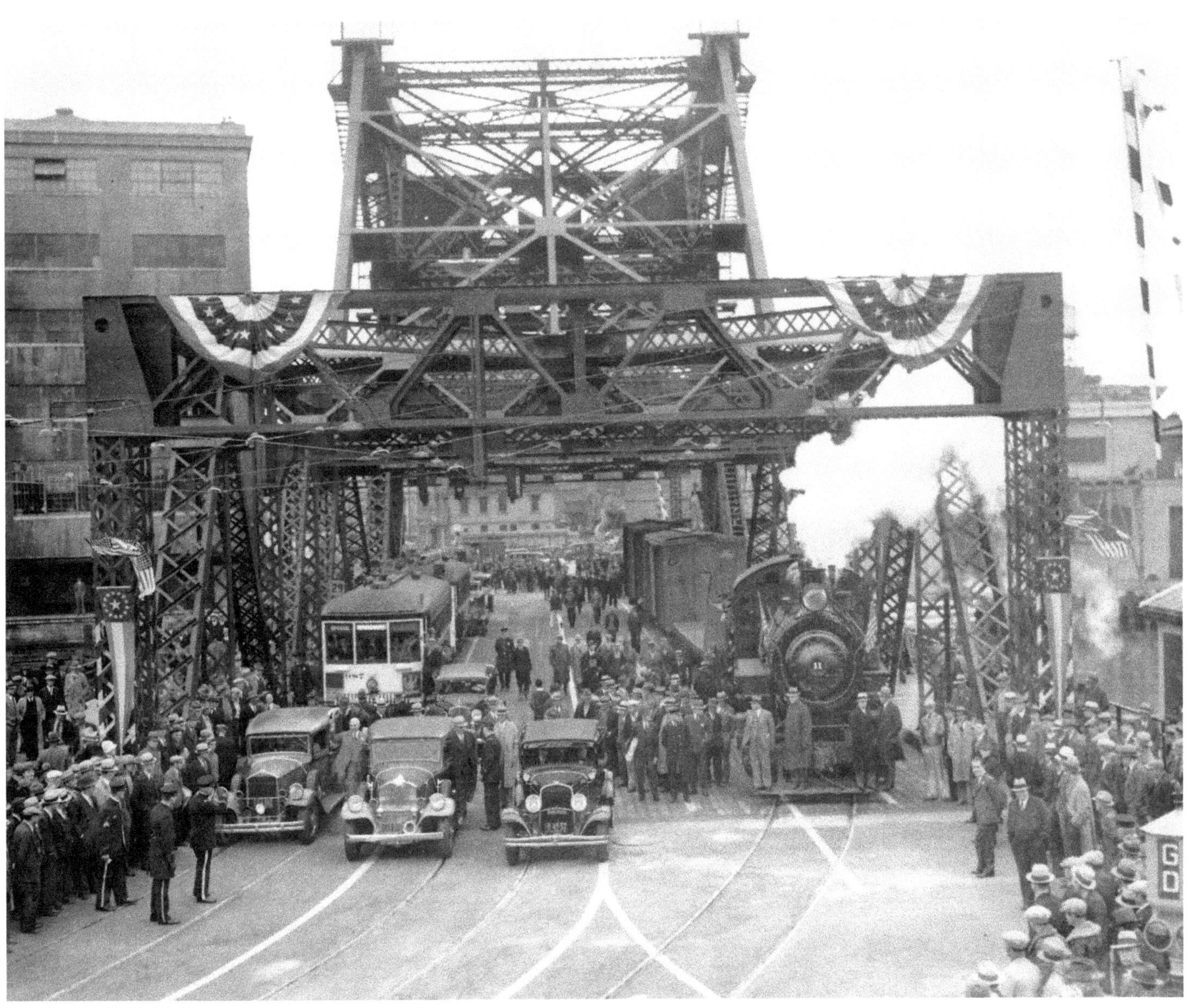

A crowd assembles for the opening ceremony of the Third Street Bridge on May 12, 1933. The bridge, designed by Joseph Strauss, designer of the Golden Gate Bridge, has since been renamed Lefty O'Doul Bridge in honor of the famous San Francisco Seals baseball player and manager, and sits next to AT&T Park, home of the San Francisco Giants. It continues to serve as an important bridge, linking the fast-developing Mission Bay area to the South of Market.

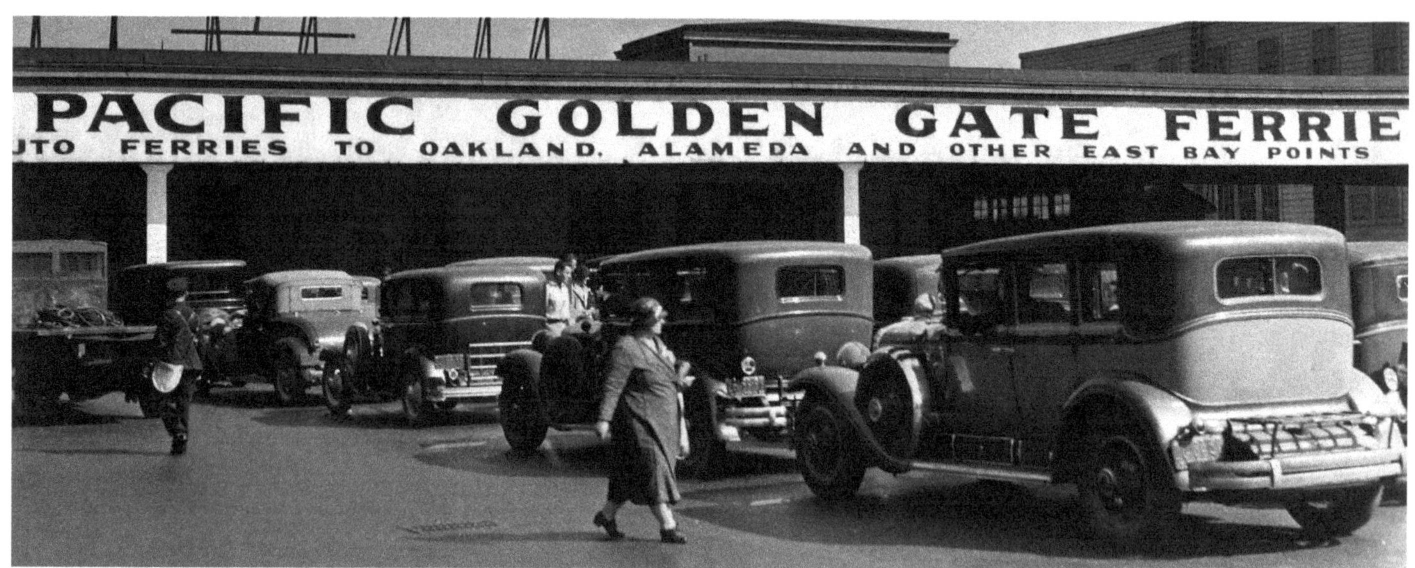

Automobiles line up to board a ferry at the Ferry Building on October 23, 1933. Before the construction of the Golden Gate and Bay bridges in the 1930s, the ferry was the sole mode of direct transportation into and out of San Francisco and the north and east, and averaged fifty million passengers every year. After the bridges were built, ferry service was discontinued in 1941, then reintroduced in the early 1960s. The double-decker Embarcadero Freeway obstructed the front of the Ferry Building from 1957 until it was razed after being damaged during the 1989 earthquake.

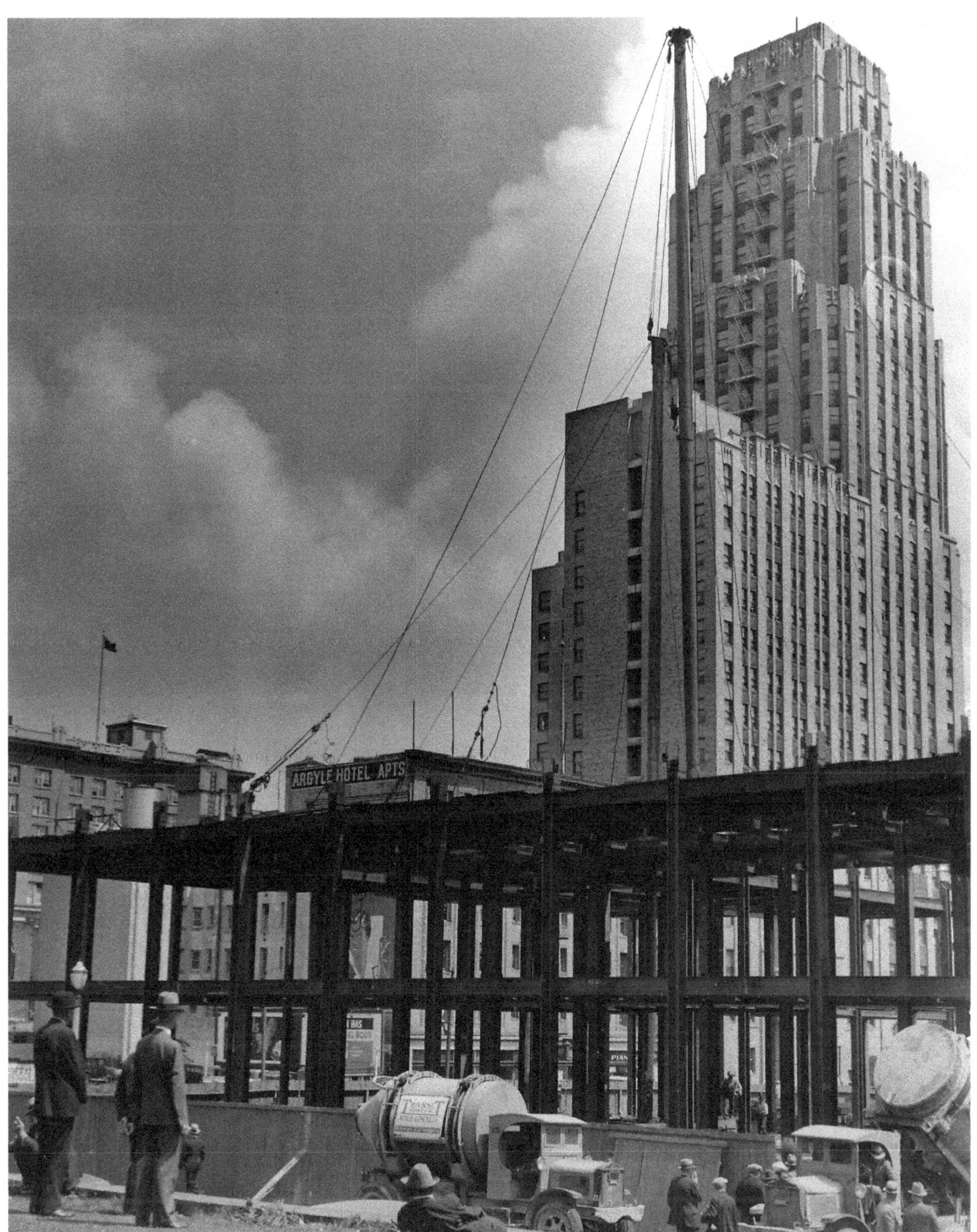

This picture, taken on April 25, 1934, shows the construction of the Federal Building at the Civic Center, with the luxurious William Taylor Hotel at McAllister and Leavenworth in the background. The hotel was renamed the Empire Hotel and was acquired in 1981 by University of California Hastings College of the Law and converted into a student dorm.

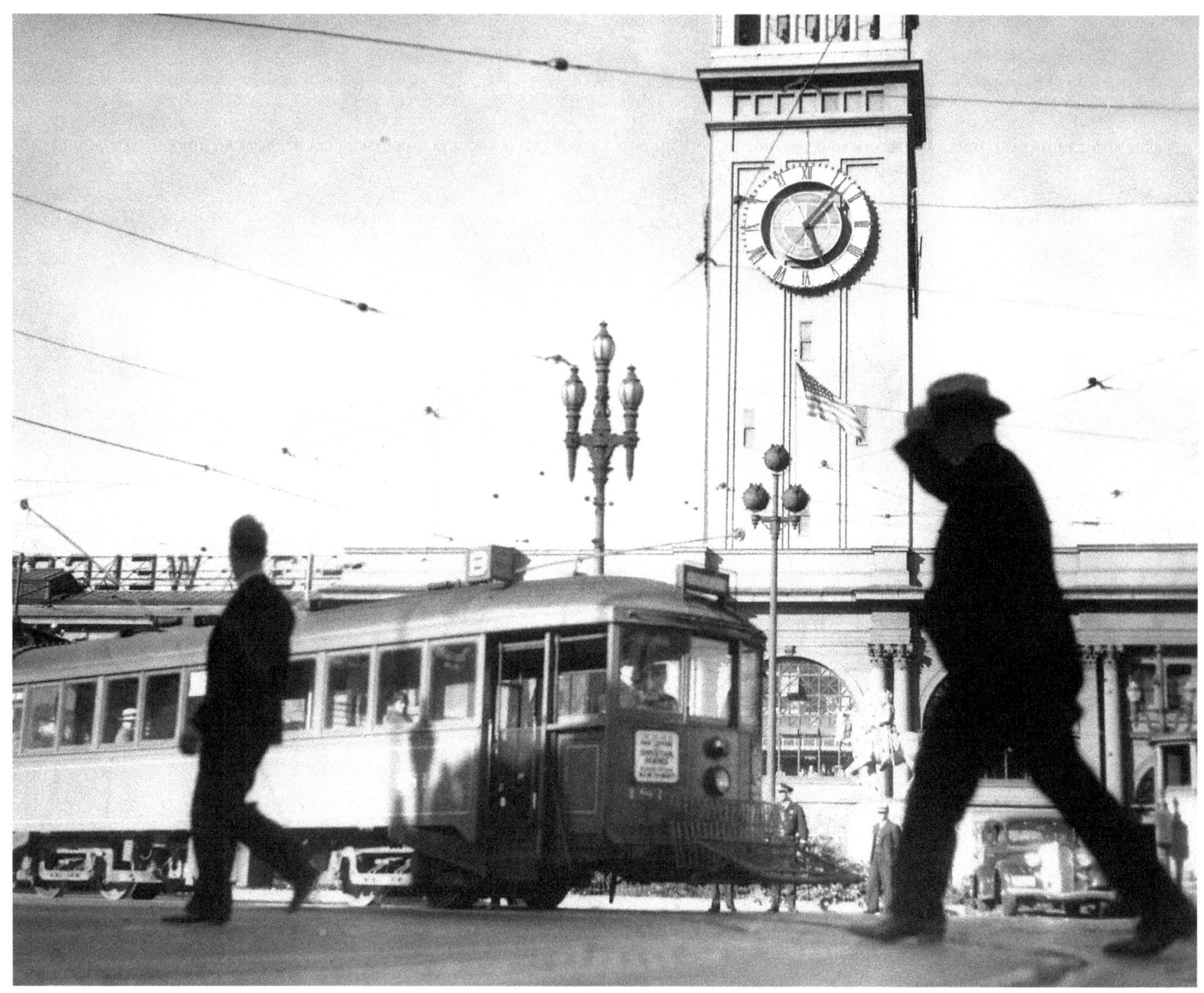

The B-Geary streetcar picks up passengers in front of the Ferry Building on July 19, 1934. This direct predecessor to the 38 Geary bus replaced a cable car line originally operated by the Geary Street, Park, & Ocean Railroad. In 1912, it became the B-Geary streetcar of MUNI, serving Ocean Beach via Geary, 33rd Avenue, and Balboa streets. In 1956, it was replaced by the 38 Geary bus, which crossed the city and went straight out Geary to Ocean Beach, though after Balboa residents protested losing their direct link to Geary. As a compromise, every third bus today follows the original B-Geary route cutting over to Balboa.

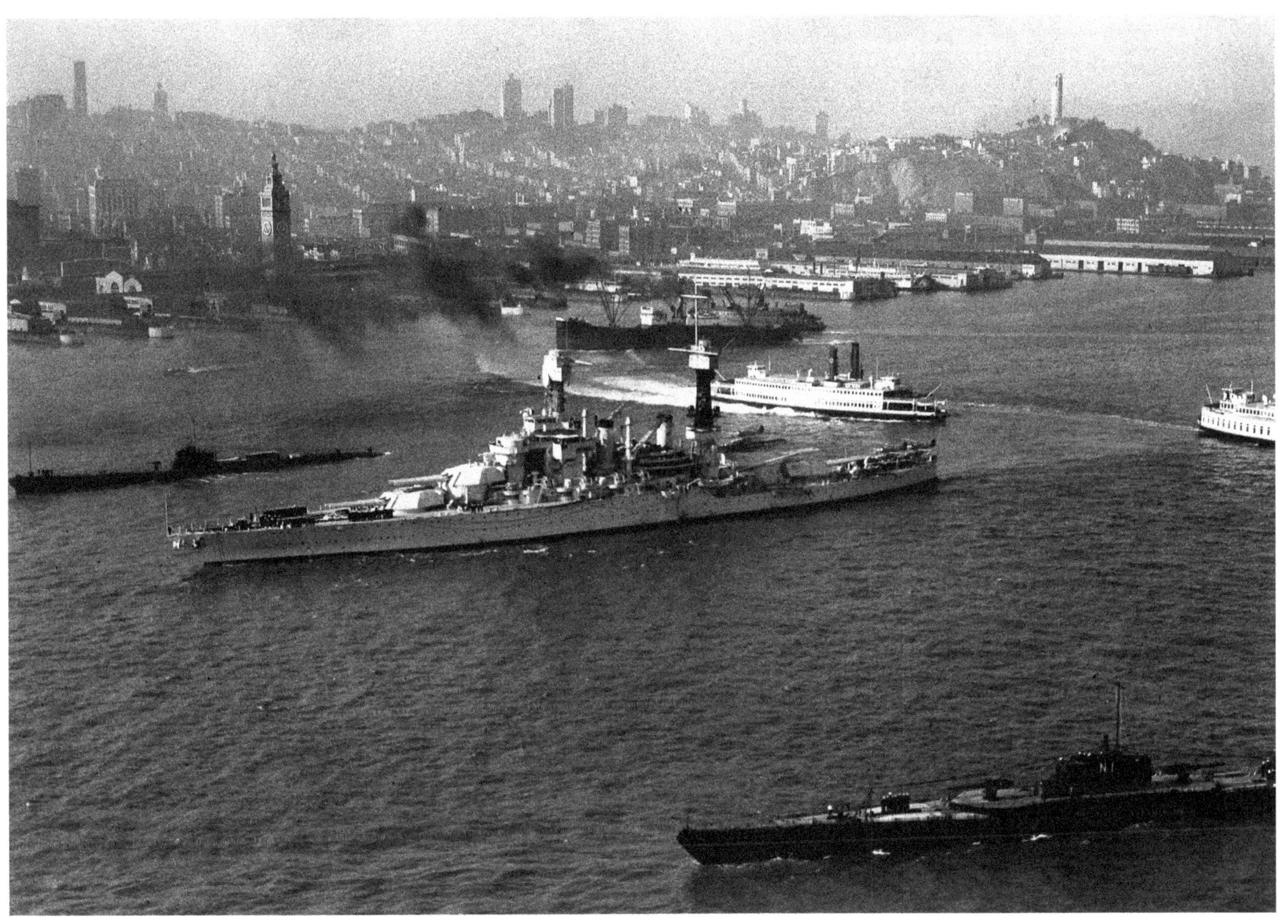

The U.S.S. *Colorado* floats in the bay flanked by two submarines, with the city visible in the background, December 8, 1934. Based in the Pacific for most of its active duty, the *Colorado* helped in the search for missing aviator Amelia Earhart in 1937.

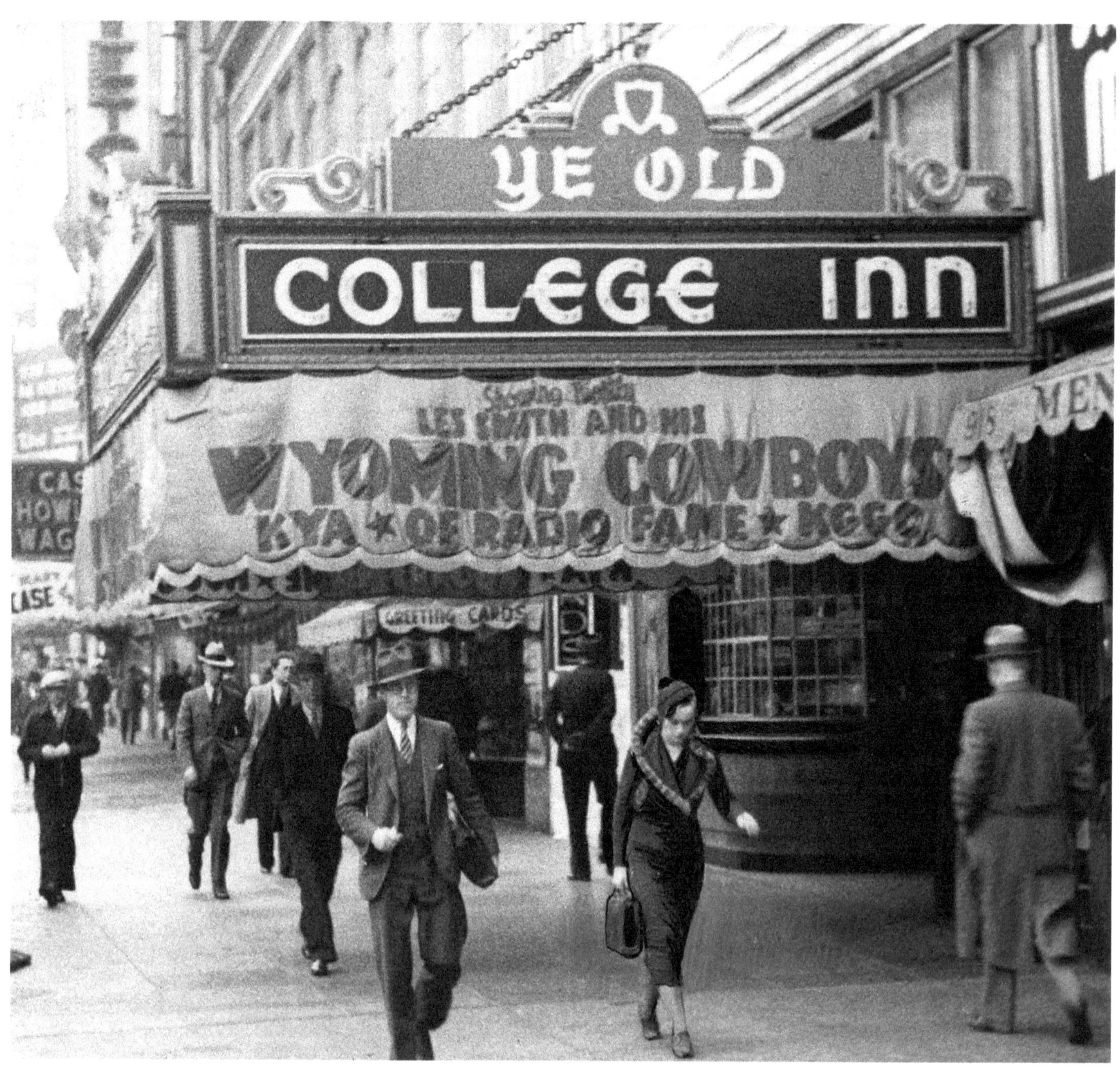

Ye Old College Inn, a San Francisco bar featuring live entertainment, is seen on February 6, 1935, before the business was closed by police.

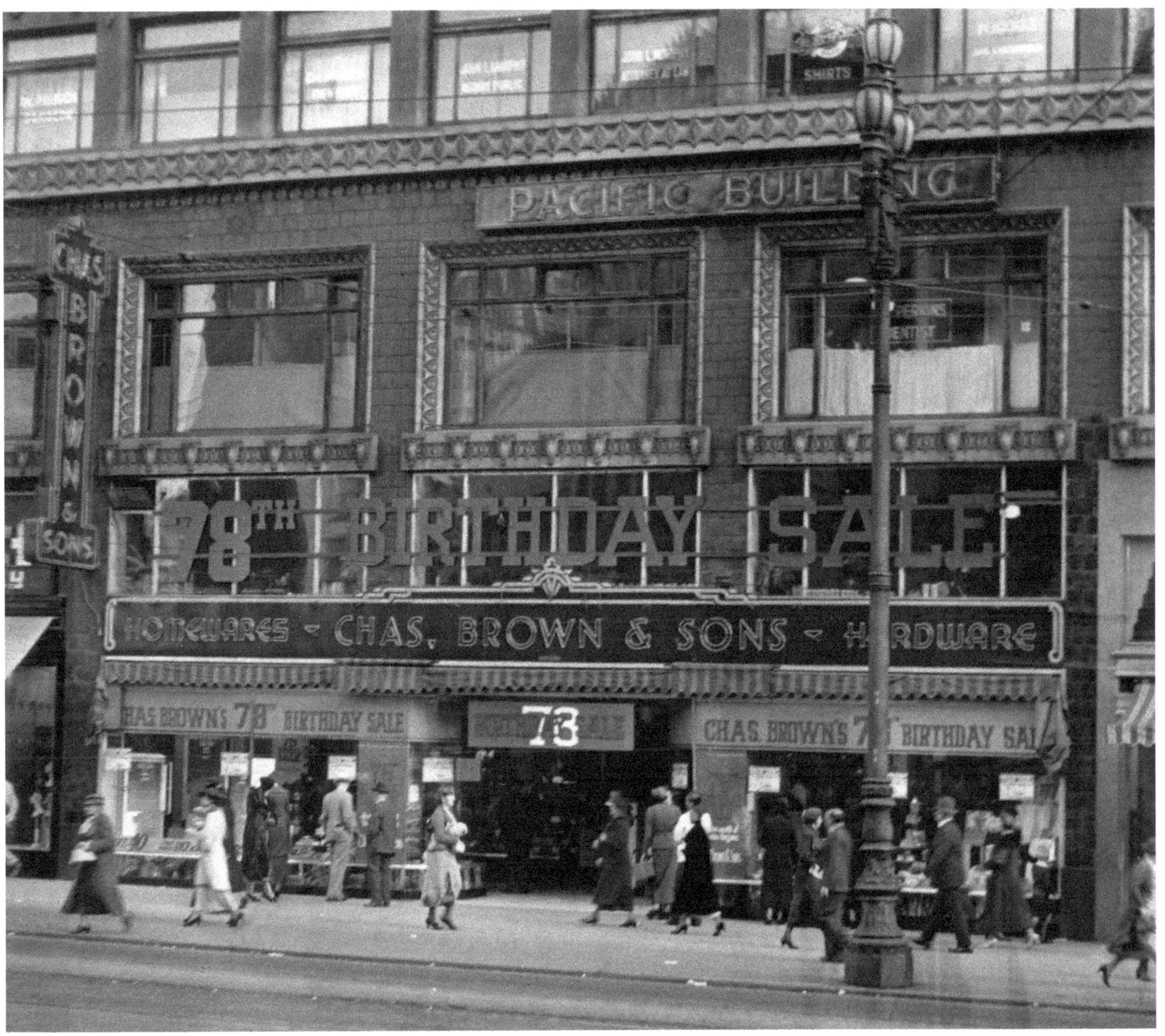

The Charles Brown and Sons hardware store at 4th and Market streets, shown here on October 14, 1935, dated back to the late 1850s.

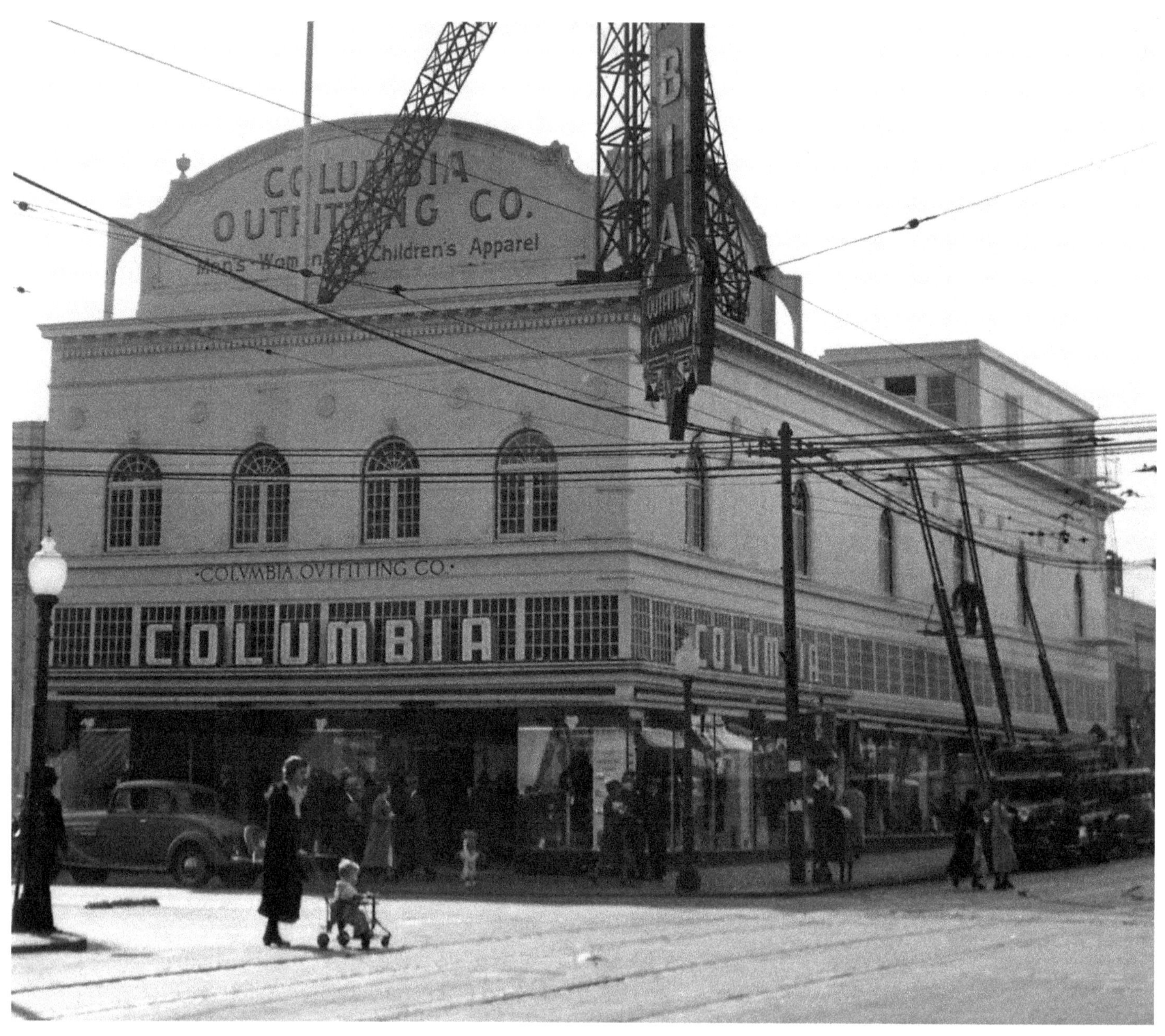

A woman pushes a baby stroller on October 14, 1935, near the Columbia Outfitting Company.

The Schmidt Lithograph Company, shown here February 28, 1936, was once the largest printing company on the West Coast. The plant housed a hospital, gardens, and handball and volleyball courts. The company no longer exists, but the clock tower of the old building remains, welcoming thousands of commuters daily at the entrance to the Bay Bridge, and giving a sense of the former industrial splendor of the South of Market area.

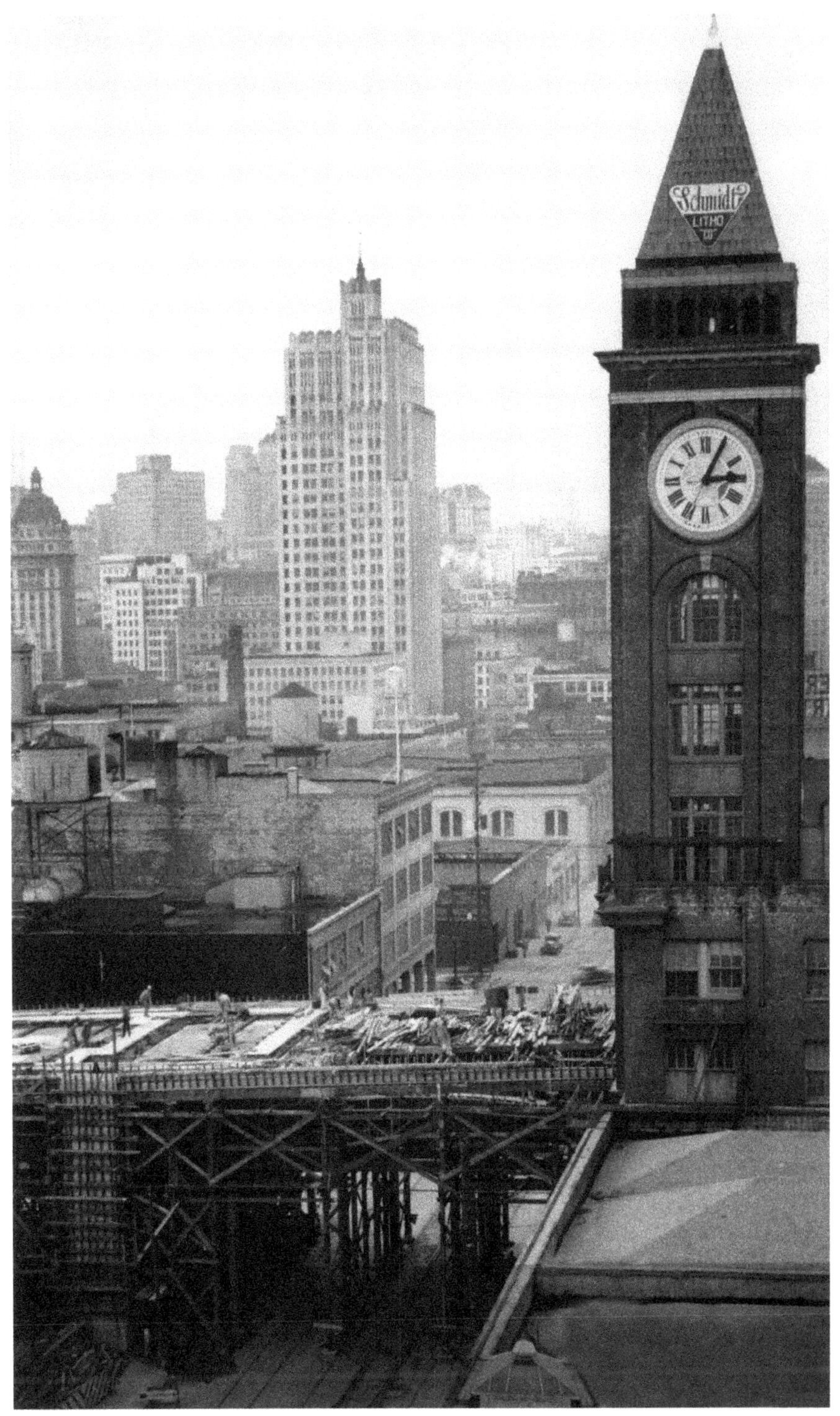

The beaux arts classicism–style U.S. Customs House Building, shown here on July 21, 1936, stands at Battery and Washington streets. Construction on the building started in early 1906 on the site of a smaller, more modest customs house, but after the earthquake, it was difficult to hire sufficient labor to finish the building on schedule. The new U.S. Customs House was not completed until 1911.

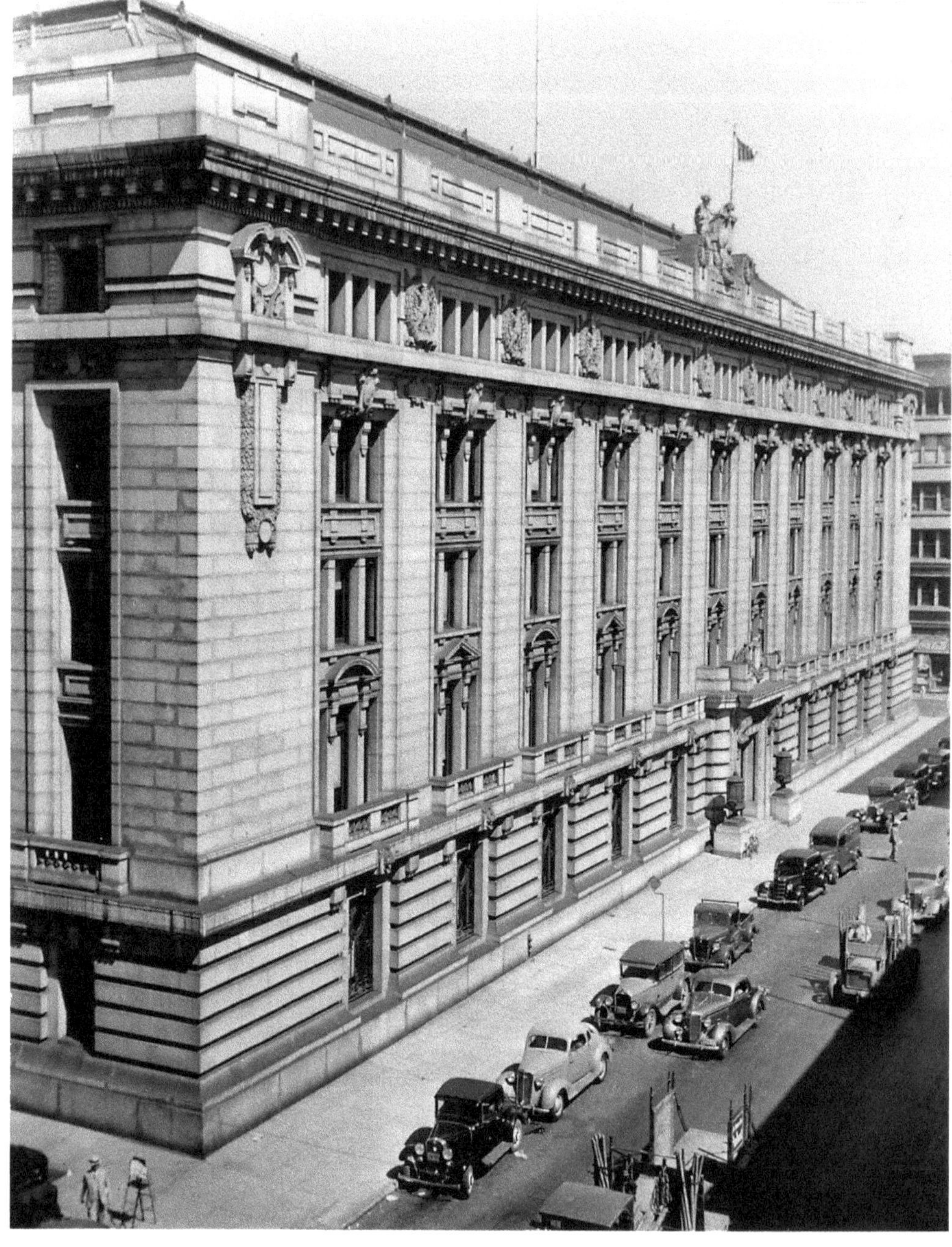

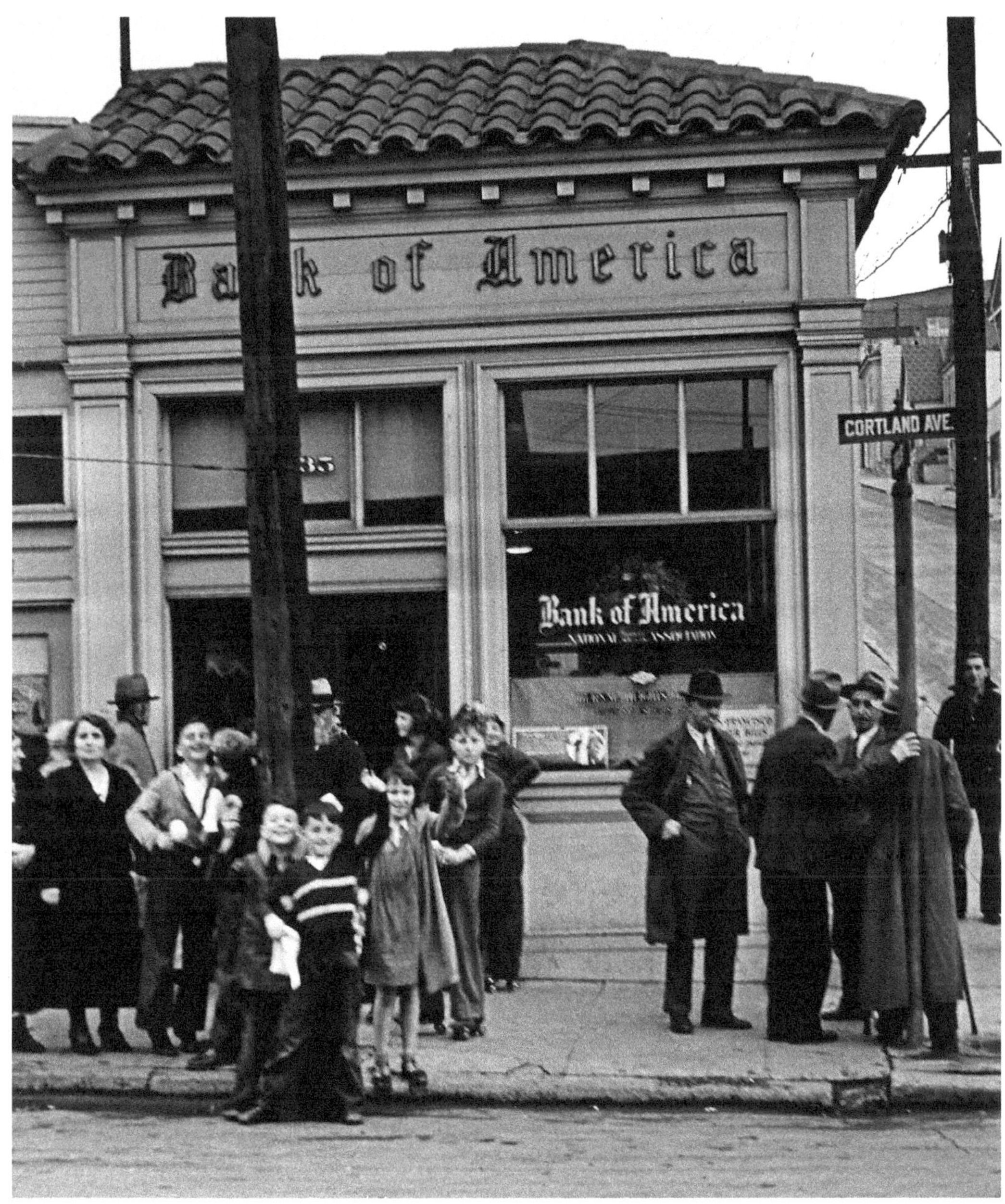

A crowd of people stands outside the Bernal Heights branch of the Bank of America, on Cortland Avenue, after a bank robbery December 24, 1936. This office almost closed in the early 1990s, but efforts by locals saved it.

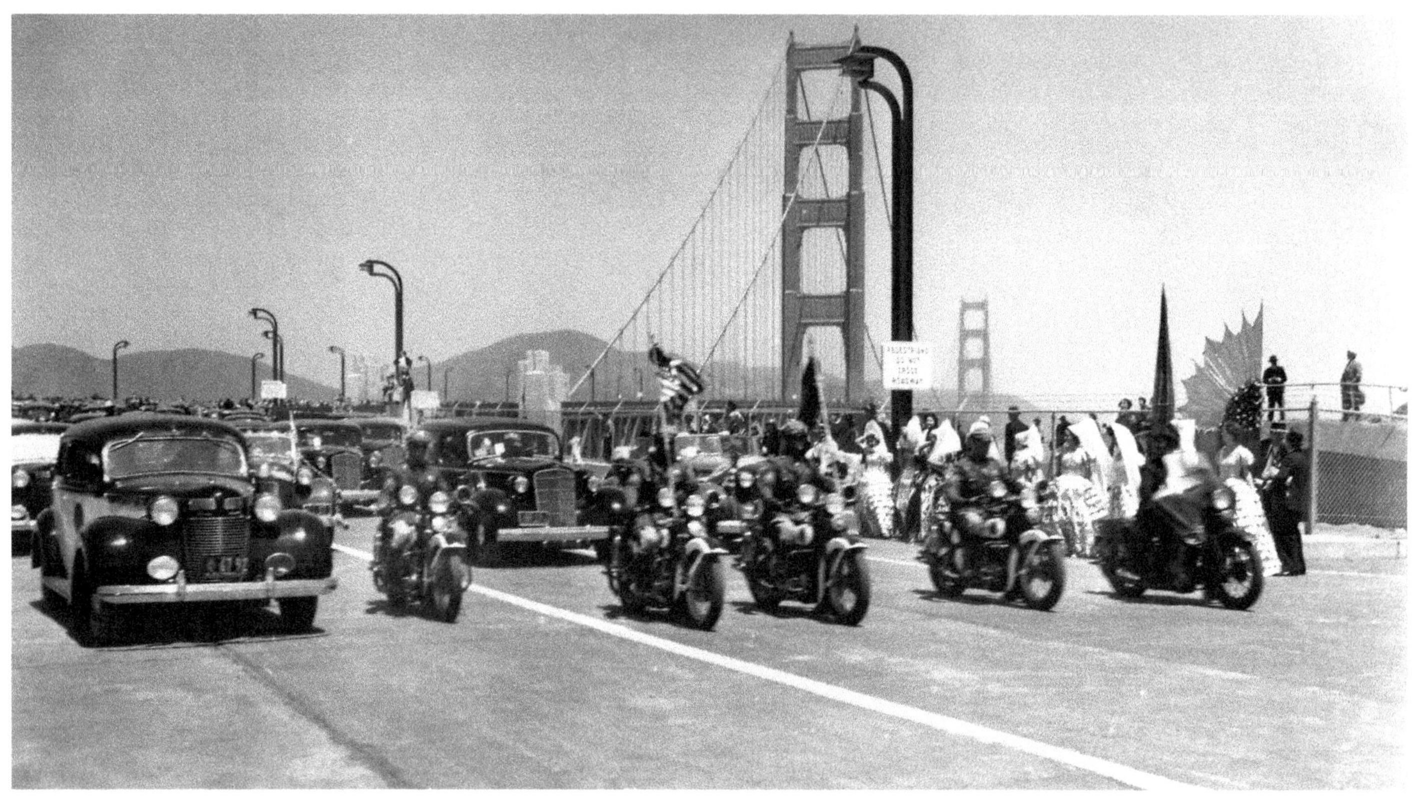

This picture shows the opening-day ceremonies of the Golden Gate Bridge, May 27, 1937. At noon on May 28, President Franklin D. Roosevelt pressed a telegraph key from Washington, D.C., signaling the official opening for vehicle traffic. This also recognized a weeklong celebration called the "Golden Gate Bridge Fiesta," which included nightly fireworks, parades, tournaments, and entertainment by the best entertainers of the day. On May 27, more than 18,000 people lined up at 6:00 A.M. to be the first to cross the new bridge, many of whom tottered across on stilts or walked backward. By midnight on May 28, 32,000 vehicles and 19,350 pedestrians had passed across.

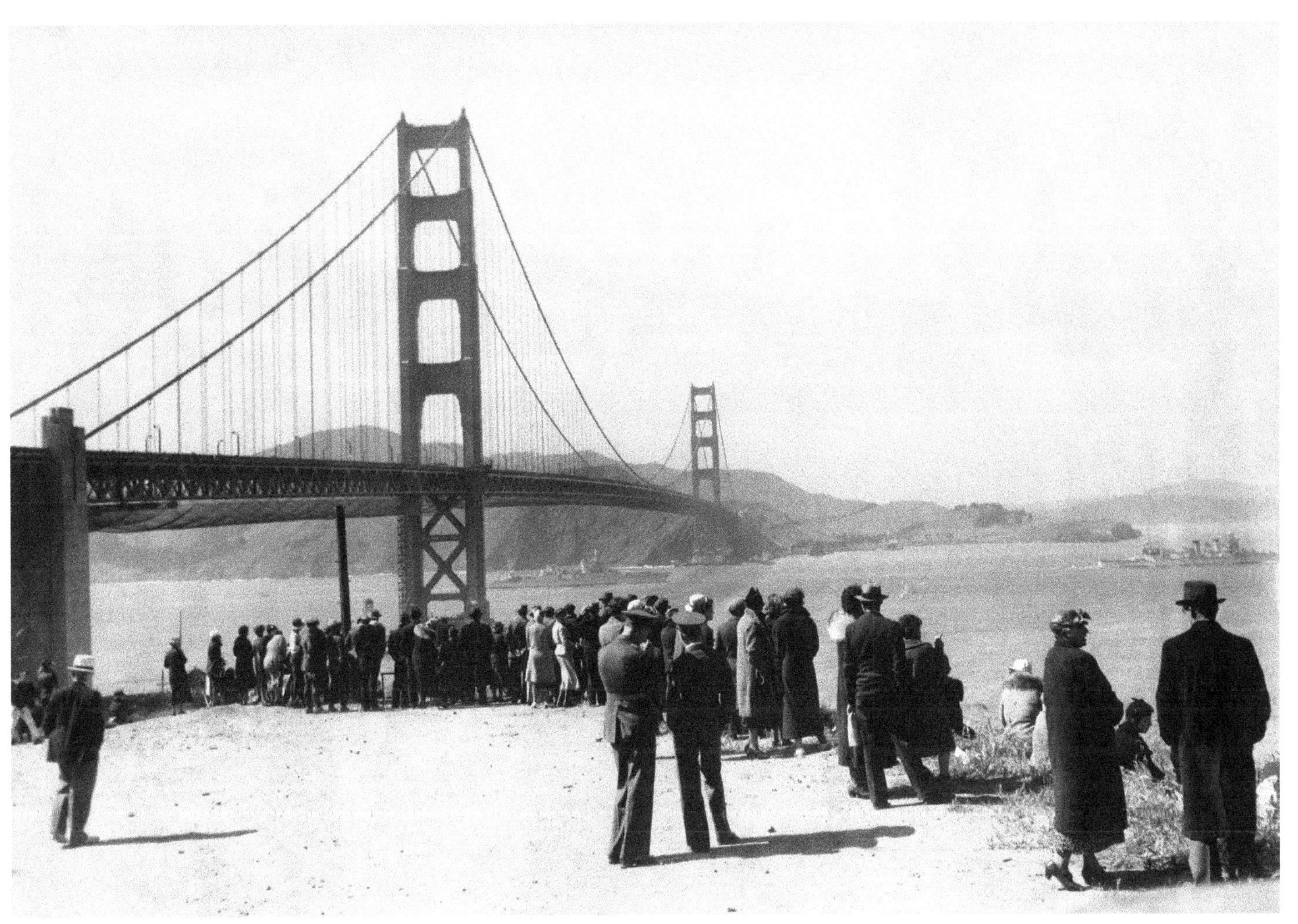

A crowd of people watches military ships enter San Francisco Bay during the Golden Gate Bridge Fiesta on May 28, 1937, as the bridge is officially ready to open. Conceived by Joseph Strauss, the majestic marvel of engineering spans 1.7 miles and connects San Francisco to Marin County. When this depression-era public works project was completed, the Golden Gate Bridge became the largest suspension bridge in the world. Painted the bold shade of "international orange" to stand out in the fog, this international symbol of San Francisco is the only road exiting the city to the north. Every day, one hundred thousand vehicles cross the Golden Gate, the most photographed bridge in the world.

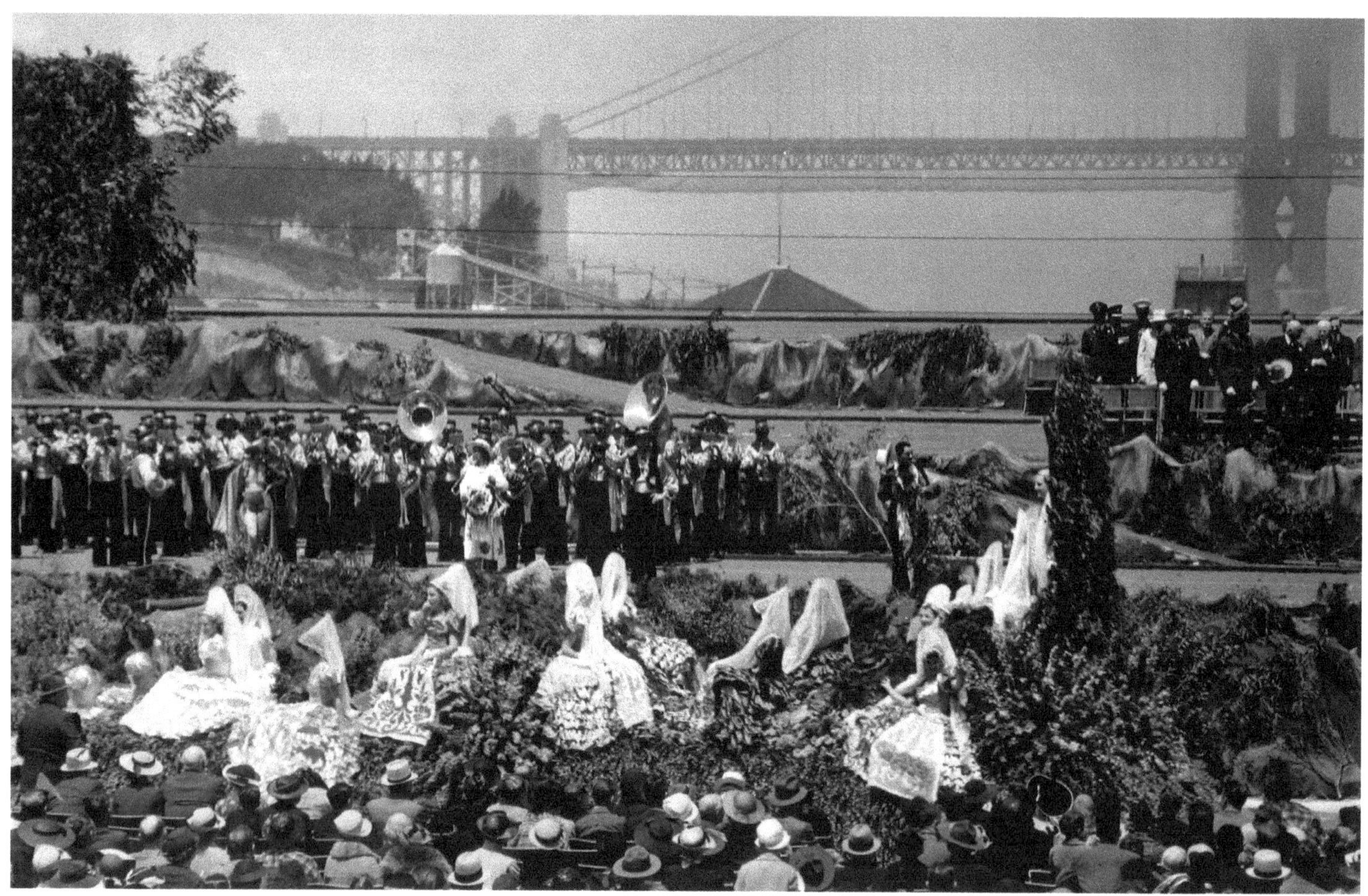

One of many events held on May 28, 1937, as part of the Golden Gate Bridge Fiesta to celebrate the opening of the bridge, a float of Fiesta Queens passes by the reviewing stand in a parade at Crissy Field.

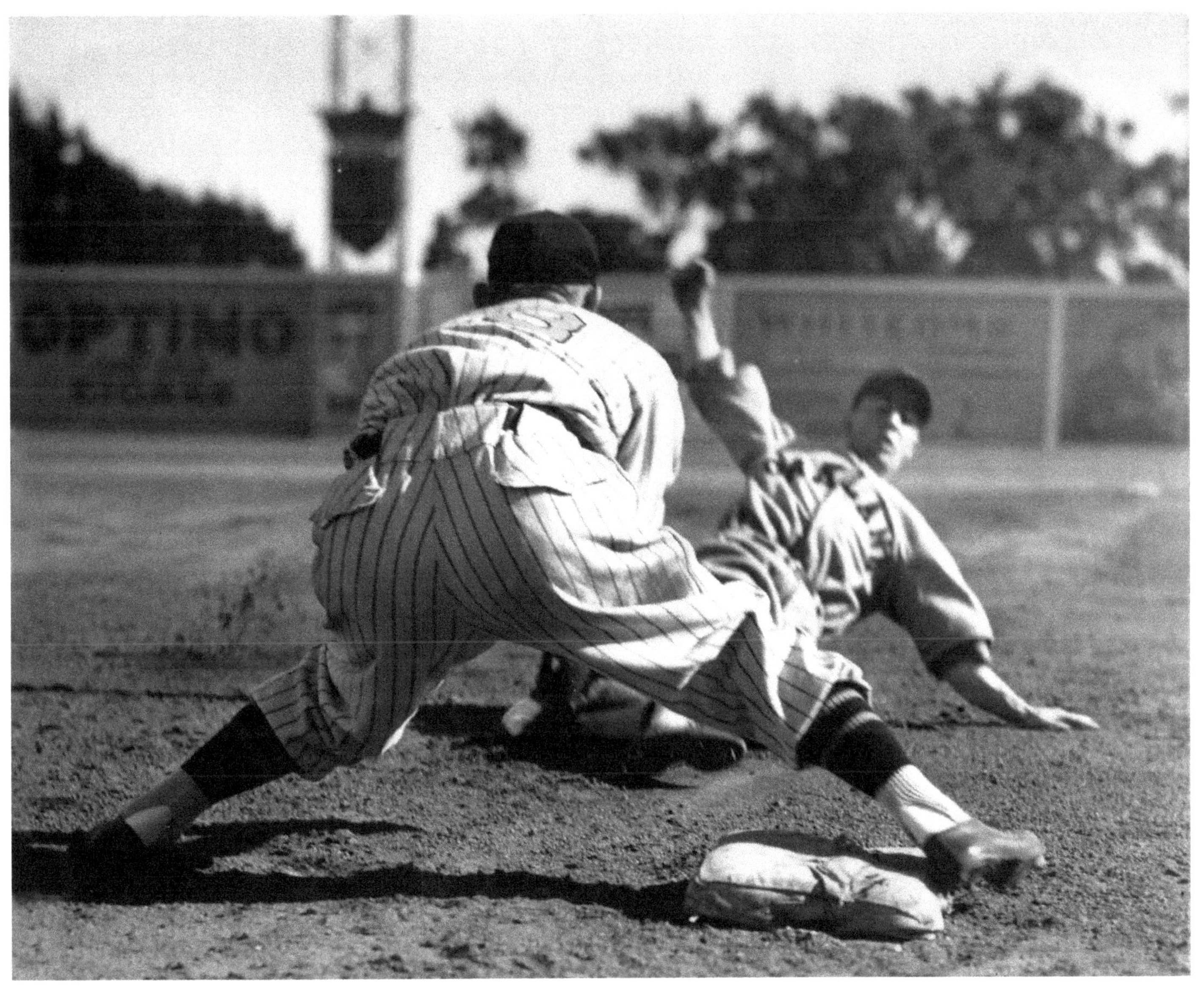

Dario Lodigiani of the Oakland Oaks slides into third base during a game with the San Francisco Seals on August 2, 1937.

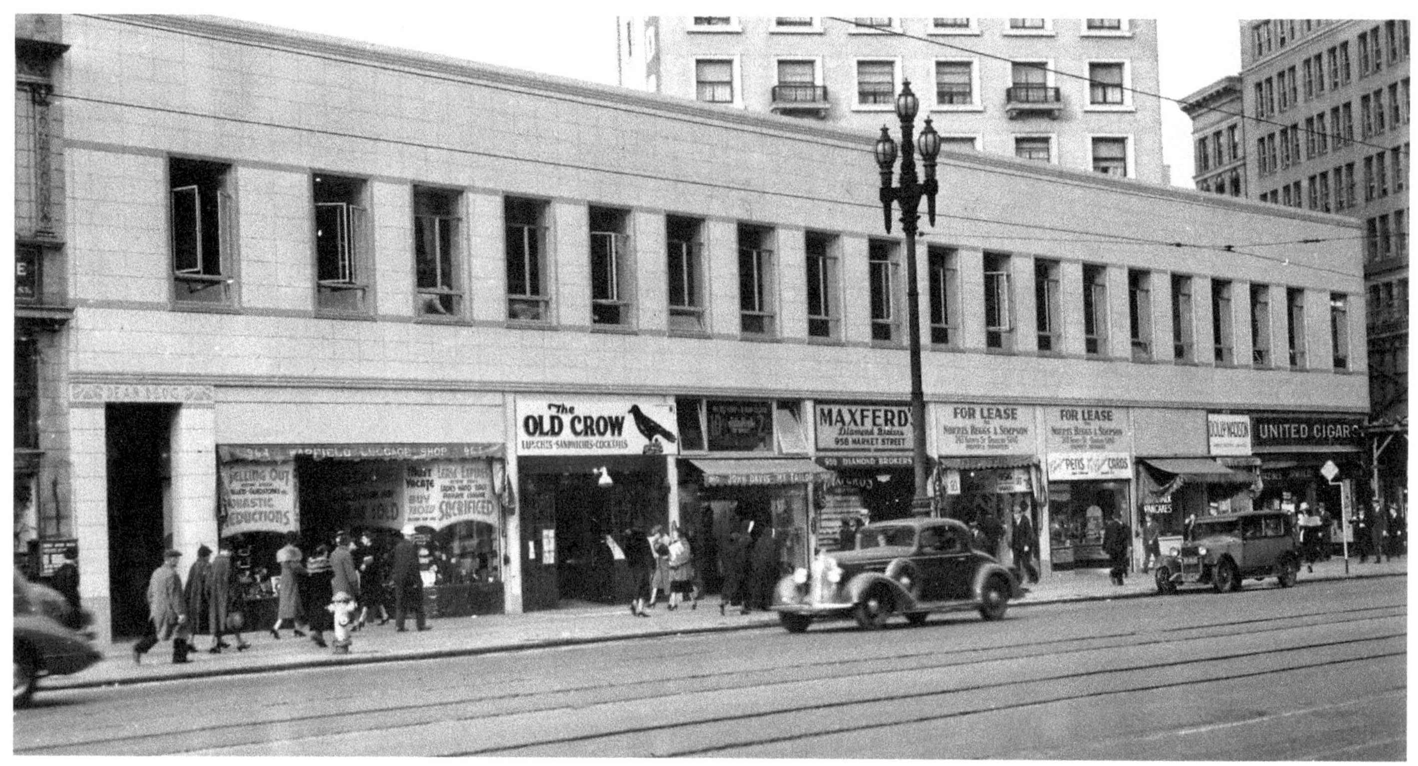

The exterior of the Dean Building at Market and Turk streets is shown here on December 11, 1937. Conspicuous by its cleanliness, this building front, renovated and newly painted, shows how business firms cooperated to improve the façades of their businesses and made their establishments more inviting during the "Start to Shine for '39" campaign.

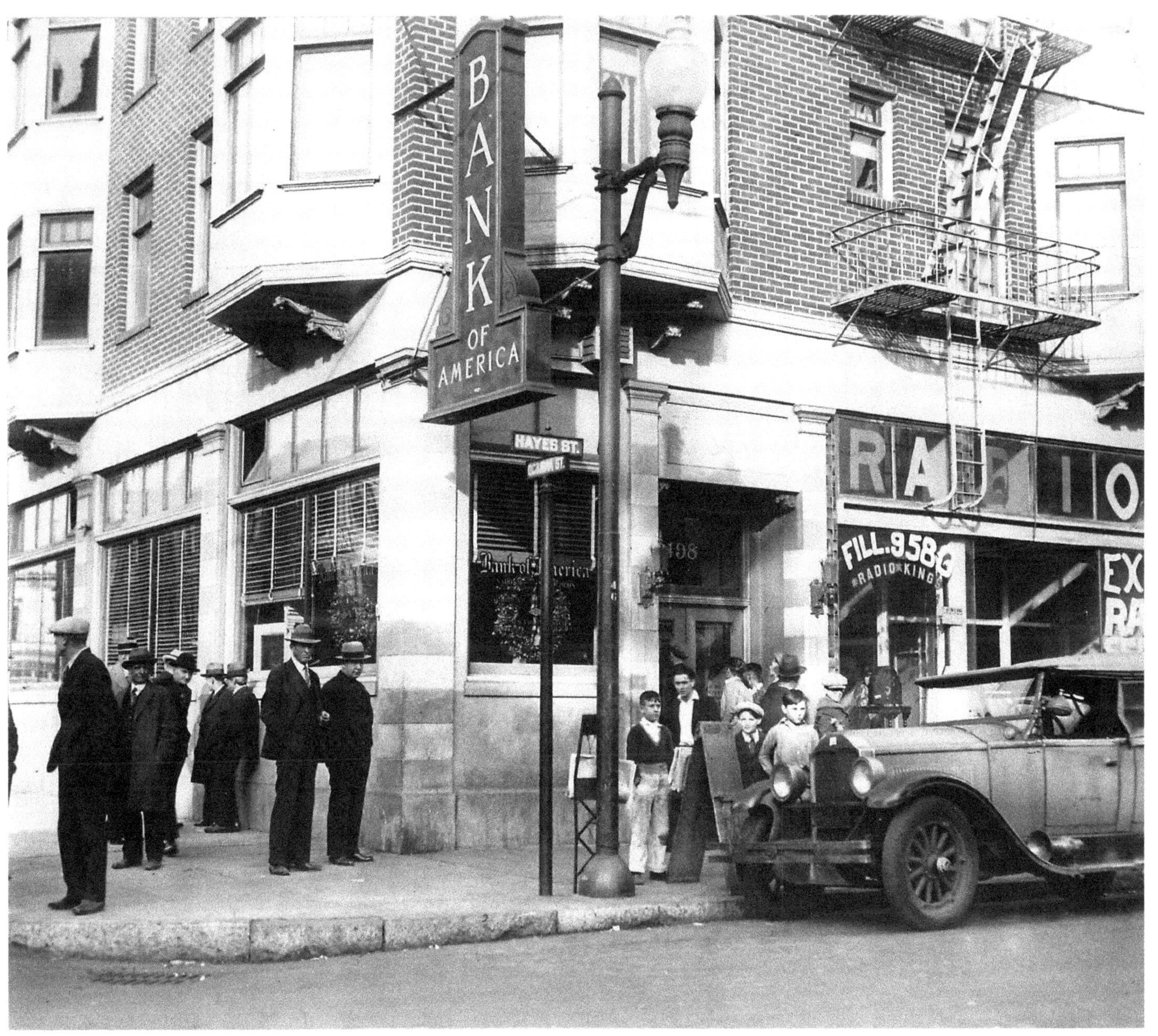

A group of people stands outside the Hayes Valley branch of the Bank of America in the 1930s.

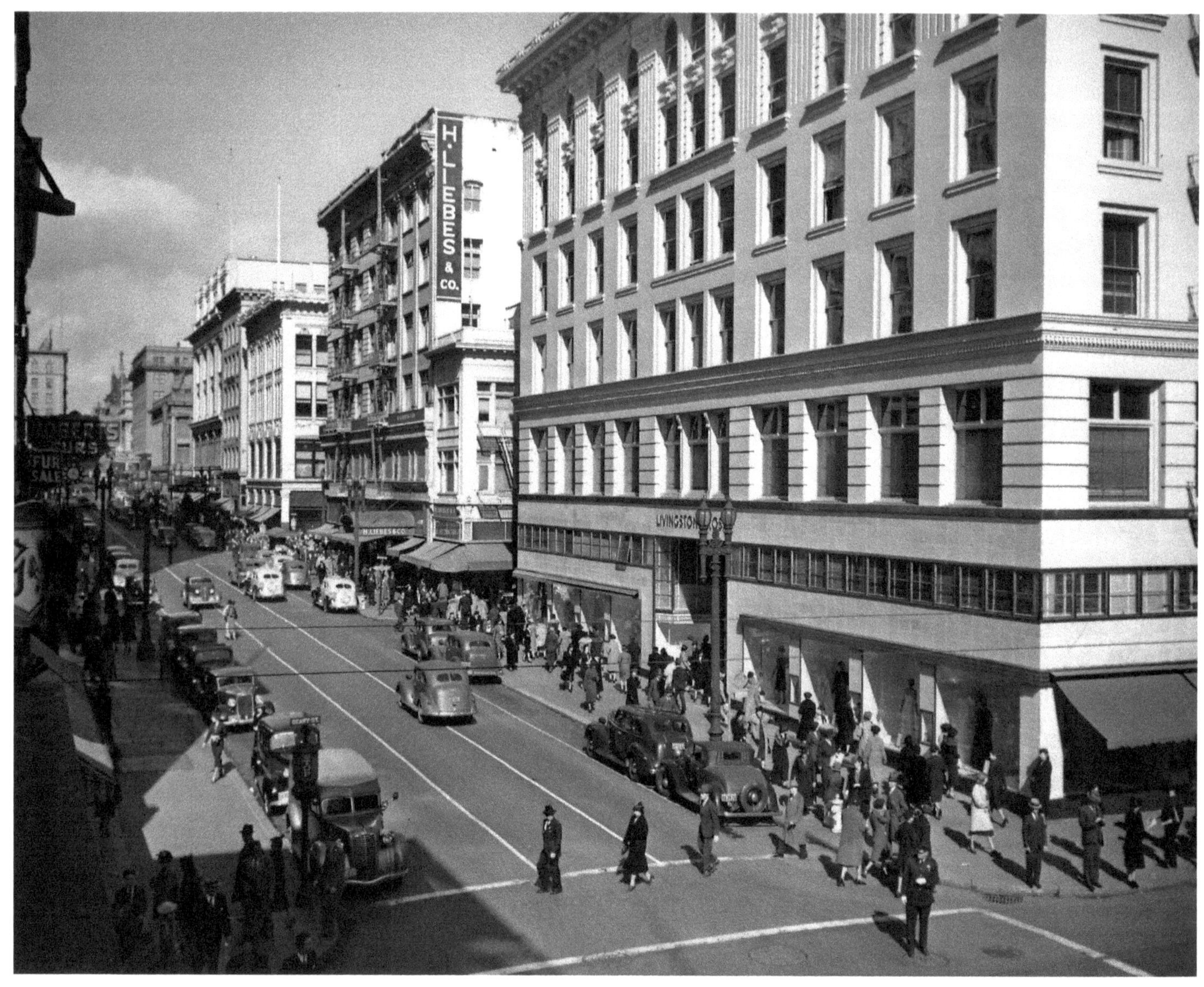

Livingston Bros., a family-owned department store in downtown San Francisco, is shown here in 1938. The store, which clothed generations of San Franciscans, closed in the 1970s.

A San Francisco Belt Train, a short-line railroad, runs along the Embarcadero in front of the Ferry Building on July 6, 1938. It began as the State Belt Railroad in 1889, and was renamed when the city bought the Port of San Francisco in 1969. With its 67 miles of track, the railroad connected the Port of San Francisco to waterfront docks and to industries and warehouses adjacent the waterfront. Its function was to switch railroad cars from four major railroads to points along its system and vice versa. Along the line south, a track along King Street (passing the location now occupied by AT&T Park) connected with the Southern Pacific. The railroad ceased operation in 1993.

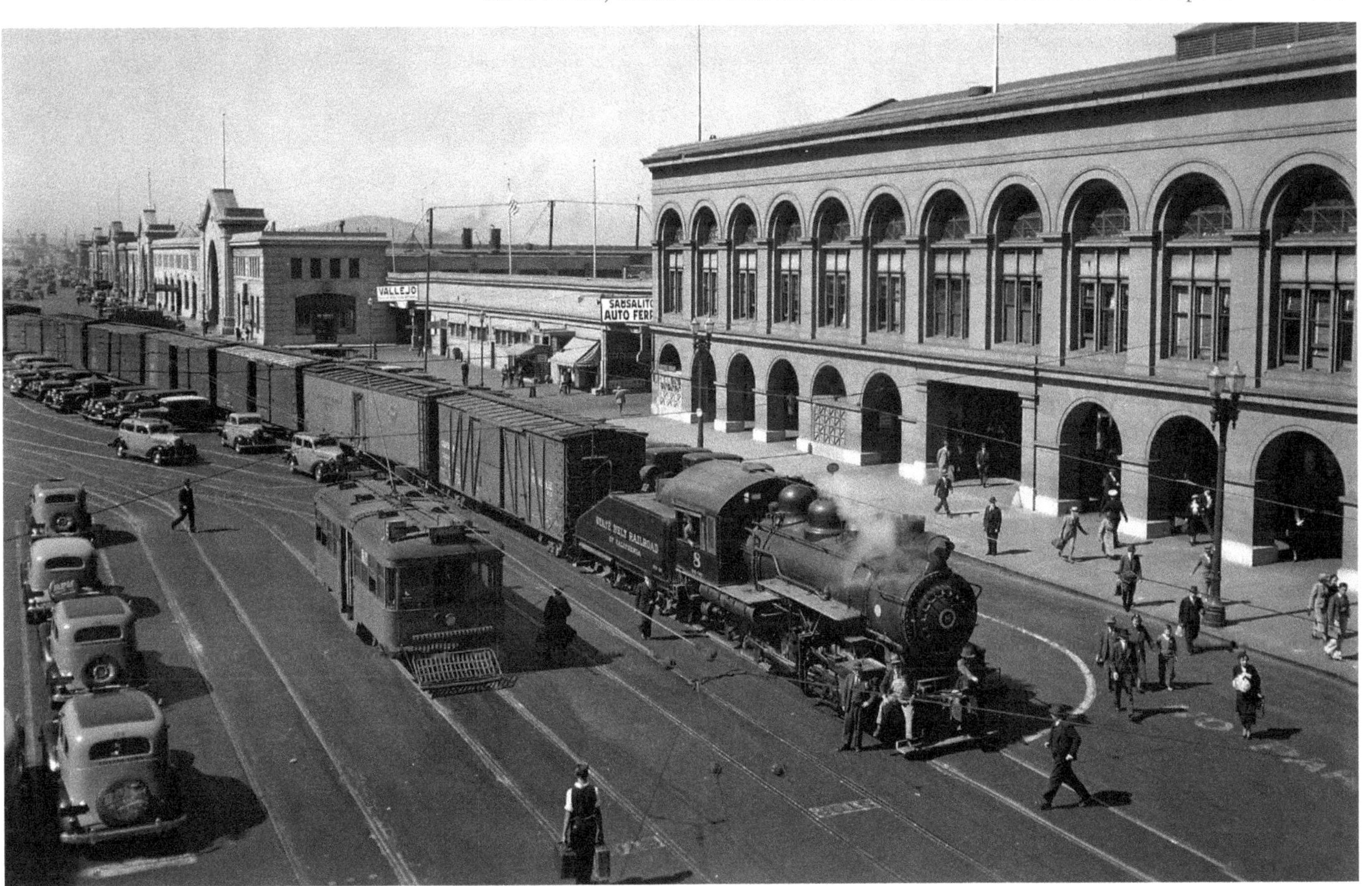

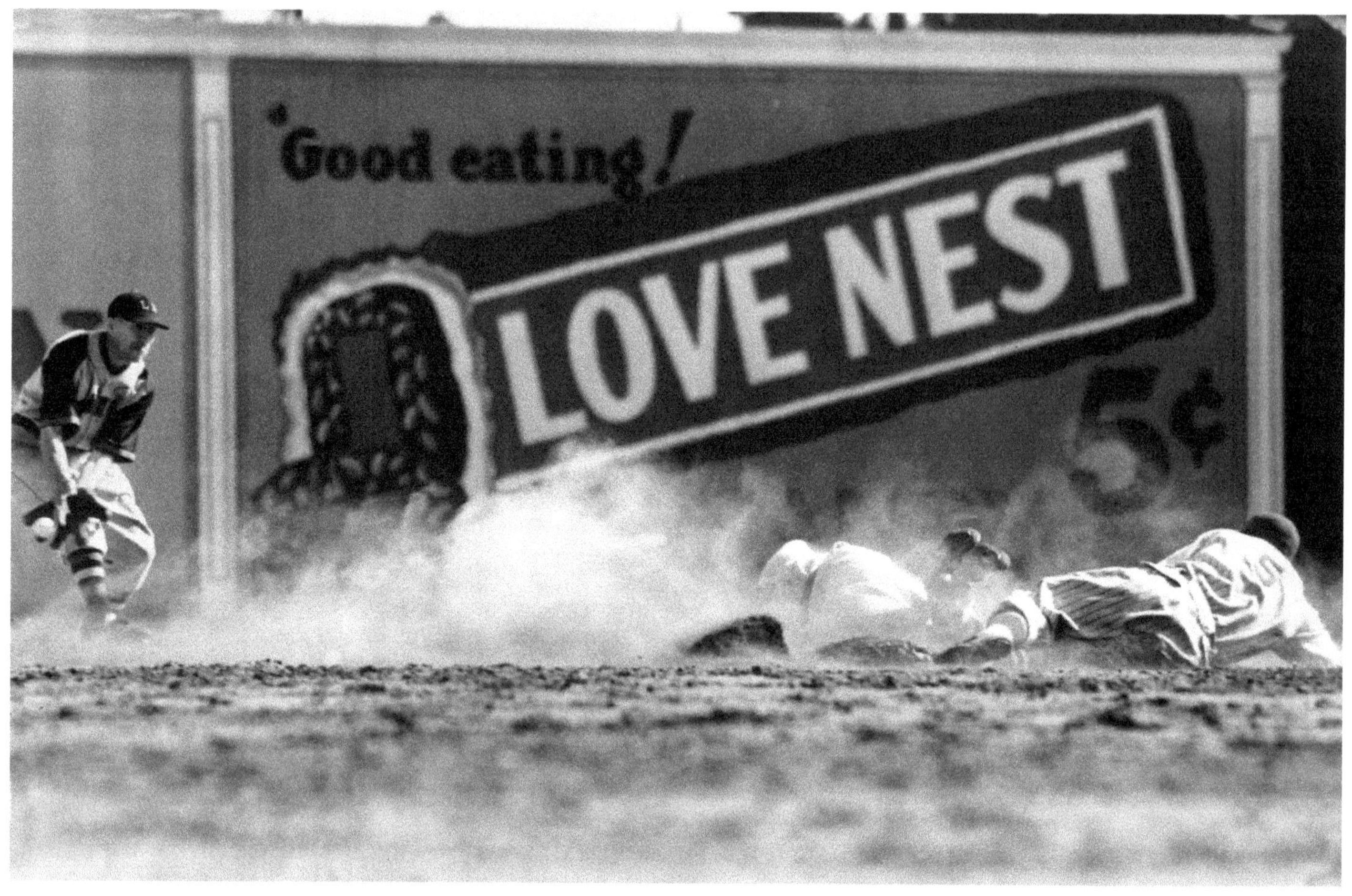

This photo shows a San Francisco Seals player stealing second base during the sixth inning in a game between San Francisco and Los Angeles at Seals Stadium on August 4, 1938. Seals Stadium was built at 16th and Bryant streets in 1931 for the minor league San Francisco baseball team of the Pacific Coast League, the Seals, and the San Francisco Missions. The Seals became the stadium's sole occupants in 1938, when the Missions moved to Hollywood and became the Stars. The Seals continued to play until the New York Giants moved to San Francisco in 1958. The Giants played in Seals Stadium for two seasons, before moving to Candlestick Park in 1960. Although Seals Stadium was demolished in 1959 and the site currently houses a Safeway grocery store and additional retail, the memory of the baseball team lives on in Lou Seal, the official mascot of the San Francisco Giants, as well as a commemorative statue along the waterfront outside AT&T Park.

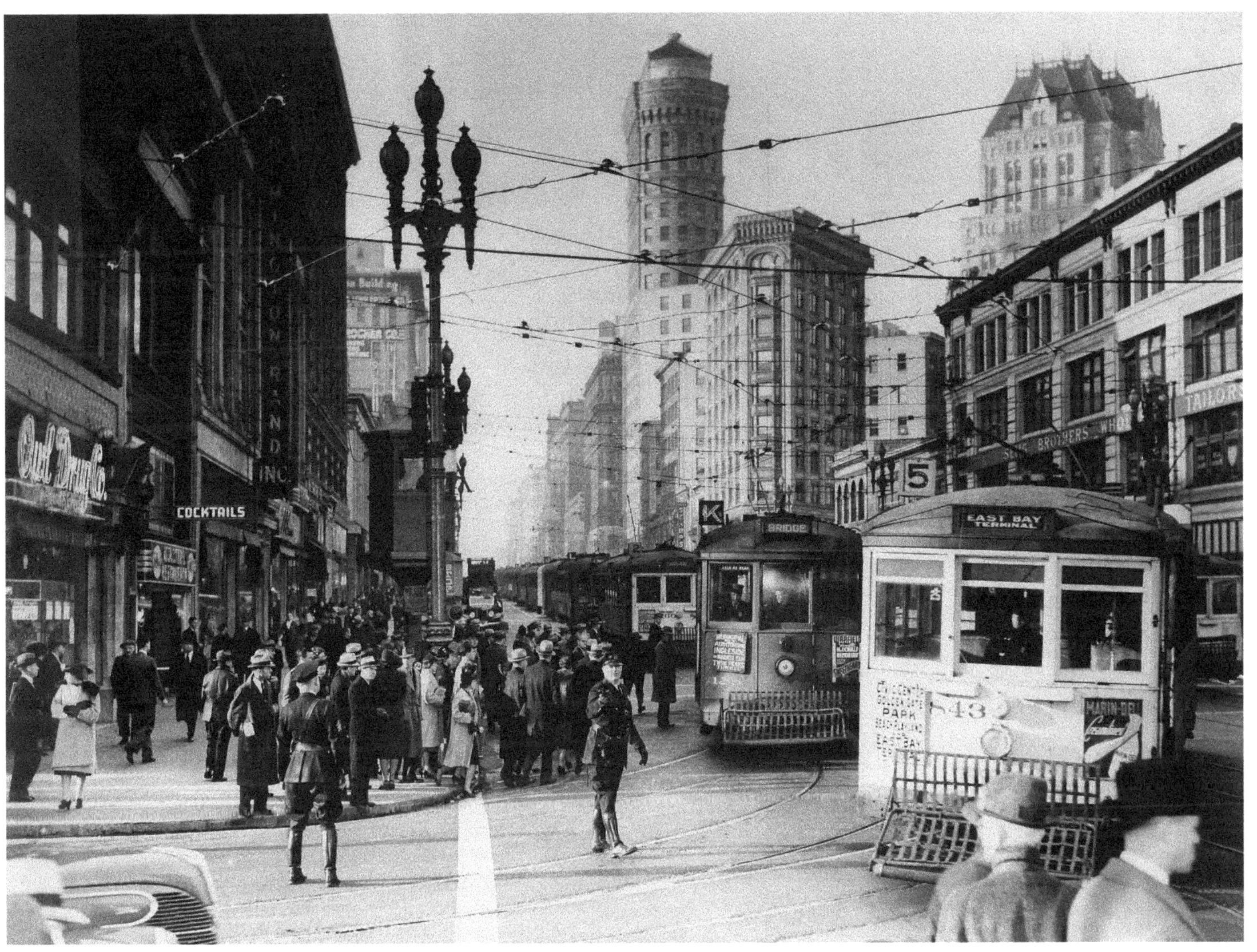

A long line of streetcars turns off Market Street en route to the East Bay Terminal, now known as the Transbay Terminal, on January 17, 1939. This was the terminus for the Key System, a streetcar system which ran on tracks on the lower deck of the Bay Bridge to points all over the East Bay. Service was discontinued in 1958, and today the system's function is covered by the BART and AC Transit systems. Currently, the Transbay Terminal serves long-distance buses and Transbay buses from San Francisco north to Marin County, east to the East Bay, and south to San Mateo County.

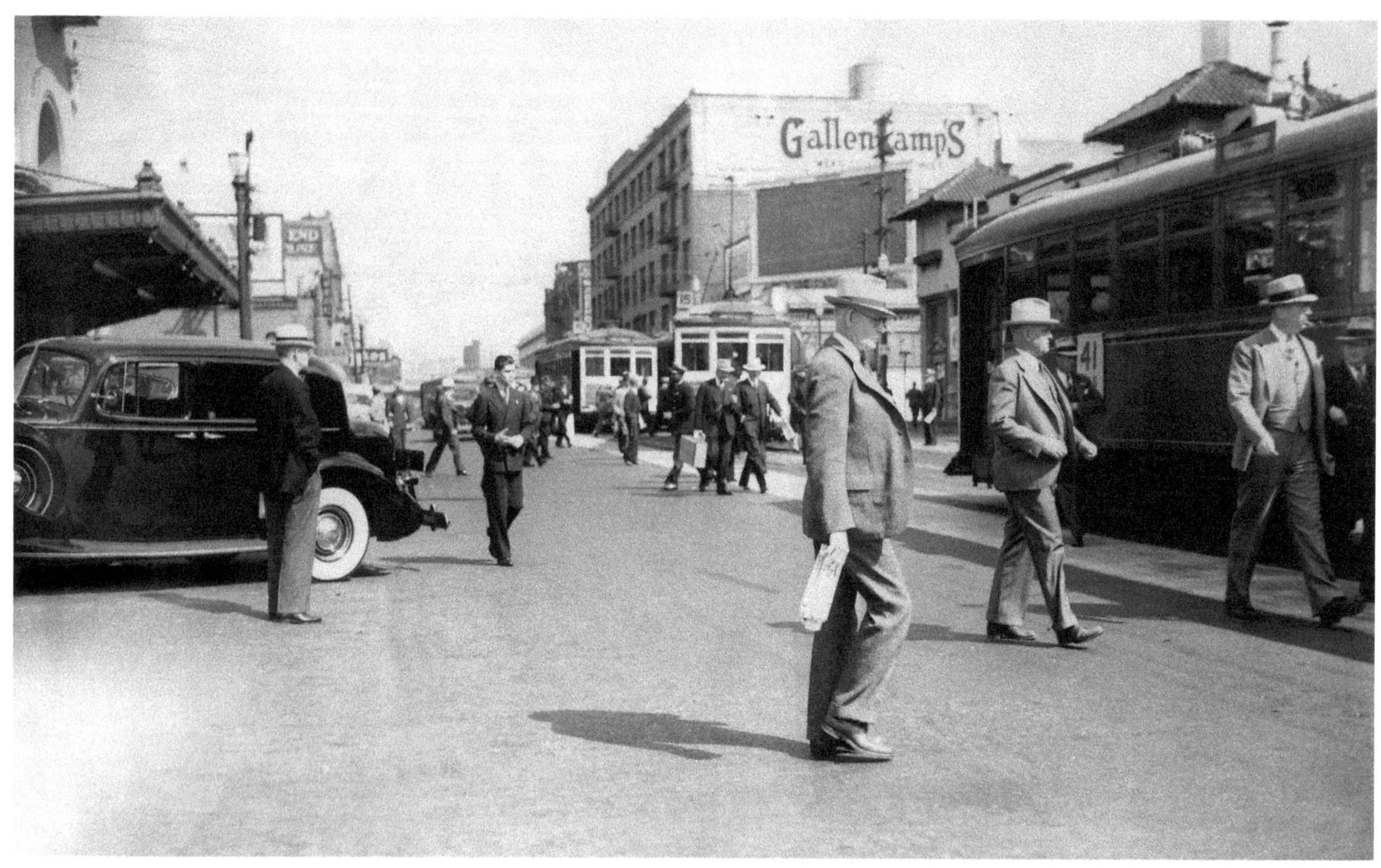

On June 14, 1939, at 3rd and Townsend streets, men dressed in suits head toward a streetcar. For many years, South of Market was a fairly industrial area, but since the mid 1990s, it has seen the construction of the San Francisco Giants new ball park, as well as many high-end condominiums, restaurants, bars, and nightlife.

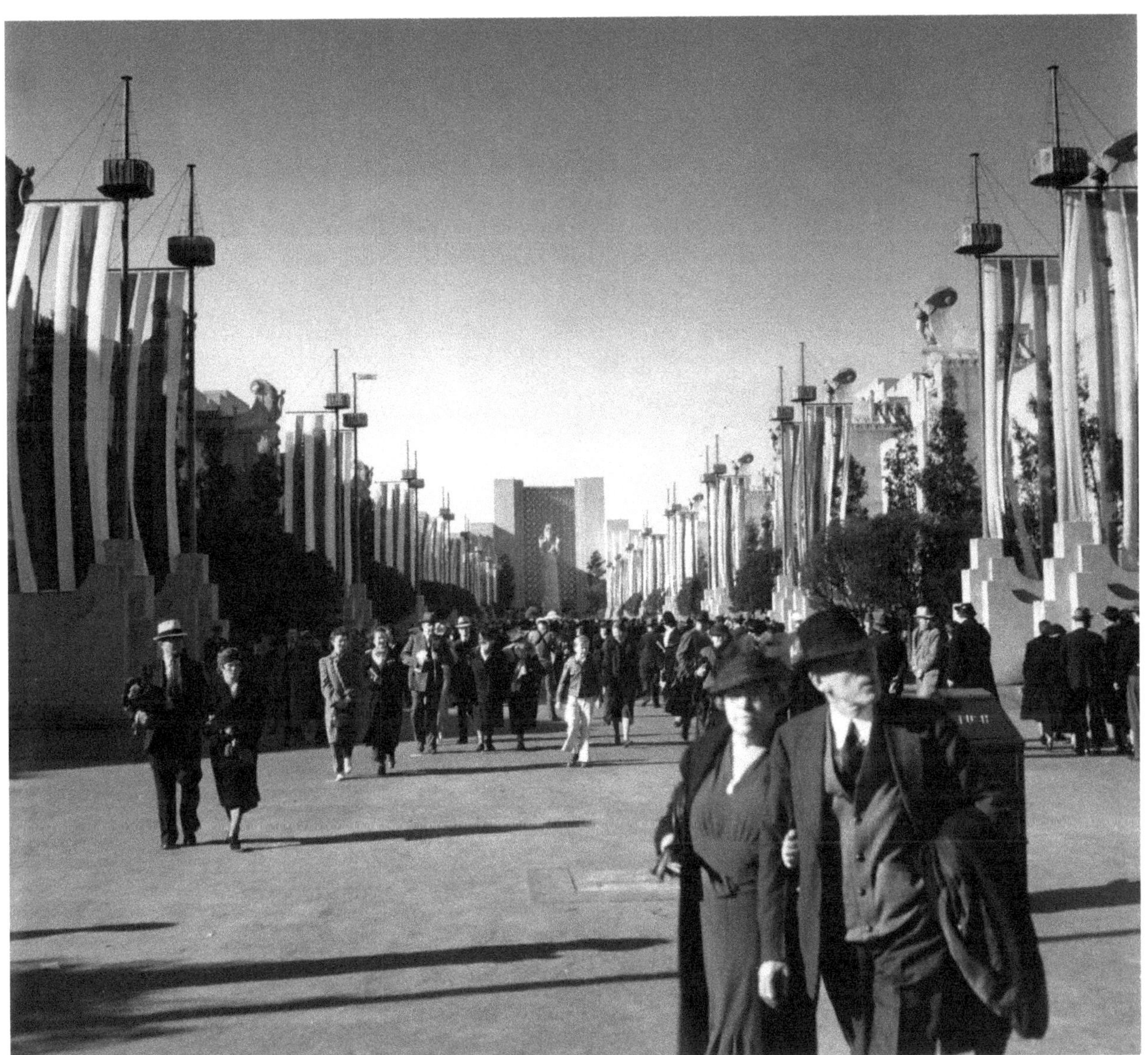

Treasure Island, shown here in 1939, was constructed as a New Deal–era WPA project to host the Golden Gate International Exposition. The massive undertaking began in February 1936 and was completed in 1939 in time to celebrate the recent completion of both the Bay and Golden Gate bridges. The 403-acre man-made island was constructed from 29 million cubic yards of sand and debris from San Francisco Bay and the Sacramento River, and 259,000 tons of rock. The exposition, themed the "Pageant of the Pacific," showcased exhibits, festivals, and music, and asserted San Francisco's rise as a strong political, economic, and cultural city in the Pacific West. It attracted many celebrities, including Irving Berlin and Judy Garland. With the start of World War II, the island was converted to a military base. Today, families rent out former officers' homes.

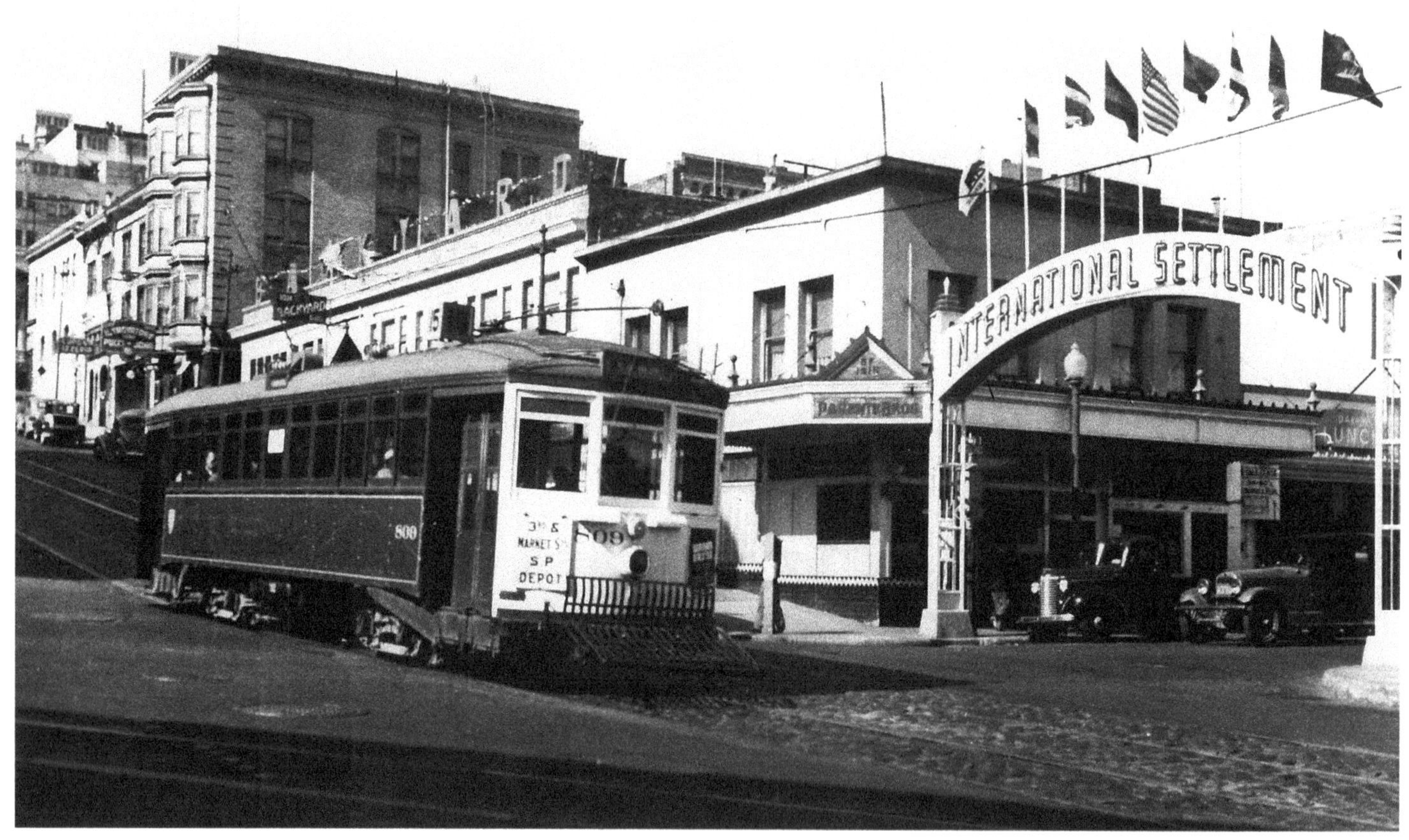

Although the Barbary Coast district tamed after the 1906 earthquake, in the 1930s and 1940s a small section of Pacific Street (today Pacific Avenue) between Montgomery and Kearny had a brief renaissance. Pictured here around 1940, the International Settlement was at its center. Contrary to its name, the area was not international, nor was it a settlement, but rather a decadent place of drinking, dancing, and prostitution. Its ambiguous and intriguing name, as well as the glittering lights and blasting music, drew in men before and during World War II. Pacific Street became known as "Terrific Street" and was so busy that cars could not pass. It was not uncommon to see bar scuffles spilling into the street. Some of its most notorious establishments included the Moulin Rouge, Sahara, Gay N'Frisky, Pago Pago, Spider Kelly's, Bela Pacific, and Arabian Nights.

Wartime Boom

(1940–1949)

At the start of the forties, San Francisco still felt like a frontier town in many ways, and was proud of its animated past. On December 7, 1941, came another turning point in San Francisco, and world history. The moment that Japan attacked the U.S. naval base at Pearl Harbor and propelled the United States into World War II, San Francisco was transformed from a city blissfully isolated from the diplomatic crises in Washington and the armed conflicts abroad into the subject of worldwide attention. Immediately, San Franciscans congregated en masse on Ocean Beach and looked out to the vast Pacific, wondering if perhaps their city would be the next target of war. Within hours of the news from Hawaii, the city declared an official state of emergency, and its citizens were forced to quickly learn to adapt to wartime life as a key military depot in the Pacific Theater.

Anxiety and paranoia gripped San Francisco in the early forties, because, following several decades of neutrality, the city was caught off guard and unprepared for war. Public figures made forceful and patriotic statements in an effort to unite the community, and military officials began aggressive campaigns to rid the area of anyone who could hurt them from within. As the city mobilized, its citizens, like the rest of the nation, were intensely patriotic, raising war bonds and participating in rationings, and at last, were ready for war.

It took a World War to truly shake the country out of the Great Depression. The war created millions of jobs, many of which, especially shipbuilding, were based in the San Francisco Bay area. Indeed, the city's population would significantly expand and diversify as California once again became a land of opportunity and a leading destination, drawing men and women from around the nation to work in the war industry.

When the war finally ended in 1945, San Francisco hosted the U.N. World Charter of Security, and the nation and the city were ready for peace.

The Orpheum Theatre in 1940, featuring the "wild" and "untamed" movie *Cimarron* starring Richard Dix. Built in 1926 at the corner of Hyde and Market, to resemble a Spanish-style palace, the theater showcased a variety of entertainment, from musical comedy to vaudeville to movies, and is still in operation today.

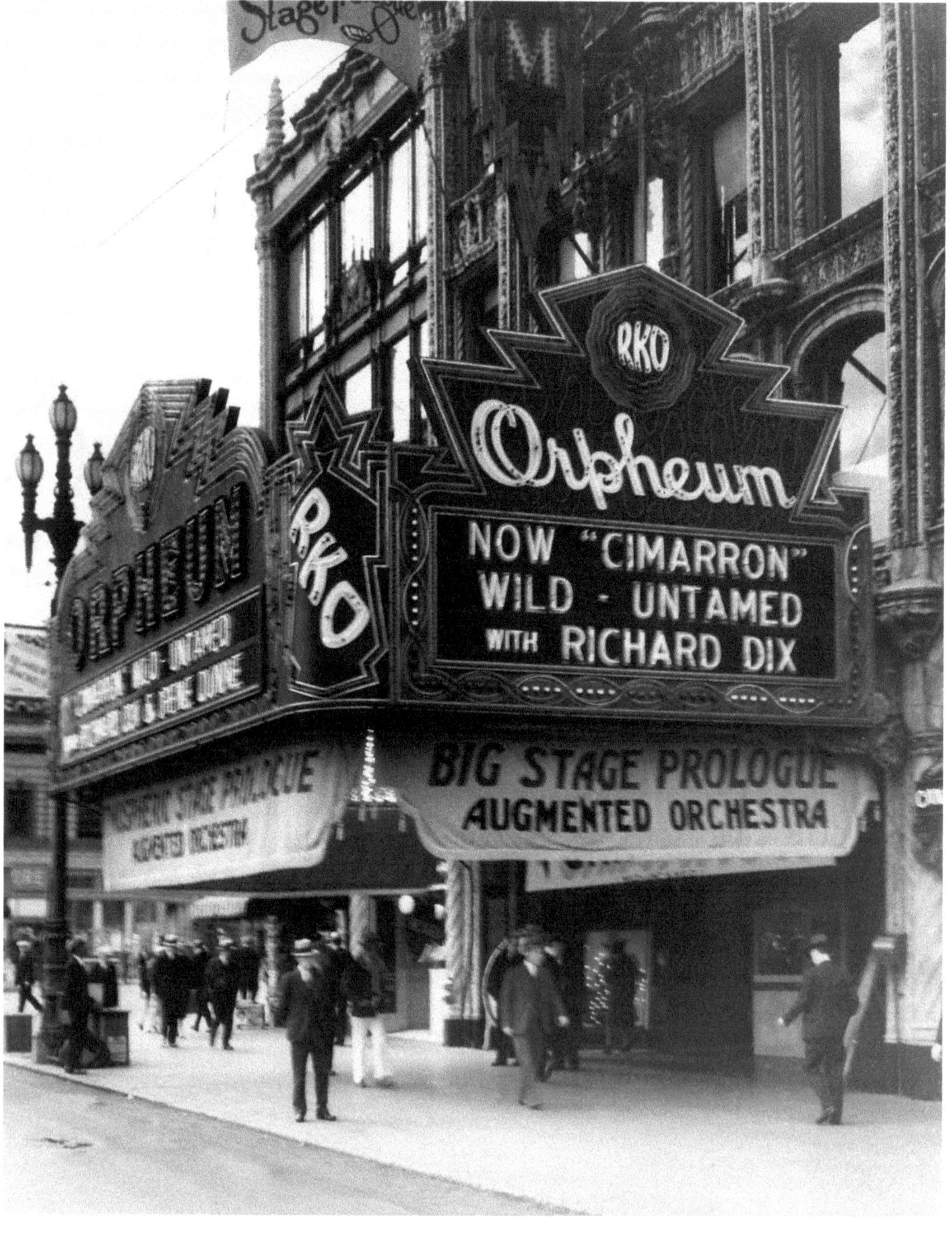

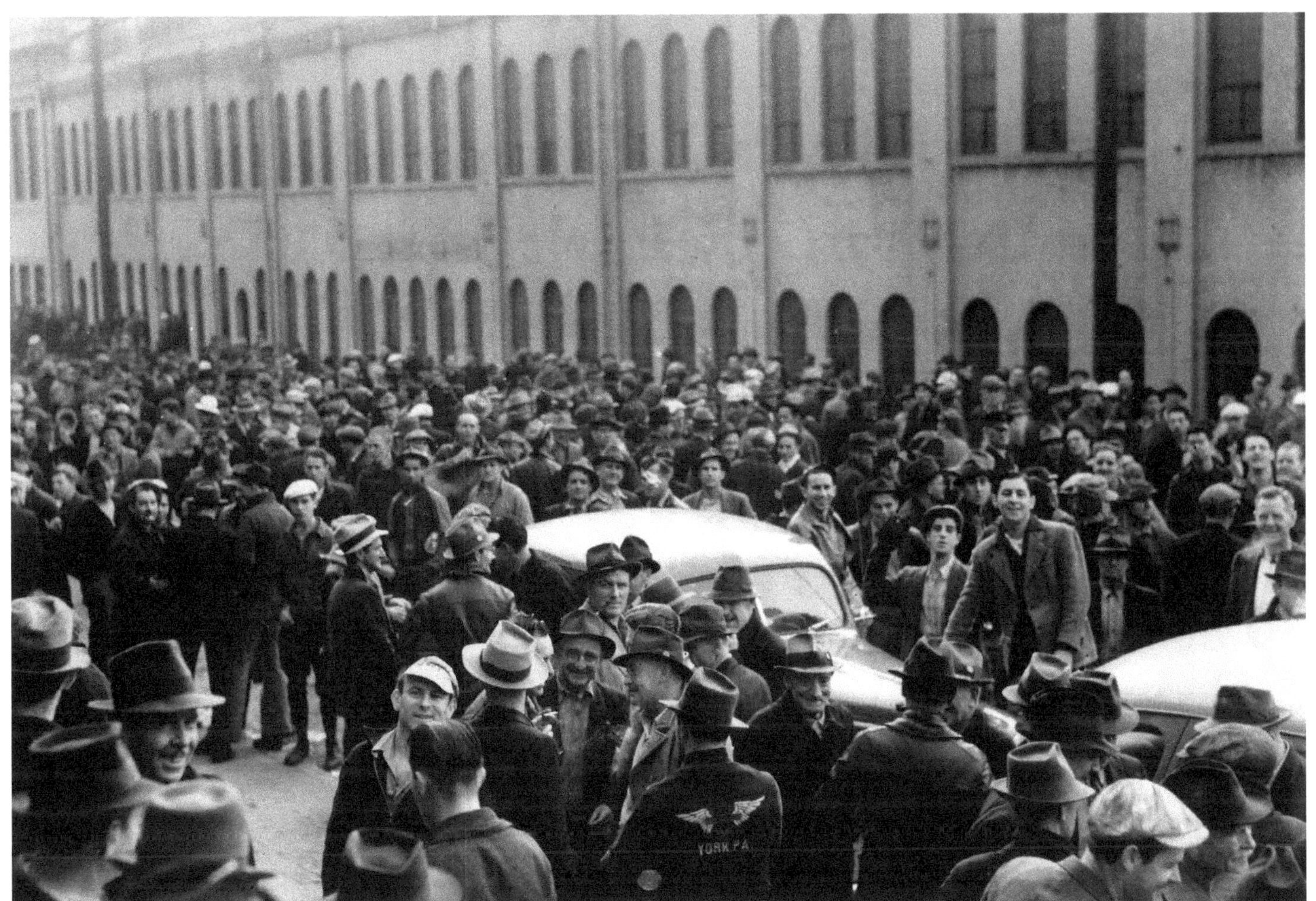

Shown here on January 17, 1941, at 20th and Illinois streets in Portrero Hill is the exterior of the Bethlehem Steel Company, one of the largest ship-building companies in the world. Over 35,000 workers gathered for a union dispute that day. The conflict was eventually settled, after a few fist fights, and tying up San Francisco shipyards for more than five hours.

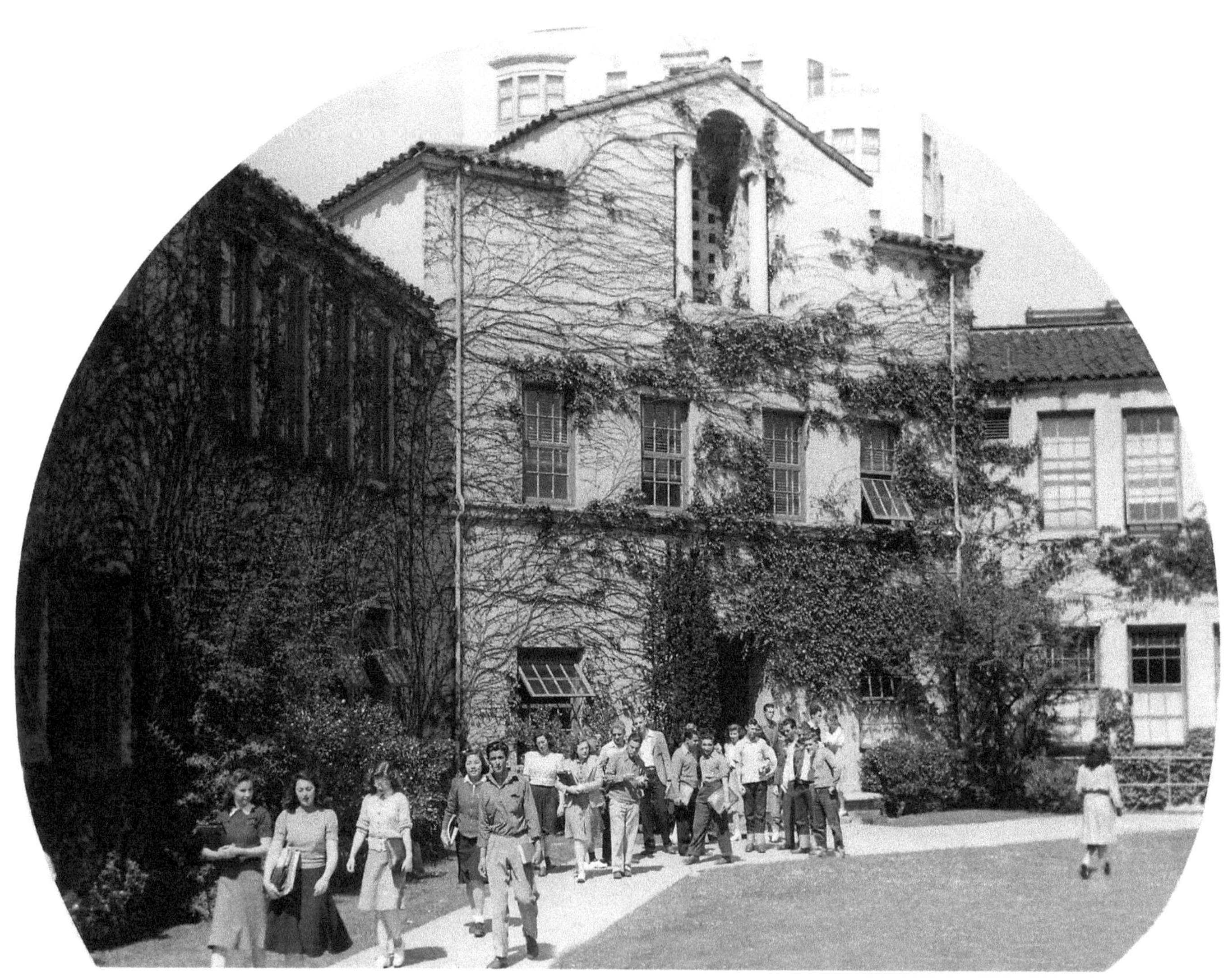

Students socialize on the old campus of San Francisco State College, at Buchanan and Haight streets on March 29, 1941. In 1953, the college moved to its present location near Lake Merced, and after receiving university status in 1972, it was renamed San Francisco State University in 1974.

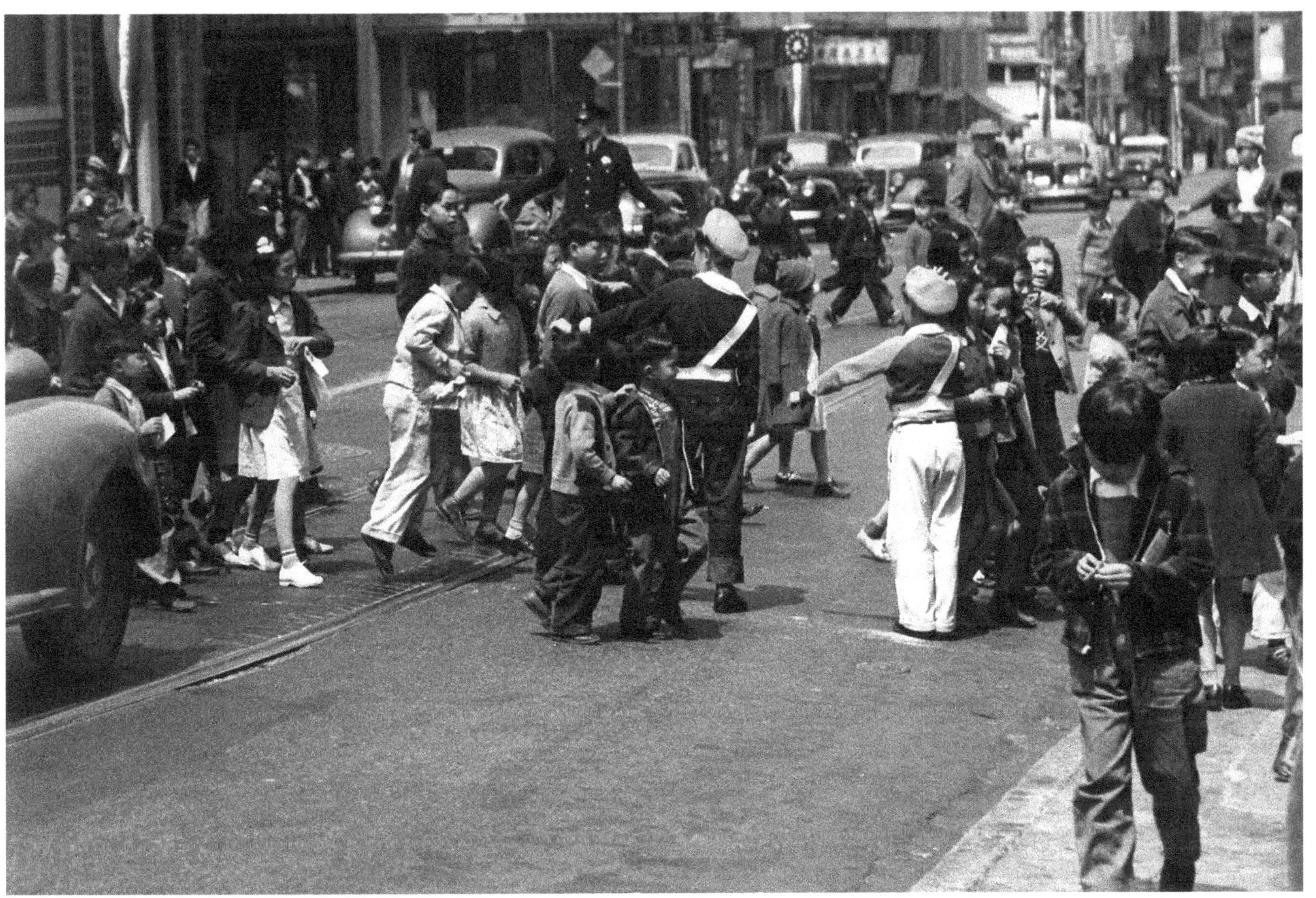

On May 1, 1941, a junior traffic patrol guides Chinese schoolchildren across the intersection of Washington and Stockton streets in Chinatown during their noon recess. After the founding of this traffic patrol, no child was killed at that intersection.

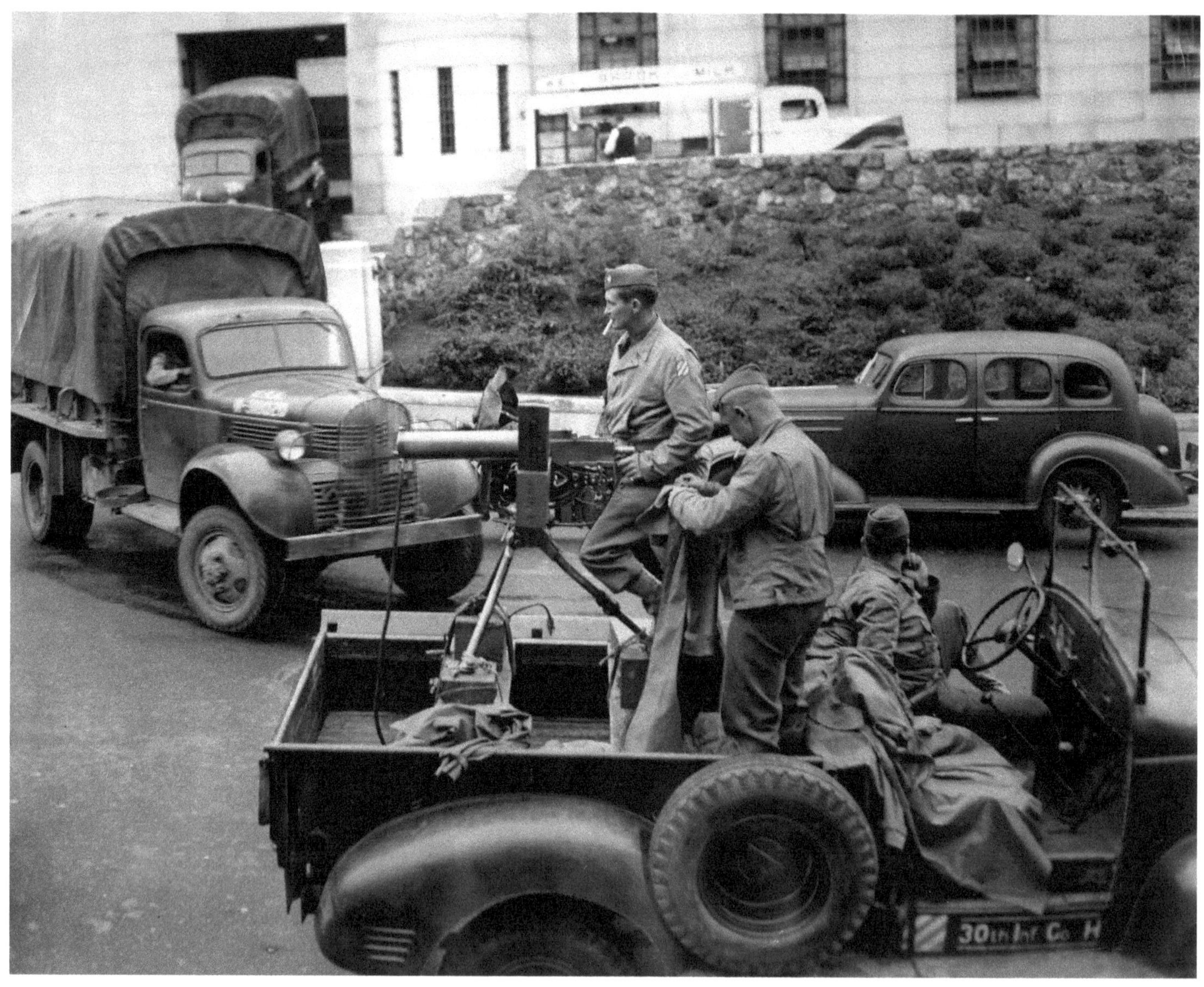

This photo shows the U.S. Army removing truckloads of money from the new Mint building at Market, Buchanan, and Duboce streets on November 4, 1941. With a machine gun mounted on a patrol car, soldiers of the Thirtieth Infantry, Company H, stand guard while trucks loaded with money roll out of the Mint headed for an undisclosed location.

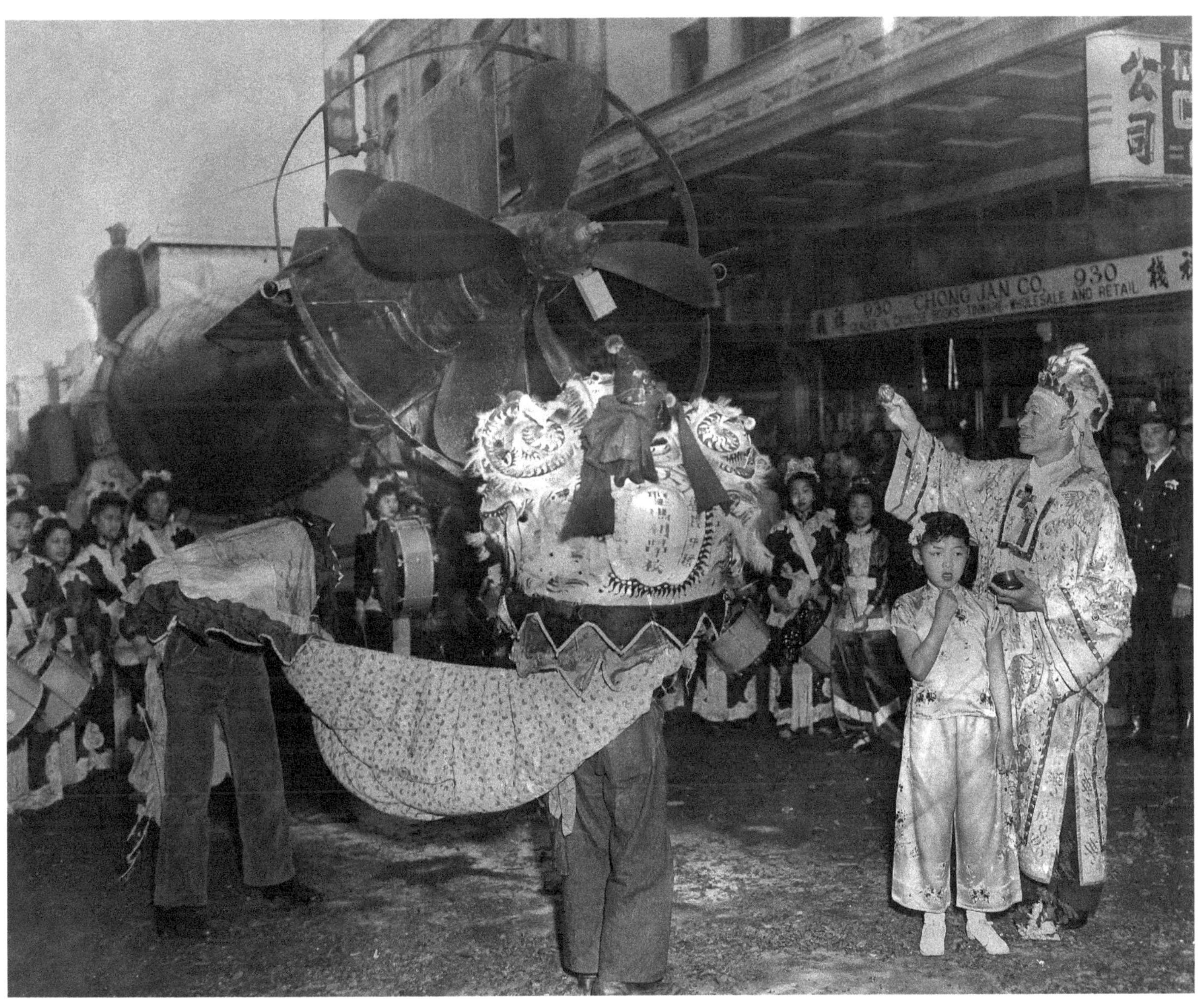

A captured Japanese midget submarine, nicknamed "Tojo's Cigar," is part of the ceremonies for San Francisco's Navy Day program on October 27, 1942, as priest Henry Yee performs ancient Chinese rites to exorcise "devils" from the craft. The formerly despised Chinese were allies now, and in 1943 Congress annulled the 1882 Exclusion Act. During World War II, the Japanese were under intense scrutiny. Under Executive Order 9066, 120,000 Japanese people in San Francisco and other West Coast cities, two-thirds of whom were American citizens, were removed from their homes and placed in internment camps for the duration of the war.

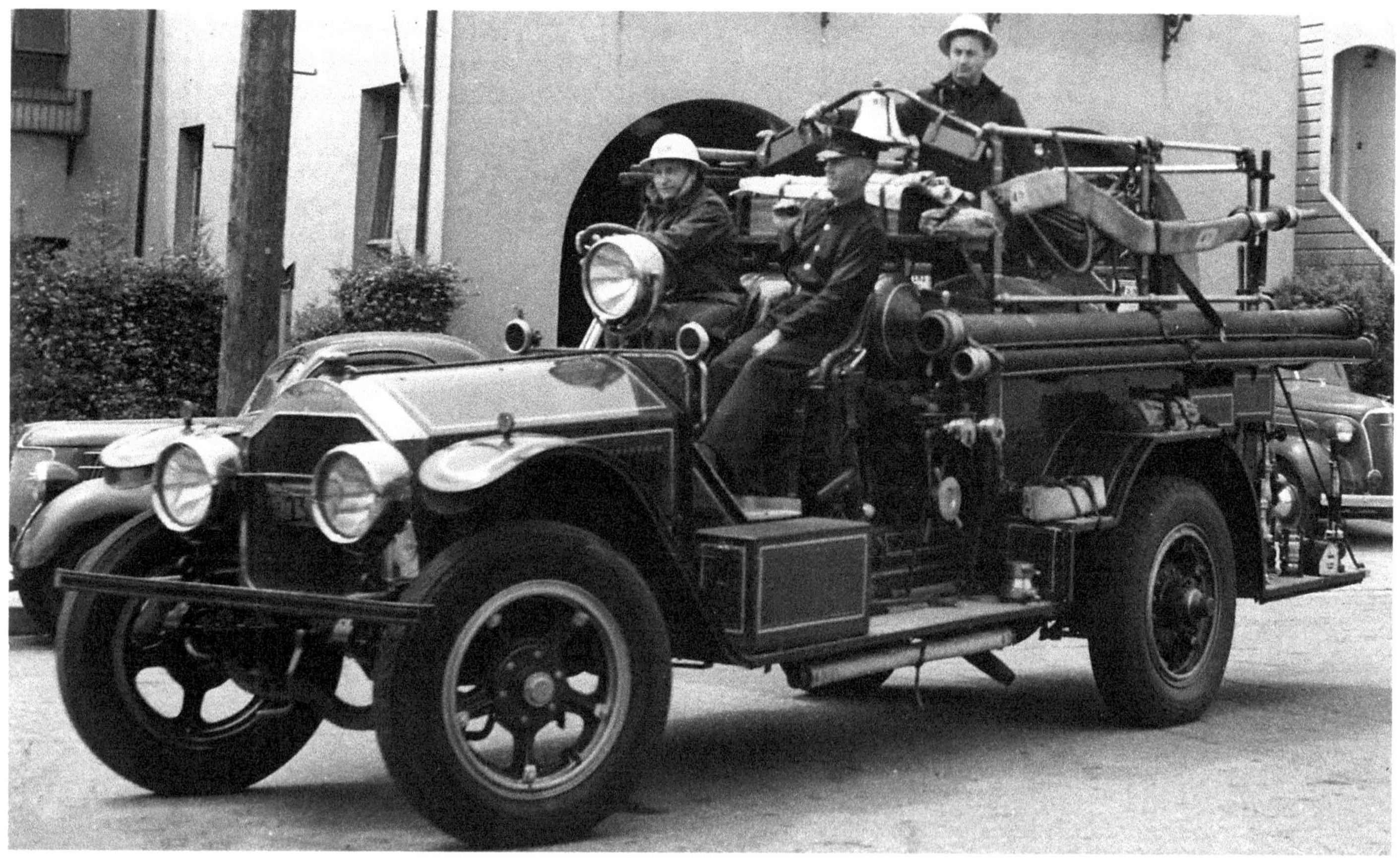

San Francisco Fire Department Engine 49, located at 2155 18th Avenue near Rivera Street in the Sunset District, May 5, 1943. The Sunset District was one of the last areas of San Francisco to be developed, as residential subdivisions gradually covered the sand dunes between the 1920s and 1940s.

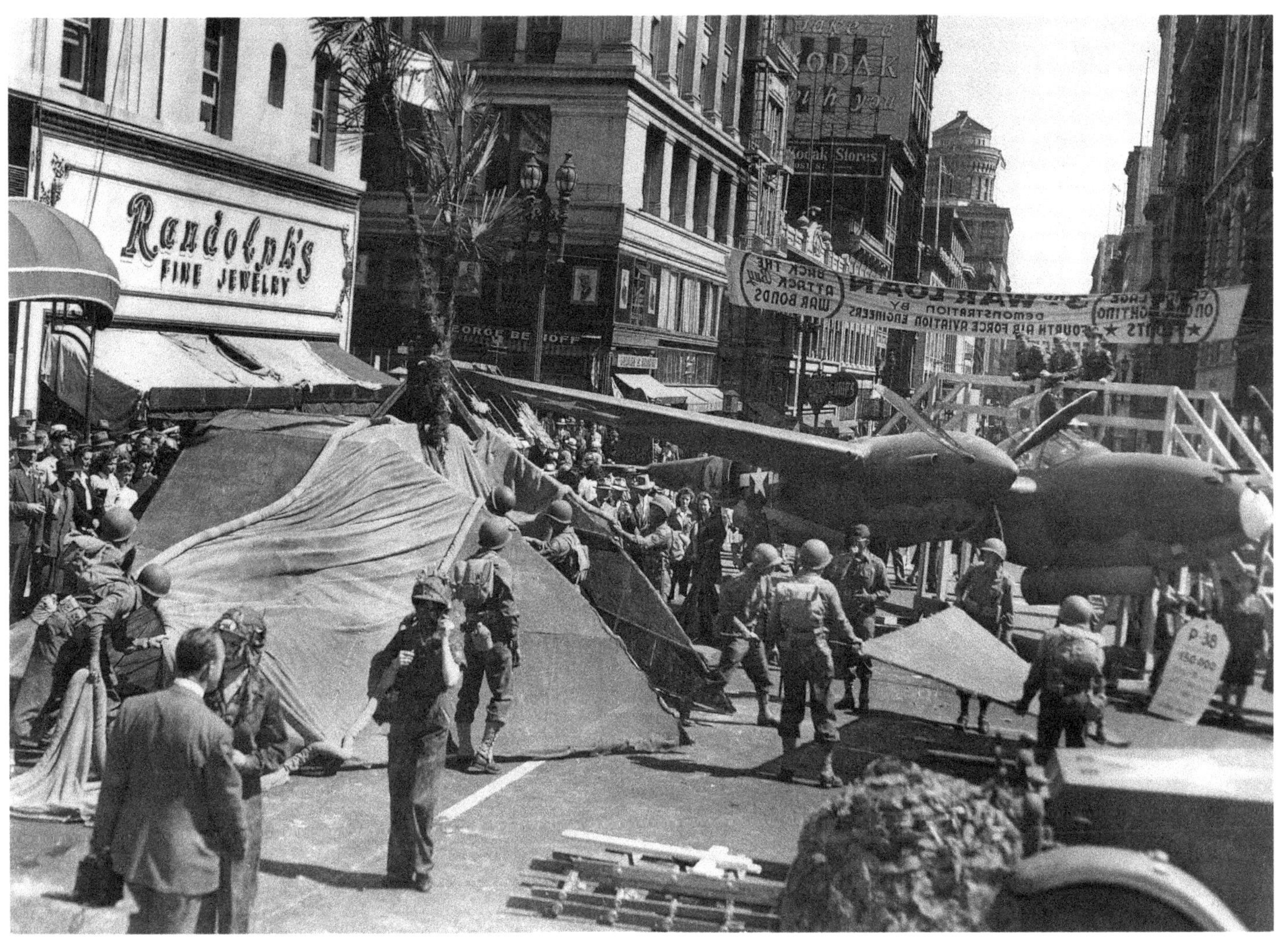

A war bond drive was held on Post Street on September 17, 1943, one of many drives held in San Francisco during World War II.

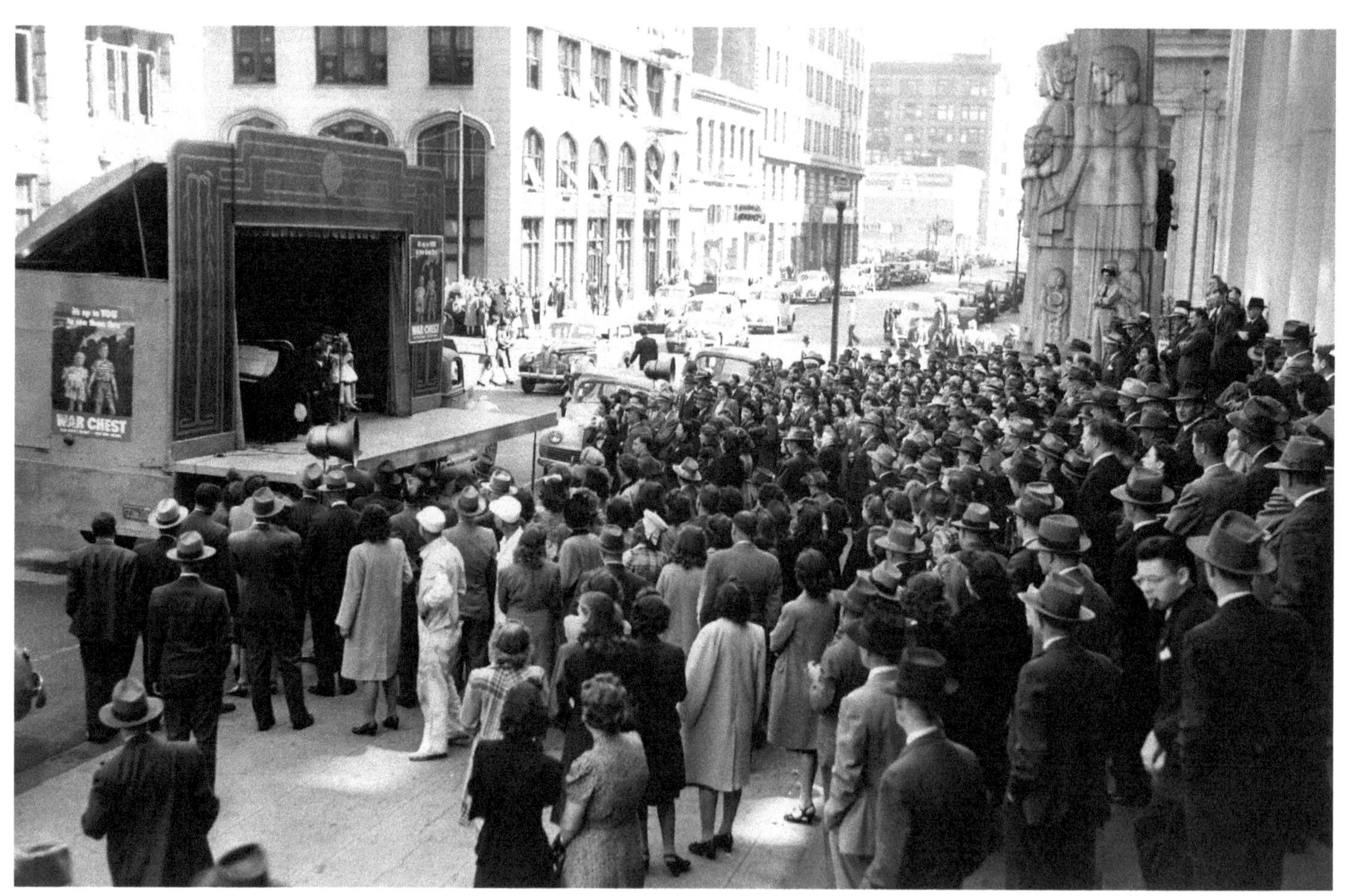

Pictured here on October 4, 1944, is the War Chest Rally in front of the Stock Exchange on Pine Street, with the goal of raising $3,792,742. The War Chest funded necessary war-front services and provided support for thousands of needy San Francisco families.

On the morning of February 21, 1945, more than 800 people lined up for cigarettes in the alley behind the Appraisers Building at Washington and Sansome streets. Seized from merchant seamen wanting to smuggle the tax-free cartons into the United States, these contraband cigarettes were sold on a first-come, first-served basis.

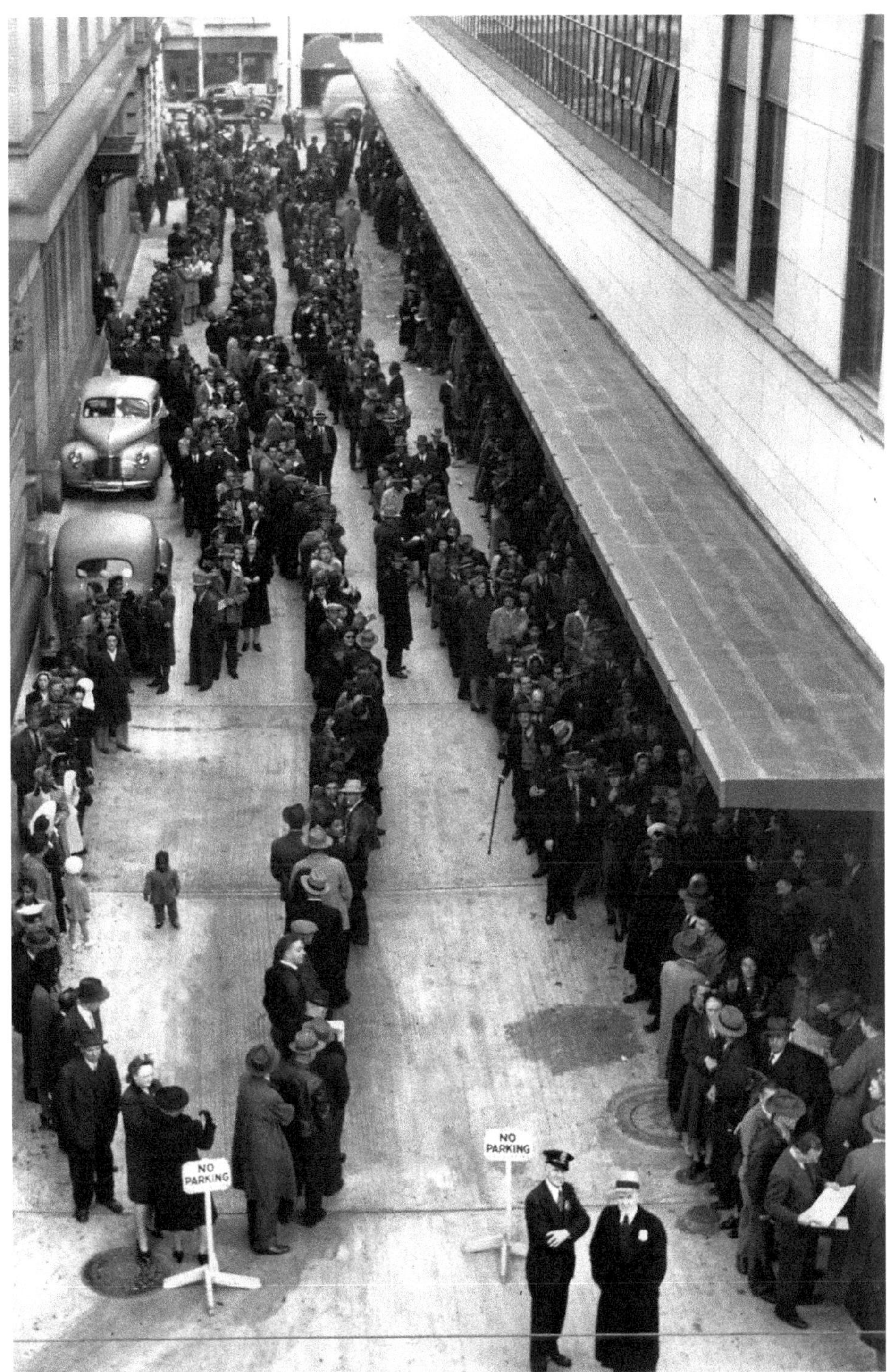

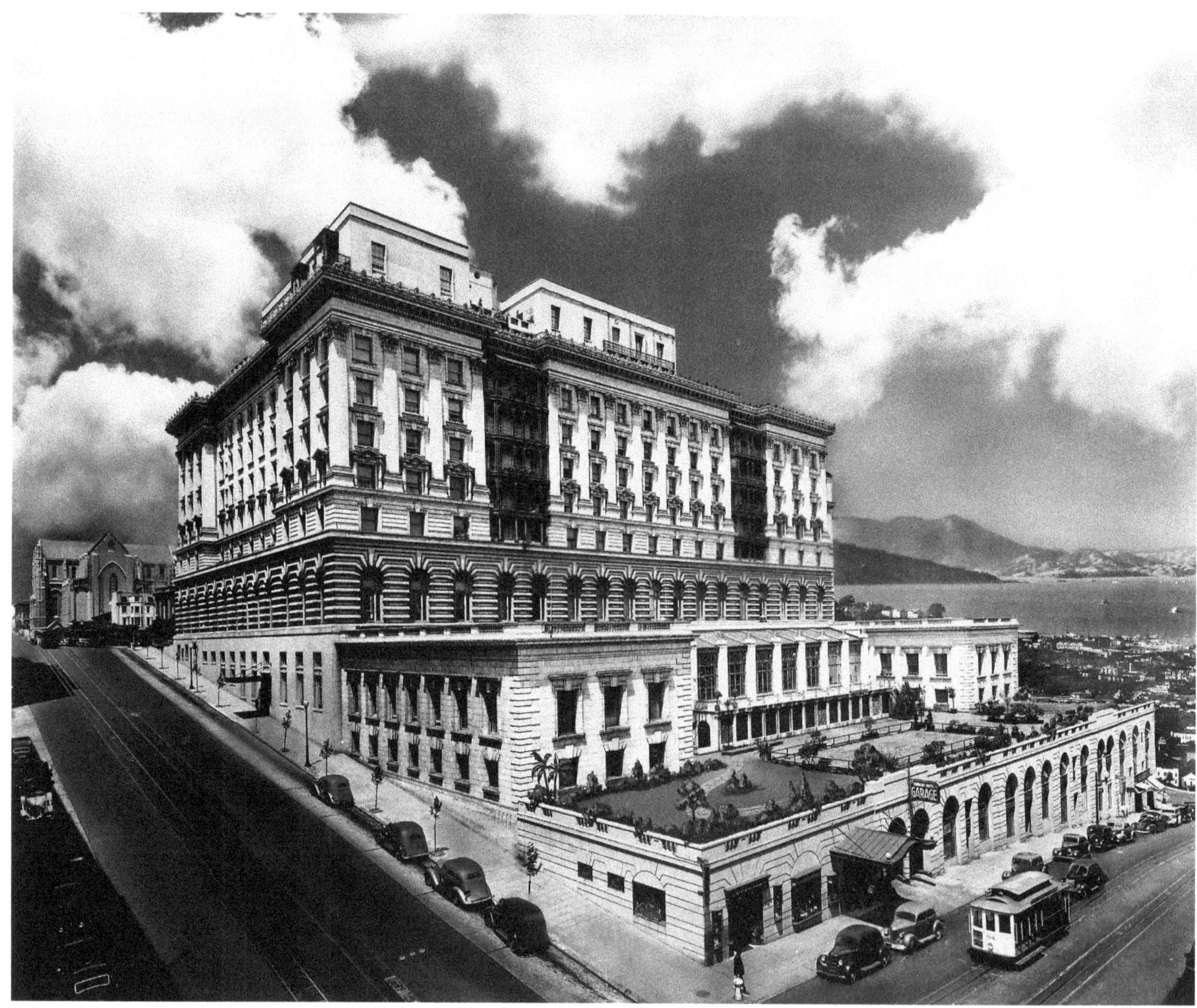

The Fairmont Hotel, shown on February 28, 1945, was started by the daughters of silver king James Fair and was sold two weeks before the 1906 earthquake to the Law brothers. Although the property was already completed at the time, it had not yet opened. With demolished mansions surrounding it, it stood like a palace atop Nob Hill during the fires. While the outer structure stood, there was some structural damage to the interior. After the fire, architect Julia Morgan reinforced the structure and redid the interior. The Fairmont opened its doors exactly one year after the earthquake and stands today as one of San Francisco's most luxurious hotels.

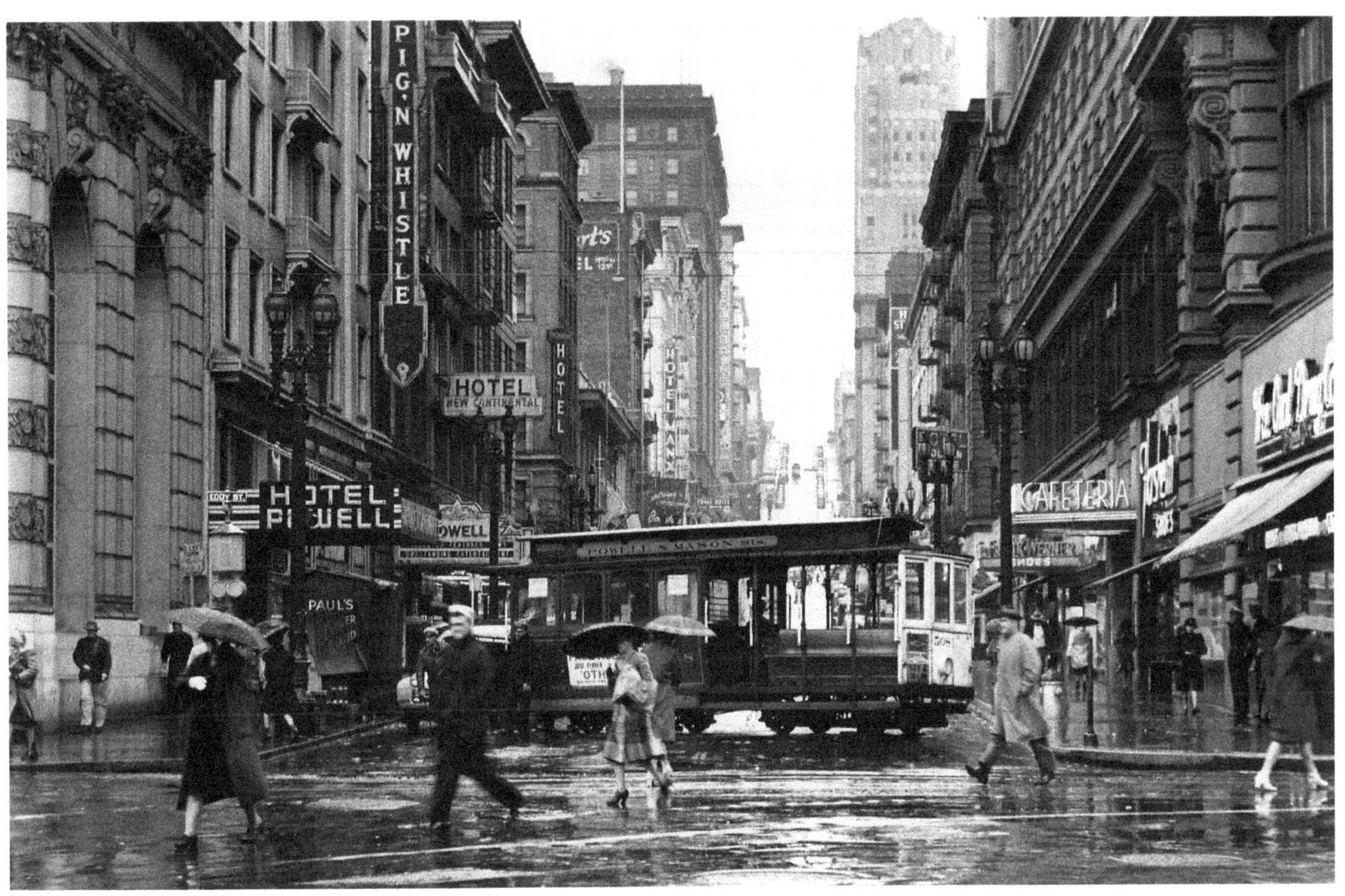

This photograph shows cable cars turning around by the old turntable on Powell Street at Market on March 24, 1945. In the 1940s, city government wanted to replace cable cars with buses, but a Mrs. Friedel Klussman created the "Committee to Save the Cable Cars," which was successful in saving three out of eight of the lines. The three remaining cable car lines still ring their bells and climb San Francisco hills to this day.

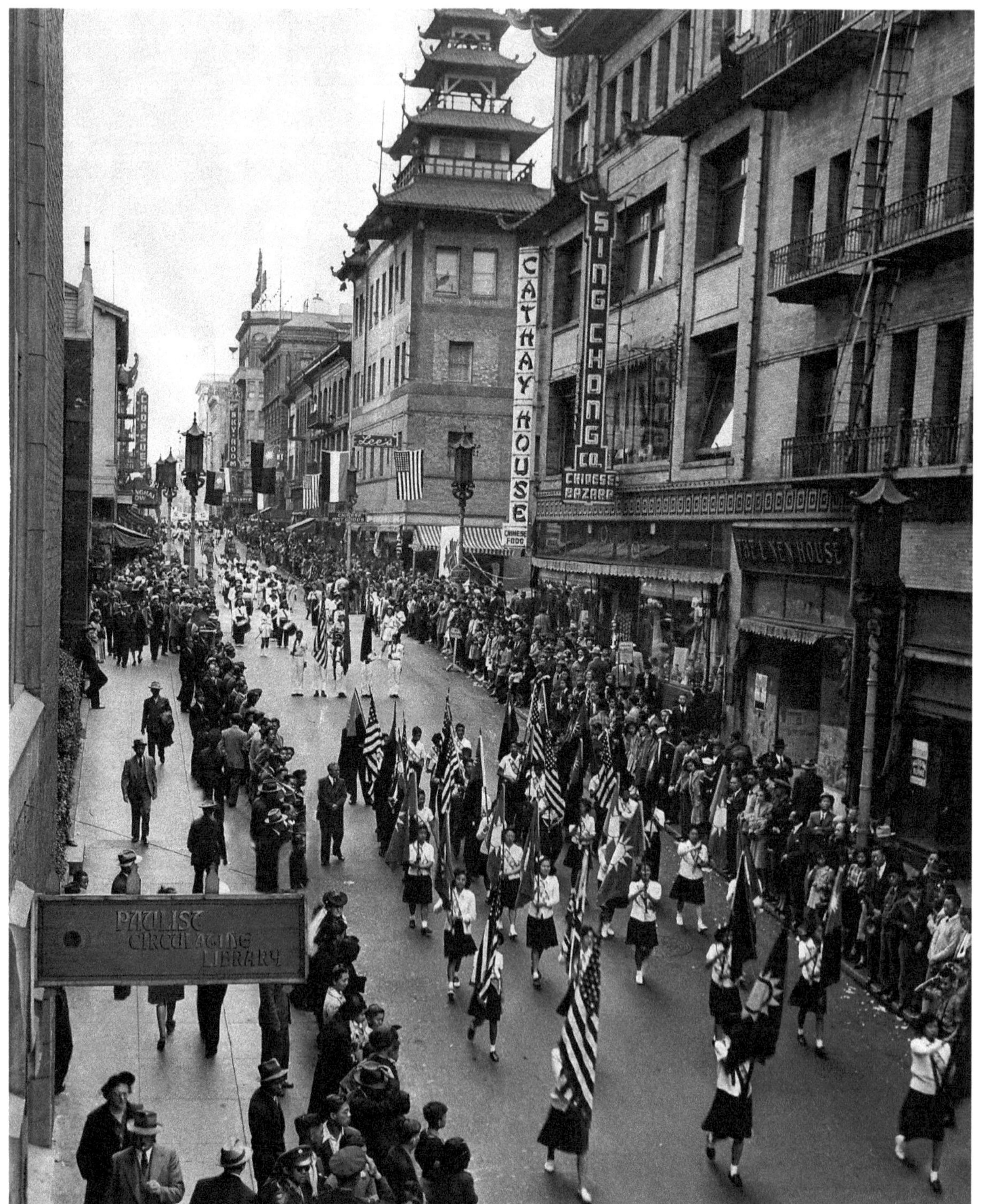

On October 11, 1945, ethnic Chinese school children march with Chinese and American flags in a parade celebrating the founding of the Republic of China in 1911.

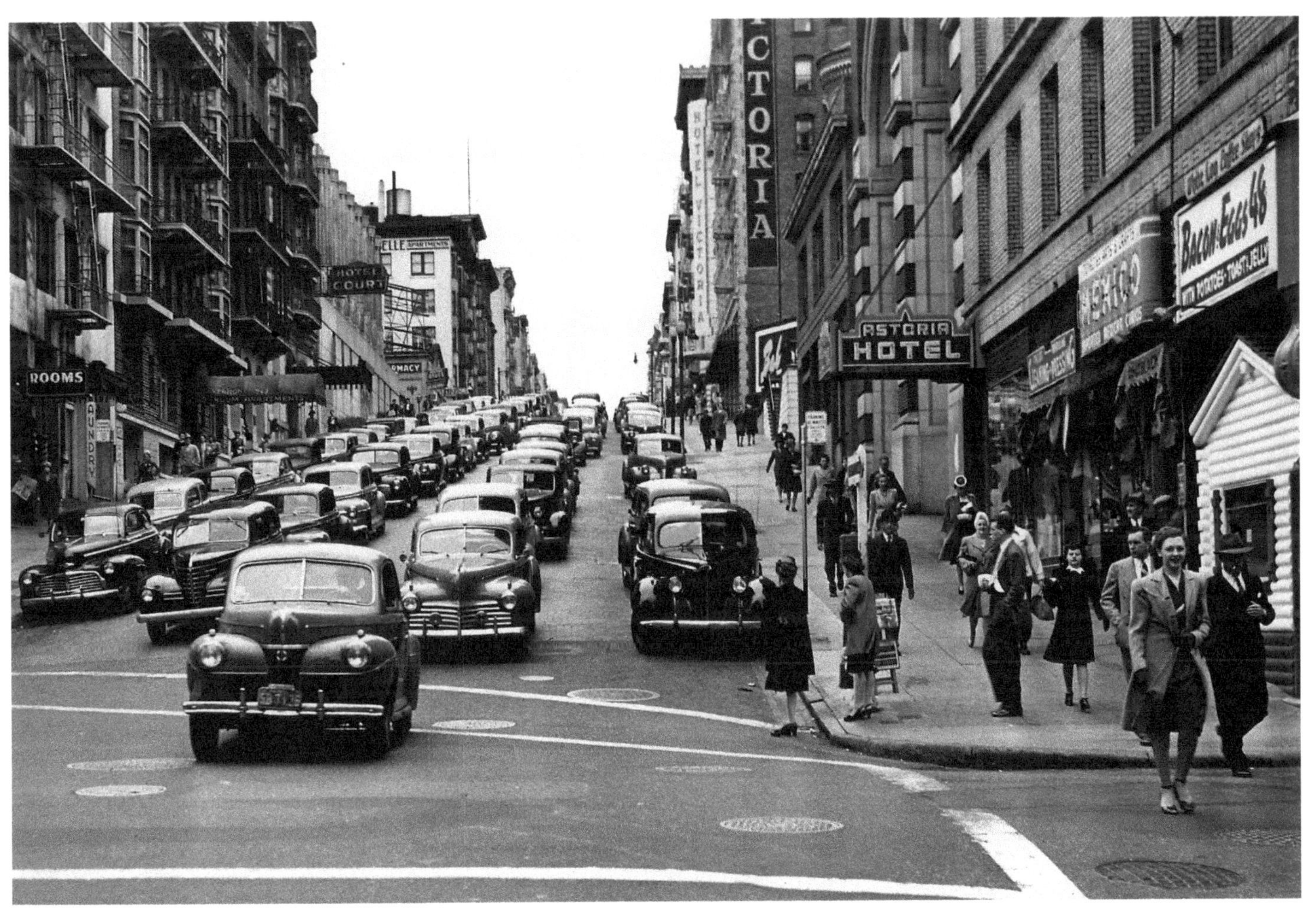

A traffic jam occurs on June 1, 1946, on Bush Street near Grant Avenue, near the entrance to Chinatown, as hundreds head downtown to work.

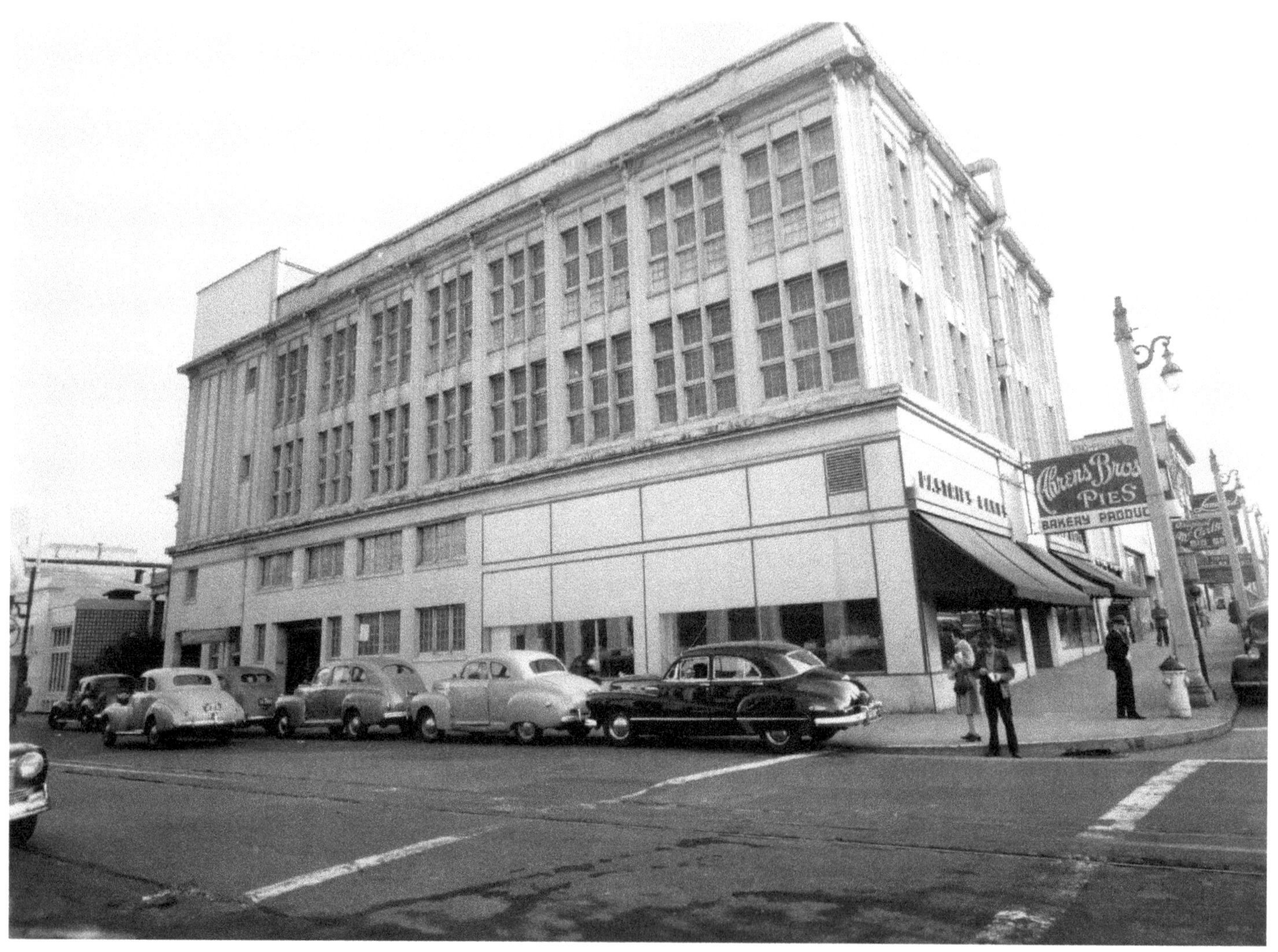

Ahrens Bakery on Van Ness Avenue, shown here in 1946, was run by the Frankensteins for more than 28 years.

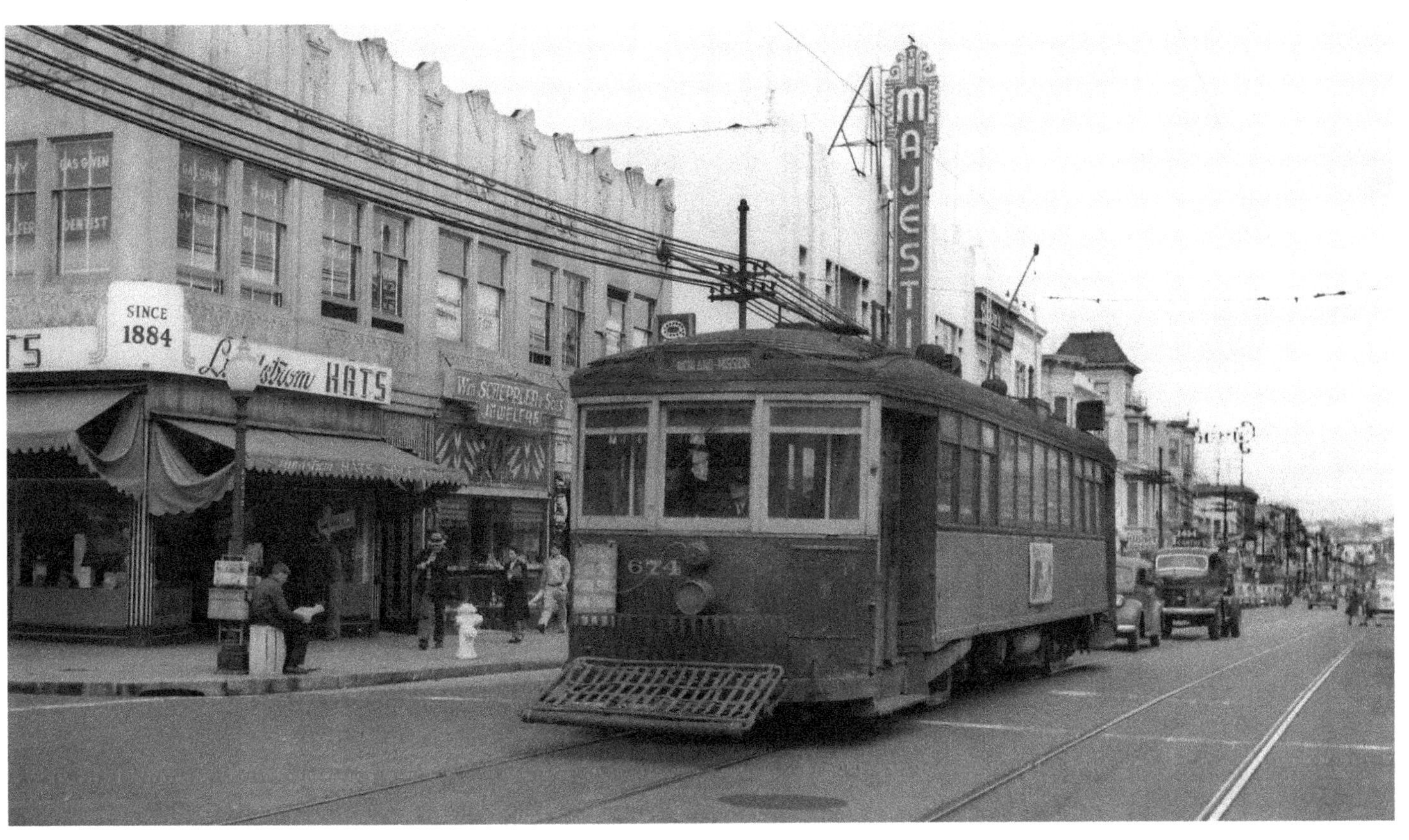

A 9 Richland streetcar travels along Mission Street near the intersection with 21st Street in 1947. A hat store dating back to 1884 is visible at left, while the Majestic Theatre sign is seen over the streetcar. Close to 20 theaters lined the Mission Street corridor from 16th Street to the San Mateo County line. In total, these theaters sat more than 15,000 people. Today, the Majestic and nearly all of the Mission Street theaters have long since closed.

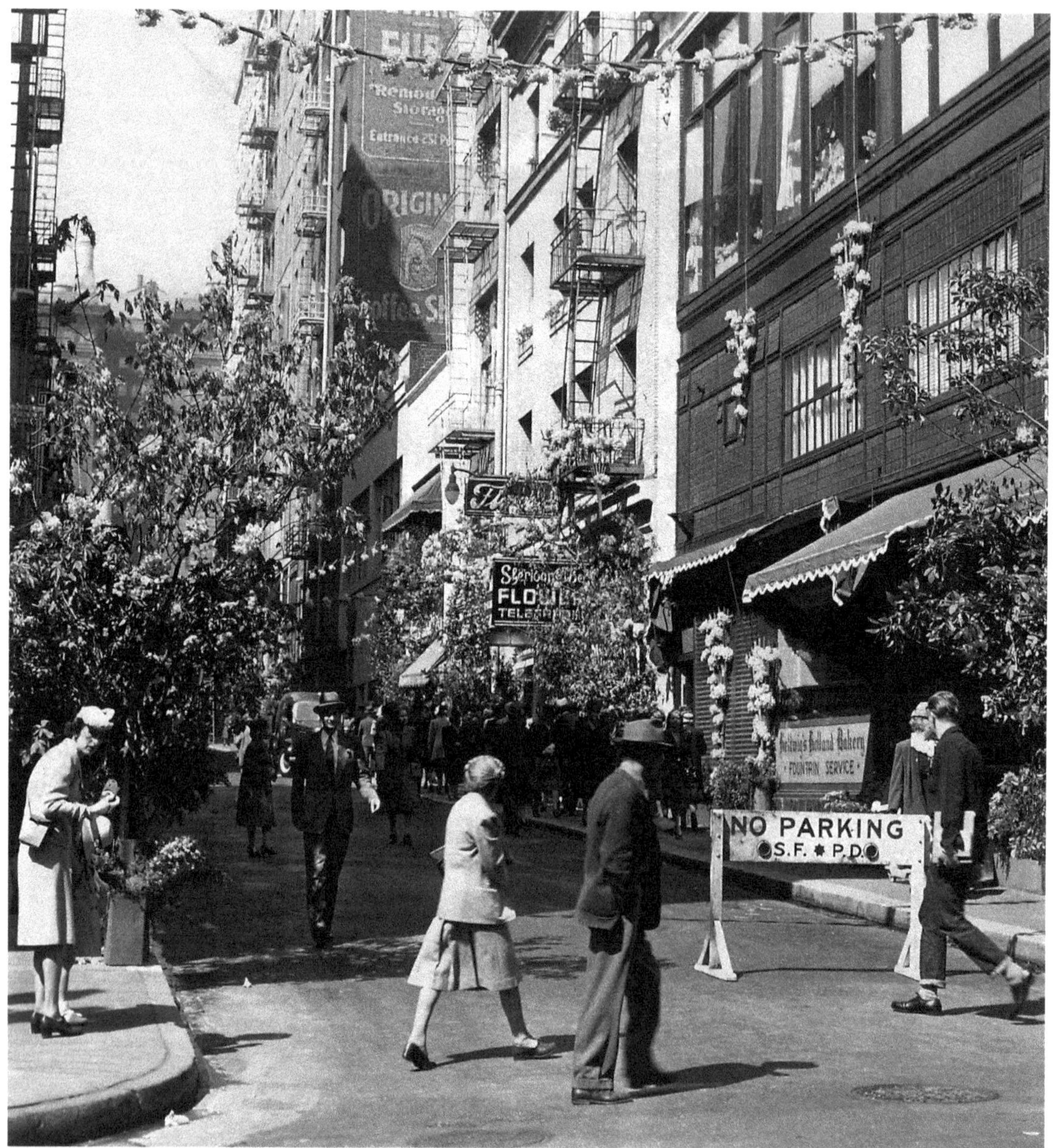

The Maiden Lane Merchants Association once held an annual "Spring Comes to Maiden Lane" festival, shown here on April 10, 1947. Bushels of daffodils and jonquils were flown from Washington for the occasion. Maiden Lane, the two-block pedestrian street between Stockton and Kearny, has a sordid history, completely obscured by the posh high-end boutiques and outdoor cafes that line the street today. Known as Morton Street in the nineteenth century, this thoroughfare was saturated with brothels and averaged a murder a week. Destroyed in the 1906 earthquake, it was renamed Maiden Lane in a biting recognition of its unsavory past.

Montgomery Street was the center of San Francisco's Financial District when this picture looking north was taken on May 6, 1947, and to this day. After World War II, more people traveled by car to work, leading to frequent traffic jams and requiring parking facilities when curbside street parking proved insufficient for the volume of cars in the area. The nearby Russ Building was first in San Francisco to have an indoor parking garage when it opened in 1927, foreshadowing the congestion that would hit the area two decades later. Cars on this one-way corridor travel south out of the Financial District to downtown, South of Market, other parts of the city, and beyond.

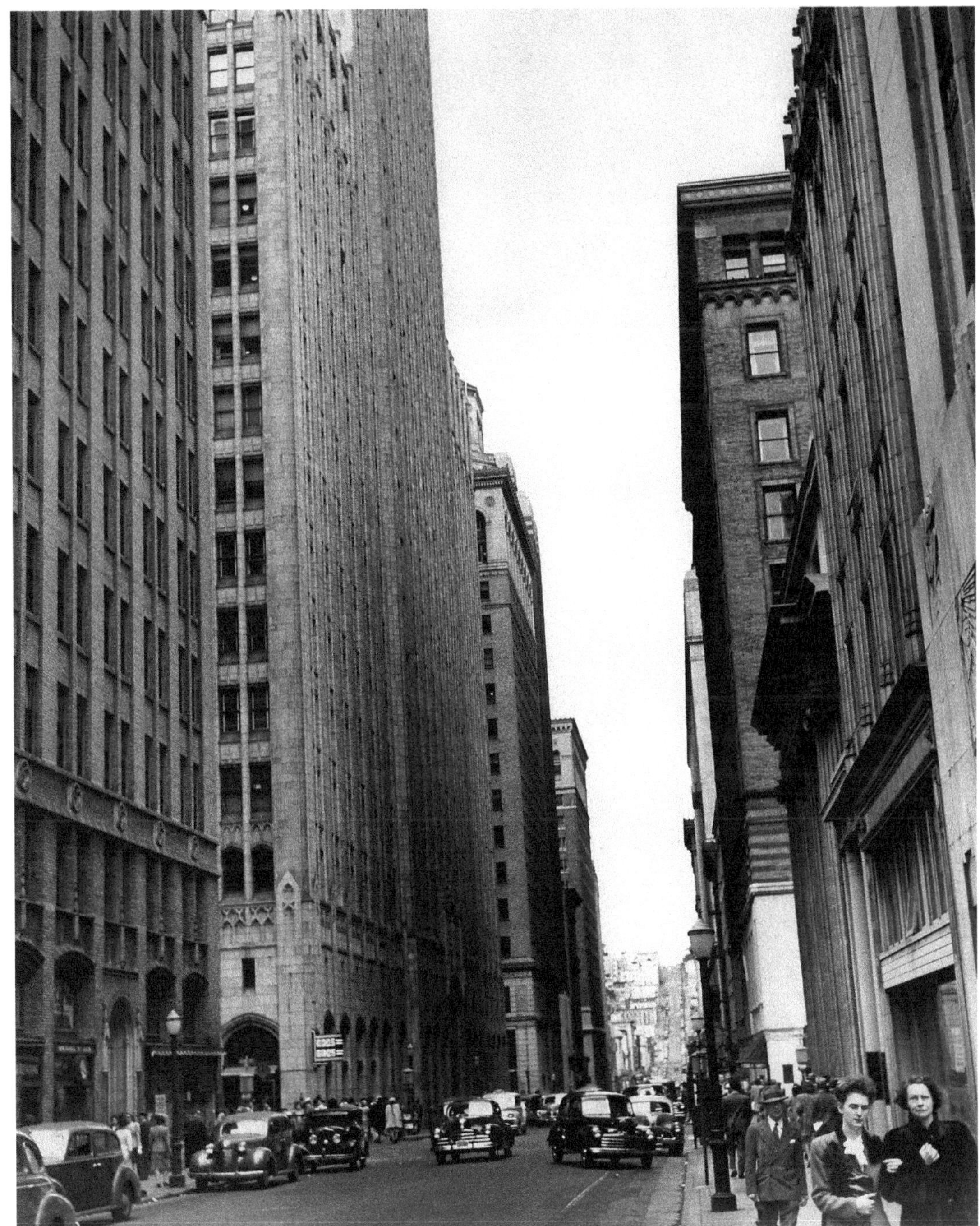

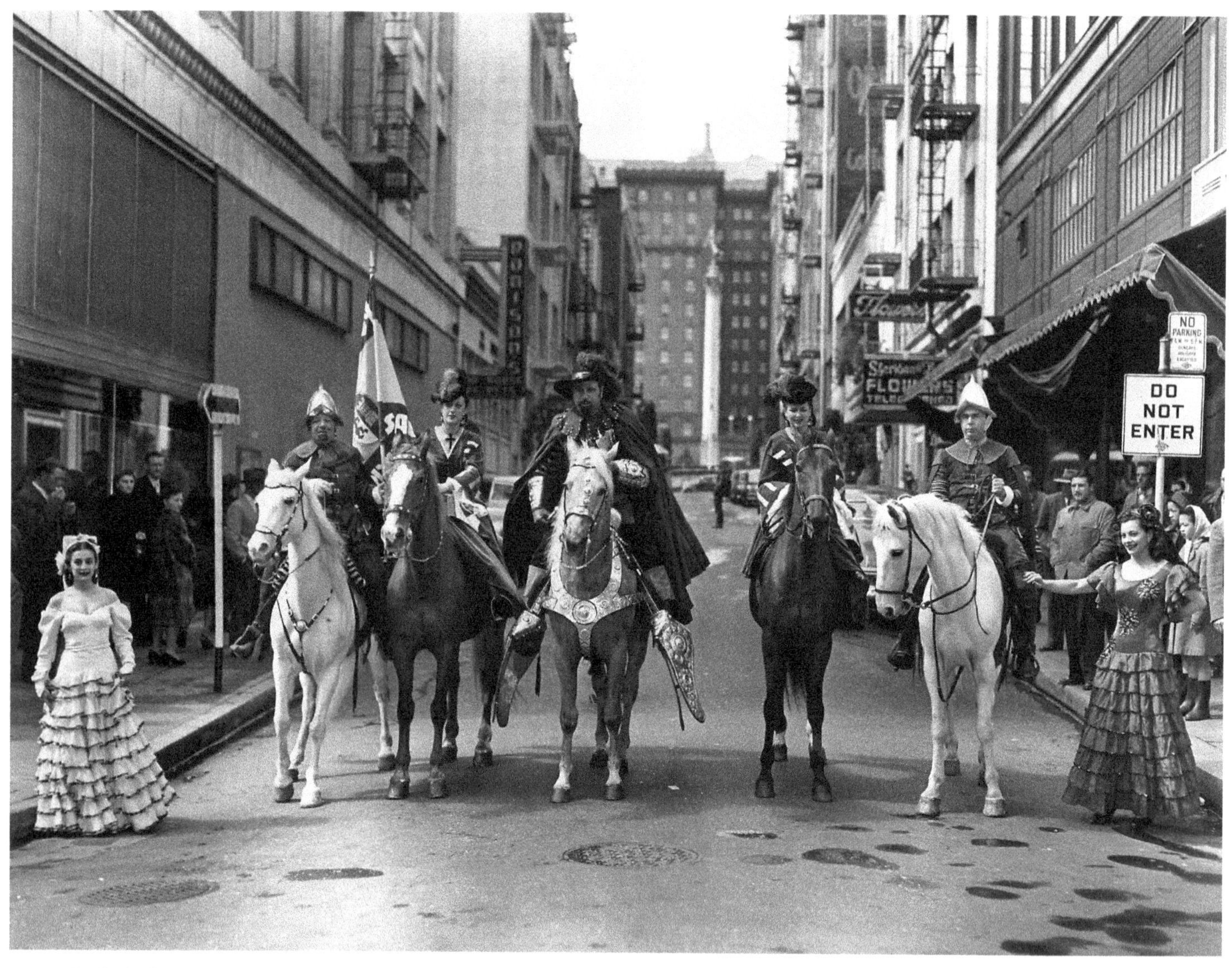

A man bedecked as Don Gaspar De Portola is flanked by two women and two bodyguards posing on horses on Maiden Lane, shown here on March 19, 1948. They are on their way to a St. Patrick's Day parade nearby.

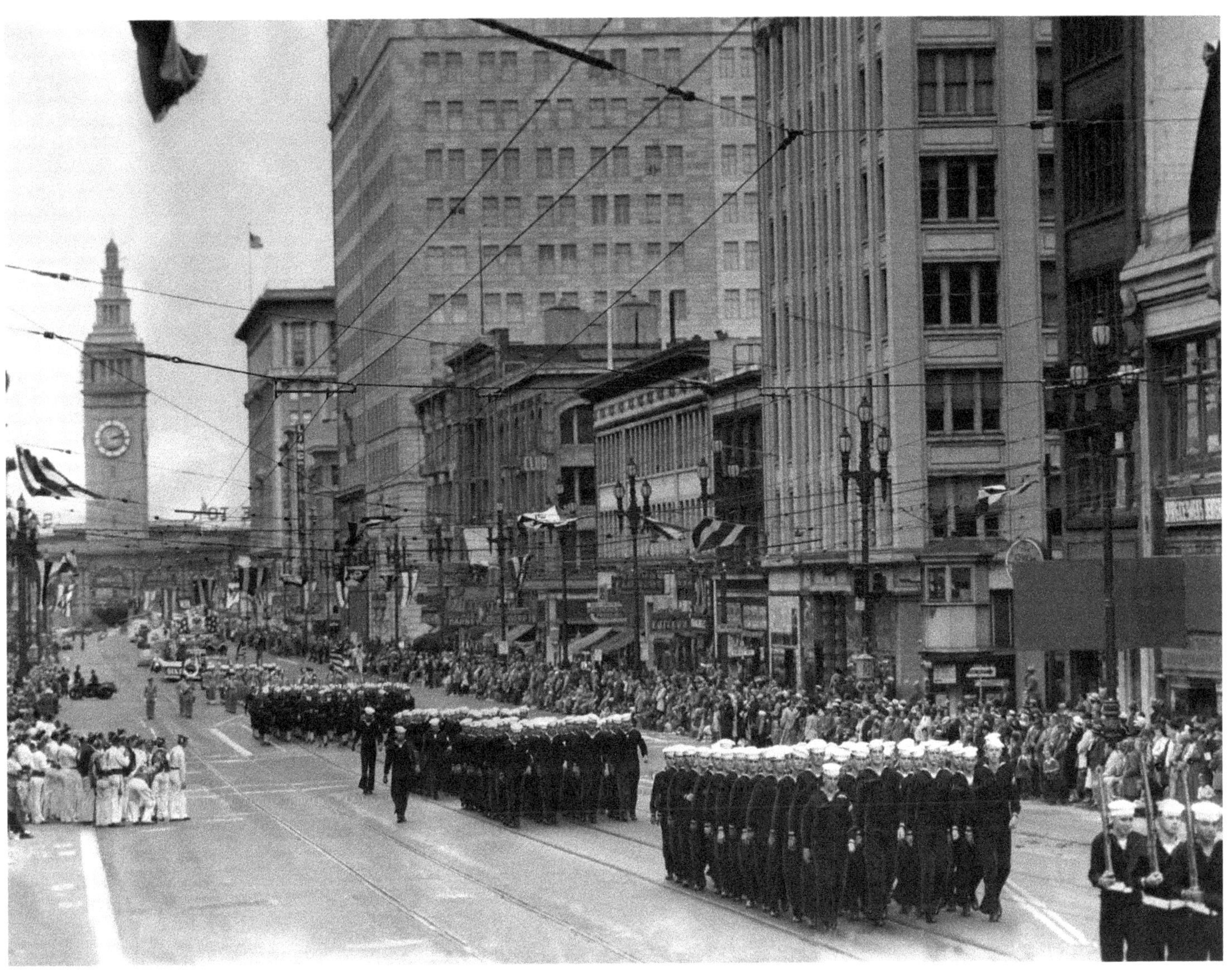

On January 3, 1949, a group of navy men strides up Market Street, signifying the opening of the 61st annual convention of Loyal Order of Moose. An estimated 65,000 people turned out for the three-hour parade.

At Stockton Street in the late morning, of March 31, 1949, large crowds of people attend the annual Maiden Lane Spring Festival. The well-dressed scene bears no resemblance to the darker (formerly Morton) street of half a century earlier.

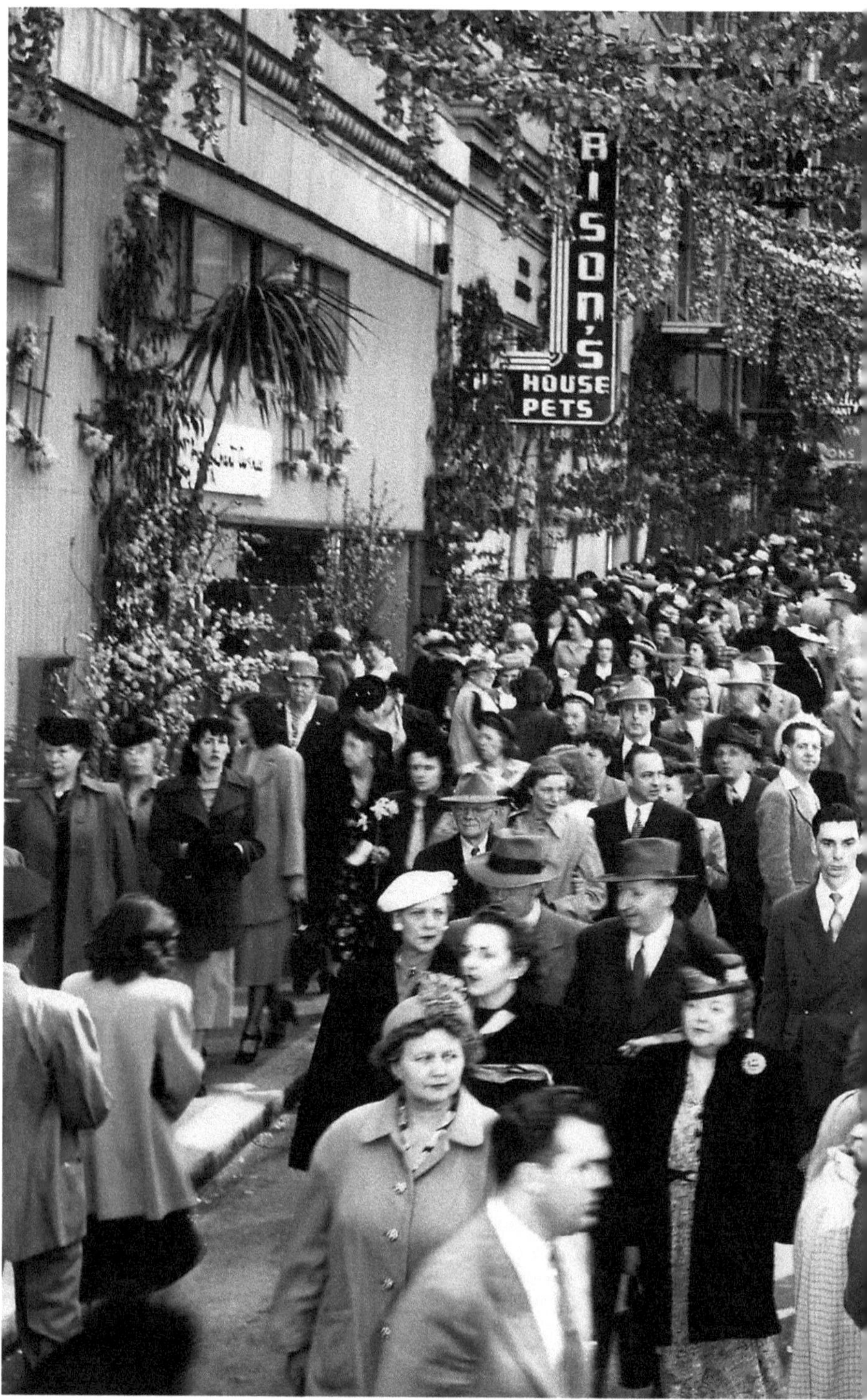

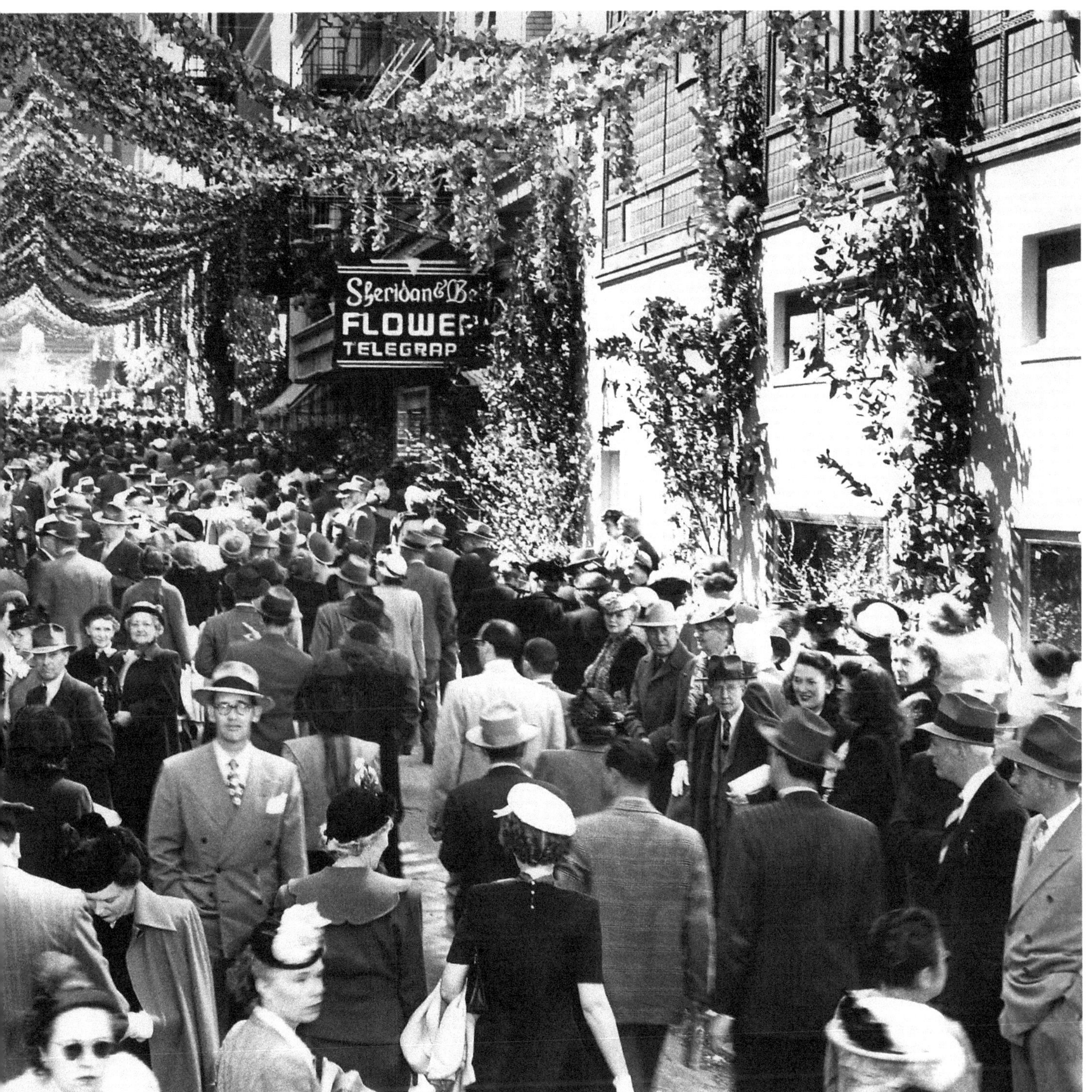
FLOWER
TELEGRAP

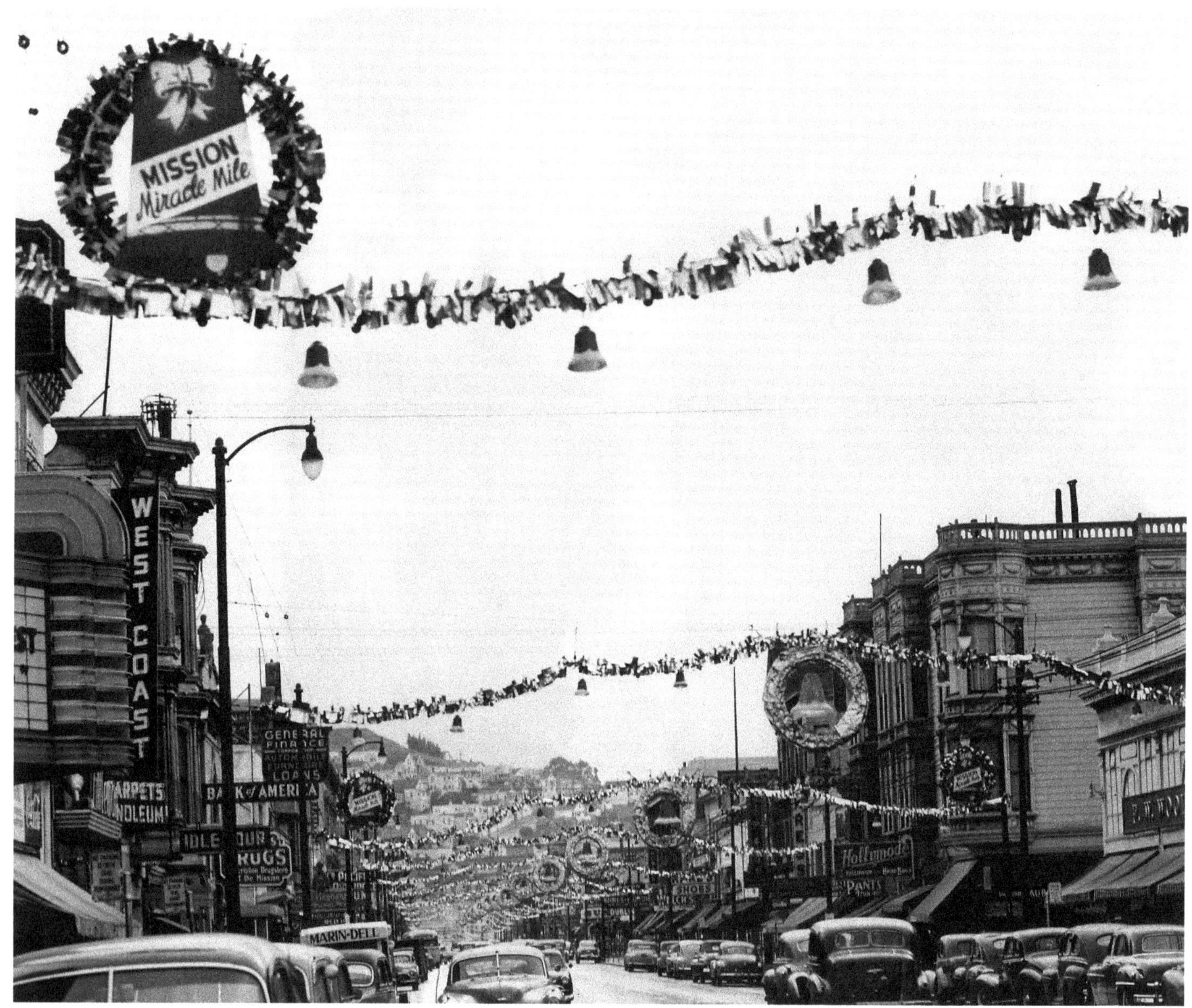

This picture, taken on December 19, 1949, shows the "Miracle Mile" on Mission Street adorned with festival holiday decorations. This area won top honors for its Christmas "dress." By the early twentieth century, Mission Street sported numerous movie theaters and a bustling array of stores, and was dubbed the "Mission Miracle Mile." Historically, the Mission District has been home to many immigrants. By day, Mission Miracle Mile is the main working-class shopping street for the 60,000 living nearby. At night, young people from all parts of the city and the Bay area flock to the Mission for its ethnic restaurants and trendy bars.

This picture, taken in the late 1940s, shows the grand staircase of the Fox Theatre. The Fox opened in 1929 at 1350 Market St., between 9th and 10th, and at the height of its popularity, the 4,651-seat theater was considered the most ornate and lavish in the country. It was demolished in the 1960s and replaced with a modern skyscraper. Various artifacts from the Fox Theatre occasionally turn up. The original curtain is still in use at the Grand Lake Theatre in Oakland.

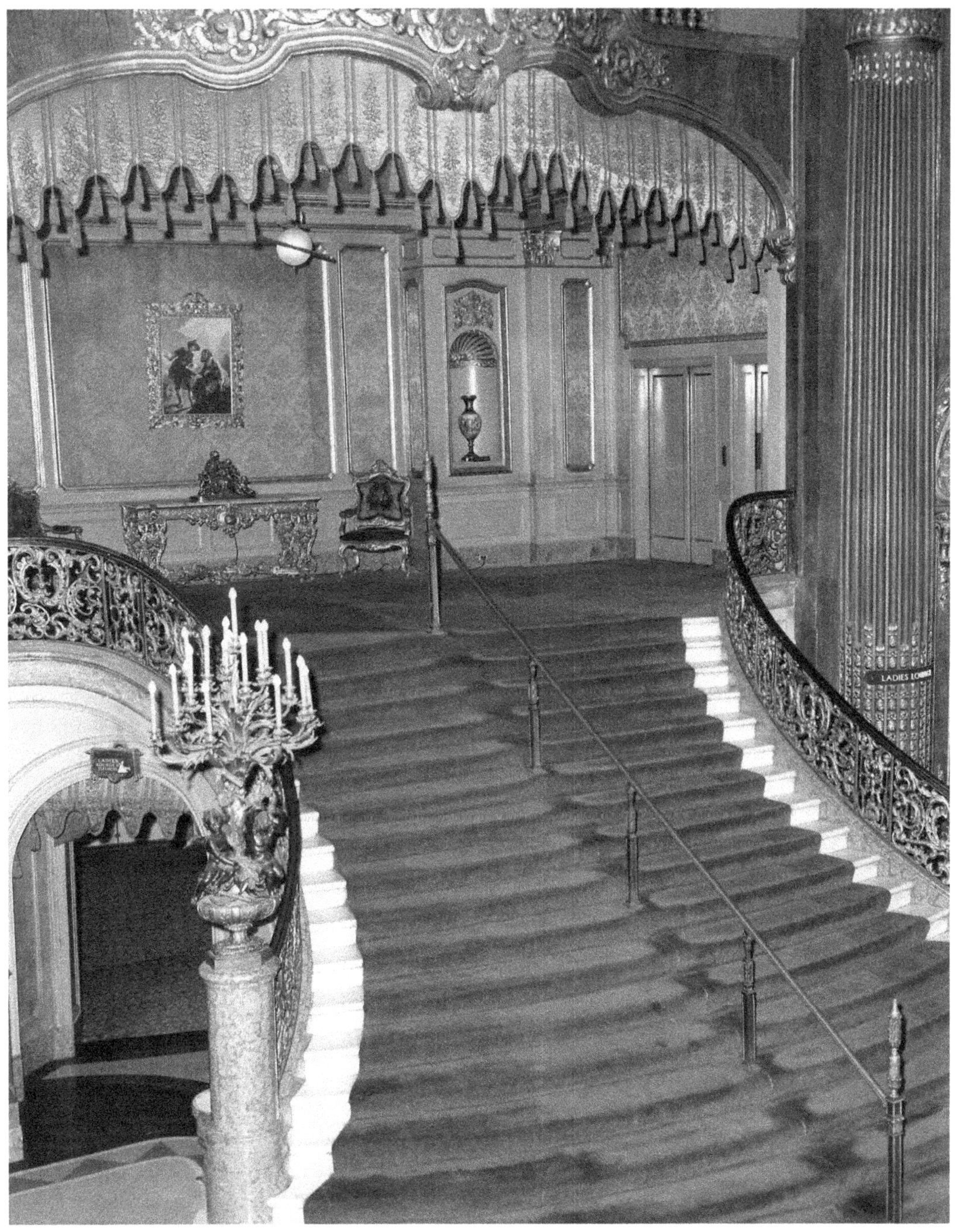

The Mobilgas Building was located at the intersection of Market and Drumm streets, as seen here on September 17, 1949. Mobilgas changed its brand name to Mobil in 1962, and merged with Exxon in 1999 to become ExxonMobil, one of the world's largest oil companies. The Hyatt Regency hotel now stands here.

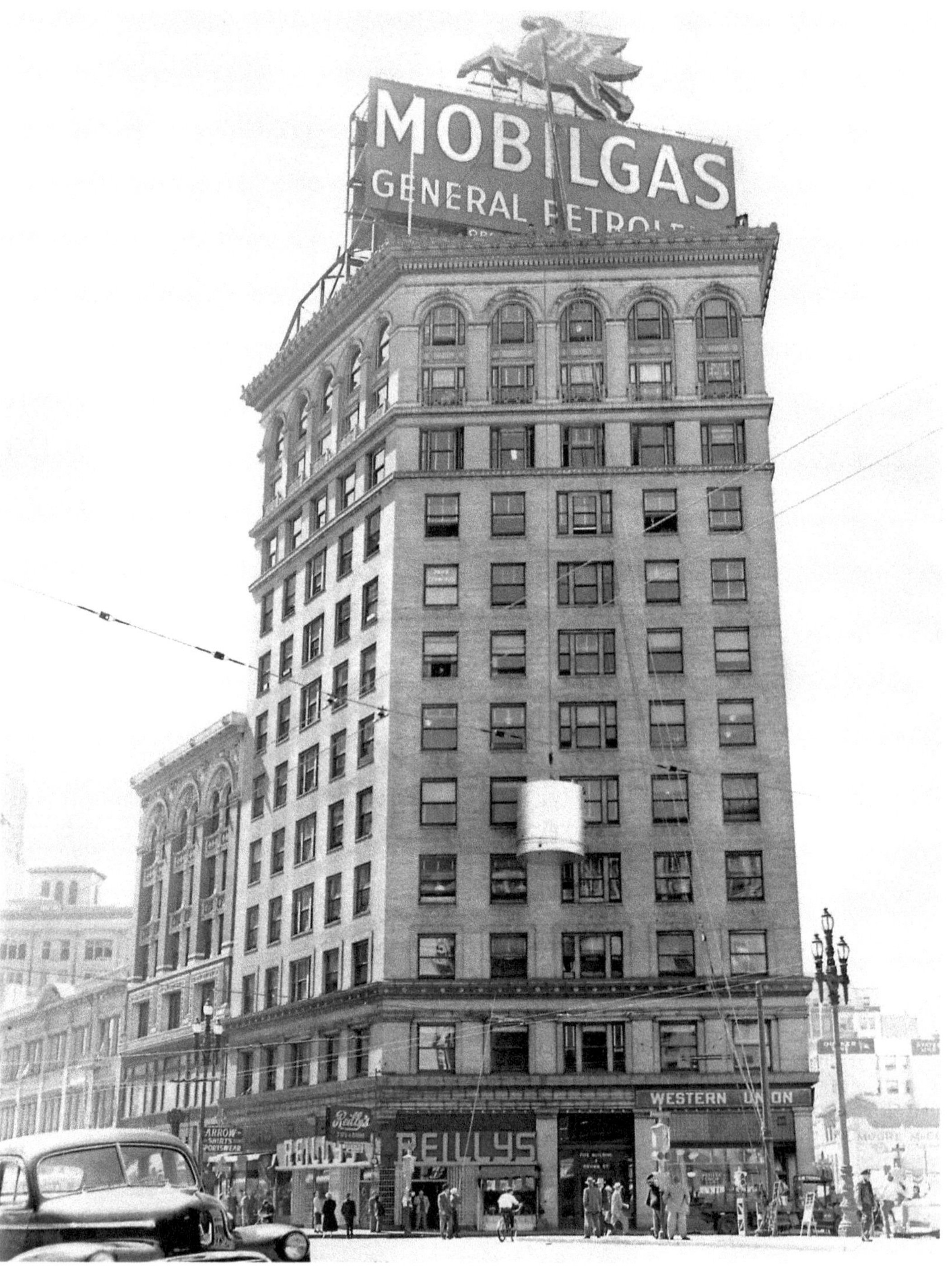

Return to "Normality"

(1950–1959)

With the end of World War II, and the jubilation of Allied victory, tens of thousands of soldiers returned home to the Bay area, and most people wanted to return to some sort of normalcy, the upshot being the Baby Boom. The fifties saw the largest rise in the economy in three decades, resulting in a period of relative economic prosperity for many, and a return to a consumer society like that of the 1920s. Wartime production had turned to peacetime production, and returning soldiers went to college for the first time with the G.I. Bill. The fifties were also a time of freeway construction, urban renewal, and the reshaping of San Francisco neighborhoods. As San Francisco's population continued to grow, the city expanded significantly in all directions; Melvina Reynold's song "Little Boxes" aptly described the cookie-cutter suburban sprawls that proliferated over the Bay area and the nation. In 1958, San Francisco got a new baseball team when the New York Giants moved to town to become the San Francisco Giants.

San Francisco, always a center for counterculture, gave birth to the Beat movement. The Beatniks used poetry and prose, art, film, and lived alternative lifestyles to express their disaffection with American consumer culture and the ethos of conformity in the nuclear age. Leaders of the Beat movement, such as Alan Ginsberg, Jack Kerouac, William Burroughs, Lawrence Ferlinghetti, and Gary Snyder, published their literature in City Lights Bookstore in North Beach, which had become the locus of the movement.

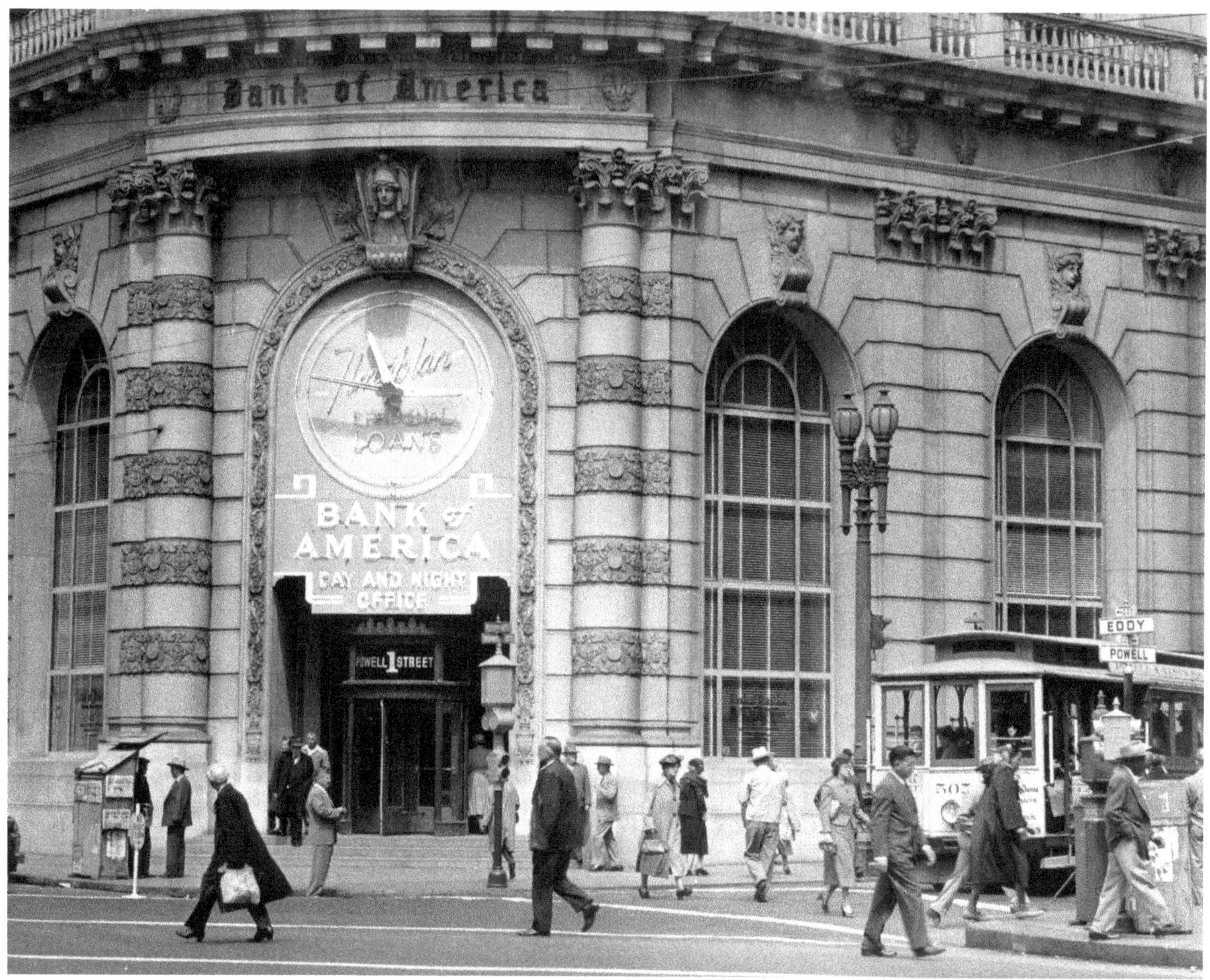

The day and night office of the Bank of America branch at Powell and Market streets, shown here July 18, 1950, was at one of the downtown's busiest intersections. It was designed by architects Walter Bliss and William Faville (also of the Bank of California Building, the Saint Francis Hotel, and many other San Francisco structures) in 1920. The building now houses a smaller branch of Bank of America on the side, while inside the main entrance is a teen fashion store.

A fireman stands next to a trolley wire downed by lightning on Sutter Street at Leavenworth on August 21, 1951. The mishap stopped trolley service for an hour.

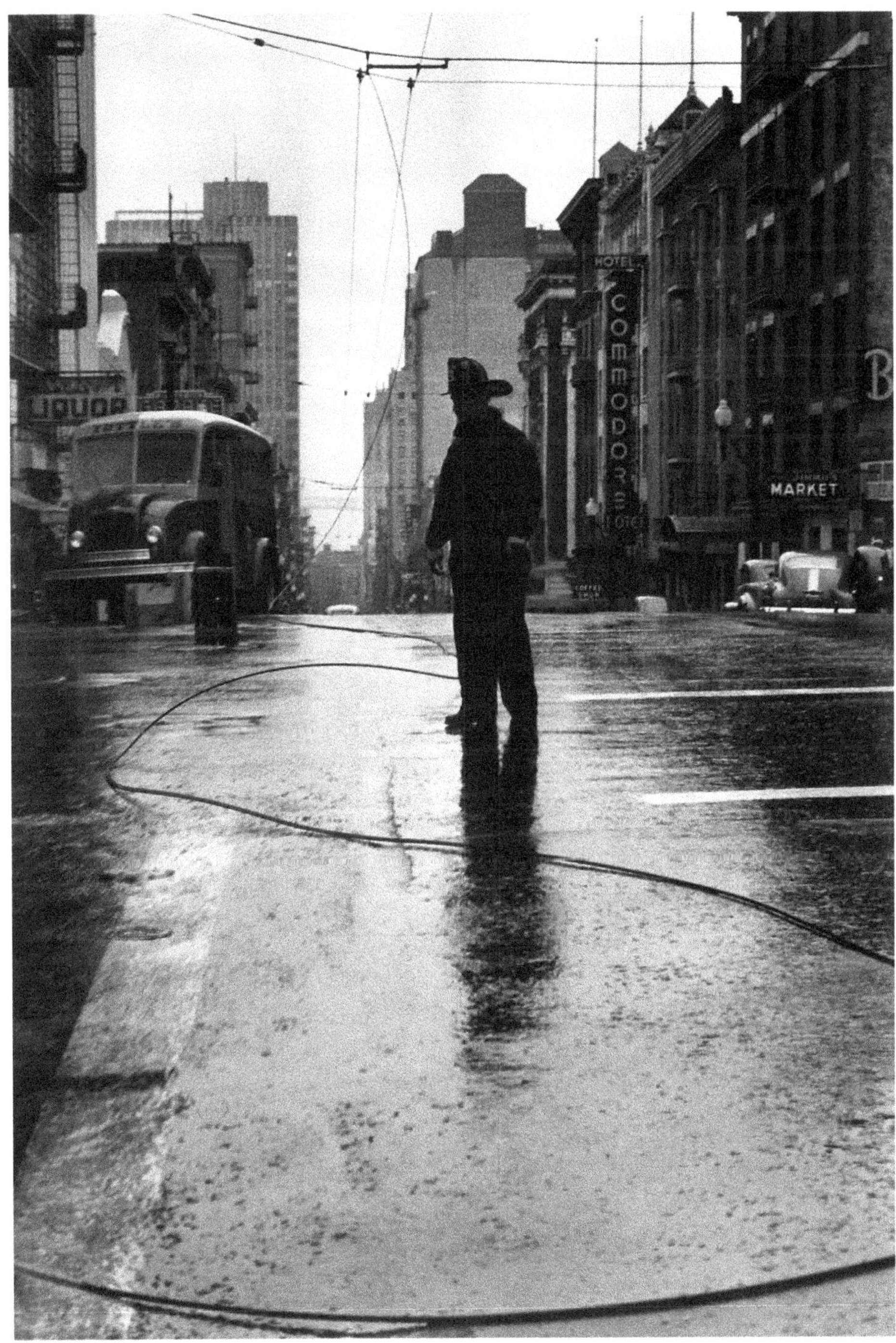

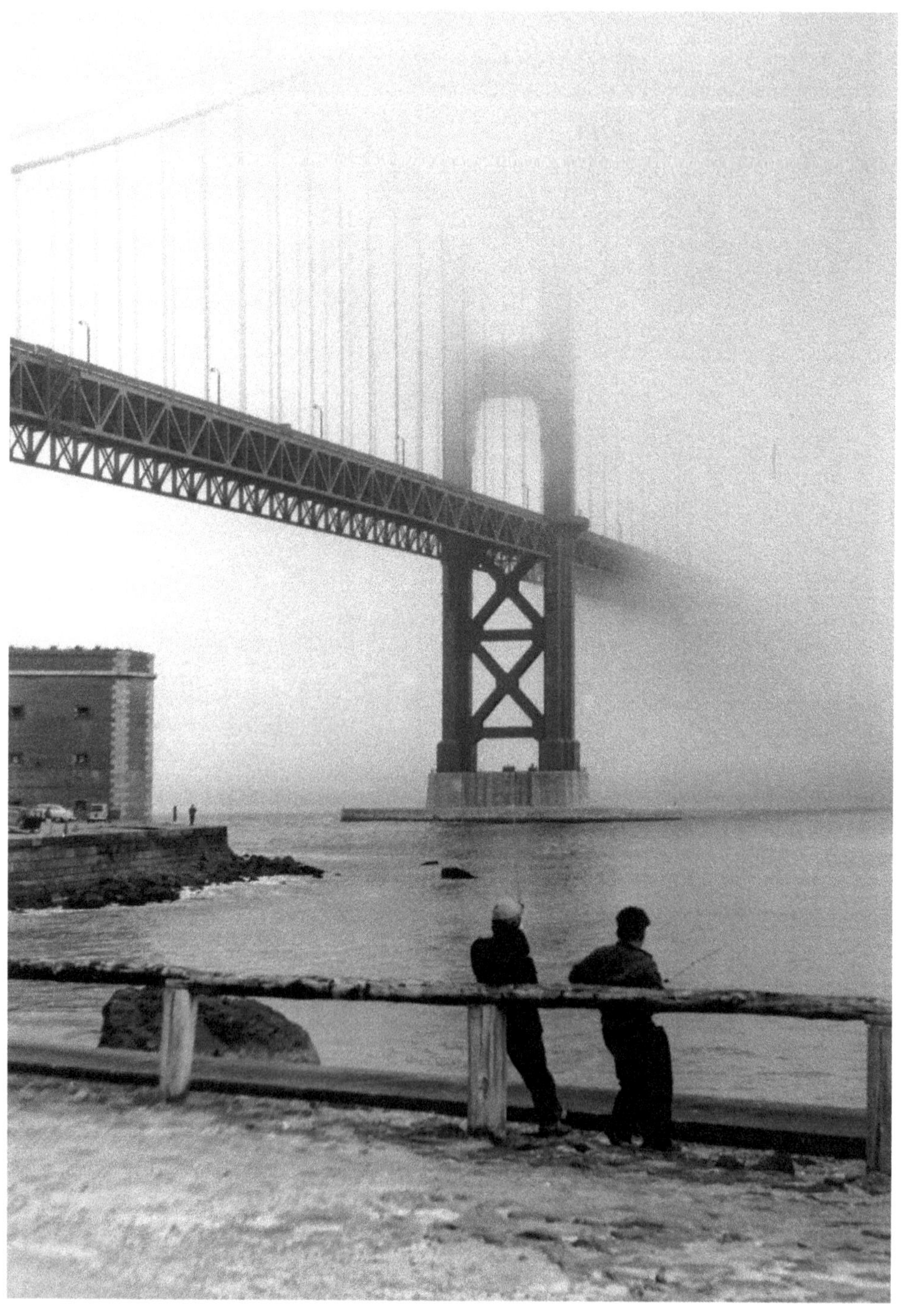

Fog envelops the Golden Gate Bridge as fishermen angle their lines at Fort Point on September 5, 1952.

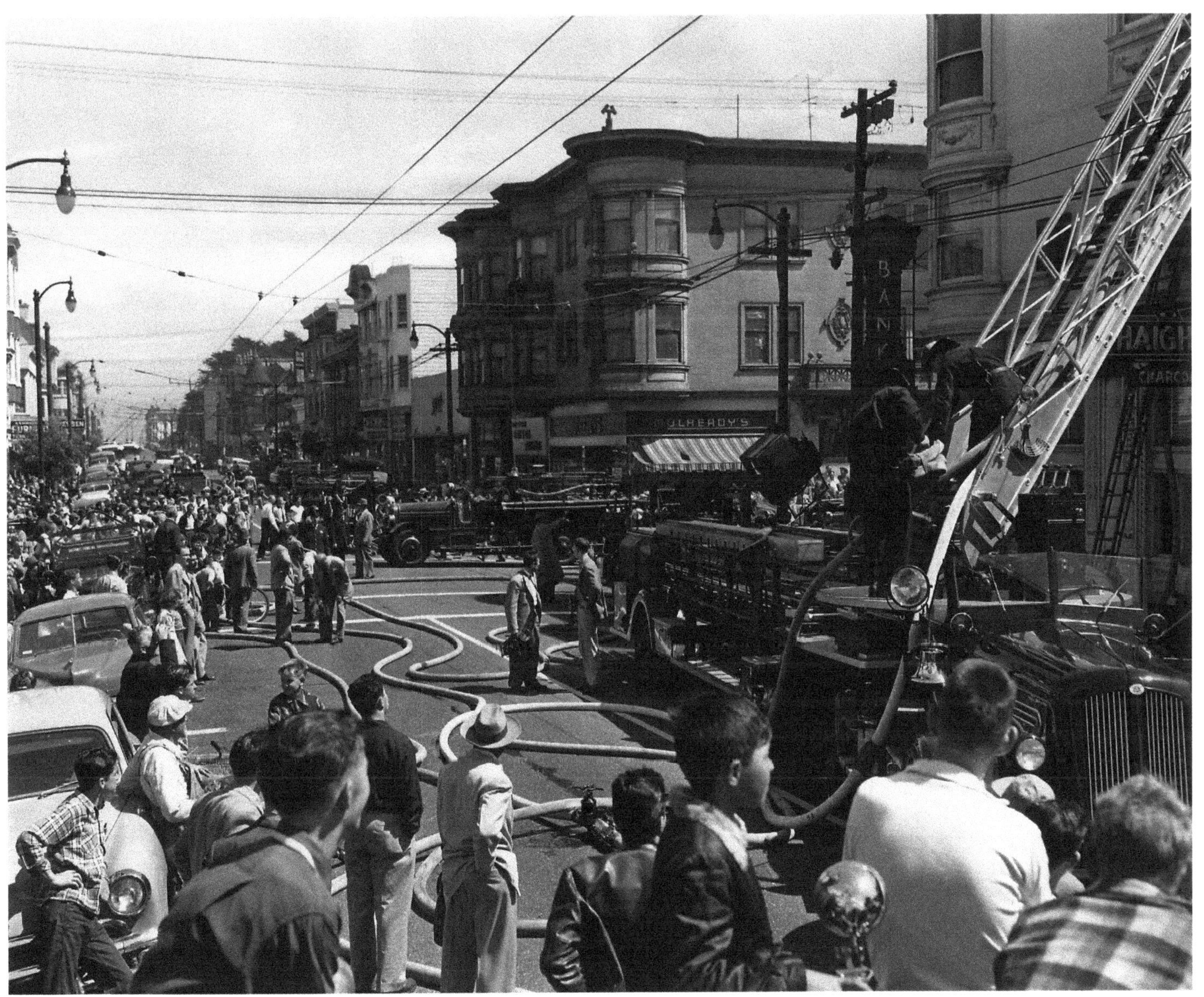

Firemen fight a three-alarm fire in an apartment building on Haight and Ashbury streets in the 1950s. Many onlookers brought their cameras to chronicle the spectacle.

General Mark Clark, an American general during World War II and the Korean War, waves to hundreds of San Franciscans lining Montgomery Street on his return from Korea in the mid 1950s. Clark served as commander of the United Nations and signed a cease-fire agreement with North Korea in 1953.

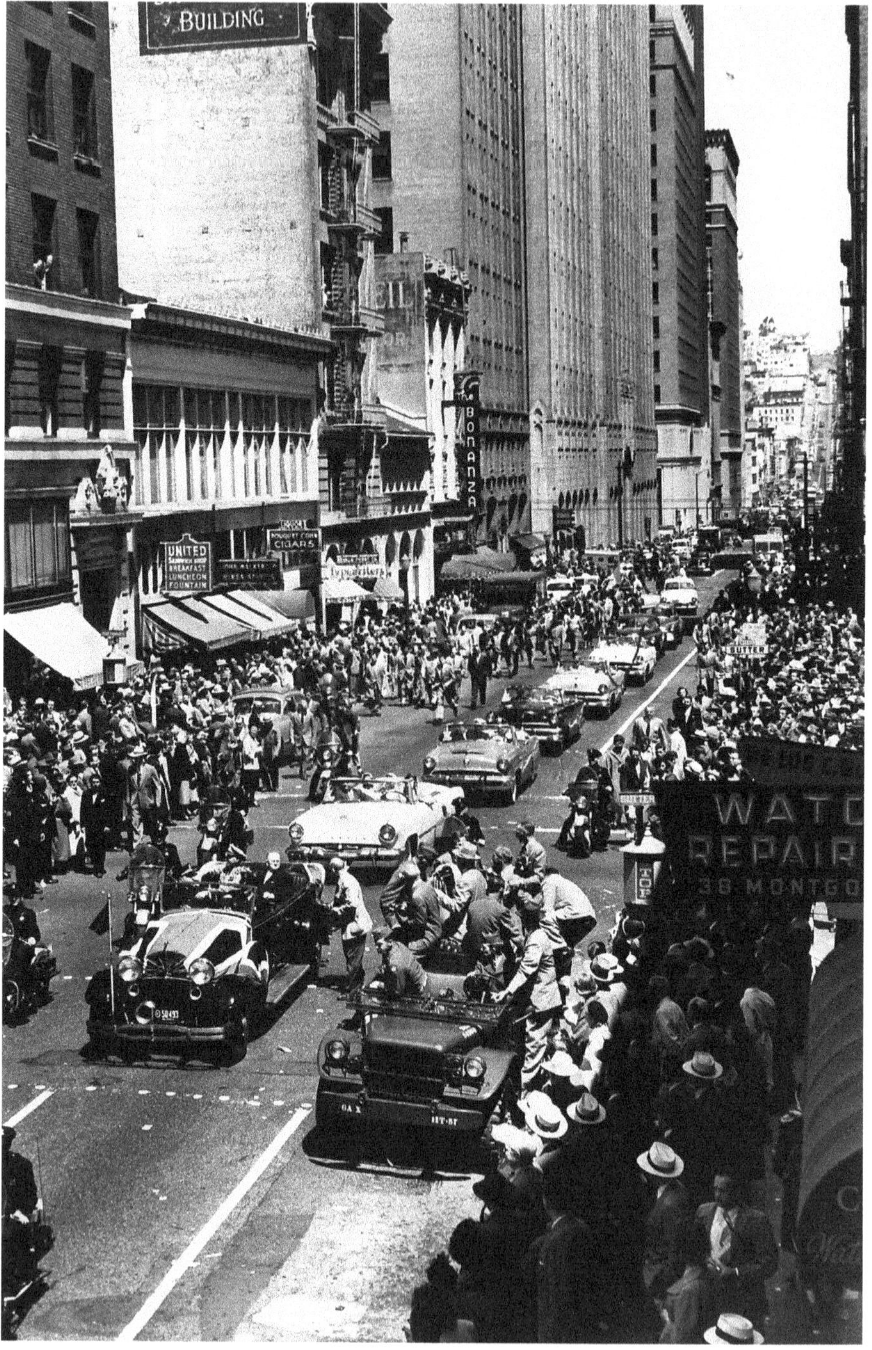

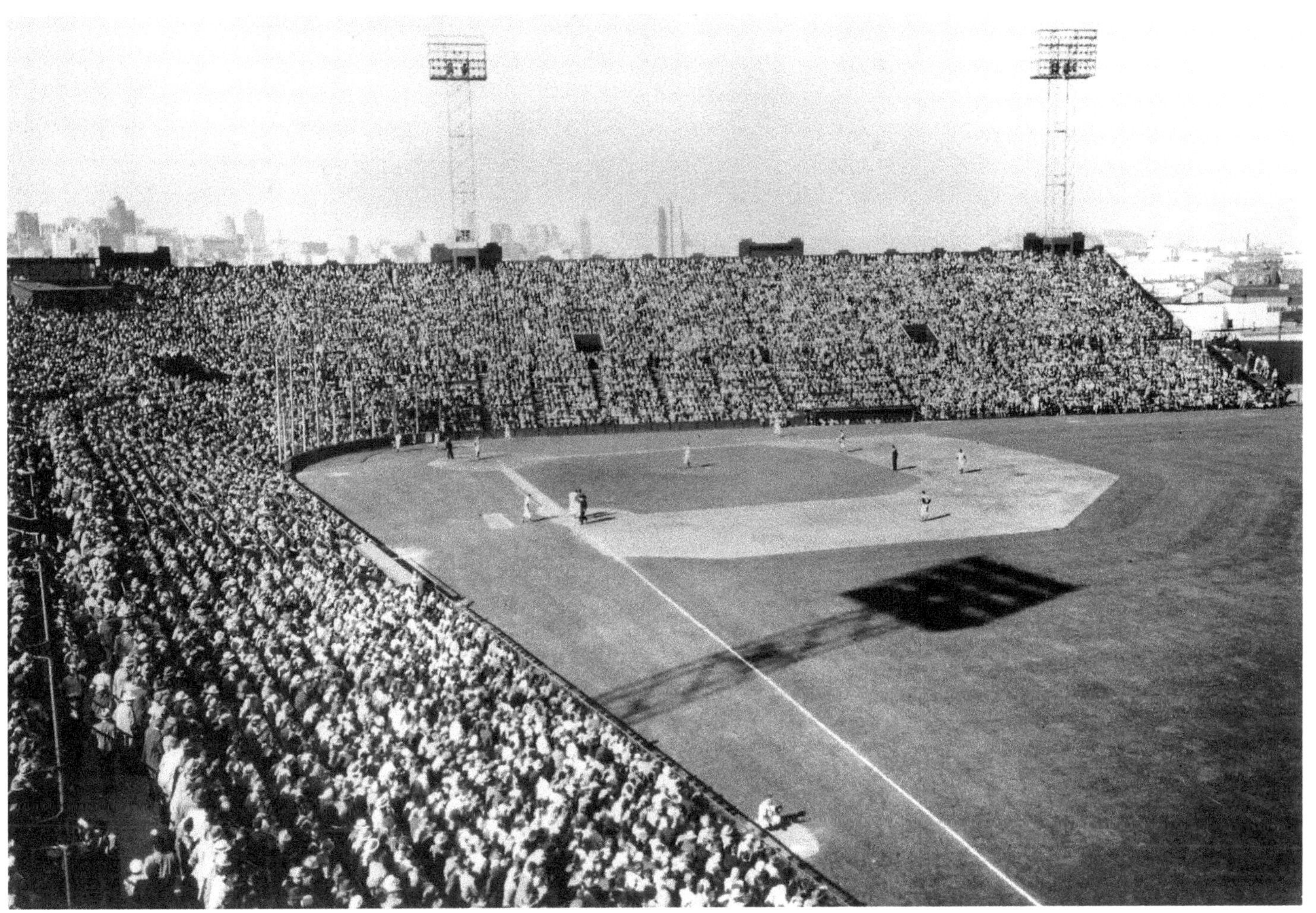

This picture shows the San Francisco Seals baseball team playing at Seals Stadium on March 20, 1954. At this event, Bay area Arvin dealers awarded new radios and television sets to Seals fans who accurately guessed the official number of fans who would turn out at the Seals game on April 6.

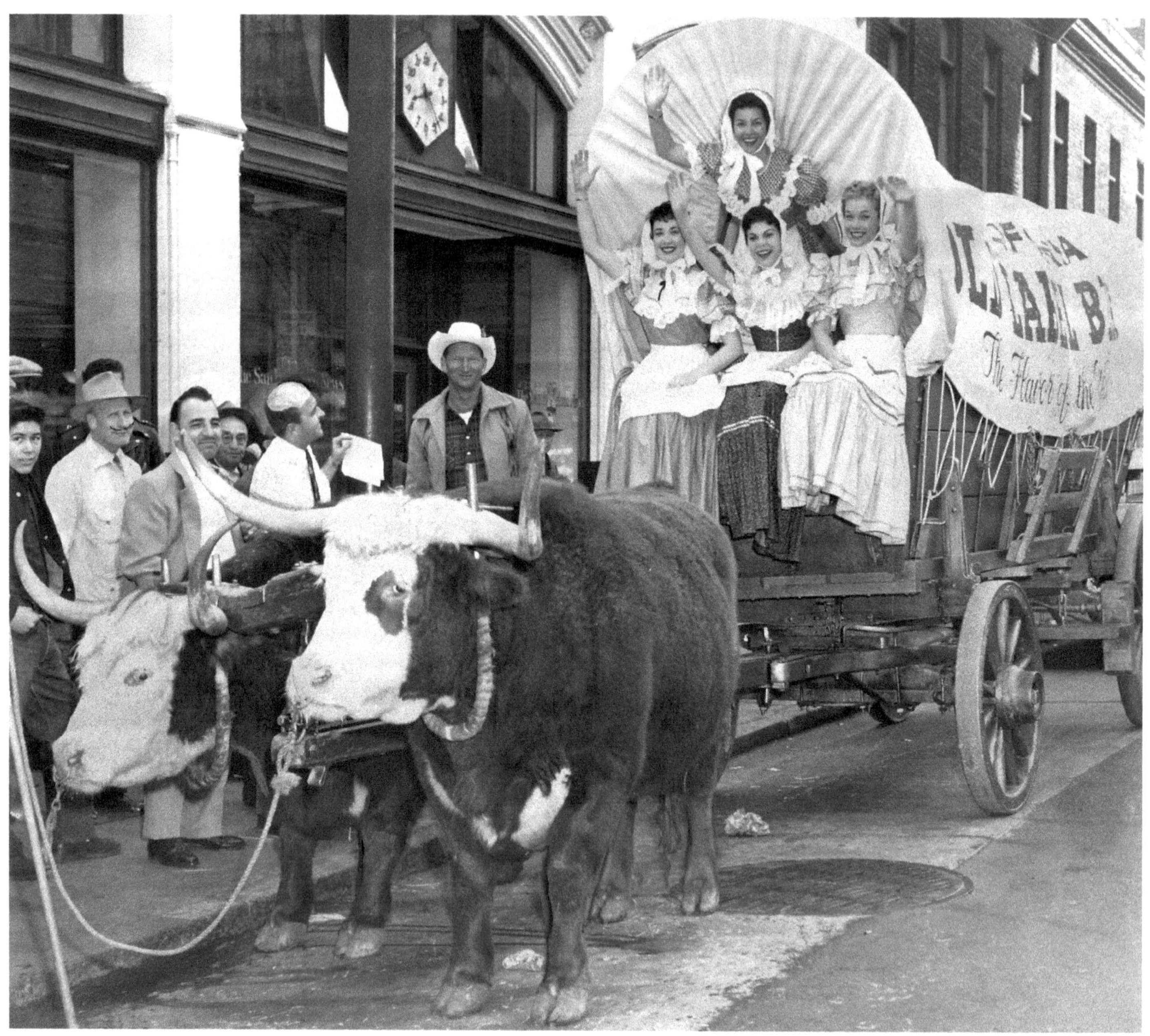

Pictured here on April 13, 1954, an ox-drawn Conestoga wagon advertises a new line of beer made by the sponsoring brewer.

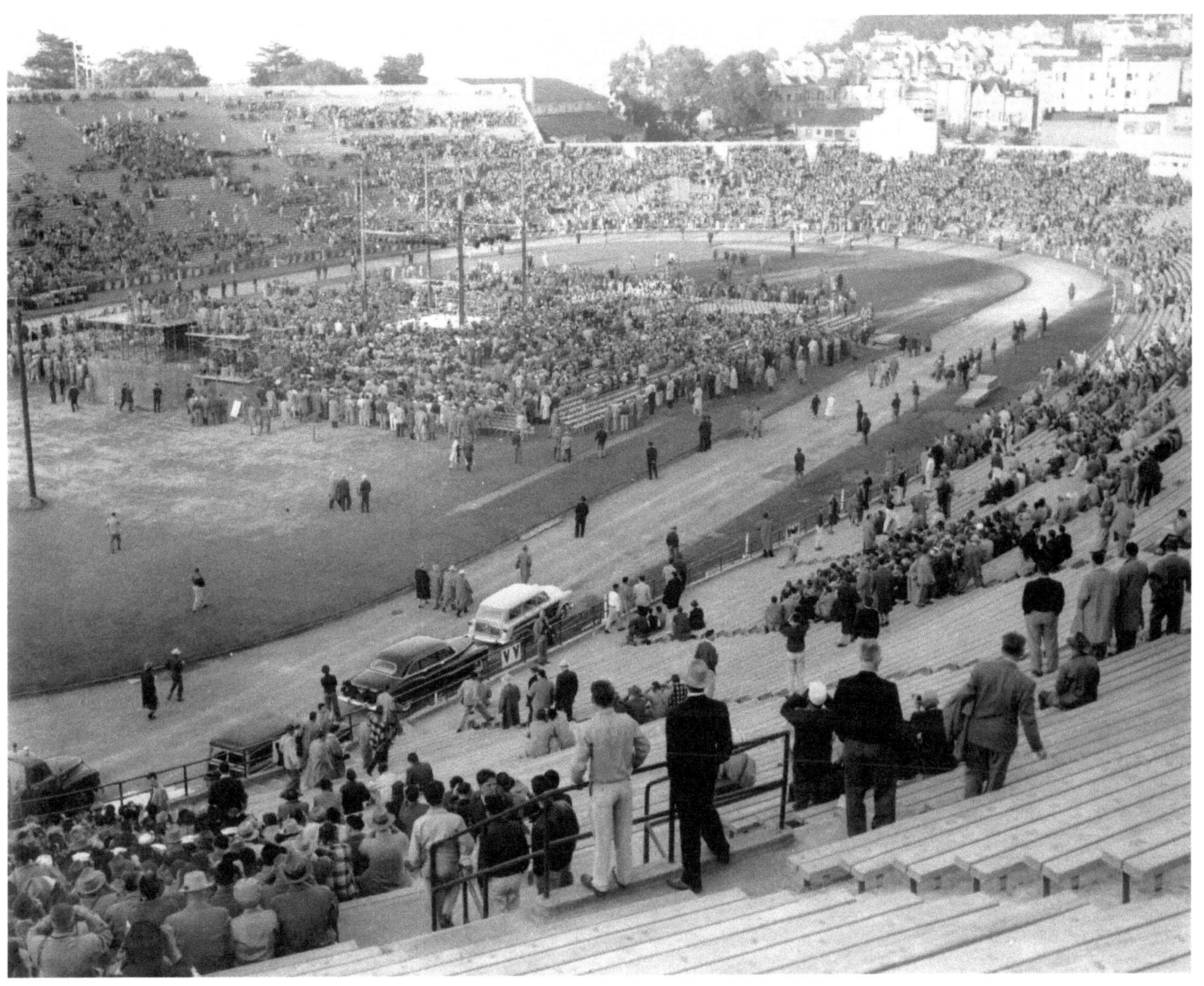

A championship heavyweight boxing match between Rocky Marciano and Don Cockell at Kezar Stadium, shown here in May 1955. Kezar Stadium, in the southeast end of Golden Gate Park, is the former longtime home to the San Francisco 49ers and, for their first year of existence in 1960, the Oakland Raiders, and is now the stadium for a professional lacrosse team, the San Francisco Dragons. In the 1970s, when football teams no longer played at Kezar, the stadium became a music venue for legendary musicians such as Led Zeppelin, Joan Baez, the Grateful Dead, Carlos Santana, and Neil Young. The stadium was heavily damaged in the 1989 earthquake, and was demolished and rebuilt with a much smaller seating capacity.

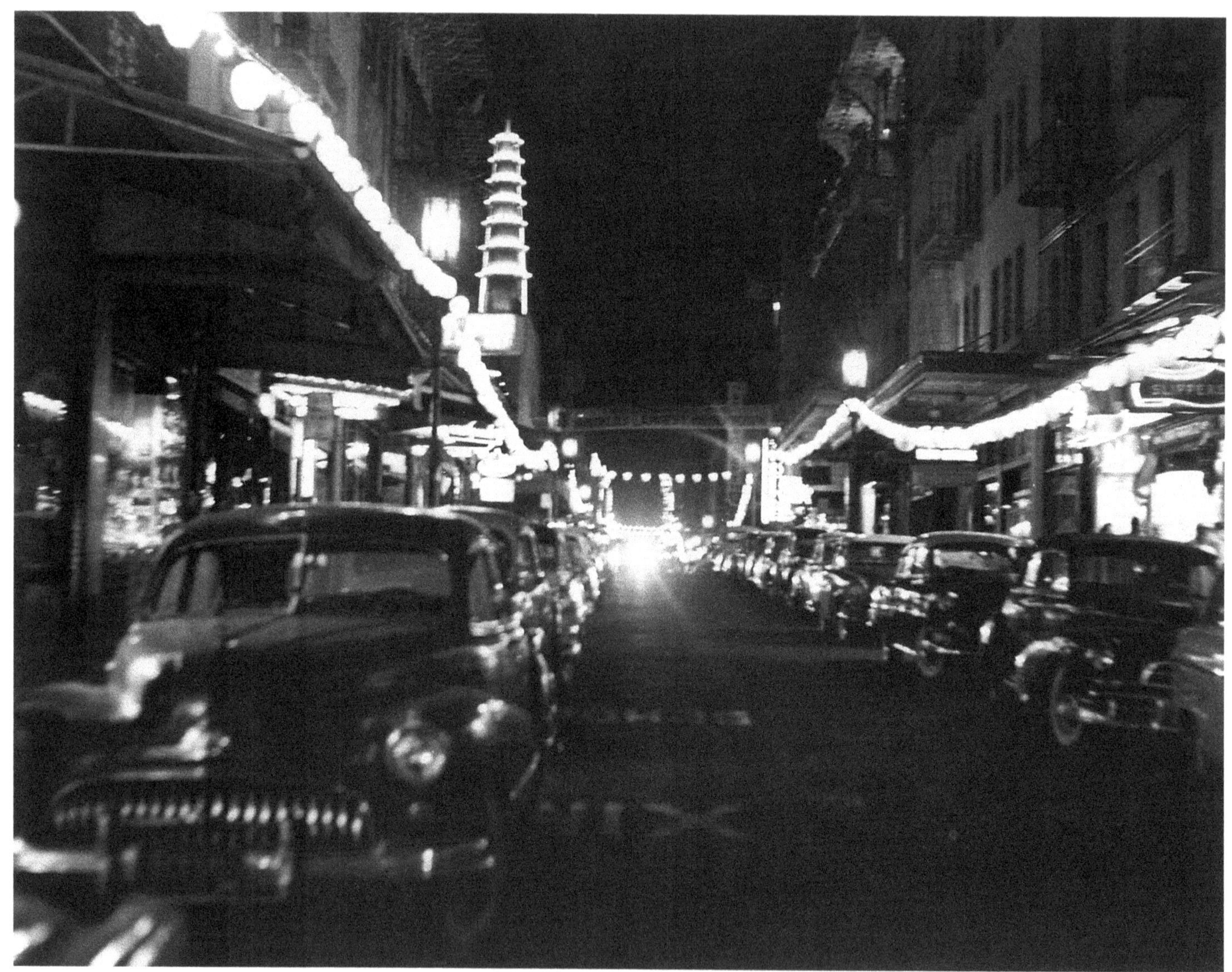

By the 1950s, the brothels, tong wars, opium dens, and other forms of crime that had plagued Chinatown in its early days existed largely in myth and legend. Lighted lanterns and colorful spotlights highlighting the street's pagodas and other Chinese-style buildings and landmarks are seen along Grant Avenue on the evening of August 11, 1955, providing an "exotic" and sanitized attraction for the thousands of tourists coming to San Francisco every year. Chinatown today remains overcrowded, with an underside that harbors clandestine sweatshops and gang activity.

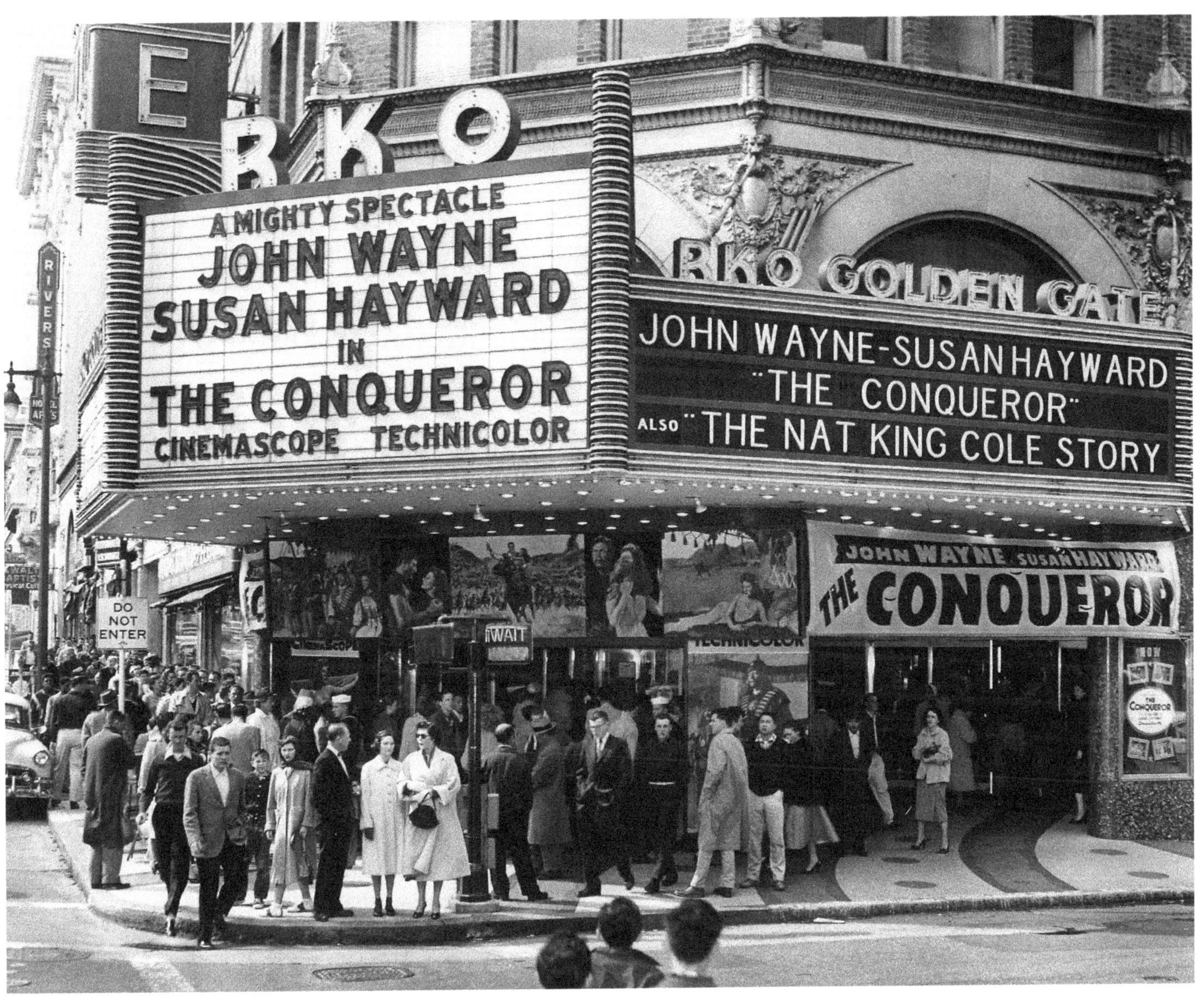

Built in 1920 at 1 Taylor Street, the Golden Gate Theatre showcased popular movies for more than half a century. Shown here February 23, 1956, scores of people line up at the Golden Gate to see John Wayne as Mongol emperor Genghis Khan in *The Conqueror,* as he battles Tartar armies to win the heart of Bortai, the Tartar princess. Since 1972, the Golden Gate Theatre has been a popular venue for the performing arts, especially traveling Broadway musicals.

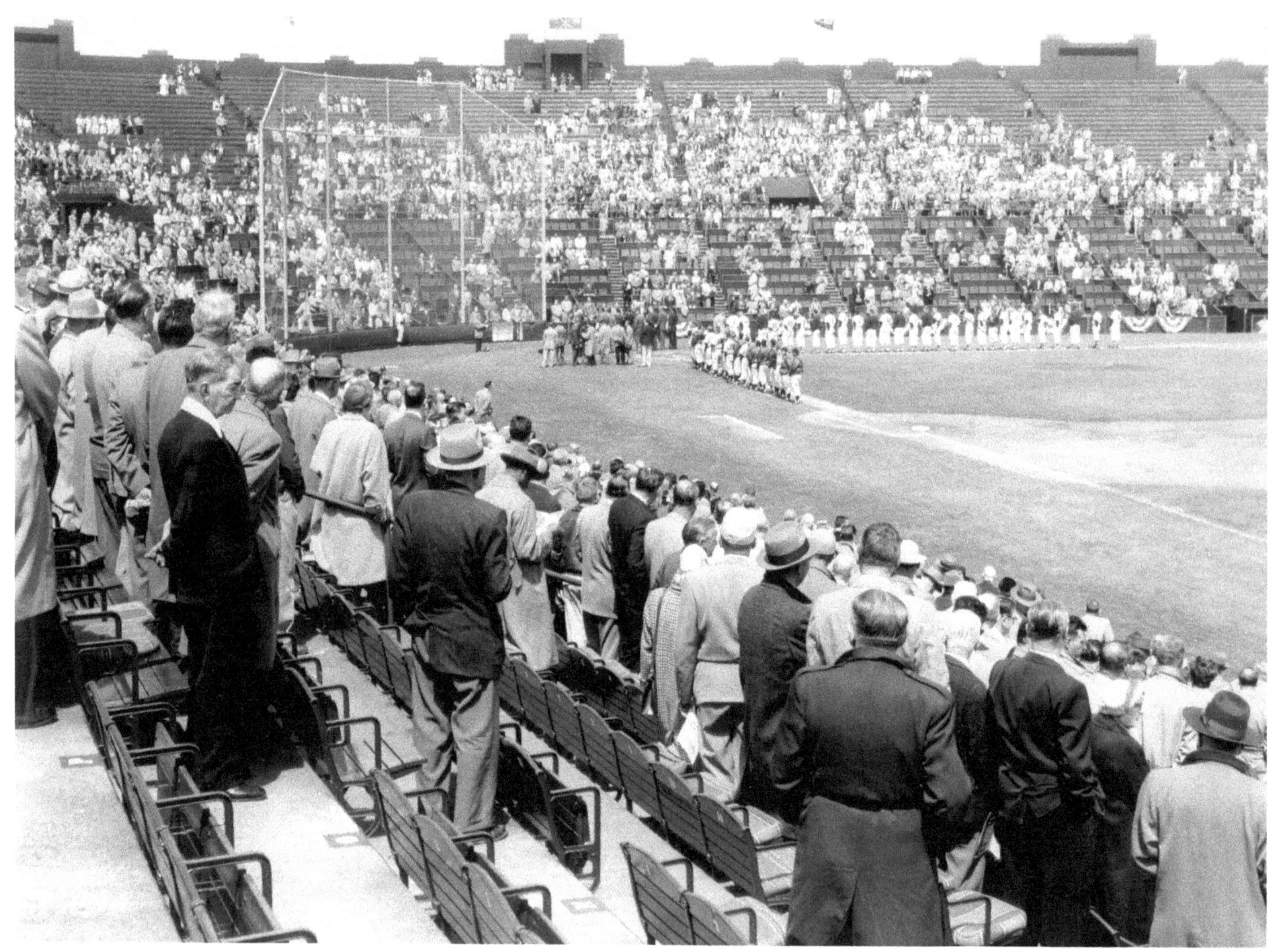

Spectators and players stand at the beginning of the opening-day game between the San Francisco Seals and the Vancouver Mounties (formerly the Oakland Oaks, who moved after the 1955 season) on April 10, 1956.

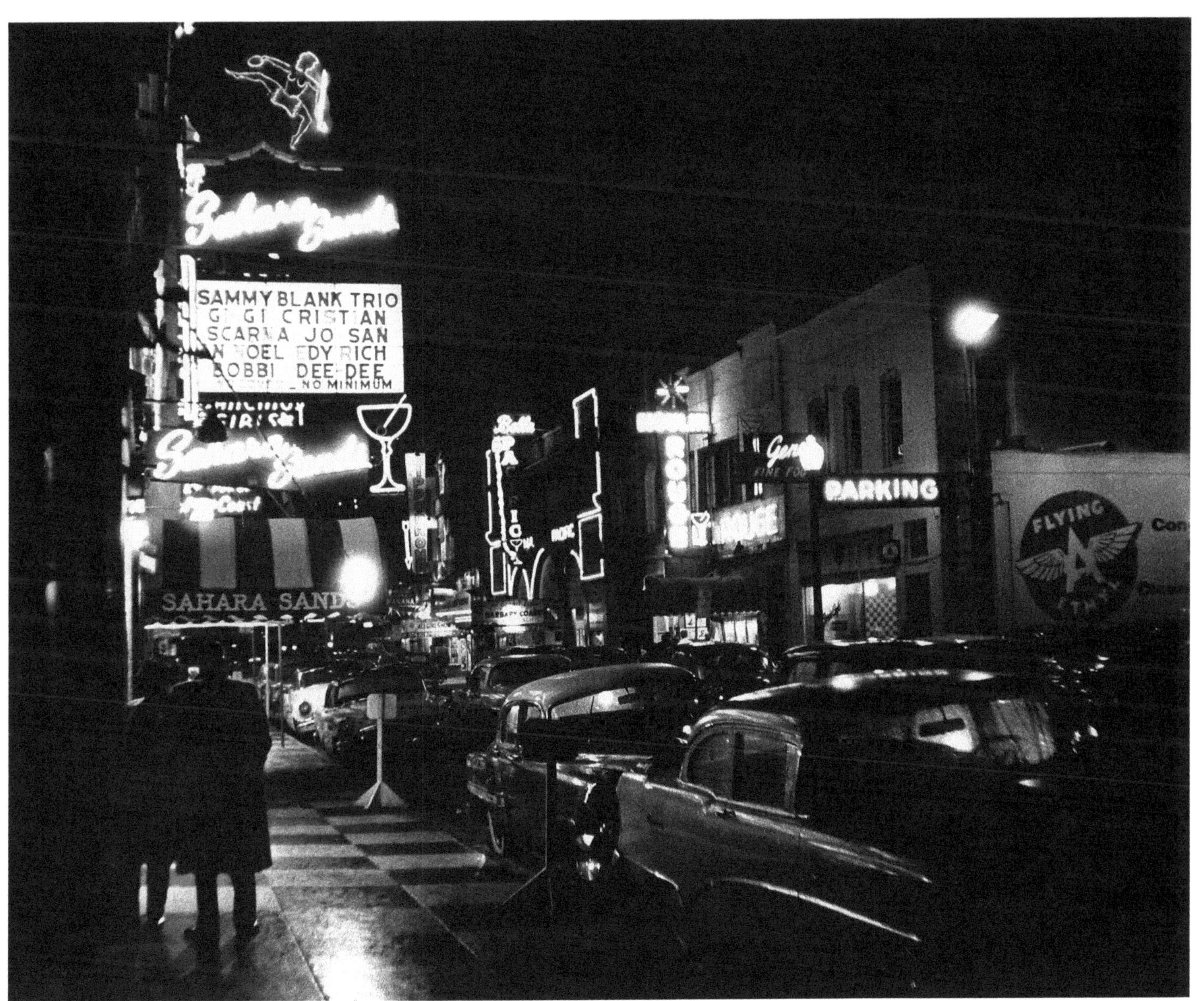

By April 30, 1956, when this picture was taken, the International Settlement on Pacific Avenue was gone, the area was much quieter, and there was not much visible evidence of the area's wild past.

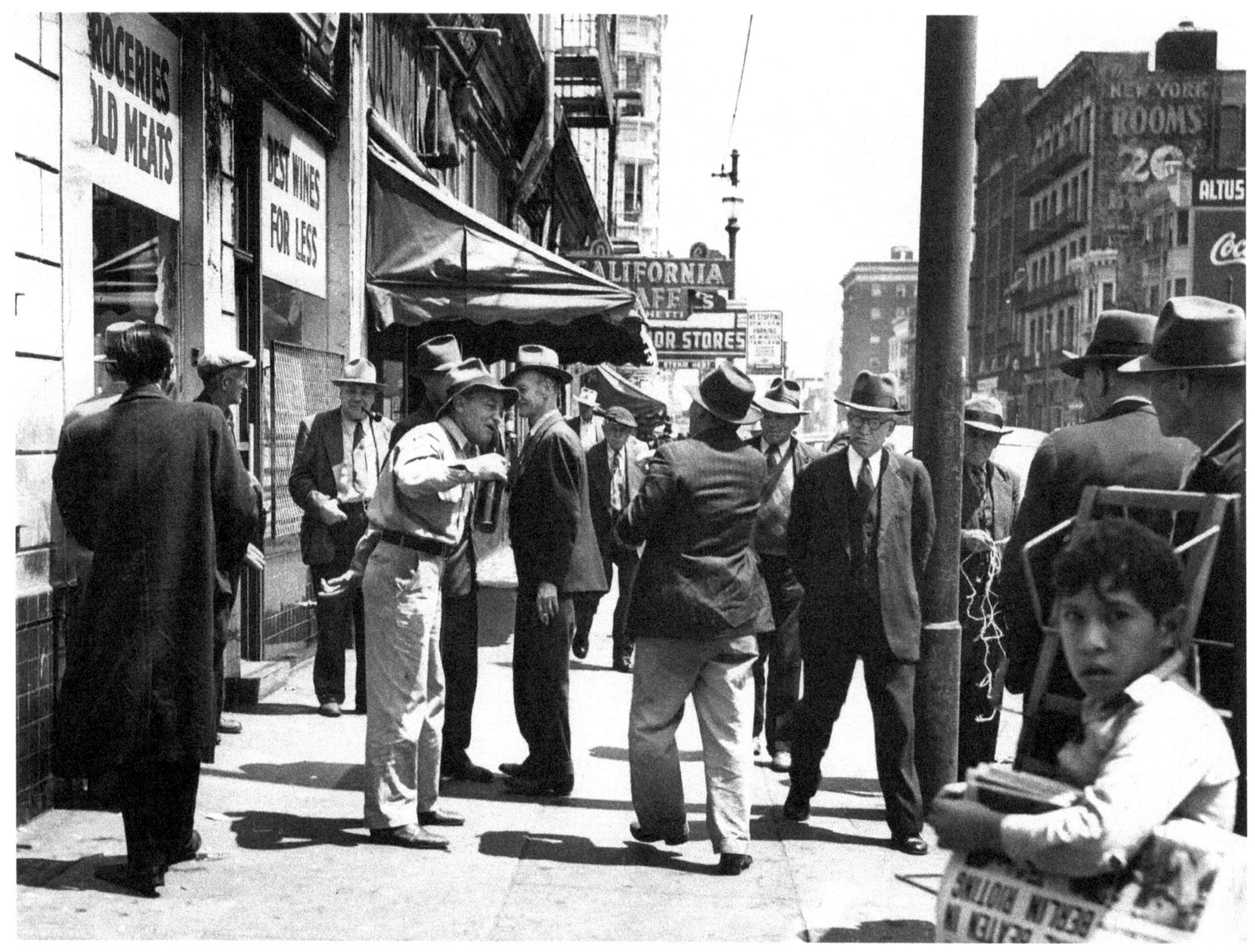

Like most large American cities, San Francisco has had several areas that could be thought of as "skid row," where unemployed, homeless, and generally down-and-out people congregate. In San Francisco, these neighborhoods tend to be areas in decline in the Tenderloin, South of Market, especially along 6th Street, and in parts of Bayview–Hunters Point. Transient hotels, cheap restaurants, liquor stores, pawn shops, and stores with "bargain" merchandise are seen here on July 23, 1956. A group of men hang out, hoping that their luck will turn and that they will find day jobs. A newspaper article of the time said, "No one along Skid Road is likely to shop carefully."

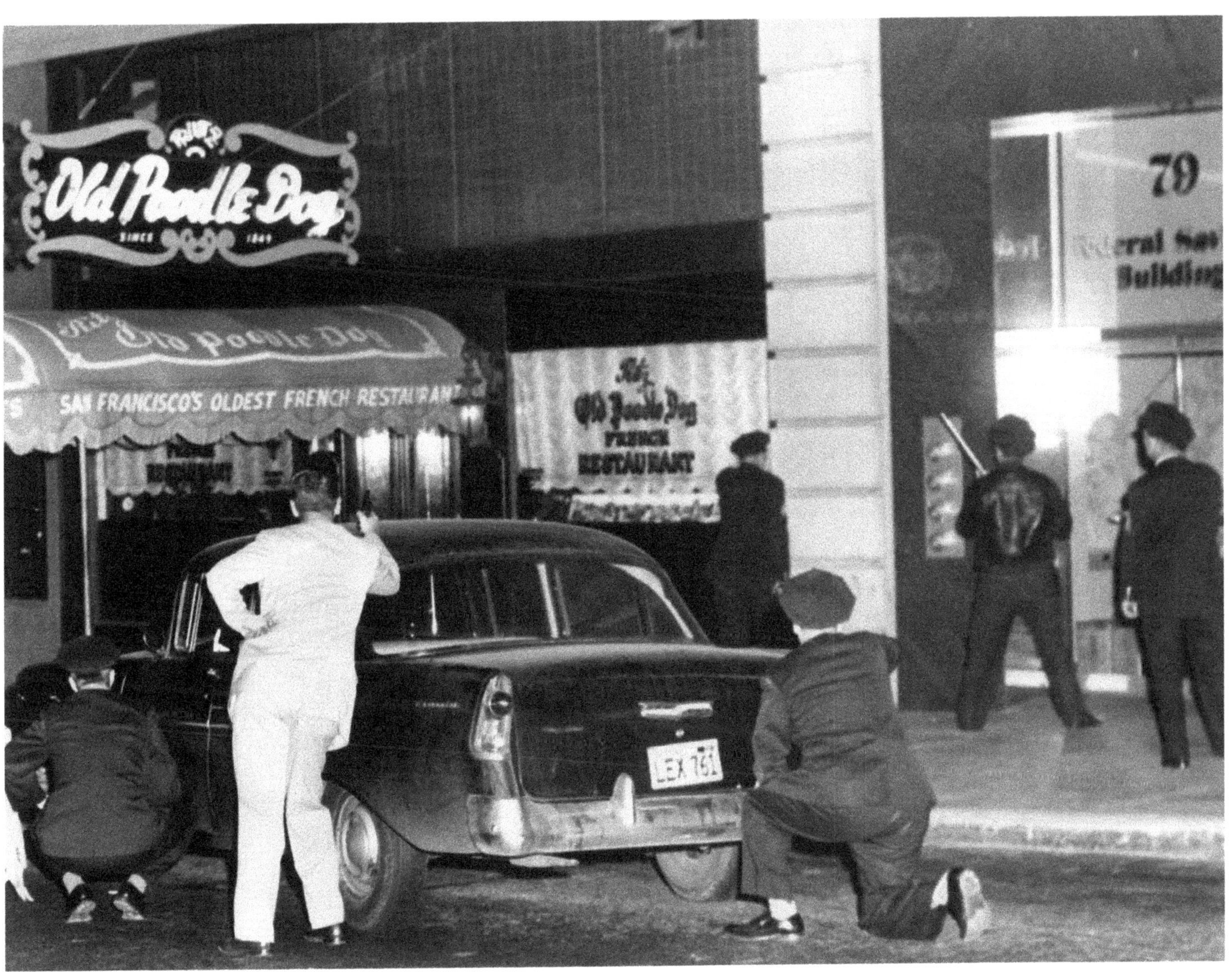

Police officers wait with guns drawn and tear gas close to hand outside the Old Poodle Dog Restaurant on Post Street, while criminals hold hostages at gunpoint inside. The four robbers escaped through a skylight with $160, but were in such a hurry that they left $920. The Poodle Dog began as a Gold Rush–era restaurant, which originally served fresh French cuisine out of a flimsy tent hotel in exchange for gold dust. Since then, there have been at least four reincarnations of the Poodle Dog Restaurant of this name, and one called Le Poudre d'Or or "Gold Dust."

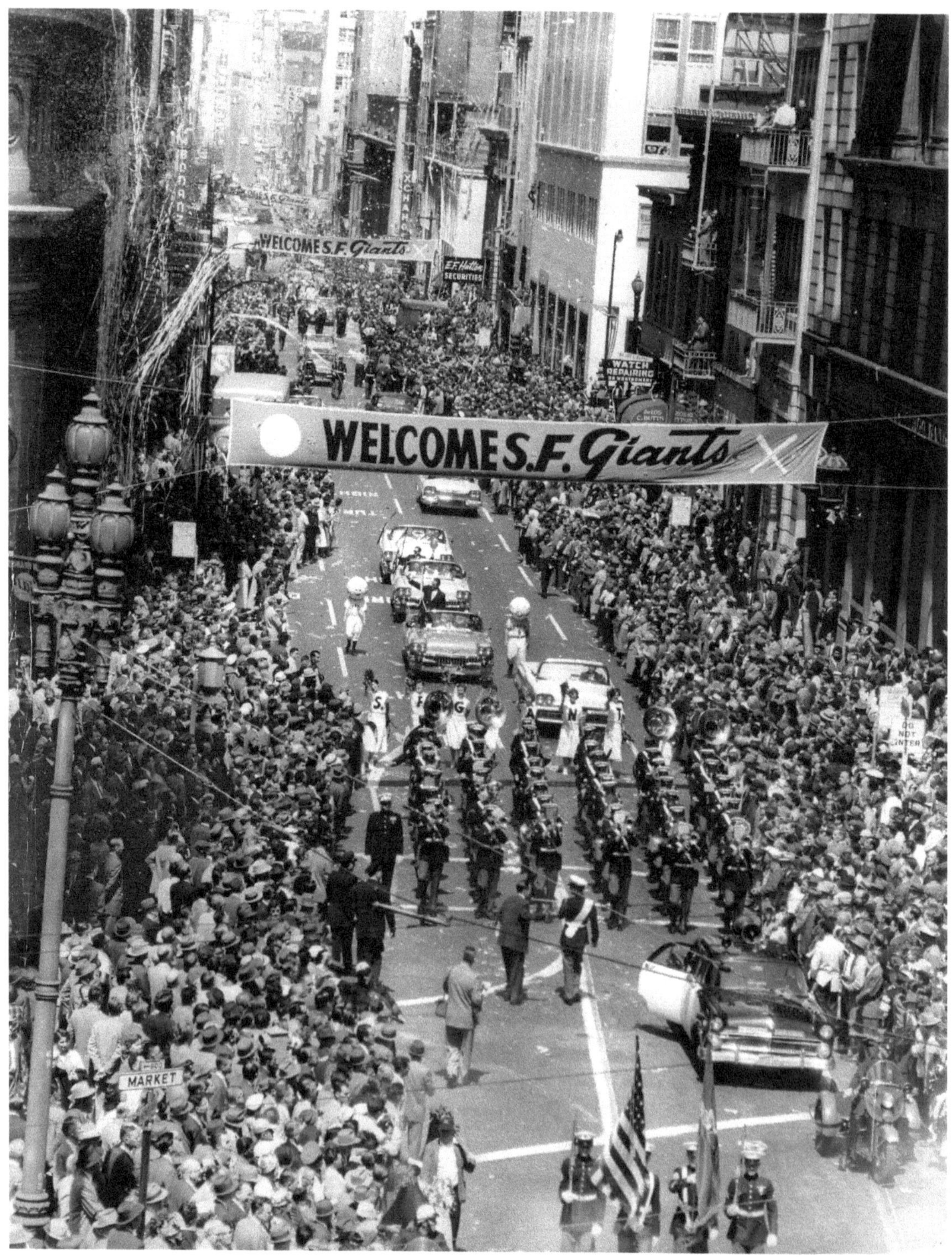

More than 100,000 baseball fans welcome San Francisco's new baseball team, the Giants, along Montgomery Street to Market, pictured here April 13, 1958. San Francisco Mayor George Christopher stands under the welcome sign, as the crowd cheers that "George brought the Giants." For nearly 50 years, San Francisco Giants fans have eagerly anticipated another Giants parade down Market Street celebrating a World Series win, but this has yet to occur. The San Francisco Giants have made only three appearances in the World Series, losing in 1962, 1989, and 2002.

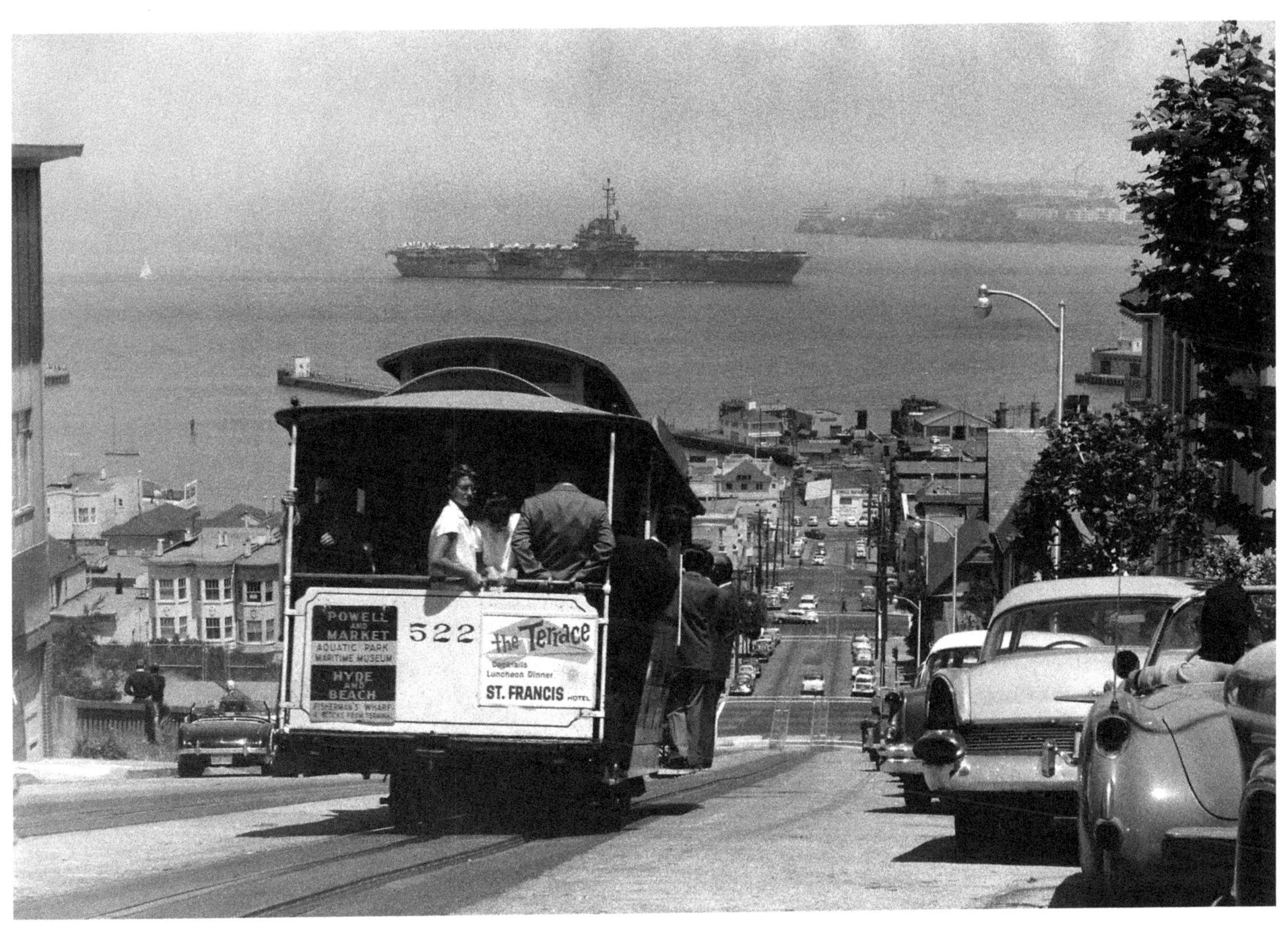

A cable car descends the Hyde Street hill, as the aircraft carrier *Ticonderoga* glides across the bay in the background, July 3, 1958.

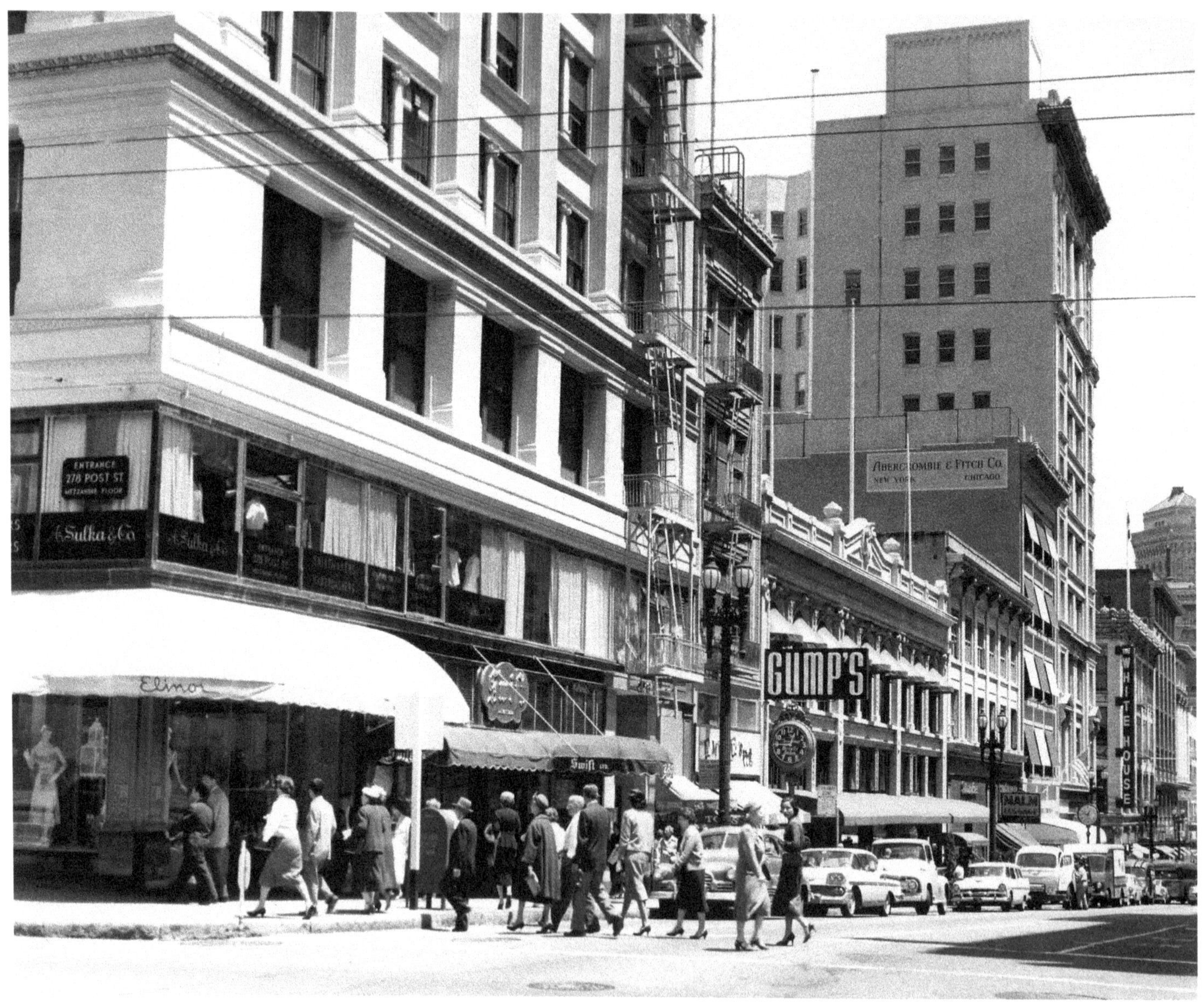

Well-dressed shoppers are seen crossing the street near Union Square at the intersection of Post and Stockton streets on May 8, 1958. The Gump's sign at lower-middle hangs outside the entrance to this eminent purveyor of unusual gifts and high-quality merchandise, especially items from the Pacific Rim. Gump's, in operation since 1861, moved in the 1990s from the location shown here.

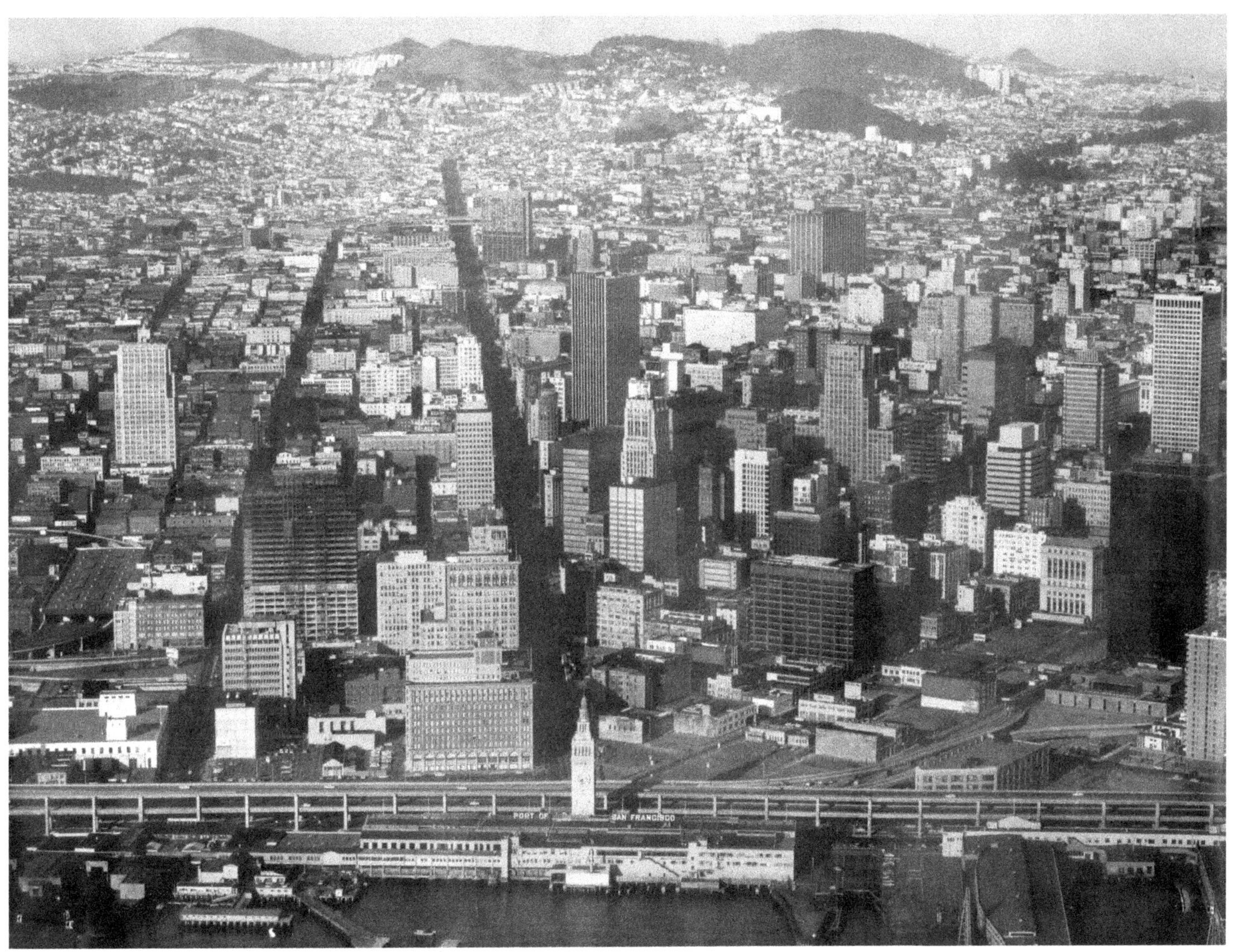

This aerial view of San Francisco looks west up Market Street. The Ferry Building is seen at bottom. Tall buildings dominate the skyline in the Financial District, downtown, South of Market, and Nob Hill areas. The double-decker Embarcadero freeway is seen running along the Embarcadero in front of the Ferry Building. Noticeably missing are the Transamerica Pyramid, completed in 1972, and the four Embarcadero Center towers, completed between 1968 and 1983, near the former Barbary Coast.

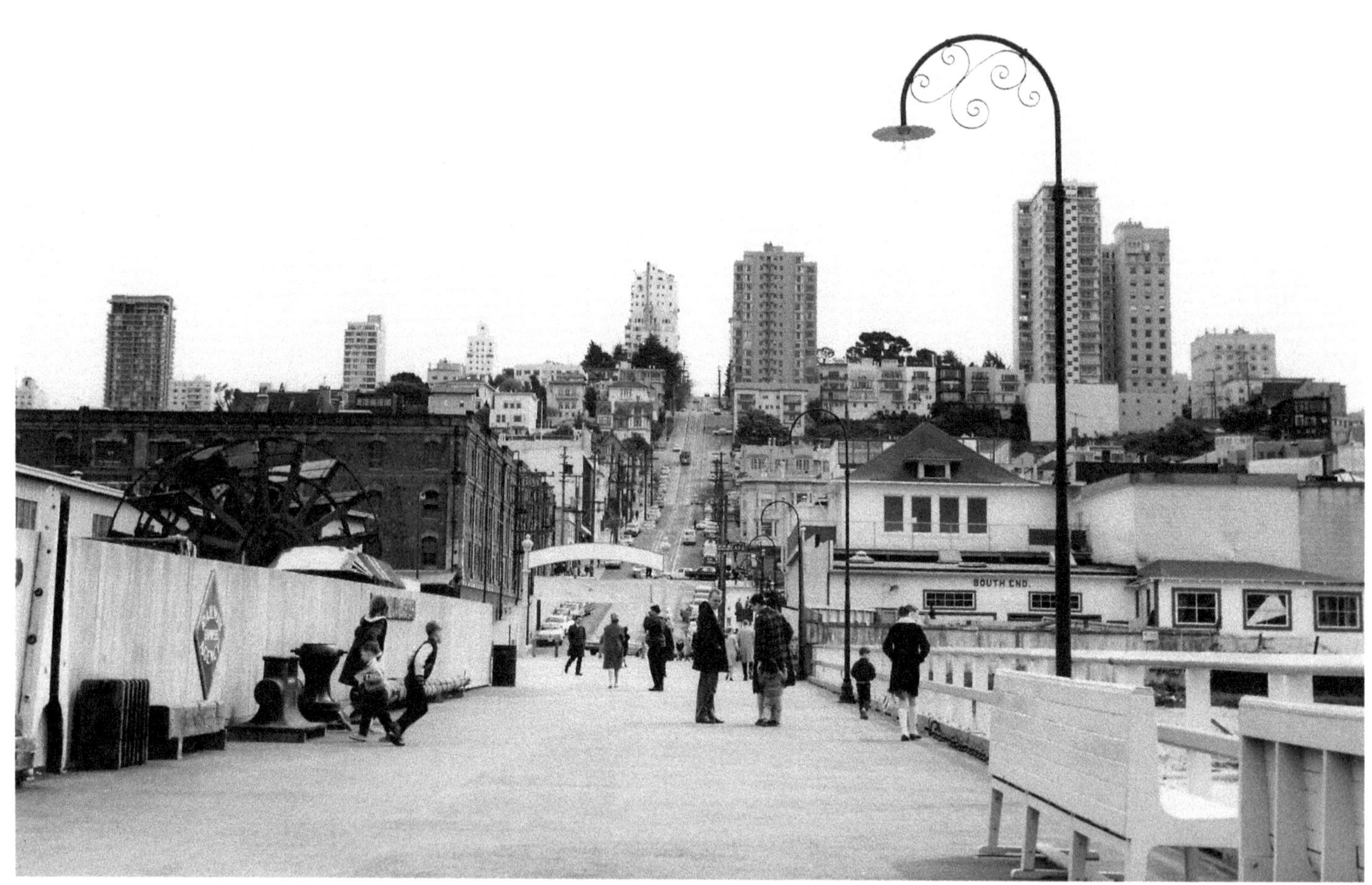

The Hyde Street hill is seen from Hyde Street Pier in this 1960s photo. Hyde Street Pier had been the site of the automobile ferry depot that operated before the Golden Gate and Bay bridges were built. Tourists regularly visit the pier, located in the Fisherman's Wharf area. The brick building at left is the Cannery, the former Del Monte fruit canning factory from the early twentieth century. Once one of the largest peach canneries in the world, today the cannery is a stylish complex of boutiques, cafes, and art galleries.

A Decade of Change

(1960s)

In the 1960s, the nation found itself fiercely divided over the Vietnam War and civil rights. The Civil Rights Movement fundamentally changed social relations in America, and this dynamic energy was pulsating in the Bay area, which emerged in the latter half of the twentieth century as extremely liberal and at the vanguard of national currents and trends. San Francisco's youth were proactive and rebelled against the established order of mainstream America, causing general social upheaval.

In 1967, 100,000 baby boomers made a pilgrimage to San Francisco's Haight-Ashbury district, the Mecca of the hippie counterculture movement. During the infamous Summer of Love, they expanded their consciousness with mind-altering drugs and lived according to the mantra of free love, drugs, and rock and roll. San Francisco also experienced a musical and cultural renaissance in the 1960s. The Grateful Dead and other bands played for free in Golden Gate Park and in the Haight. The gay rights movement also began in the sixties.

In the decades to come, San Francisco would cement its reputation as one of the world's great cities. Known worldwide for its diversity, natural beauty, high quality of life, culture, and cuisine, San Francisco today is home to approximately 750,000 people. The city has come a long way from its humble beginnings as a rough-and-tumble frontier town, and recovered greatly from the ashes of the 1906 earthquake which nearly destroyed it. In spite of the ebb and flow of economic prosperity through the decades, another massive earthquake in 1989, and the high cost of living, San Francisco is consistently ranked as one of the top cities in the nation and the world to live in and to visit.

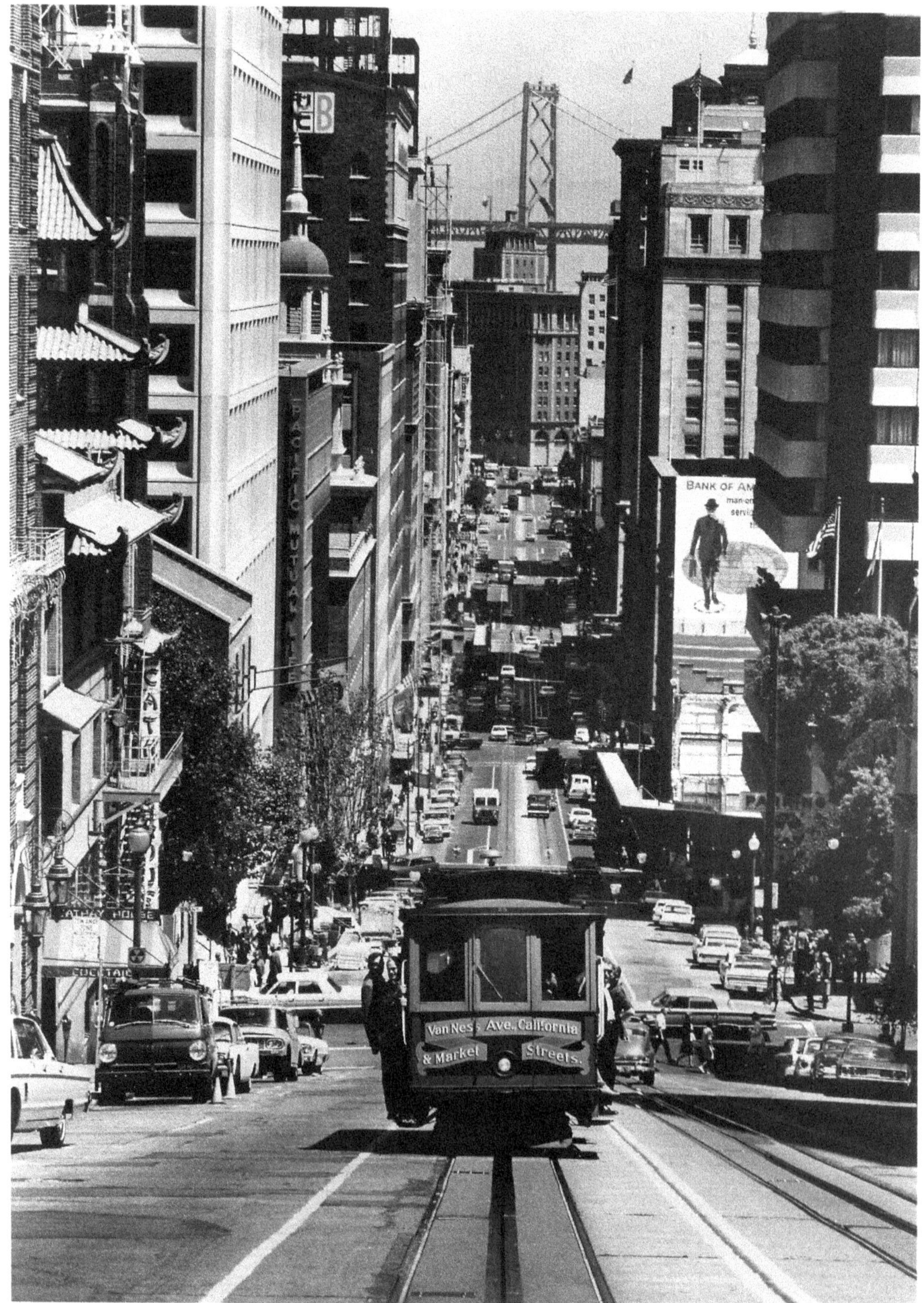

This California Street cable car slowly climbs "halfway to the stars" in the 1960s, passing the buildings in the Financial District, luxury hotels, and Chinatown, with the Bay Bridge in the distance.

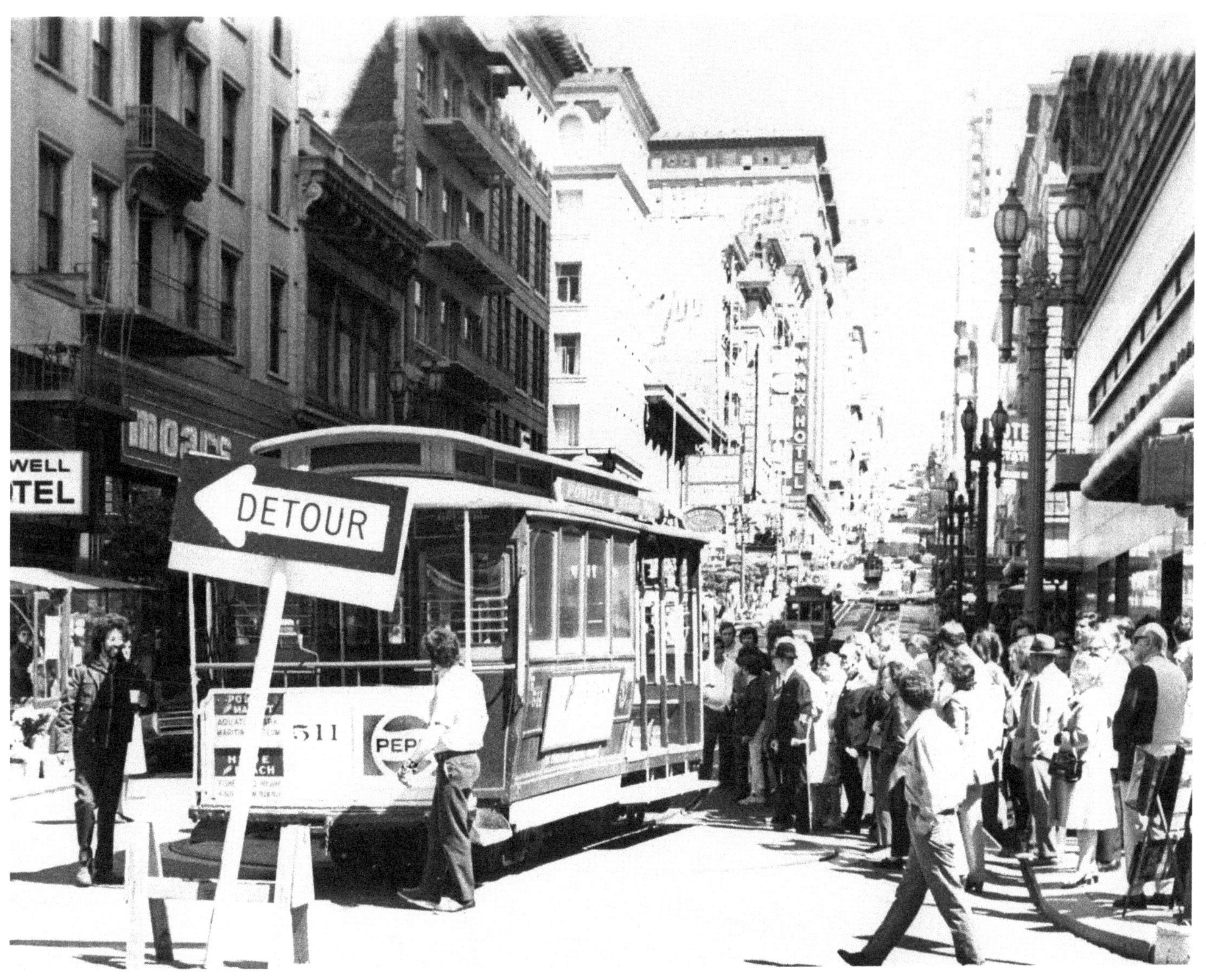

A crowd of people waits to ride a cable car on Powell Street, shown here in the 1960s.

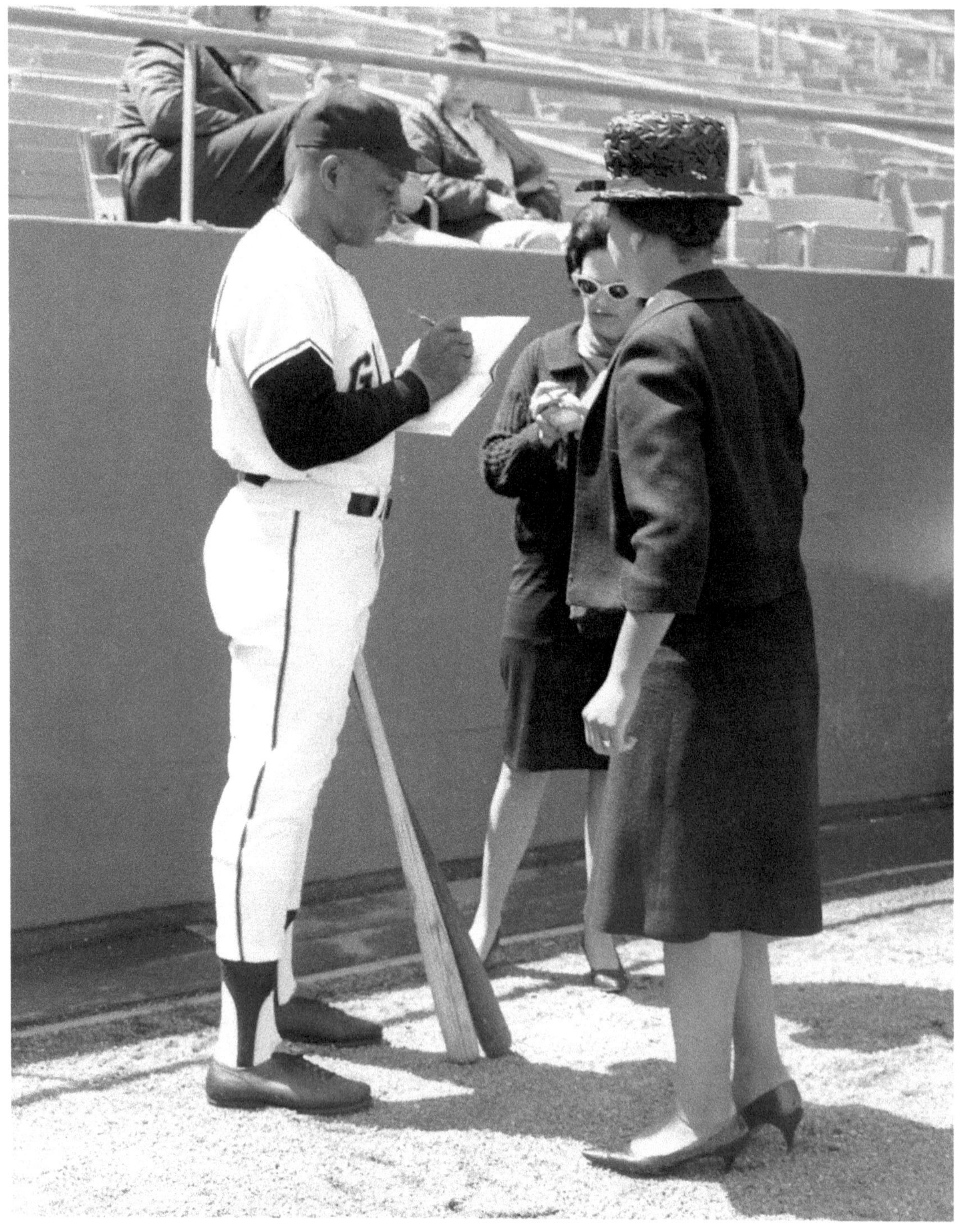

San Francisco Giants All-Star Willie Mays signs autographs for his fans in the 1960s. Today's AT&T Park is located at 24 (Willie's playing number) Willie Mays Plaza, with a statue of Mays and 24 palm trees gracing the front.

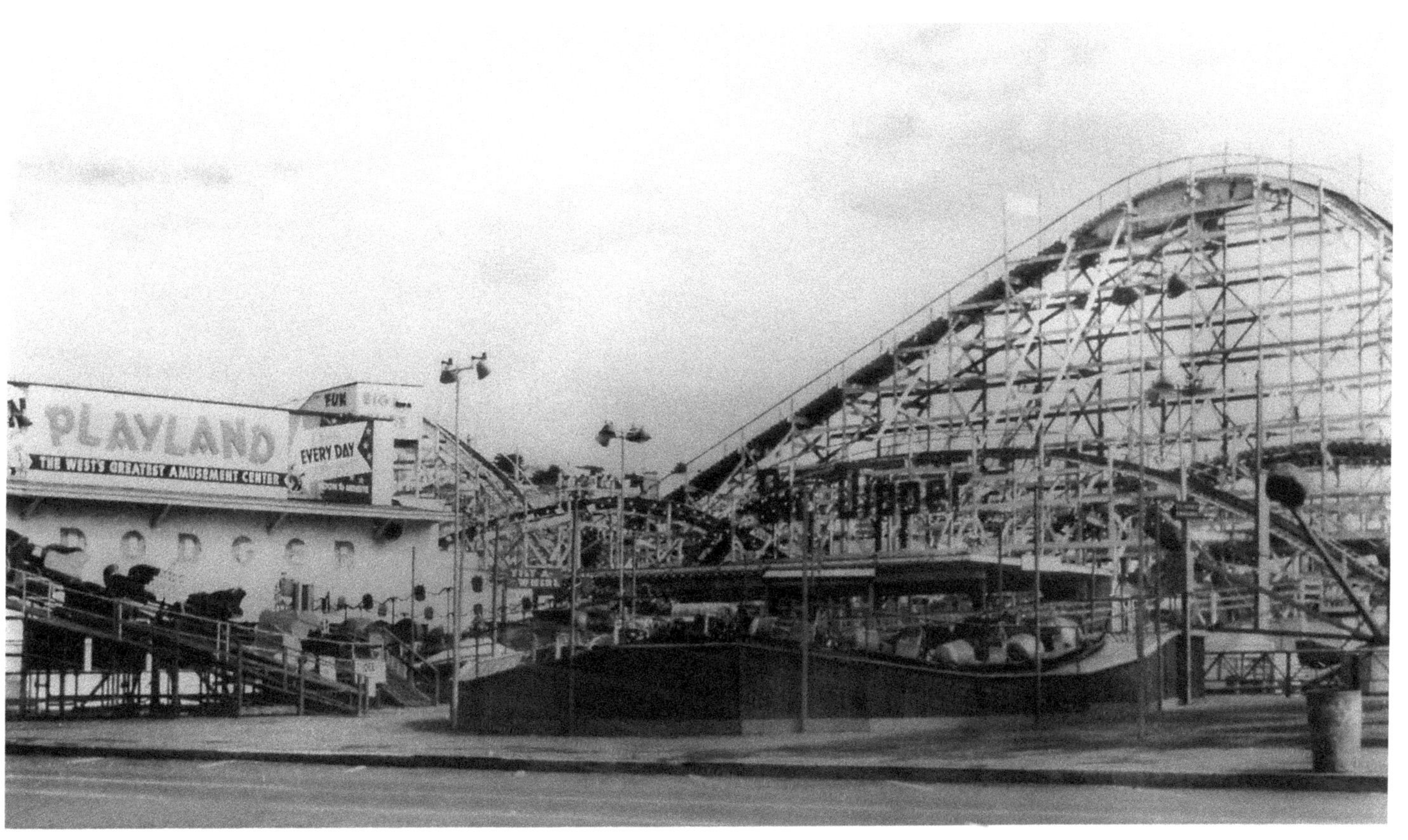

The famous Playland at the Beach at Ocean Beach is shown here in 1960. This amusement park was open from 1921 to 1972 and flourished during the Depression and World War II, attracting people from all over the Bay area, especially families, couples, and soldiers, to its inexpensive, old-fashioned fun. Many San Franciscans have fond memories of Topsy's Roost Restaurant, Chutes at the Beach water ride, the carousel, the Big Dipper wooden roller coaster, and Laughing Sal, the huge, mechanical, gap-toothed, freckled woman with rust-colored ringlet hair that greeted people and scared children at the entrance to the Fun House in Playland, beginning in the 1940s. Playland was also the birthplace of It's-It ice cream sandwiches, created by the owner of the park, George Whitney. In the 1960s, Playland was in decline and the area was past its prime. Non-descript condominiums replaced Playland after it was finally demolished in 1972.

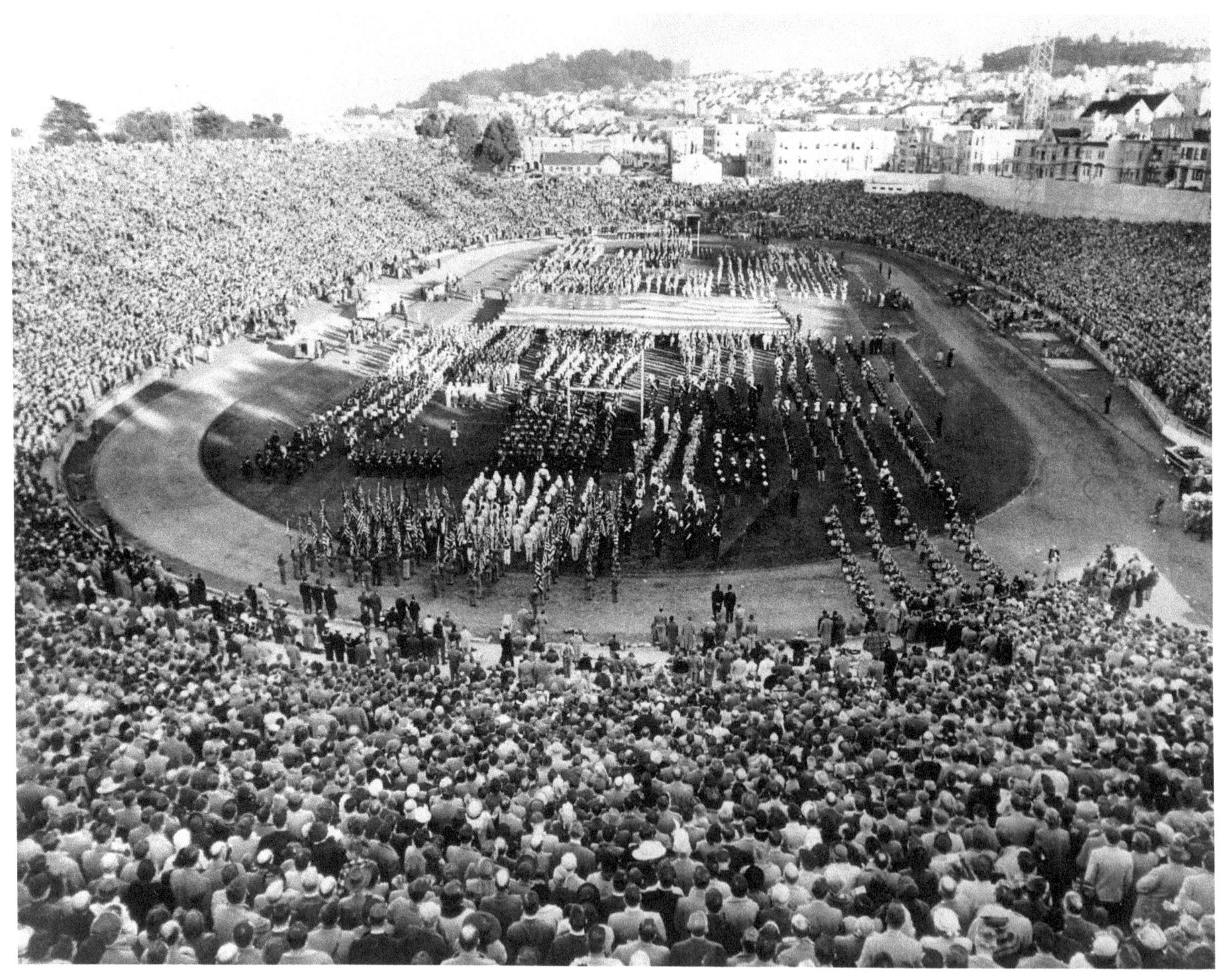

A crowd watches a marching band on the field at Kezar Stadium on May 11, 1960.

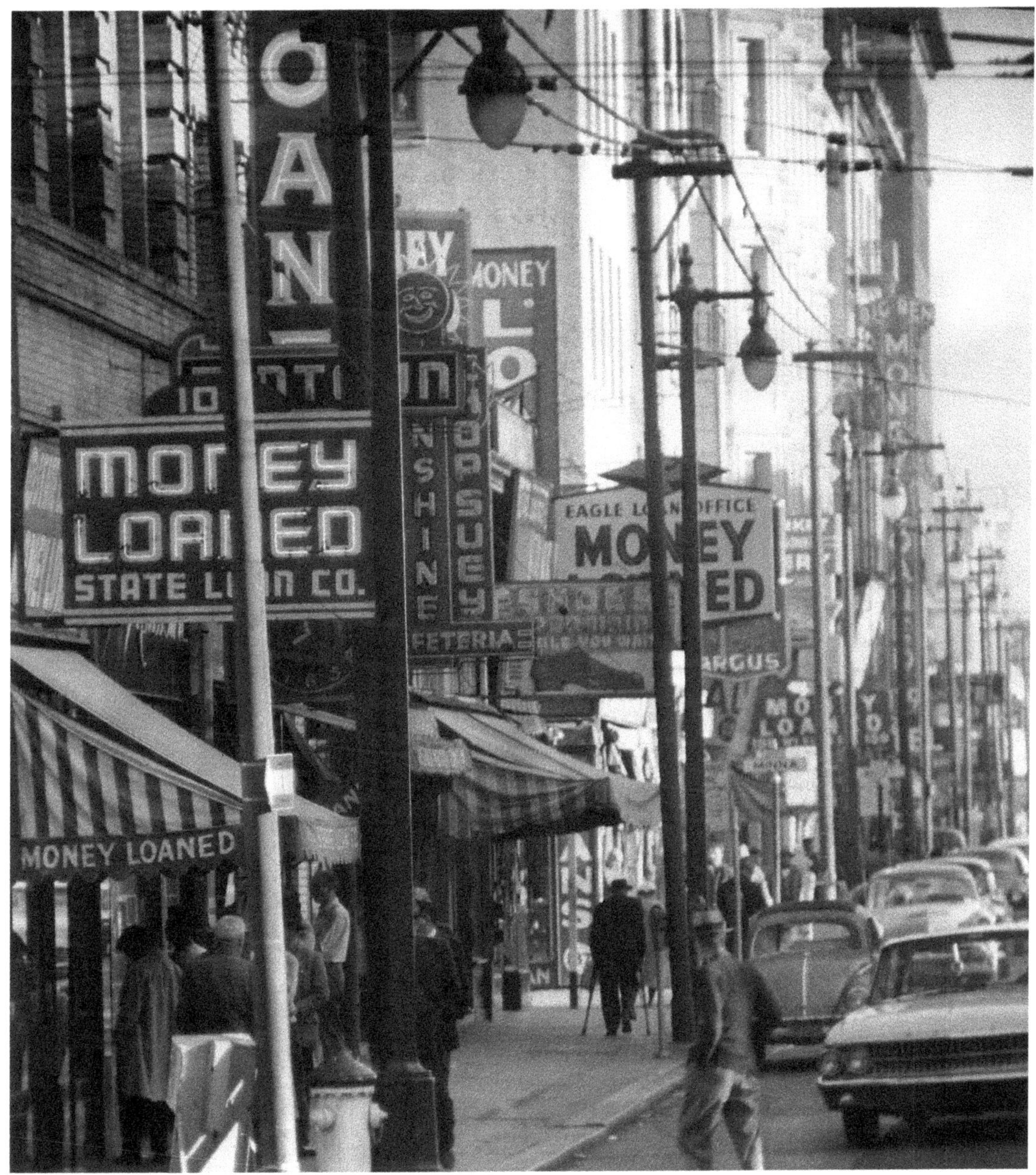

When this photograph was taken on January 10, 1961, Third Street, looking south from Mission Street, was run down and seedy. Pawn shops and loan offices were prominent on every block. At the time, the area was being considered for renovation by the San Francisco Redevelopment Agency. Within a couple of years, gentrification of the entire South of Market area began as block after block was torn out, making room for huge modern buildings, including the Moscone Convention Center, built in 1981 and named for George Moscone, the former San Francisco mayor who was assassinated in 1978, the Marriott Hotel, which opened its doors in 1989, the San Francisco Museum of Modern Art, completed in 1995, and the Metreon entertainment complex, completed in 1999.

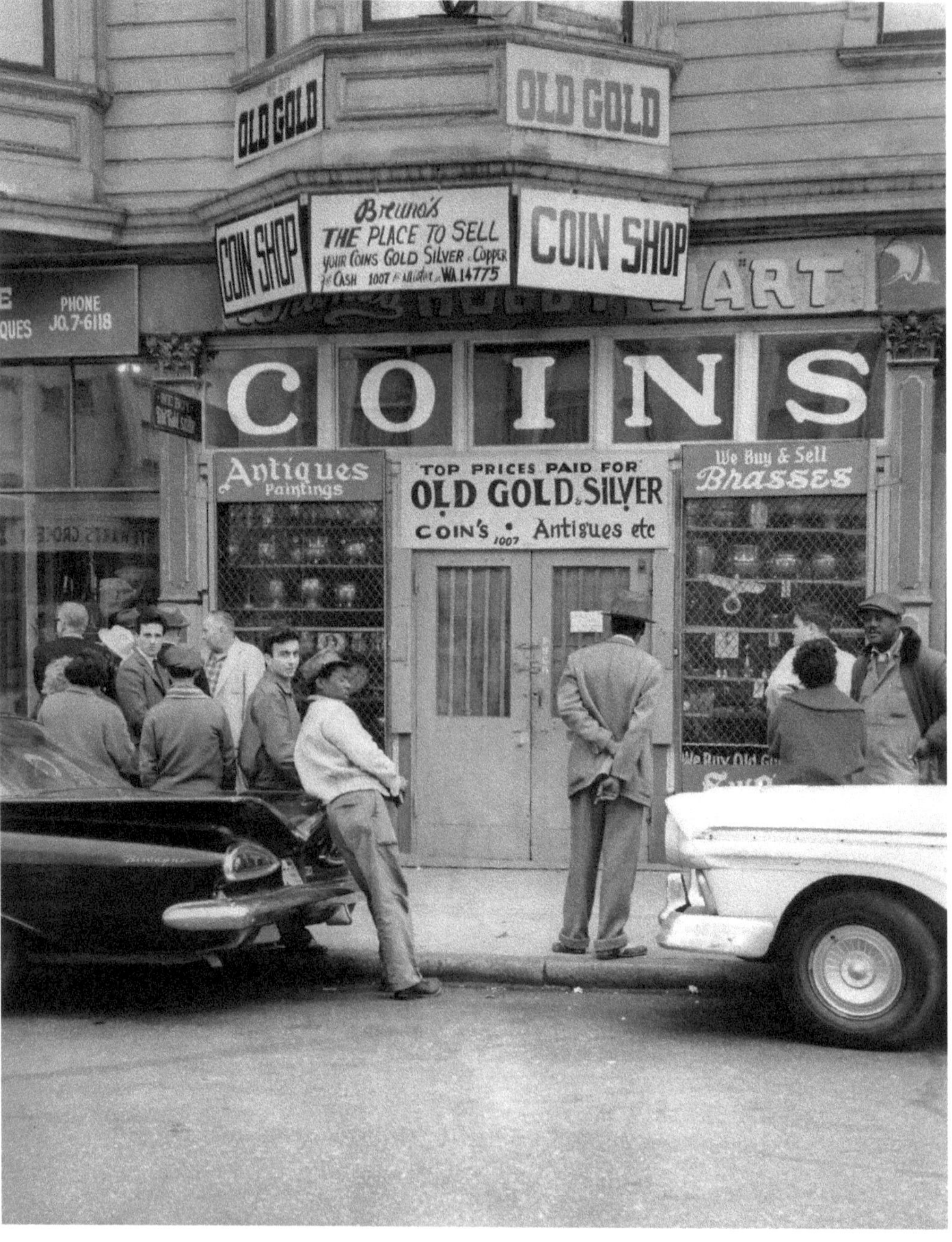

Bruno's Coin Shop at 1007 McAllister Street is pictured here on February 8, 1962, after owner Bruno Crossfield, an antique and coin dealer, was found murdered.

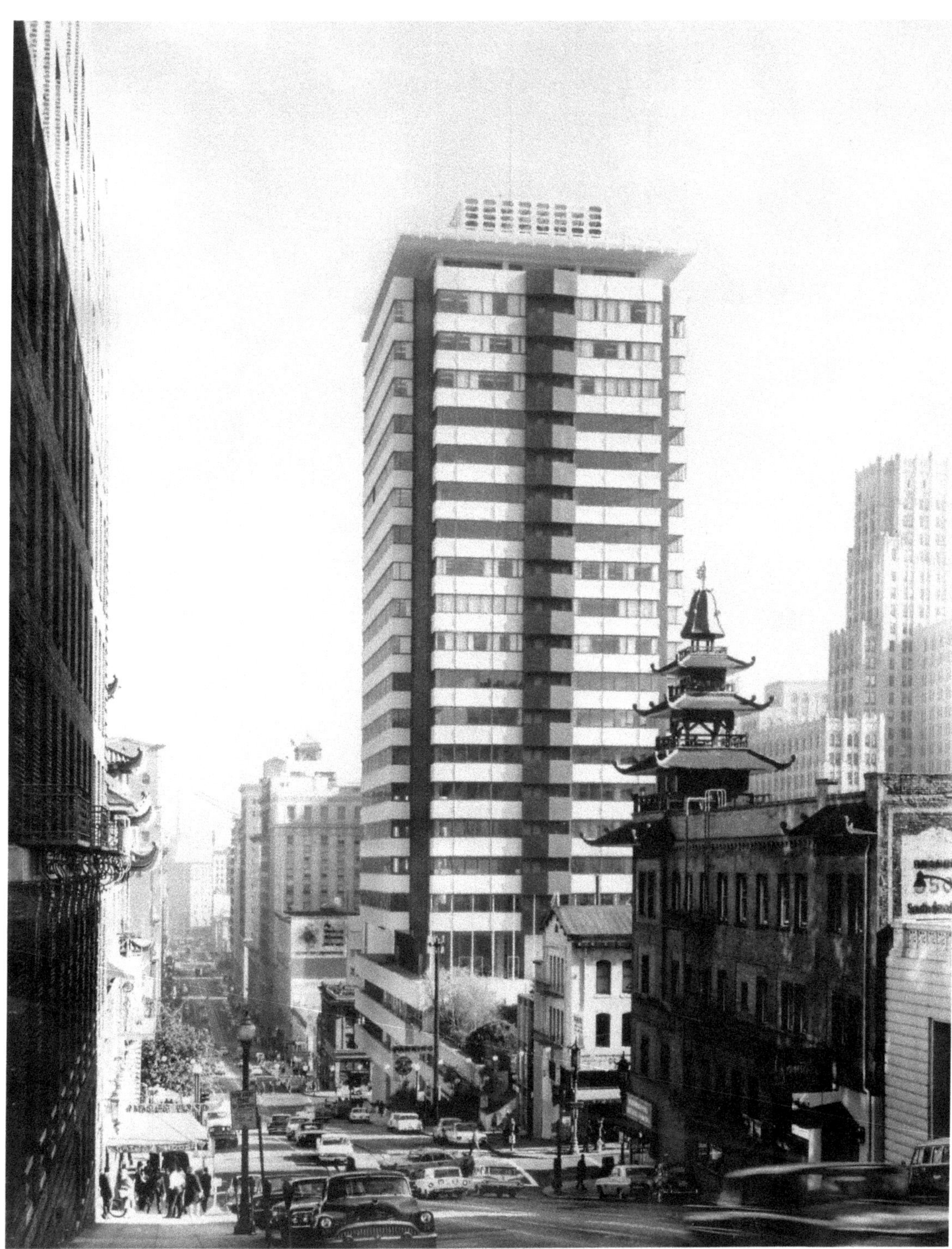

Anshell and Allen, the architects of the elegant International Building at 601 California Street at Kearny, pictured here May 22, 1962, were awarded an Architectural Award of Excellence by the American Institute of Steel Construction for the building's sophistication and earthquake fitting.

The De Young Building (formerly the Chronicle Building) is shown here on March 26, 1963, at the intersection of Geary, Kearny, and Market streets. Built in 1889, it was modernized in the early 1960s with exterior steel cladding and numerous other improvements. Its original brick exterior is currently being restored as the building is converted to luxury residences.

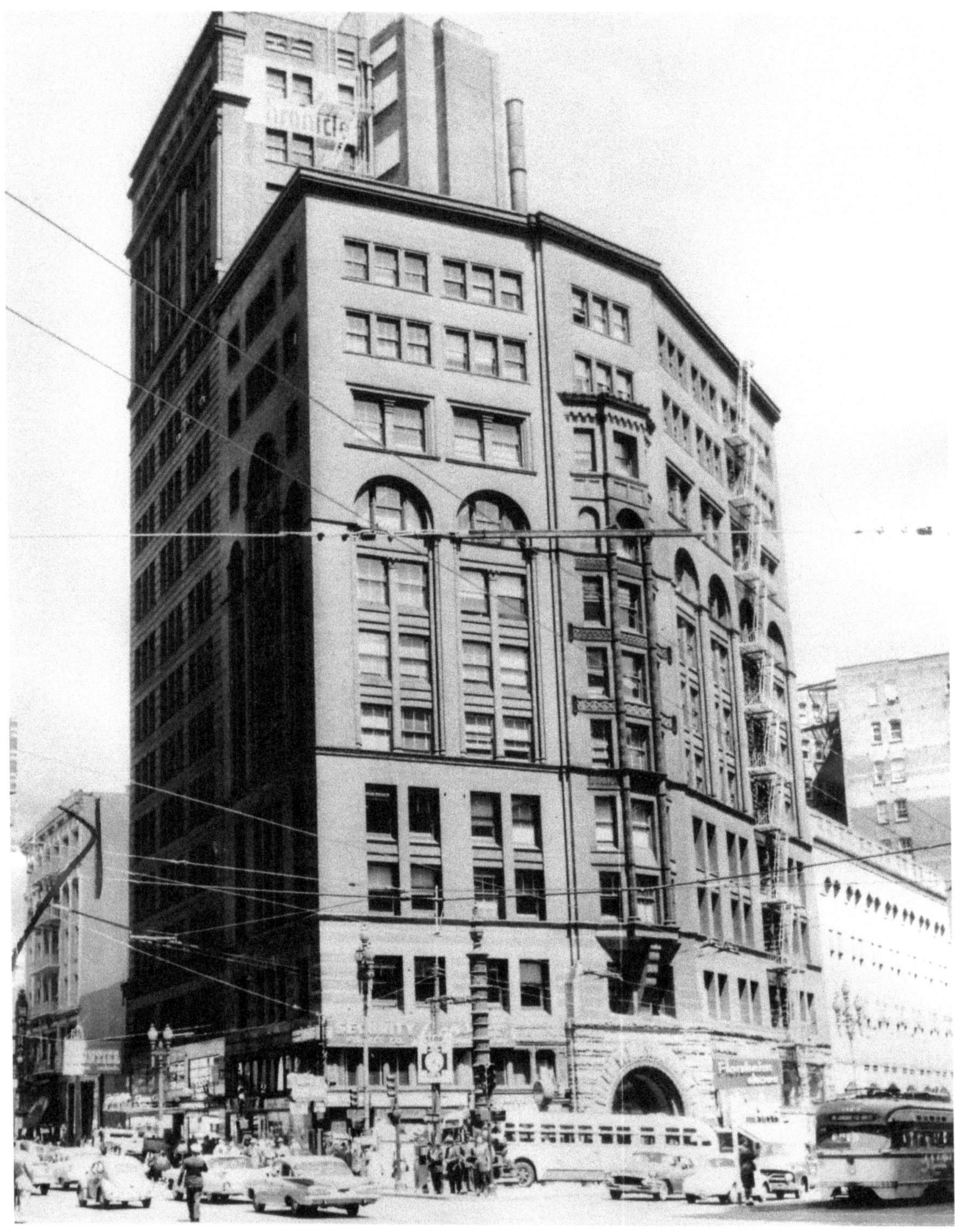

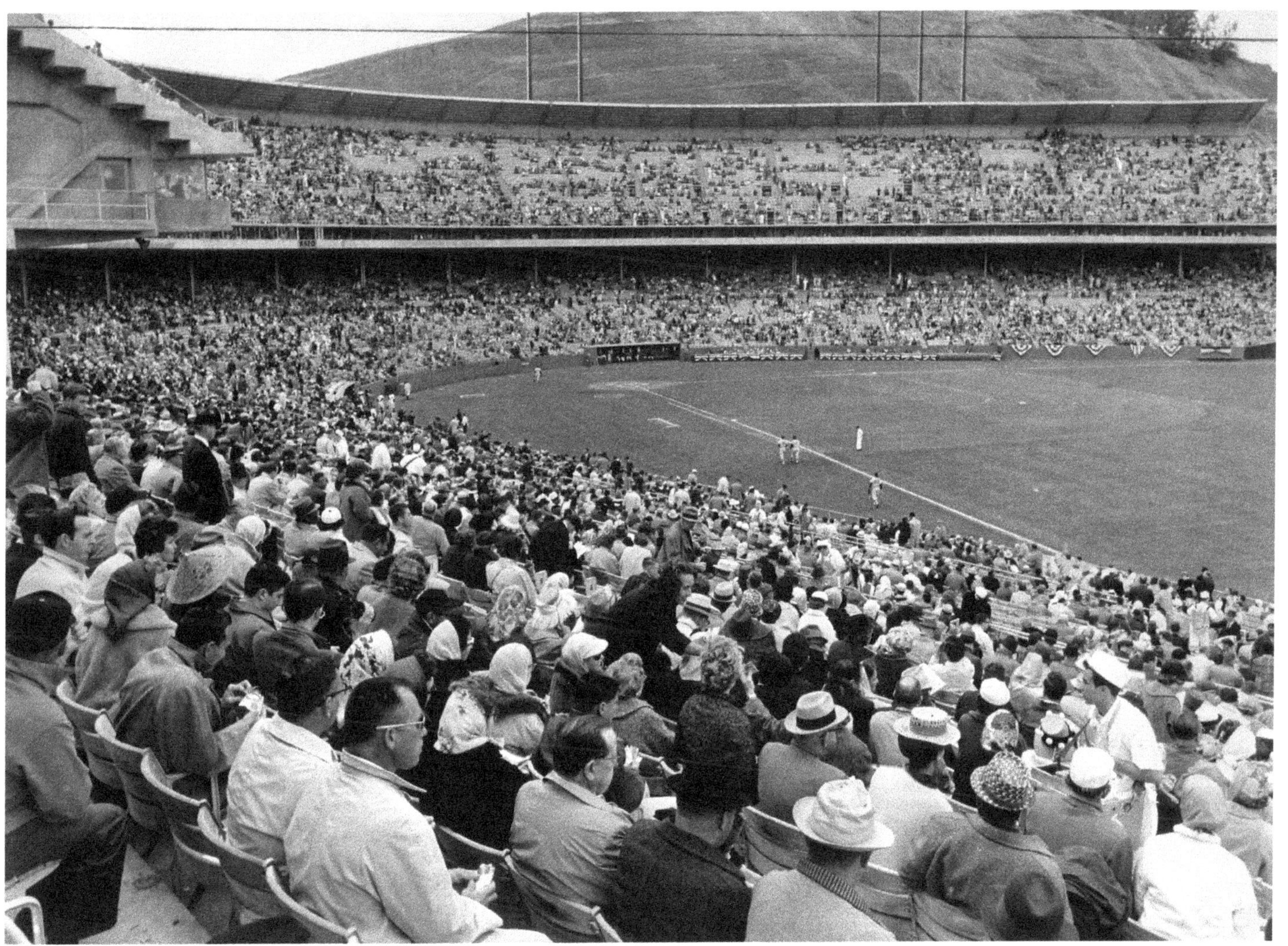

Baseball fans watch as the Giants play the Houston Colt 45s at Candlestick Park on April 16, 1963. Candlestick Park was the home of the Giants until they moved into their new ball park in China Basin in 2000. The San Francisco 49ers football team continues to play at Candlestick pending construction of a new stadium.

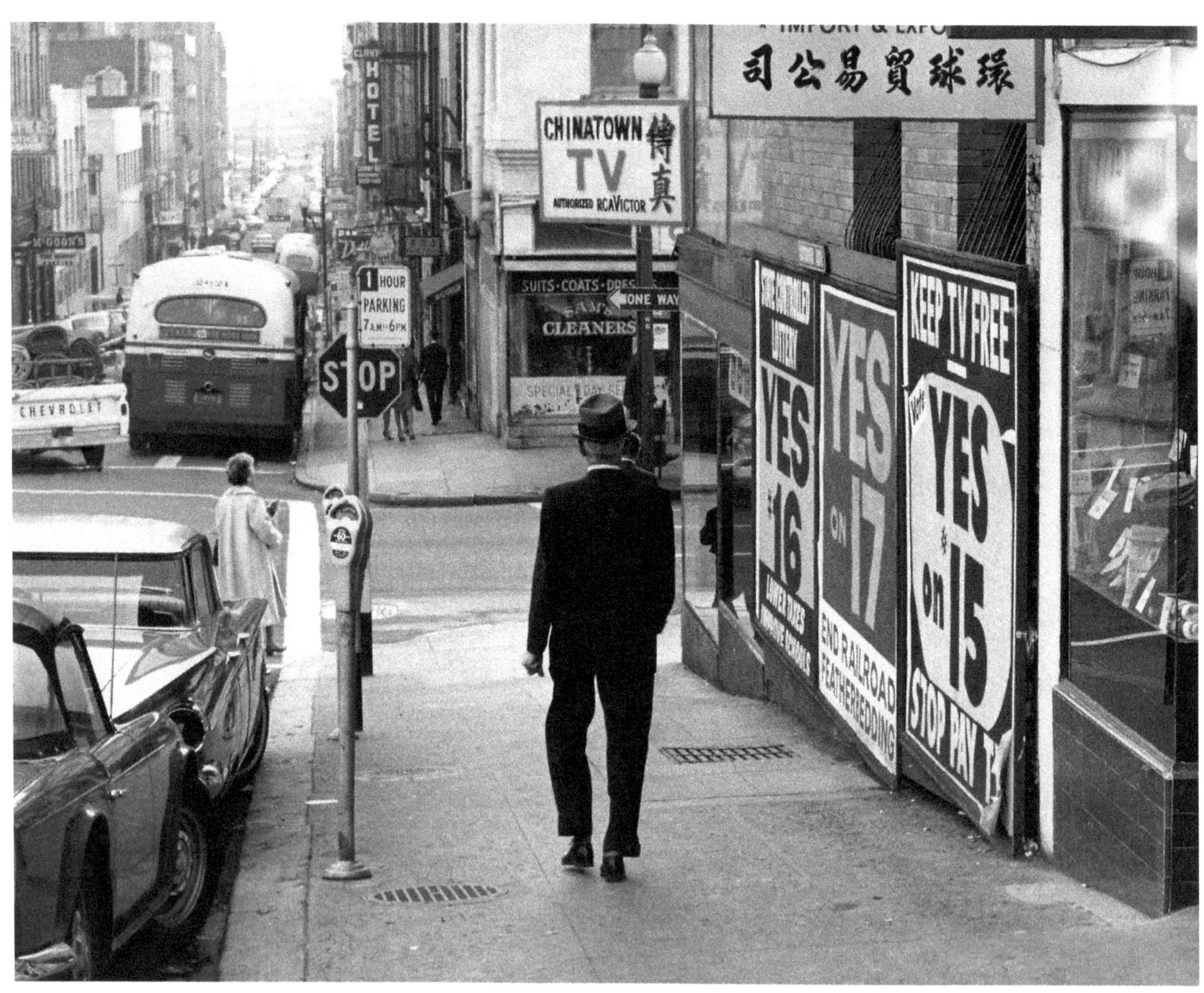

Chinatown and the Financial District are seen in this November 9, 1964, picture taken on Clay Street.

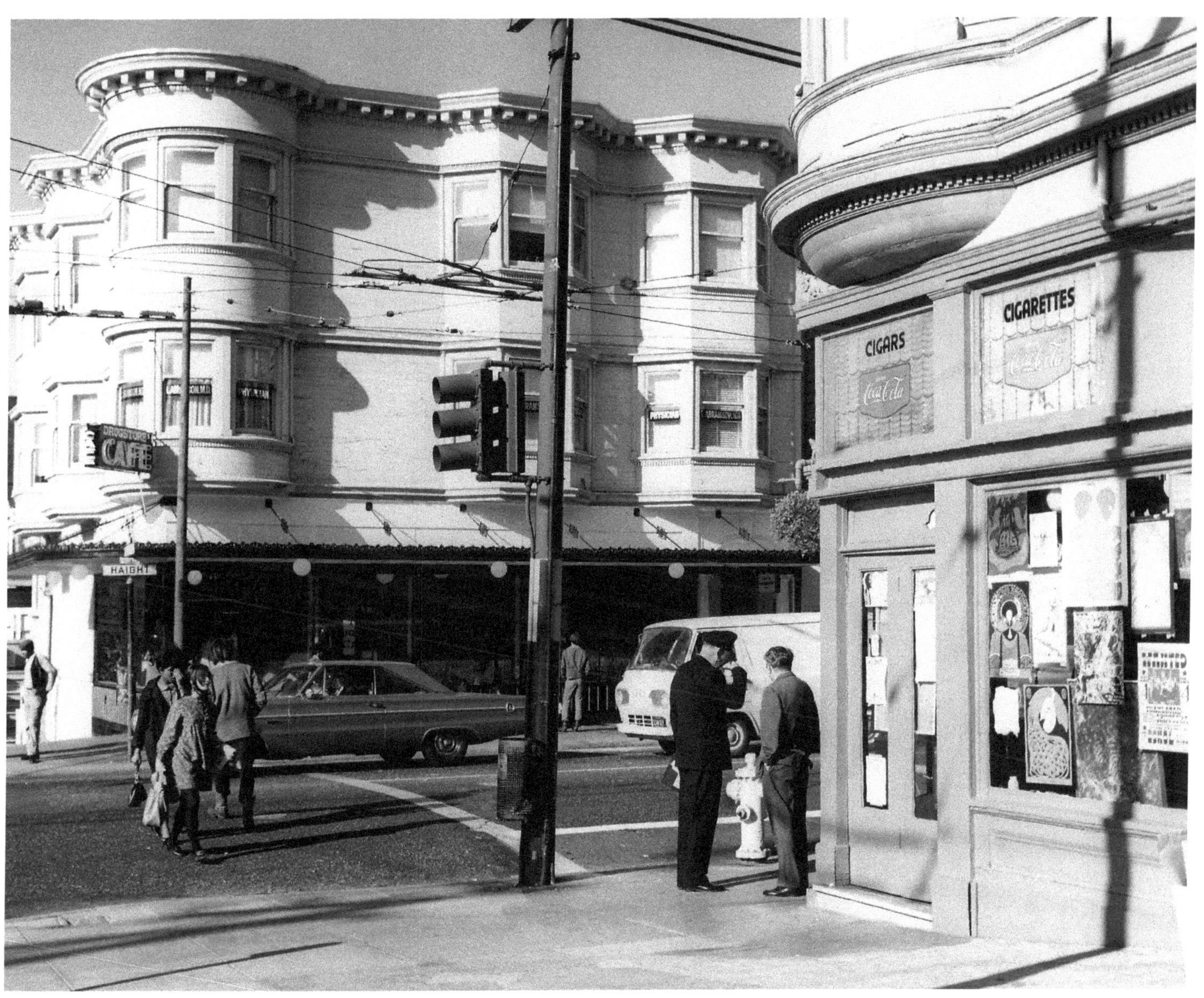

Haight Street in 1967. Before the 1880s, the underdeveloped area around this street was dominated by sand dunes and a few farms. In the late nineteenth century, the Haight developed into an upper-middle-class residential district, which fortuitously escaped destruction from the 1906 earthquake and fires. By the 1950s, the neighborhood was in decline, and by the 1960s, its deteriorating and cheap-rent Victorian houses were a haven for hippies and the counterculture movement. During this time, the Black Panthers across the bay in Oakland fought for black power, while the hippies in the Haight were endorsing free love.

Notes on the Photographs

These notes, listed by page number, attempt to include all aspects known of the photographs. Each of the photographs is identified by the page number, photograph's title or description, photographer and collection, archive, and call or box number when applicable. Although every attempt was made to collect all available data, in some cases complete data was unavailable due to the age and condition of some of the photographs and records.

II **Golden Gate Bridge-Aerial**
San Francisco Public Library
AAD-1264

VI **Kearny Street Traffic**
San Francisco Public Library
AAB-4196

X **Eddie Hanlon's Bar-1949 Post Street**
San Francisco Public Library
AAB-1810

2 **Wells, Fargo & Co.**
San Francisco Public Library
AAC-4622

3 **SW Corner-Pine & Montgomery St.**
San Francisco Public Library
AAC-5176

4 **Portsmouth Square**
San Francisco Public Library
AAA-7032

5 **Fourth of July Parade-Old St. Mary's Church**
San Francisco Public Library
AAB-0722

6 **Post and Market St. Crowd**
San Francisco Public Library
AAB-4861

7 **What Cheer House**
San Francisco Public Library
AAB-2501

8 **San Francisco Waterfront**
San Francisco Public Library
AAC-1825

9 **St. Ignatius College**
San Francisco Public Library
AAE-0965

10 **California Street-Looking South**
San Francisco Public Library
AAB-7366

11 **Dashaway Hall**
San Francisco Public Library
AAC-4741

12 **Horse Drawn Ambulance**
San Francisco Public Library
AAD-0052

13 **Chinatown**
San Francisco Public Library
AAB-6772

14 **Babcock and Wilcox Employees**
San Francisco Public Library
AAC-6307

15 **Warner's Cobweb Palace-Group**
San Francisco Public Library
AAB-1891

16 **Chinatown-Man with Baskets**
San Francisco Public Library
AAB-7041

17 **Mission Dolores**
San Francisco Public Library
AAB-0684

18 **San Francisco Fire Co. Firemen**
San Francisco Public Library
AAE-1239

19 **Long Bridge-Fishing**
San Francisco Public Library
AAD-1532

20 **Dupont Street**
San Francisco Public Library
AAB-3522

21 **Bush Street, West of Kearny**
San Francisco Public Library
AAB-3021

22 **Grand Hotel**
San Francisco Public Library
AAB-2248

23 **Old Engine 8 Firehouse**
San Francisco Public Library
AAE-1124

24 **Alcatraz Island**
San Francisco Public Library
AAC-9297

25 **J.M. Heinold's Saloon**
San Francisco Public Library
AAB-1770

26 **Palace Hotel**
San Francisco Public Library
AAB-2286

27 **Ferry Building**
San Francisco Public Library
AAD-6246

28 **Phelan Building**
San Francisco Public Library
AAC-5149

29 **View from Market Street**
San Francisco Public Library
AAB-4887

30 **Chinatown District, Waverly Place and Clay Street**
San Francisco Public Library
AAB-6784

31 **Bancroft History Building**
San Francisco Public Library
AAC-4680

32 **Kearny at Commercial Street**
San Francisco Public Library
AAB-4187

33 **Bush Street, East from Montgomery**
San Francisco Public Library
AAB-2978

34 **Market Street, East from Third**
San Francisco Public Library
AAB-4943

35 **Chinatown Squad of S.F. Police Dept.**
San Francisco Public Library
AAD-9019

36 **Baldwin Hotel**
San Francisco Public Library
AAB-1946

37 **Market and McAllister Streets**
San Francisco Public Library
AAB-4941

38 **United Presbyterian Church**
San Francisco Public Library
AAB-1622

39 **Market Street at Mason**
San Francisco Public Library
AAB-4944

40 **Artillery Drill, Presidio**
San Francisco Public Library
AAC-0412

43 **Ocean Beach Crowds**
San Francisco Public Library
AAB-9811

44 **Union Trust Building**
San Francisco Public Library
AAC-5456

45 **Market Street-Christmas Day 1903**
San Francisco Public Library
AAB-6148

46 **Market Street, Between Grant and Kearny**
San Francisco Public Library
AAB-2977

47 **Folger's Coffee Building -Construction**
San Francisco Public Library
AAC-6974

48 **Market Street-West from Ferry Building**
San Francisco Public Library
AAB-6181

49 **Kearny Street**
San Francisco Public Library
AAB-4215

50 **Third Street**
San Francisco Public Library
AAB-5760

51 **Crocker Building, Market and Post Streets**
San Francisco Public Library
AAC-4734

52 **Streetcars in Water-Sixteenth St./Folsom**
San Francisco Public Library
AAB-5929

53 **Hearst Building**
San Francisco Public Library
AAC-4927

54 **History Building-Market St. b/t 3rd & 4th St.**
San Francisco Public Library
AC-4914

55 **Call Building on Fire**
San Francisco Public Library
AAC-2812

56 **Palace Hotel and Lotta's Fountain**
San Francisco Public Library
AB-2283

57 **U.S. Mint-1906 Earthquake**
San Francisco Public Library
AAC-4031

58 **China Town**
San Francisco Public Library
AAC-2872

59 **Market Street-Earthquake**
San Francisco Public Library
AAC-3443

60 **Market Street-Automobile**
San Francisco Public Library
AC-2586

61 **City Hall-Earthquake Ruins**
San Francisco Public Library
AAC-2934

62 **Four Women-Leaning Building**
San Francisco Public Library
AAC-3885

63 **Fook Wah & Co. Importers**
San Francisco Public Library
AAB-6826

64 **Men and Boys-Outside Bar After Earthquake**
San Francisco Public Library
AAC-2611

66 **Bank of Italy Earthquake Ruins**
San Francisco Public Library
AAC-2566

67 **Bank of California-Earthquake**
San Francisco Public Library
AAC-2588

68 **S.F. Fire Dept.-Truck Co.9**
San Francisco Public Library
AAD-8189

69 **Mission Street-West of Third**
San Francisco Public Library
AAB-4731

70 **Newspapers Boys**
San Francisco Public Library
AAB-4563

71 **Nightclubs on Pacific Street**
San Francisco Public Library
AAB-6692

72 **St. Francis Hotel**
San Francisco Public Library
AAB-2404

73 **Civic Center-Hot Air Balloon**
San Francisco Public Library
AB-/399

74 **Horse Car-Market and Battery St.**
San Francisco Public Library
AAC-8191

75 **Imperial (United Artists) Theater**
San Francisco Public Library
AAA-8893

76 **Streetcar on Geary Street**
San Francisco Public Library
AAB-3718

78 **Market Street Crowds**
San Francisco Public Library
AAB-6233

79 **Civic Center Plaza Crowds**
San Francisco Public Library
AAB-7172

80 **Fort Point**
San Francisco Public Library
AAC-1027

81 **Frist San Francisco Airport**
San Francisco Public Library
AAB-9355

82 **Bank of Italy**
San Francisco Public Library
AC-4288

83 **Market at 4th Street**
San Francisco Public Library
AAB-6249

84 **McNab and Smith Co.-Horse-Drawn Wagon**
San Francisco Public Library
AAC-7241

85 **St. Ignatius Field-U. of S.F.**
San Francisco Public Library
AAD-8012

86 **Burnett Brother's**
San Francisco Public Library
AAC-6536

87 **Fillmore Street**
San Francisco Public Library
AAB-3596

88 **Alcatraz Island**
San Francisco Public Library
AAC-9267

89 **View of Downtown**
San Francisco Public Library
AAB-8474

90 **Ferry Building-Diamond Jubilee**
San Francisco Public Library
AAD-6384

91 **St. Francis Theater**
San Francisco Public Library
AAA-9197

92 **Mission and 4th Streets-Policeman**
San Francisco Public Library
AAB-4662

93 **Montgomery and California Street**
San Francisco Public Library
AAB-7290

94 **Third Street at Minna**
San Francisco Public Library
AAB-5829

95 **Mission and 22nd Street**
San Francisco Public Library
AAB-9520

96 **California Theater**
San Francisco Public Library
AAA-8604

97 **French American Bank**
San Francisco Public Library
AAC-4524

98 **Granat Bros. Jewelers**
San Francisco Public Library
AAC-6825

99 **Siberia Maru Leaving Port of S.F.**
San Francisco Public Library
AAC-1973

100 **Men Loading American Railway Express Truck**
San Francisco Public Library
AAC-6346

101 **McLeran Building**
San Francisco Public Library
AAC-4974

102 **Dreamland Auditorium**
San Francisco Public Library
AAC-4744

103 **S.F. Curb Exchange**
San Francisco Public Library
AAC-4738

104 **Chinatown District**
San Francisco Public Library
AAB-6780

105 **Stock Exchange**
San Francisco Public Library
AAC-5436

106 **Bay City Markets**
San Francisco Public Library
AAC-6866

108 **Odeon Theater**
San Francisco Public Library
AAA-8988

109 **Nuestra Senora de Guadalupe**
San Francisco Public Library
AAB-0708

110 **Ocean Beach**
San Francisco Public Library
AAB-9759

111 **Downtown Skyline**
San Francisco Public Library
AAB-8481

112 **Savings Union Bank & Trust Company**
San Francisco Public Library
AAC-4617

113 **City National Bank Crowd**
San Francisco Public Library
AAC-4380

114 **American Trust Company Crowd**
San Francisco Public Library
AAC-4263

115 **Acme Beer Delivery Truck**
San Francisco Public Library
AAC-6420

116 **Third Street Bridge Firefighters**
San Francisco Public Library
AAD-1680

117 **Third Street Bridge-Opening Crowd**
San Francisco Public Library
AAD-1645

118 **Ferry Building-Automobiles**
San Francisco Public Library
AAD-6318

119 **Federal Building at Civic Center**
San Francisco Public Library
AAC-4888

120 **Streetcar at Ferry Building**
San Francisco Public Library
AAD-6319

121 **USS Colorado in Bay**
San Francisco Public Library
AAC-2094

122 **College Inn**
San Francisco Public Library
AAB-1797

123 **Charles Brown and Sons Hardware**
San Francisco Public Library
AAC-6574

124 **Columbia Apparel**
San Francisco Public Library
AAC-6705

125 **Schmidt Lithograph Company**
San Francisco Public Library
AAD-7406

126 **U.S. Customs House**
San Francisco Public Library
AAC-4712

127 **Bank of America-Bernal Heights**
San Francisco Public Library
AAC-4316

128 **Golden Gate Bridge-Opening Ceremonies**
San Francisco Public Library
AAD-1281

129 **Golden Gate Bridge Fiesta**
San Francisco Public Library
AAD-1244

130 **Float of Fiesta Queens**
San Francisco Public Library
AAD-1229

131 **Dario Lodigiani-Oakland Oaks**
San Francisco Public Library
AAD-3330

132 **Dean Building Exterior**
San Francisco Public Library
AAC-4750

133 **Bank of America**
San Francisco Public Library
AAC-4324

134 **Livingston Bros. Dept. Store**
San Francisco Public Library
AAC-7186

135 **Train at Embarcadero**
San Francisco Public Library
AAB-3535

136 **Seals Player**
San Francisco Public Library
AAD-3332

137 **Streetcars, Market St.**
San Francisco Public Library
AAB-6414

138 **Third and Townsend Streets**
San Francisco Public Library
AAB-5815

139 **Golden Gate International Expo**
San Francisco Public Library
AAD-3785

140 **International Settlement**
San Francisco Public Library
AAB-9093

142 **Orpheum Theater Exterior**
San Francisco Public Library
AAA-8995

143 **Bethlehem Steel Co. Union Dispute**
San Francisco Public Library
AAC-6376

144 **San Francisco State College-Students**
San Francisco Public Library
AAD-7849

145 **Junior Traffic Patrol**
San Francisco Public Library
AAB-6877

146 **U.S. Army Removing Money from Mint**
San Francisco Public Library
AAD-3400

147 **San Francisco Navy Day Submarine**
San Francisco Public Library
AAB-7086

148 **San Francisco Fire Dept. Engine 49**
San Francisco Public Library
AAD-8183

149 **War Bond Drive-Post Street**
San Francisco Public Library
AAB-5102

150 **War Chest Rally**
San Francisco Public Library
AAB-5039

151 **Appraisers Building-Line for Cigarettes**
San Francisco Public Library
AAC-4715

152 **Fairmont Hotel**
San Francisco Public Library
AAB-1979

153 **Powell Street at Market**
San Francisco Public Library
AAB-5194

154 **Chinese-American Parade**
San Francisco Public Library
AAB-7204

155 **Traffic on Bush Street**
San Francisco Public Library
AAB-3032

156 **Ahrens Bakery**
San Francisco Public Library
AAC-6294

157 **Streetcar on Mission and 21st**
San Francisco Public Library
AAB-4683

158 **Maiden Lane Festival**
San Francisco Public Library
AAB-4441

159 **Montgomery Street**
San Francisco Public Library
AAB-7343

160 **Don Gaspar De Portola**
San Francisco Public Library
AAB-4427

161 **Parade of Navy Men**
San Francisco Public Library
AAB-6460

162 **Maiden Lane Spring Festival**
San Francisco Public Library
AAB-4467

164 **Mission St. Christmas Decorations**
San Francisco Public Library
AAB-4704

165 **Fox Theater Stairway**
San Francisco Public Library
AAA-8772

166 **Mobilgas Building**
San Francisco Public Library
AAC-5048

168 **Bank of America-Powell and Market**
San Francisco Public Library
AAC-4337

169 **Fireman with Trolley**
San Francisco Public Library
AAB-7343

170 **Fog Over Golden Gate & Fishermen**
San Francisco Public Library
AAD-1279

171 **Firemen at Haight and Ashbury**
San Francisco Public Library
AAB-3958

172 **General Mark Clark**
San Francisco Public Library
AAB-7349

173 **San Francisco Seals**
San Francisco Public Library
AAD-3297

174 **California Brewing Company-Conestoga**
San Francisco Public Library
AAC-6455

175 **Kezar Stadium Boxing**
San Francisco Public Library
AAC-5240

176 **Chinatown-Grant Ave.**
San Francisco Public Library
AAB-3836

177 **Golden Gate Theater**
San Francisco Public Library
AAA-8833

178 **Opening Day-S.F. Seals**
San Francisco Public Library
AAD-3328

179 **International Settlement**
San Francisco Public Library
AAB-9094

180 **"Skid Road"**
San Francisco Public Library
AAC-0682

181 **Old Poodle Dog Restaurant**
San Francisco Public Library
AAC-9024

182 **Giants Team Welcome**
San Francisco Public Library
AAD-3340

183 **Hyde Street Cable Car**
San Francisco Public Library
AAB-4124

184 **Post Street**
San Francisco Public Library
AAB-5106

185 **View of S.F. from Bay**
San Francisco Public Library
AAC-9105

186 **Hyde Street**
San Francisco Public Library
AAB-4127

188 **Cable Car-California Street**
San Francisco Public Library
AAB-3201

189 **Powell Street Cable Car**
San Francisco Public Library
AAB-5209

190 **San Francisco Giants-Willie Mays**
San Francisco Public Library
AAD-3345

191 **Playland on the Beach**
San Francisco Public Library
AAB-9985

192 **Kezar Stadium**
San Francisco Public Library
AAC-5299

193 **Third Street Looking from Mission Street**
San Francisco Public Library
AAB-5836

194 **Bruno's Coin Shop**
San Francisco Public Library
AAC-6532

195 **International Building**
San Francisco Public Library
AAC-4972

196 **De Young Building**
San Francisco Public Library
AAC-4742

197 **Candlestick Park**
San Francisco Public Library
AAC-5200

198 **Downtown Clay Street**
San Francisco Public Library
AAB-3347

199 **Haight Street**
San Francisco Public Library
AAB-3961

206 **Haight Theater**
San Francisco Public Library
AAB-8820

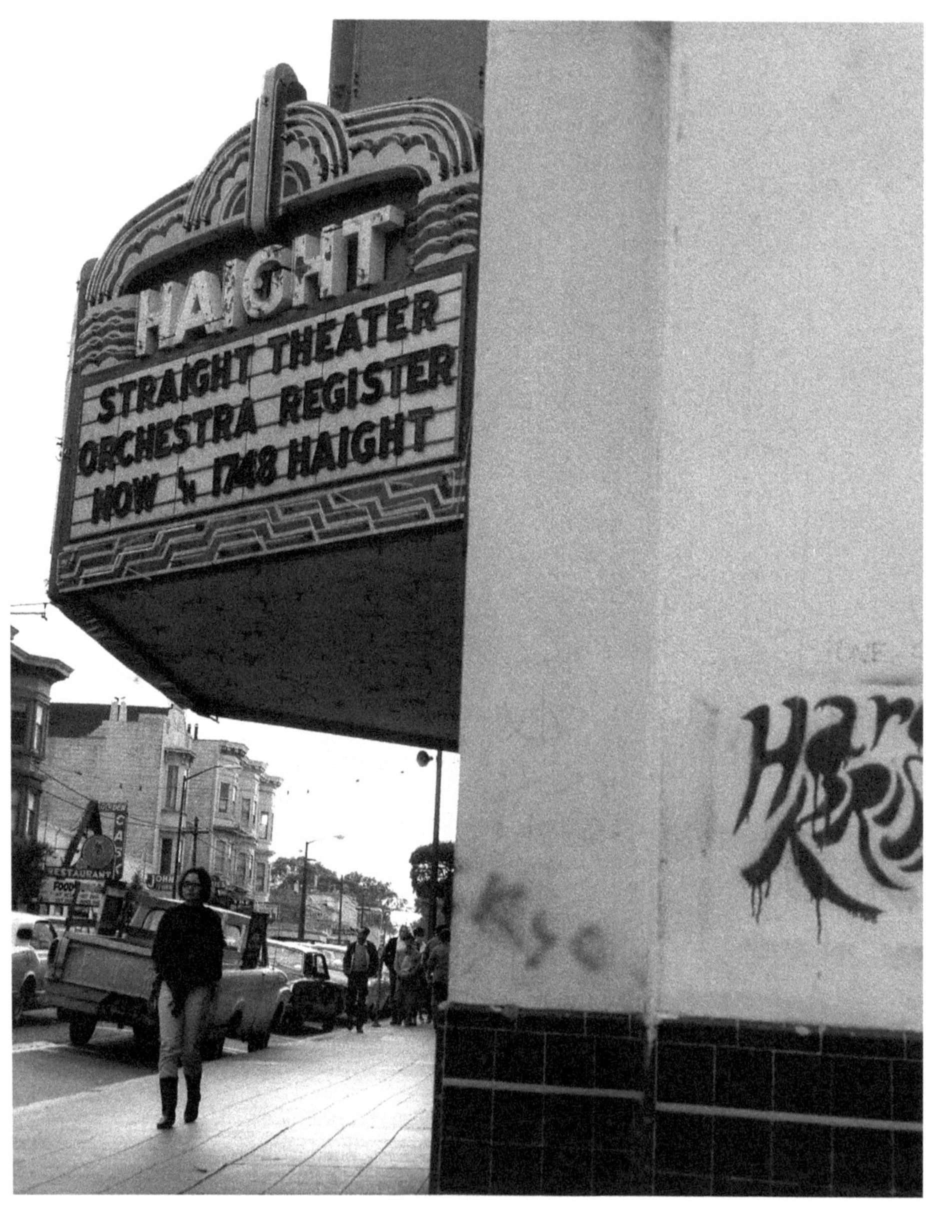

A woman walks by the Haight Theatre at 1748 Haight Street in 1967, the year immortalized as "the Summer of Love." The theater was a key part of the Haight for nearly 60 years before it stopped showing movies in the mid-1960s. Haight Ashbury evokes images of flower children, hippies, drugs, and counterculture. At the famous intersection of Haight and Ashbury streets, made legendary in songs by rock bands such as Janis Joplin and the Grateful Dead, now stands a Ben and Jerry's and a Gap store, a strong statement on the neighborhood's gentrification. Yet in many ways, the diverse atmosphere along Haight Street still embodies elements of its liberal 1960s persona. The area draws busloads of tourists every week in search of the area's hippy legacy, as well as teen runaways, hipsters, and bohemians.

HISTORIC PHOTOS OF SAN FRANCISCO

Before the discovery of silver and gold, San Francisco was a frontier missionary town. From these modest beginnings, the city overcame great adversity to become one of the world's most significant metropolitan centers. Throughout its history San Francisco has been an entrepreneurial center. Beginning with new transportation technologies of railroads and shipping, to services such as banking and insurance, the entrepreneurial community has a long history of overcoming challenges to reach prosperity.

This volume, *Historic Photos of San Francisco,* captures the evolution of this great city in still photography from various collections of the San Francisco Public Library. The book follows life, government, education, and events spanning two centuries of San Francisco's history. It captures unique and rare scenes as depicted in nearly 200 historic photographs. These images portray the events and people that have played a part in the building of a unique and prosperous city.

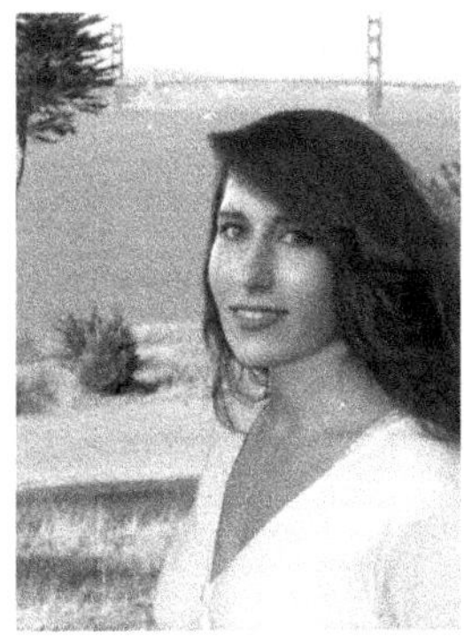

Rebecca Schall grew up in the Richmond District of San Francisco, near the Presidio, and has always been fascinated by the city's rich historical and cultural landscape. She has been involved in numerous local activities, including an archaeological dig in the Presidio, and conducted extensive research on topics in San Francisco and European history. After completing her graduate studies in history, Rebecca spent time studying and researching in Paris. Rebecca now lives in the San Francisco Bay Area, where she teaches history and continues historical research and writing. Schall has also written *Historic Photos of Paris* and *Historic Photos of the Presidio,* both available from Turner Publishing. For more information on the author, visit her Web site: www.rebeccaschall.com

WWW.TURNERPUBLISHING.COM

www.ingramcontent.com/pod-product-compliance
Lightning Source LLC
LaVergne TN
LVHW060613110826
845154LV00003B/80
* 9 7 8 1 6 8 3 3 6 9 3 8 7 *